LEO STRAUSS ON MOSES MENDELSSOHN

LEO STRAUSS
ON
MOSES MENDELSSOHN

Translated and edited, with an interpretive essay, by Martin D. Yaffe

THE UNIVERSITY OF CHICAGO PRESS
CHICAGO AND LONDON

Leo Strauss (1899–1973) was one of the preeminent political philosophers of the twentieth century. He is the author of many books, among them *The Political Philosophy of Hobbes*, *Natural Right and History*, and *Spinoza's Critique of Religion*, all published by the University of Chicago Press.

Martin D. Yaffe is professor of philosophy and religion studies at the University of North Texas and the author or editor of several books, including *Shylock and the Jewish Question*.

The University of Chicago Press, Chicago 60637
The University of Chicago Press, Ltd., London
© 2012 by The University of Chicago
All rights reserved. Published 2012.
Printed in the United States of America

21 20 19 18 17 16 15 14 13 12   1 2 3 4 5

ISBN-13: 978-0-226-92278-2   (cloth)
ISBN-13: 978-0-226-92279-9   (e-book)
ISBN-10: 0-226-92278-2   (cloth)
ISBN-10: 0-226-92279-0   (e-book)

Library of Congress Cataloging-in-Publication Data

Strauss, Leo.
　　Leo Strauss on Moses Mendelssohn / translated and edited, with an interpretive essay, by Martin D. Yaffe.
　　　　pages. cm.
　　Includes bibliographical references and index.
　　"This book is an annotated translation of the introductions written by the young Leo Strauss to ten of Mendelssohn's writings."
　　ISBN-13: 978-0-226-92278-2 (cloth : alk. paper)
　　ISBN-10: 0-226-92278-2 (cloth : alk. paper)
　　ISBN-13: 978-0-226-92279-9 (e-book)
　　ISBN-10: 0-226-92279-0 (e-book)   1. Mendelssohn, Moses, 1729–1786.   I. Yaffe, Martin D. II. Title.
　　B2693.S873 2012
　　193—dc23
　　　　　　　　　　　　　　　　　　　　　　　　　　　　　　　　　　2012022901

♾ This paper meets the requirements of ANSI/NISO Z39.48-1992 (Permanence of Paper).

To (Rabbi) Jack Bemporad

Yet wisdom, where can she be found?
Which is the place of understanding?
—Job 28:12

CONTENTS

Translator's Preface xi
Chronology of Writings Mentioned in Strauss's Introductions xxi
Abbreviations xxvii

PART I   Leo Strauss's Introductions to Ten Writings of Moses Mendelssohn

Preliminary Remark by Alexander Altmann 3
1. Introduction to *Pope a Metaphysician!* 7
2. Introduction to "Epistle to Mr. Lessing in Leipzig" 14
3. Introduction to *Commentary on Moses Maimonides' "Logical Terms"* 18
4. Introduction to *Treatise on Evidence in Metaphysical Sciences* 19
5. Introduction to *Phädon* 29
6. Introduction to *Treatise on the Incorporeality of the Human Soul* 50
7. Introduction to "On a Handwritten Essay of Mr. de Luc's" 55
8. Introduction to *The Soul* 57
9. Introduction to *Morning Hours* and *To the Friends of Lessing* 59
10. Introduction to *God's Cause, or Providence Vindicated* 146

APPENDIX 1: Strauss, Preliminary Remark to *A Reminder of Lessing* 162
APPENDIX 2: Supplements to Translator's Notes in Strauss's Introductions 163
APPENDIX 3: From Mendelssohn's "Epistle to Mr. Lessing in Leipzig" (Passage cited in Strauss, *Natural Right and History*, p. 275, n. 41) 213
APPENDIX 4: From Lessing's "The Education of the Human Race" (§§70–73) 214

PART II   An Interpretive Essay

Strauss on Mendelssohn: An Interpretive Essay by Martin D. Yaffe 219

Index of Proper Names 319

TRANSLATOR'S PREFACE

I

Leo Strauss on Moses Mendelssohn is a translation of ten introductions by the political philosopher Leo Strauss (1899–1973) to various philosophical writings by Moses Mendelssohn (1729–86), the leading Jewish figure of the German Enlightenment and the philosophical founder of modern Jewish thought. Strauss composed the introductions in the 1930s as a junior editor of the *Moses Mendelssohn Gesammelte Schriften Jubiläumsausgabe*—the Jubilee Edition of Mendelssohn's collected writings. This multivolume collaboration among leading German-Jewish scholars, begun in Weimar Germany in commemoration of the bicentennial of Mendelssohn's birth, was soon suppressed and all but destroyed by the Nazi regime. Not until the 1970s were the Jubilee Edition's previously published volumes reprinted (including two of the three volumes that Strauss worked on), delayed volumes published (including Strauss's third volume), and new ones undertaken.

The Mendelssohnian writings that Strauss edited, annotated, and introduced—and translated from the Hebrew in the case of two of them—span Mendelssohn's celebrated literary career. They culminate in *Morning Hours* (1785) and *To the Friends of Lessing* (1786), written as philosophical defenses of the moral and theological respectability of the late Gotthold Ephraim Lessing (1729–81), Mendelssohn's dearest friend and the German Enlightenment's outstanding literary figure and theological polemicist. Mendelssohn was responding to the shocking claim by Friedrich Heinrich Jacobi (1743–1819) that toward the end of his life, having long since moved from Berlin and close proximity to Mendelssohn, Lessing had secretly become a devotee of the philosophy of Benedict Spinoza (1632–77). To Jacobi and Mendelssohn and their German contemporaries—indeed, to any thoughtful reader in Europe during the century or so since Spinoza—this would be another way of saying that Lessing had become an atheist.

To judge by initial impressions, the shocking character of Spinozist atheism shows up less in Spinoza's magnum opus, *Ethics Demonstrated in a Geometrical Order* (1677), than in his *Theologico-Political Treatise* (1670), which is a sort of introduction to the *Ethics*. The elaborate argument of the *Ethics* is perhaps shocking enough, theologically at any rate. It collapses God into nature and, at the same time, elevates nature into God. Spinoza cushioned this dual shock to some extent by giving his *Ethics* the rhetorical look of a geometrical treatise, so as to limit its readership to those who could be expected or encouraged to negotiate its complicated internal cross-references and chains of deductive reasoning. He also took the precaution of publishing the *Ethics* posthumously and anonymously. Meanwhile, he interrupted writing the *Ethics* to publish the *Treatise*, also anonymously. The *Treatise* is the philosophical founding document of both modern liberal democracy and modern biblical criticism. In the course of its lively, spirited, semipopular yet formidable argument, it denies the Mosaic authorship of the Pentateuch and, with that, any divinely revealed basis for morality. Not surprisingly, the *Treatise* gained widespread notoriety almost right away among its intended, theologically minded Christian readership. Compounding the notoriety was the fact that readers soon pinpointed its anonymous author, accurately, as an excommunicated Jew from Amsterdam who—for reasons made plain enough in the *Treatise* itself—declined to convert to Christianity.

A century later, the moral opprobrium attached to Spinoza reached Lessing in the following way. Spinozist biblical criticism had found its practitioners in Lutheran Germany. These included above all Hermann Samuel Reimarus (1694–1768), whose unpublished *Apology or Defense for the Rational Worshipers of God* broadens and thickens Spinoza's argument about the Old Testament to include the New Testament. After his death, Reimarus's daughter Elise presented her father's manuscript in confidence to Lessing, who by then was librarian at the Ducal Library at Wolfenbüttel, in Brunswick, and as editor of the library's quarterly publication was exempt from routine theological censorship. By 1774, Lessing began publishing excerpts from Reimarus's manuscript, while preserving their author's anonymity by calling them "Fragments of an Unnamed." To the several "Fragments," Lessing added editorial "Counterpropositions" designed to contextualize the radical views of the "Fragmentist" and separate his own views somewhat from them. Even so, publishing the "Fragments" upset orthodox Lutheran theologians, and Lessing soon found himself drawn into a lengthy controversy over the "Fragments" with Pastor Johann Melchior Goeze of Hamburg. Neither the Fragmentist nor Lessing as his editor presents himself as a doctrinaire Spinozist. Reimarus in his other writings had adhered to the natural or rational theology of Gottfried Wilhelm Leibniz (1646–

1716), which was predominant in the German universities of Lessing's day in the version promulgated by Leibniz's first-generation disciple Christian Wolff (1679–1754) and was a respectable, if controversial, theist alternative to revelation-believing Christianity among Enlightened Lutherans. In the glare of the "Fragments" controversy, however, Lessing could appear to have abandoned Leibnizianism for Spinozism. Mendelssohn in *Morning Hours* gives voice to this opinion—if only in order to rebut it while countering Jacobi's assertion that Lessing had confessed his recent Spinozism to him in private conversations during the summer of 1780. Among other things, *Morning Hours* asserts instead that Lessing's Spinozism had been known to Mendelssohn since the beginning of their friendship but that it was a "purified" Spinozism consisting of a morally harmless Pantheism, rather than atheism.

Yet with the memory of the "Fragments" controversy still fresh, Jacobi's assertion had a certain plausibility. The resulting dispute over Lessing's Spinozism, which started in the summer of 1783 as a private exchange of letters between Jacobi and Mendelssohn with Elise Reimarus as initial go-between, ended up in four books, two by each disputant, each hurrying to preempt the other's. Jacobi's *On Spinoza's Doctrine, in Letters to Mr. Moses Mendelssohn* narrowly preceded Mendelssohn's *Morning Hours*; and Mendelssohn's quick follow-up, *To the Friends of Lessing*—which the chronically ill Mendelssohn hand-delivered to his publisher on a cold New Year's eve but in doing so caught a chill that caused his untimely death four days later—soon prompted Jacobi's *Against Mendelssohn's Accusations in "To the Friends of Lessing."* In its published format, the dispute drew considerable attention and became known as the Pantheism Controversy. It marked the formal reception of Spinoza in Germany and, with it, the eclipse of the philosophy of Leibniz. Thanks to Mendelssohn's rhetorically engaging defense of Lessing, Spinoza gained public respectability as a Pantheist—the label he still wears among latter-day scholars.

II

The foregoing details are more or less familiar to historians nowadays, and Strauss's introductions recount and analyze them as appropriate. Why then, one might ask, does Strauss's analysis merit special attention? There are two reasons.

First, the most authoritative recent account of the Pantheism Controversy—by Frederick Beiser—considers Strauss's treatment of the complicated background to it as the best, along with Alexander Altmann's.[1] Beiser adds that his own treatment of it is "greatly indebted" to both Strauss and Altmann. Yet apart from the fact that Strauss and Altmann do not entirely agree concerning the events giving rise to the controversy, Beiser does not spell out in any detail his debt to Strauss in particular. The present translation makes up for that omission. It allows the anglophone reader to compare Beiser's account with Strauss's directly. As for the differences between Strauss and Altmann—who, as it happened, also became the editor and literary executor of Strauss's unpublished manuscript containing the critical text, editorial apparatus, and philosophical introduction to *Morning Hours* and *To the Friends of Lessing*—I consider those at some length in my interpretive essay.

But second, Beiser's account differs markedly from Strauss's as regards each of the three figures at the center of the controversy (besides Spinoza).

Beiser considers Jacobi's critique of Spinoza, and of the Enlightenment in general, definitive and unanswerable, and also determinative as such for subsequent German philosophy.[2] In Beiser's formulation, it was a critique of the Enlightenment's "faith in reason." As Beiser shows, Jacobi contends that Spinoza's argument in the *Ethics* is the fullest expression of the use of reason to prove everything scientifically and take nothing for granted. According to Jacobi, this tendency originates in the will not to depend on anything one cannot in principle control; and yet, if followed out resolutely, it leads necessarily to determinism and fatalism, as Spinoza makes clear. The corrective, says Jacobi, is to return to the starting point that precedes and underlies all scientific proof, namely, "knowledge of ignorance" as arrived at from the standpoint of prescientific belief—a standpoint that in the circumstances is recoverable only by means of a *salto mortale* (or leap of faith). According to Beiser, Jacobi's indictment of Spinoza and the Enlightenment is thus an indictment of reason as such. According to Strauss, on the other hand, Jacobi like the Enlightenment generally (including Mendelssohn) presupposes that reason is at bottom what it is said to be by Thomas

---

1. Bei, 335n12. For Altmann, see his "Preliminary Remark" to the *Jubiläumsausgabe* volume containing Mendelssohn's *Morgenstunden* and *An die Freunde Lessings*, translated in the present volume.

2. Bei, 1ff., 9–10, 46–47, 85, 108, with Strauss, IMH XXVI. Cf. Beck, 360; David Janssens, *Between Athens and Jerusalem: Philosophy, Prophecy, and Politics in Leo Strauss's Early Thought* (Albany: State University of New York Press, 2008), 78–81, 89f.; Bruce Rosenstock, *Philosophy and the Jewish Question: Mendelssohn, Rosenzweig, and Beyond* (New York: Fordham University Press, 2010), 83–106; Beth Lord, *Kant and Spinozism: Transcendent Idealism and Immanence from Jacobi to Deleuze* (London: Palgrave Macmillan, 2011), 23f., 29–31; Michah Gottlieb, *Faith and Freedom: Moses Mendelssohn's Theological-Political Thought* (New York: Oxford University Press, 2011), 67–71.

Hobbes (1588–1679)—the philosophical founder of the Enlightenment, as Strauss argues elsewhere—namely, an instrument of the passions.[3] At the same time, Strauss suggests that Lessing, in contrast to Jacobi, had freed himself from that narrow presupposition by turning to premodern thinkers like Horace and Plato. That is to say, although Jacobi may conceivably have been, in Strauss's words, "the most understanding adherent that Lessing found among his contemporaries," he nevertheless failed to consider the possibility that Lessing had come to question the very view of reason that Jacobi was ascribing to him in calling him a Spinozist.

As regards Lessing, moreover, Beiser accepts Jacobi's report of his Spinozism at face value.[4] He notes that Mendelssohn's first response to that report was to consider Lessing's putative confession of Spinozism merely an example of Lessing's characteristic irony and love of paradox. But Beiser discounts this response on the grounds that Jacobi in an earlier publication relates that Lessing had told him personally that (in Beiser's words) "he would never indulge in paradox for its own sake, and . . . would never attack a true belief unless it were based on poor arguments." Strauss, however, vindicates Mendelssohn's first response. He points out, among other things, that according to the plain wording of Jacobi's report, Lessing was not confessing Spinozism unqualifiedly. As Strauss documents, Lessing had preceded his confession by saying to Jacobi, "*If* I am to name myself after anyone . . ." (the emphasis is Strauss's); and a bit later, after Jacobi had protested that his own credo was not in Spinoza, Lessing had replied, "I would hope that it is not in any book."

Finally, as regards Mendelssohn, Beiser considers that his attributing Spinozism qua Pantheism to Lessing is warranted and accurate.[5] But Strauss argues that none of the documentation that Mendelssohn cites or could

---

3. See the epilogue to my interpretive essay on what Strauss says elsewhere about Hobbes et al.

4. Bei, 63–64, 71, 73–74, with Strauss, IMH XXIII, XXXI, XC–XCI. Cf. All, 72, 147; Beck, 358–59; Hermann Timm, *Gott und die Freiheit: Studien zur Religionsphilosophie der Goethezeit, Band 1, Die Spinoza Renaissance* (Frankfurt am Main: Vittorio Klostermann, 1974), 5; Bell, 72–73, 85–93; Gérard Vallée, introduction to *The Spinoza Conversations between Lessing and Jacobi: Text with Excerpts from the Ensuing Controversy*, trans. Gérard Vallée, J. B. Lawson, and C. G. Chapple (Lanham, MD: University Press of America, 1988), 16–36; George di Giovanni, introduction to Friedrich Heinrich Jacobi, *The Main Philosophical Writings and the Novel "Allwill,"* trans. George di Giovanni (Montreal and Kingston: McGill-Queen's University Press, 1994), 74–98; Dominique Bourel, *Moses Mendelssohn: La naissance du judaïsme moderne* (Paris: Gallimard, 2004), 412ff.; William F. H. Altman, *The German Stranger: Leo Strauss and National Socialism* (Lanham, MD: Lexington Books, 2011), 39–57.

5. Bei, 55-57, 104, with Strauss, IMH XCI–XCV. Cf. Bell, 27–37; Vallée, introduction, 36-62; Alan Arkush, *Moses Mendelssohn and the Enlightenment* (Albany: SUNY Press, 1994), 72; Willi Goetschel, *Spinoza's Modernity: Mendelssohn, Lessing, and Heine* (Madison: University of Wisconsin

have cited actually supports the attribution. Nor, Strauss goes on to show, could Lessing ever have thought of himself seriously as a Pantheist. Moreover, Mendelssohn evidently knew as much. Needless to say, Strauss's argument here has possible implications for what we are to make of latter-day characterizations of Spinoza and Spinozism as well.[6]

III

My translation includes Alexander Altmann's editorial preface to the *Jubiläumsausgabe* volume containing Mendelssohn's *Morning Hours* and *To the Friends of Lessing*. Since that particular volume did not come into print until shortly after Strauss's death, Altmann's preface doubles as a brief eulogy of Strauss. It includes three letters that Strauss wrote to Altmann about their scholarly disagreements concerning the Pantheism Controversy. I consider the disagreements at some length in my interpretive essay, which goes on to analyze each of Strauss's introductions in turn and show how these culminate in his masterful treatment of the writings of Mendelssohn, Lessing, and Jacobi that generated the controversy. My essay confines itself mostly to looking at the introductions on their own terms, though I include an epilogue that summarizes what Strauss says elsewhere about the broader theological and political themes broached in the introductions. Those themes include the fate of Spinoza and Spinozism post-Mendelssohn, as sketched in the mature Strauss's autobiographical retrospective on the theological and political backdrop to his early Spinoza studies, which in turn were indispensable for his Mendelssohn introductions.[7]

In the introductions, Strauss often refers the reader to his extensive editorial annotations to the Mendelssohnian texts he edited. I have therefore translated all the annotations he refers to explicitly and many he refers to implicitly. Occasionally he also refers to annotations by his fellow *Jubiläumsausgabe* editors, as well as to passages from their introductions to other Mendelssohnian texts. I have translated those too. Here and there, I have translated various other annotations by Strauss's fellow editors, and passages I have excerpted from their introductions, for the purpose of supply-

---

Press, 2004), 170-80; Benjamin Lazier, *God Interrupted: Heresy and the European Imagination between the World Wars* (Princeton: Princeton University Press, 2008), 110.

6. See the epilogue to my interpretive essay on what Strauss says elsewhere about Spinoza and Spinozism.

7. Strauss, "Preface to the English Translation" to *Spinoza's Critique of Religion* (New York: Schocken Books, 1965), 1–31; reprinted in Strauss, *Liberalism Ancient and Modern* (New York: Basic Books, 1968), 224–59. See also notes 18–19 and 27–29 of my interpretive essay, pp. 223–24, below.

ing further background information as appropriate. In their German originals, all editorial annotations to the Mendelssohnian texts are formatted as entries in editorial apparatuses appended to the respective *Jubiläumsausgabe* volumes. With some (self-evident) exceptions, I have likewise formatted the annotations I have translated for the present volume as appendix entries. I have done the same with the passages excerpted from Strauss's fellow editors.

To ease the reader's way from Strauss's introductions to the appendix entries and back as needed, and to simplify references to and within the introductions themselves, I have devised a distinctive citation format. It is as follows.

The German originals of Strauss's introductions lack footnotes, in keeping with the *Jubiläumsausgabe*'s use of running (parenthetical) notes exclusively. These I have reformatted as numbered footnotes and interspersed among my own translator's footnotes.

When citing a particular footnote, I do so according to the particular introduction to which it belongs and the pagination of the *Jubiläumsausgabe* volume in which the introduction appears in German. Thus, for example, the first of Strauss's running notes in his introduction to Mendelssohn's *Pope a Metaphysician!* is on page xv of that introduction in the *Jubiläumsausgabe* volume and is footnote 4 in my numbering. I include the *Jubiläumsausgabe* page numbers in the running text of my translation of the introduction; these are readily visible inside curly brackets in boldface—as {**xv**}, for example. This format allows, as well, easy cross-reference to the German original.[8]

I also abbreviate the titles of Strauss's introductions by their initials.[9] Thus, to take the present example, "Introduction to *Pope a Metaphysician!*" becomes IPM.

In short, I cite the aforementioned footnote as IPM xvn4.

To indicate the difference between my footnotes and Strauss's, I add his initials in curly brackets to the end of each of his: {LS}. Whenever a footnote of Strauss's refers the reader to an editorial annotation or excerpted passage, I supplement that footnote in one of two ways. If the annotation is short enough or is best consulted right away, I simply quote it (without

---

8. The *Jubiläumsausgabe* page numbers are also reproduced in Strauss's "*Einleitungen zu Moses Mendelssohn Gesammelte Schriften,*" in Strauss, *Gesammelte Schriften, Band II: Philosophie und Gesetz—Frühe Schriften*, ed. Heinrich Meier (Stuttgart and Weimar: J. B. Metzler Verlag, 1997), 465–605. This version of his *Einleitungen* ("Introductions") does not include the editorial annotations, etc.

9. For a complete list of the abbreviations used in this volume, see pages xxvii–xxxiv, below.

quotation marks) and identify its source in the curly brackets immediately following. Otherwise, I refer the reader to the appropriate appendix entry, by using the rubric "appendix 2, supplement to . . ." and inserting the appropriate footnote abbreviation.

Occasionally, too, I have expanded, updated, corrected, and repositioned Strauss's original citations as appropriate.

IV

Besides the editorial annotations, my appendixes contain English translations of the following: Strauss's preface to a book on Lessing that he contemplated but never wrote; a hitherto untranslated Mendelssohnian passage that Strauss cites in his *Natural Right and History* (1953); and an important passage from Lessing's "The Education of the Human Race" to which Strauss's introductions call attention.

In addition, I have translated Strauss's German renderings of (selections from) Mendelssohn's *Commentary on Maimonides' "Logical Terms"* and of Mendelssohn's *The Soul*. These two Hebrew writings Strauss also annotated extensively for his German-speaking reader. I have therefore translated Strauss's annotations as well. My translations, along with the annotations, do not appear in the present volume but may be found online at www.press.uchicago.edu/sites/strauss/.

Generally, my efforts as translator to convey the forcefulness, eloquence, and economy of Strauss's German prose have been guided by these same features as they show up in his untranslated English prose. This has meant translating Strauss and the sources he quotes (in German and other languages) as literally as a proper and fluid English diction, and my own modest abilities, would allow me to. It has especially meant keeping his important terms as consistent as possible in English, on the premise that he himself understood and wrote them consistently in his native German. Where I found that English idiom now and then required me to insert a word or phrase that does not appear as such in Strauss's German, I often indicated as much either by means of a translator's footnote or else by attaching to the insertion a small circle in superscript—thus°.

V

I undertook the translation at the kind invitation of Kenneth Hart Green, then editor of a series of volumes elsewhere that was devoted to the Jewish writings of Leo Strauss. Before my volume on Strauss's Mendelssohnian writings—and Green's on Strauss's Maimonidean writings[10]—became ready for publication, the series was interrupted by the publisher and our volumes left homeless. Thanks in part to Ken's efforts, each volume found a new home at University of Chicago Press. Meanwhile, Ken has been a thoughtful, patient, and encouraging friend to my volume and to me, especially by offering helpful advice and criticism as needed. We have shared an appreciation of the scholarly demands facing anyone drawn to the Jewish and philosophical issues that Strauss articulates, and of the joy accompanying the strenuous efforts often required for thinking these through.

Ian Moore, then still an undergraduate, perused my translation of Strauss's German with a critical eye and saved me from occasional infelicities and outright blunders. So did two anonymous readers for the press, whose substantive comments on my interpretive essay as well prompted me to refocus and reformulate parts of it. I hasten to add that any and all translator's errors or other howlers are my own. (Needless to say, I take no pride in ownership of these.)

Other scholarly friends have helped in ways too varied to mention all at once. I hope that they (or their memories) will pardon me for merely listing them here. Sincere thanks to the late Eve Adler, Gisela Berns, the late Laurence Berns, Curtis Bowman, Zac Cadwalader, Dennis Erwin, David Gilner, Trish Glazebrook, Willi Goetschel, Richard Golden, Lenn Goodman, Michah Gottlieb, Gene Hargrove, Reid Heller, Antonio Lastra, Monica Lindemann, Thomas Meyer, Svetozar Minkov, Josh Parens, Michael Platt, Marty Plax, the late Ellis Rivkin, Ricardo Rozzi and Pancha Massardo, Nathan Tarcov, Alan Udoff, and Hartwig Wiedebach.

I am grateful to Friedrich Frommann Verlag Günther Holzboog of Stuttgart–Bad Cannstatt, to Heinrich Meier, to J. B. Metzler Verlag of Stuttgart and Weimar, and to the Leo Strauss Center at the University of Chicago for permissions to use copyright materials. Thanks also to *La Torre del Virrey: Revista de Estudios Culturales* (and its editor Antonio Lastra) of Valencia, Spain, for permission to recycle an article that appeared in volume 4 (Winter 2007–8) as "Interpretación de la *Ética* de Spinoza como un 'sistema': las *Horas matinales* de Moses Mendelssohn."

My wife Connie has remained steadfastly loving, patient, and supportive even as this volume was consuming much of my attention not just during

---

10. Kenneth Hart Green, *Leo Strauss and the Rediscovery of Maimonides,* and Leo Strauss, *On Maimonides: The Complete Writings.* Both volumes are now forthcoming from University of Chicago Press.

workday hours but after hours and on weekends and holidays too. So have our two sons Michael and David, now loving, patient, and supportive husbands and parents in families of their own.

Finally, I dedicate the volume to (Rabbi) Jack Bemporad, who ever so gently prodded me into writing my first scholarly publication, and directly or indirectly has motivated and encouraged others since. I hope he finds here a small token of my heartfelt fondness, deep appreciation, and long-standing esteem.

CHRONOLOGY OF WRITINGS CITED IN STRAUSS'S INTRODUCTIONS[11]

c. 399– BCE	Plato, *Apology, Crito, Phaedo, Republic*
c. 263–71	Plotinus, *Enneads*
1151	Moses Maimonides, *Millot HaHiggayon*[12] [*Logical Terms*]
1190	Maimonides, *Moreh Nevuchim*[13] [*Guide of the Perplexed*]
1641	René Descartes, *Meditationes de prima philosophia* [*Meditations on First Philosophy*]
1651	Thomas Hobbes, *Leviathan, or the Matter, Form and Power of a Commonwealth, Ecclesiastical and Civil*
1662	Blaise Pascal, *Pensées* [*Thoughts*] (posthumously published)
1663	Benedict Spinoza, *Principia philosophiae cartesiensis* [*Principles of Cartesian Philosophy*]
1670	Spinoza, *Tractatus theologico-politicus* [*Theologico-Political Treatise*]
1677	Spinoza, *Ethica ordine geometrico demonstrata* [*Ethics Demonstrated in a Geometrical Order*] (posthumously published)
1678	Ralph Cudworth, *The True Intellectual System of the Universe: the first part, wherein all the reason and philosophy of atheism is confuted and its impossibility demonstrated* (*imprimatur* dated 1671)
1680	Nicolas Malebranche, *Traité de la nature et de la grâce* [*Treatise on Nature and Grace*]
1686	Gottfried Wilhelm Leibniz, *Discours de métaphysique* [*Discourse on Metaphysics*]
1697f.	Pierre Bayle, *Dictionnaire historique et critique* [*Historical and Critical Dictionary*]
1689	John Locke, *Essay Concerning Human Understanding*

11. In this chronology, I limit myself by and large to authors mentioned in the text and notes of LS's ten introductions. As for those authors cited in Strauss's editorial annotations to JA II, III.1 and III.2—many of which I have translated and appended to his introductions as appropriate—LS himself generally adds the pertinent bibliographical information, including publication dates.

12. Mendelssohn used a Hebrew translation of the Arabic original; the latter was no longer extant in full at that time. See also p. 251 n. 143, below.

13. Mendelssohn used a Hebrew translation of the Arabic original.

1695 Leibniz, "Système nouveau de la nature et de la communication des substances, aussi bien que de l'union qu'il y a entre l'âme et le corps" [New System of the Nature and Communication of Substances, as well as of the Union that there is between Soul and Body]

1703f. Leibniz, *Nouveaux essais sur l'entendement* [*New Essays on Understanding*]

1710 Leibniz, *Essais de théodicée sur la bonté de Dieu, la liberté de l'homme et l'origine du mal* [*Essays in Theodicy on the Goodness of God, the Freedom of Man, and the Origin of Evil*]

Leibniz, *Causa Dei asserta per justitiam ejus, cum caeteris ejus perfectionibus, cunctisque actionibus conciliatam* [*God's Cause Upheld through His Justice having been Reconciled with His Remaining Perfections and the Entirety of Actions*] (appended to *Essais de théodicée*)

1711 Shaftesbury [Anthony Ashley Cooper], *Characteristics of Men, Manners, Opinions, Times*

1714 Leibniz, "Principes de la nature et de la grâce, fondées en raison" [Principles of Nature and Grace, Founded in Reason]

Leibniz, *Monadologie* [*Monadology*]

1723 Christian Wolff, *Vernünftigen Gedancken von der Menschen Thun und Lassen* [*Rational Thoughts on Men's Acting and Forbearing*]

1725 Georg Bernhard Bilfinger, *Dilucidationes philosophicae de Deo, animâ humanâ, mundo et generalibus rerum affectionibus* [*Philosophical Clarifications of God, the Human Soul, the World, and the General Dispositions of Things*]

1732 Voltaire [François Marie Arouet], *Zaïre*

1733f. Alexander Pope, "An Essay on Man"

1736 Voltaire, *Alzire*

1736f. Wolff, *Theologia naturalis* [*Natural Theology*]

1737 Jean Pierre de Crousaz, *Examen de l'Essai de Herr Pope sur l'homme* [*Examination of Mr. Pope's "Essay on Man"*]

1738 William Warburton, *A Vindication of Herr Pope's "Essay on Man" from the Misinterpretations of Herr de Crousaz*

1738f. Wolff, *Philosophia practica universalis* [*Universal Practical Philosophy*]

1741ff. Jean Henri Samuel Formey, *La belle wolfienne ou Abrégé de la philosophie wolfienne* [*The Beautiful Wolffian, or Epitome of the Wolffian Philosophy*]

1745 Pierre Louis Moreau de Maupertuis, *Venus physique* [*Physical Venus*]

1748 Johann Joachim Spalding, *Die Bestimmung des Menschen* [*The Destiny of Man*]

1749 Gotthold Ephraim Lessing, *Die Juden* [*The Jews*]

c. 1753 Lessing, "Das Christenthum der Vernunft" [The Christianity of Reason] (unpublished)

1753 Jean Jacques Rousseau, *Discours sur l'origine et les fondements de l'inégalité parmi les hommes* [*Discourse on the Origin and Foundations of Inequality among Men*]

1754 Lessing, "Rettungen des Horaz" [Vindications of Horace]

Lessing, "Rettung des Hieronymus Cardanus" [Vindication of Hieronymus Cardanus]

Hermann Samuel Reimarus, *Die vornehmsten Wahrheiten der natürlichen Religion* [*The Noblest Truths of Natural Religion*]

1755 MENDELSSOHN, *PHILOSOPHISCHE GESPRÄCHE* [*PHILOSOPHICAL DIALOGUES*]

MENDELSSOHN, *ÜBER DIE EMPFINDUNGEN* [*ON THE SENTIMENTS*]

MENDELSSOHN and Gotthold Ephraim Lessing, *POPE EIN METAPHYSIKER!* [*Pope a Metaphysician!*]

1755f. MENDELSSOHN, GERMAN TRANSLATION OF ROUSSEAU'S *DISCOURS SUR L'ORIGINE ET LES FONDEMENTS DE L'INÉGALITÉ PARMI LES HOMMES* [*DISCOURSE ON THE ORIGIN AND FOUNDATIONS OF INEQUALITY AMONG MEN*] (published anonymously)

MENDELSSOHN, "SENDSCHREIBEN AN DEN HERRN MAGISTER LESSING IN LEIPZIG" [EPISTLE TO MR. LESSING IN LEIPZIG] (published as an Appendix to Mendelssohn's Rousseau translation)

1756 MENDELSSOHN, *GEDANKEN VON DER WAHRSCHEINLICHKEIT* [*THOUGHTS ON PROBABILITY*] (published anonymously)

1758 Pierre Louis Moreau de Maupertuis, *Examen philosophique de la preuve de l'existence de Dieu employée dans l'Essai de Cosmologie* [*Philosophical Examination of the Proofs of the Existence of God employed in the "Essay on Cosmology"*]

1759 Roger Joseph Boscovich, *Philosophiae naturalis Theoria* [*Theory of Natural Philosophy*]

Johann Georg Hamann, *Sokratische Denkwürdigkeiten für die lange Weile des Publikums* [*Socratic Memorabilia for the Boredom of the Public*]

Voltaire, *Candide, ou l'optimisme* [*Candide, or Optimism*]

1760 MENDELSSOHN, *BIUR MILLOT HAHIGGAYON* [*COMMENTARY ON MOSES MAIMONIDES' "LOGICAL TERMS"*] (in Hebrew)

1761 André Pierre le Guay de Prémontval, *Vues philosophiques, ou Protestations et déclarations sur les principaux objets des connoissances humaines* [*Philosophical Views, or Professings and Declarations on the Principal Objects of Human Knowledge*]

Rousseau, *Julie, ou la nouvelle Héloise* [*Julie, or the New Heloise*]

1762 Rousseau, *Émile, ou de l'éducation* [*Emile, or on Education*]

1763 Lessing, "Über die Wirklichkeit der Dinge außer Gott" [On the Actuality of Things Outside God]

1764 MENDELSSOHN, *ABHANDLUNG ÜBER DIE EVIDENZ IN METAPHYSISCHEN WISSENSCHAFTEN* [*TREATISE ON EVIDENCE IN METAPHYSICAL SCIENCES*]

Thomas Abbt, "Zweifel über die Bestimmung des Menschen" [Doubt concerning the Destiny of Man]

MENDELSSOHN, "ORAKEL DIE BESTIMMUNG DES MENSCHEN BETREFFEND" [ORACLE APROPOS THE DESTINY OF MAN]

Johann Bernhard Basedow, *Philalethie*

Johann Heinrich Lambert, *Neues Organon oder Gedanken über die Erforschung und Bezeichnung des Wahren* [*New Organon, or Thoughts on the Investigation and Designation of Truth*]

1765 Basedow, *Theoretische System der gesunden Vernunft* [*Theoretical System of Sound Commonsense*]

1766 Johann Gottfried Herder, *Fragmente über die neuere deutsche Literatur* [*Fragments on Recent German Literature*]

1767 MENDELSSOHN, *PHÄDON ODER ÜBER DIE UNSTERBLICHKEIT DER SEELE, IN DREY GESPRÄCHEN* [*PHÄDON, OR ON THE IMMORTALITY OF THE SOUL IN THREE DIALOGUES*]

1769 Lessing, *Hamburgische Dramaturgie* [*Hamburg Dramaturgy*]

Charles Bonnet, *La palingénésie philosophique, ou idées sur l'état passée et l'état futur des êtres vivants* [*Philosophical Palingenesis, or Ideas on the Past and Future States of Living Beings*]

Johann Caspar Lavater, German translation of Bonnet's *La palingénésie*

MENDELSSOHN, "GEGENBETRACHTUNGEN ÜBER BONNET'S PALINGENESIE" [COUNTERREFLECTIONS ON BONNET'S *PALINGENESIS*] (unpublished)

1770 MENDELSSOHN, *SCHREIBEN AN DEN HERRN DIACONUS LAVATER* [*LETTER TO DEACON LAVATER*]

Lavater, *Antwort an den Herrn Moses Mendelssohn* [*Reply to Mr. Moses Mendelssohn*]

MENDELSSOHN, *NACHERINNERUNG* [*EPILOGUE*] (appended to Lavater's *Antwort*)

1772 Lessing, *Emilia Galotti*

Johann August Eberhard, *Neue Apologie des Sokrates oder Untersuchung der Lehre von der Seligkeit der Heiden* [*New Apology of Socrates, or Investigation of the Blessedness of the Heathens*]

1773 Johann Wolfgang Goethe, "Prometheus"

Lessing, "Leibniz von den ewigen Strafen" [Leibniz on Eternal Punishments]

Lessing, "Des Andreas Wissowatius Einwürfe wider den Dreieinigkeit" [Andreas Wissowatius's Objections to the Trinity]

1774 Reimarus, "Von Duldung der Deisten" [On Toleration of the Deists] (excerpt from Reimarus's unpublished *Apologie oder Schutzschrift für die vernünftigen Verehrer Gottes* [*Apology or Defense for Rational Worshippers of God*]; published anonymously by Lessing as "Fragment einer Ungennante" [Fragment of an Unnamed]; subsequently referred to, together with five other excerpts published anonymously by Lessing in 1777f., as the "Wolfenbüttel Fragments")

1776f. Johann Nikolaus Tetens, *Philosophische Versuche über die menschliche Natur und ihre Entwicklung* [*Philosophical Essays on Human Nature and its Development*]

1777f. Reimarus, "Von Verschreyung der Vernunft auf den Kanzeln" [On the Decrying of Reason in the Pulpits][14]

Reimarus, "Unmöglichkeit einer Offenbarung, die all Menschen auf einer gegründete Art glauben könnten" [Impossibility of a Revelation that All Men Could Believe on a Rational Basis]

Reimarus, "Durchgang der Israeliten durchs rothe Meer" [Passage of the Israelites through the Red Sea]

Reimarus, "Daß die Bücher A.T. nicht geschrieben worden, eine Religion zu offenbaren" [That the Old Testament Books Were Not Written to Reveal a Religion]

Reimarus, "Über die Auferstehungsgeschichte" [On the Resurrection Story]

Lessing, "Die Erziehung des Menschengeschlechts" [The Education of the Human Race] (first half; completed text published 1780)

1778 Lessing, *Anti-Goeze*, etc.

1779 Lessing, *Nathan der Weise* [*Nathan the Wise*]

Friedrich Heinrich Jacobi, *Woldemar. Erster Theil* [*Woldemar: First Part*]

Jean André de Luc, *Lettres physiques et morales sur l'histoire de la terre et de l'homme* [*Physical and Moral Writings on the History of the Earth and of Man*]

1781 Dohm, Christian. *Über die bürgerliche Verbesserung der Juden* [*On the Civil Amelioration of the Jews*]

Jacobi, *Vermischte Schriften. Erster Theil.* [*Miscellaneous Writings: First Part*]

Immanuel Kant, *Kritik der reinen Vernunft* [*Critique of Pure Reason*] (1st ed.)

1782 MENDELSSOHN, ANMERKUNGEN ZU ABBTS FREUNDSCHAFTLICHER CORRESPONDENZ [ANNOTATIONS TO ABBT'S FRIENDLY CORRESPONDENCE]

MENDELSSOHN. VORREDE [PREFACE] to Menasseh ben Israel, *Rettung der Juden* [*Vindication of the Jews*].

1782 Jacobi, *Etwas, das Lessing gesagt hat. Ein Kommentar zu den "Reisen der Päpste" nebst Betrachtungen von einem Dritten* [*Something that Lessing Said: A Commentary on the "Journeys of the Popes" with Meditations by a Third Party*]

1783 MENDELSSOHN, JERUSALEM ODER ÜBER RELIGIÖSE MACHT UND JUDENTUM [JERUSALEM, OR ON RELIGIOUS POWER AND JUDAISM]

MENDELSSOHN et al., "GEDANKEN VERSCHIEDENER BEY GELEGENHEIT EINER MERKWÜRDIGE SCHRIFT" [THOUGHTS OF VARIOUS MEN APROPOS A REMARKABLE WRITING]

---

14. This and the four following entries are the remaining "Wolfenbüttel Fragments." See the Reimarus entry for 1774, above.

Jacobi, "Erinnerungen gegen die in den Januar des Museums eingerückte 'Gedanken über eine merkwürdige Schrift...'" [Objections to "Thoughts of Various Men about a Remarkable Writing" Which Appeared in the January Issue of *Museum*...]

1784 MENDELSSOHN, "ERINNERUNGEN HERR JACOBIS" [OBJECTIONS OF MR. JACOBI]

MENDELSSOHN, *SACHE GOTTES ODER DIE GERETTETE VORSEHUNG* [*GOD'S CAUSE, OR PROVIDENCE VINDICATED*] (unpublished)

1785 MENDELSSOHN, *ABHANDLUNG VON DER UNKÖRPERLICHKEIT DER MENSCHLICHEN SEELE* [*TREATISE ON THE INCORPOREALITY OF THE HUMAN SOUL*] (German original; Latin translation by J. Grossinger published in 1784)

MENDELSSOHN, *MORGENSTUNDEN ODER VORLESUNGEN ÜBER DAS DASEIN GOTTES* [*MORNING HOURS, OR LECTURES ON THE EXISTENCE OF GOD*]

Jacobi, *Über die Lehre des Spinozas in Briefen an den Herrn Moses Mendelssohn* [*On Spinoza's Doctrine, in Letters to Mr. Moses Mendelssohn*]

1786 MENDELSSOHN, *AN DIE FREUNDE LESSINGS* [*TO THE FRIENDS OF LESSING*]

Jacobi, *Wider Mendelssohns Beschuldigungen betreffend die Briefen über die Lehre des Spinoza* [*Against Mendelssohn's Accusations apropos the "Letters on Spinoza's Doctrine"*]

1787 MENDELSSOHN, *SEFER HANEFESH* [*THE SOUL*] (in Hebrew; published posthumously)

Jacobi, *David Hume über den Glauben, oder Idealismus und Realismus* [*David Hume on Belief, or Idealism and Realism*]

Kant, *Kritik der reinen Vernunft* [*Critique of Pure Reason*] (2nd ed.)

Reimarus, J. A. H. *Über die Gründe der menschlichen Erkenntniß und der natürlichen Religion* [*On the Bases of Human Knowledge and of Natural Religion*]

ABBREVIATIONS

AA Alexander Altmann

Adelung Adelung, Johann, Christoph. *Grammatisch-kritische Wörterbuch der hochdeutschen Mundart*. 4 Bände. Vienna: B. P. Bauer, 1811.

All Allison, Henry E. *Lessing and the Enlightenment: His Philosophy of Religion and Its Relation to Eighteenth-Century Thought*. Ann Arbor: University of Michigan Press, 1966.

Ar Ariew, Roger, ed. *G. W. Leibniz and Samuel Clarke: Correspondence*. Indianapolis: Hackett, 2000.

ArGa Ariew, Roger, and Daniel Garber, eds. and trans. *G. W. Leibniz: Philosophical Essays*. Indianapolis: Hackett, 1989.

Ark Mendelssohn, Moses. *Jerusalem, or On Religious Power and Judaism*. Translated by Alan Arkush. Introduction and commentary by Alexander Altmann. Hanover, NH: University Press of New England, 1983.

AT Descartes, René. *Oeuvres*. Édités par Charles Adam et Paul Tannéry. Nouvelle édition. 12 tomes. Paris: Vrin, 1957–68.

Bai Bailey, Cyril, ed. *Epicurus: The Extant Remains*. Oxford: Clarendon Press, 1926. Reprint. Hildesheim and New York: Olms, 1975.

Bch Voltaire. *Oeuvres complètes*. Nouvelle edition . . . conforme pour le texte à l'édition de [A. J. Q.] Beuchot. 54 tomes. Paris: Garnier frères, 1877–85.

Beck Beck, Lewis White. *Early German Philosophy: Kant and His Predecessors*. Cambridge, MA: Harvard University Press, 1969.

Bei Beiser, Frederick C. *The Fate of Reason: German Philosophy from Kant to Fichte*. Cambridge, MA: Harvard University Press, 1987.

Bell Bell, David. *Spinoza in Germany from 1670 to the Age of Goethe*. London: Institute of Germanic Studies, University of London, 1984.

Beu Spalding, Johann Joachim. *Die Bestimmung des Menschen*. Herausgegeben von Albrecht Beutel, Daniela Kirschkowski, und Dennis Prause. Tübingen: Mohr Siebeck, 2006.

Blm Rousseau, Jean Jacques. *Emile: or On Education*. Translated by Allan Bloom. New York: Basic Books, 1979.

CCJR Jacobs, Louis. *A Concise Companion to the Jewish Religion*. Oxford: Oxford University Press, 1999.

Cha *Lessing's Theological Writings*. Translated by Henry Chadwick. Stanford: Stanford University Press, 1956.

CM Strauss, Leo, *The City and Man*. Chicago: Rand McNally, 1964.

Cul Mendelssohn, Moses. *Phaedon, or The Death of Socrates*. Translated by Charles Cullen. London: J. Cooper, 1789. Reprint, New York: Arno, 1973.

DaDy Mendelssohn, Moses. *Morning Hours: Lectures on God's Existence*. Translated by Daniel O. Dahlstrom and Corey Dyck. Dordrecht, Heidelberg, London, and New York: Springer, 2011.

Dah Mendelssohn, Moses. *Philosophical Writings*. Translated by Daniel O. Dahlstrom. Cambridge: Cambridge University Press, 1997.

DHC Bayle, Pierre. *Dictionnaire historique et critique*. 5me éd. 4 tomes. Amsterdam, 1640.

Dilucidationes Bilfinger, Georg Bernhard. *Dilucidationes philosophicae, de deo, anima humana, mundo*. Tübingen, 1725, 1746, 1768.

Empfindungen Mendelssohn, Moses. *Briefe über die Empfindungen*, JA I 41–123 (1. Auflage); JA I 227–337 (2. Auflage)

Enthusiast Mendelssohn, Moses. "Enthusiast, Visionair, Fanatiker," JA III.1 315–17

EP Baumgarten, Alexander Gottlieb. *Ethica Philosophica*. Halle, 1740.

Erd Leibniz, Gottfried Wilhelm. *Opera Philosophica*. Instruxit J. E. Erdmann. Faksimiledruck der Ausgabe 1840, durch weitere Textstücke ergänzt und mit einem Vorwort versehen von Renate Vollbrecht. Aalen: Scientia, 1959.

ET Strauss, Leo. "Exoteric Teaching." Edited by Kenneth Hart Green. *Interpretation: A Journal of Political Philosophy* 14 (1986): 51–59.

Evidenz Mendelssohn, Moses. *Abhandlung über die Evidenz*, JA II 267–30

Fai Horace. *Satires, Epistles and Ars Poetica*. Edited and translated by H. Rushton Fairclough. Rev. ed. Cambridge, MA: Harvard University Press, 1929.

Fr. French

Freunde Mendelssohn, Moses. *An die Freunde Lessings*, JA III.2 177–218

FrWo Francks, Richard, and R. S. Woolhouse, trans. *Gottfried Wilhelm Leibniz: Philosophical Texts*. Oxford: Oxford University Press, 1998.

GaKa *Basic Writings of Nietzsche*. Introduction by Peter Gay. Translated by Walter Kaufman. New York: Modern Library, 2000.

Gal Gallagher, Paul B. "'Pope a Metaphysician!' An Anonymous Pamphlet in Defense of Leibniz." *Fidelio* 8.4 (Winter 1999): 45–59.

GAW von Harnack, Adolf. *Geschichte der Königliche Preußische Akademie der Wissenschaft*. 3 Bände in 4. Berlin: Reichsdruckerei, 1900.

Gay Voltaire. *Philosophical Dictionary*. Translated by Peter Gay. New York: Harcourt, Brace & World, 1962.

ABBREVIATIONS xxix

Geb Spinoza, Benedictus de. *Opera*. Herausgegeben von Carl Gebhart. 4 Bände. Heidelberg: Carl Winters Universitätsbuchhandlung, 1925.

Gegenbetrachtungen Mendelssohn, Moses. "Gegenbetrachtungen über Bonnets Palingenesis," JA VII 65–107

Ger Leibniz, Gottfried Wilhelm. *Philosophischen Schriften*. Herausgegeben von C. J. Gerhart. 7 Bände. Reprint, Hildesheim: Olms, 1960–61.

Ger. German

Gespräche Mendelssohn, Moses. *Philosophische Gespräche*, JA I 1–40 (1. Auflage); 337–77 (2. Auflage)

Gio Jacobi, Friedrich Heinrich. *The Main Philosophical Writings and the Novel "Allwill."* Translated by George di Giovanni. Montreal and Kingston: McGill-Queen's University Press, 1994.

Goe *Goethes sämtliche Werke*. Mit Einleitungen von Karl Goedeke. Neu durchgesehene und ergänzte Ausgabe. 36 Bände. Stuttgart: J. G. Cotta: Gebrüder Kröner, 1893–96.

Got Mendelssohn, Moses. *Writings on Judaism, Christianity, & the Bible*. Edited by Michah Gottlieb. Translations by Curtis Bowman, Elias Sacks, and Allan Arkush. Waltham, MA: Brandeis University Press, 2011.

HaNefesh Mendelssohn, Moses. הנפש, JA XIV 121–44.

Hav Voltaire. *Candide*. Edited by George R. Havens. Rev. ed. New York: Holt, Rinehart and Winston, 1969.

HCR Strauss, Leo. *Hobbes's Critique of Religion and Related Writings*. Translated and edited by Gabriel Bartlett and Svetozar Minkov. Chicago: University of Chicago Press, 2011.

Heb. Hebrew

Hef Descartes, René. *Meditations on First Philosophy/Meditationes de Prima Philosophia*. Edited and translated by George Heffernan. Notre Dame, IN: University of Notre Dame Press, 1990.

Higgayon Mendelssohn, Moses. ביאור מלות ההגיון, JA XIV 23–119.

Hug Leibniz, Gottfried Wilhelm. *Theodicy: Essays on the Goodness of God, the Freedom of Man and the Origin of Evil*. Edited by Austin Farrer. Translated by E. M. Huggard. London: Routledge & Kegan Paul, 1951. La Salle, IL: Open Court, 1985.

IdL Strauss, Leo. "Introduction to Mendelssohn's 'On a Literary Essay of Mr. de Luc's.'" Translated in the present volume.

IEL Strauss, Leo. "Introduction to Mendelssohn's 'Epistle to Mr. Lessing in Leipzig.'" Translated in the present volume.

IGC Strauss, Leo. "Introduction to Mendelssohn's *God's Cause, or Providence Vindicated*." Translated in the present volume.

IIS Strauss, Leo. "Introduction to Mendelssohn's *Treatise on the Incorporeality of the Human Soul.*" Translated in the present volume.

IKW *Immanuel Kants Werke.* Herausgegeben von Ernst Cassirer. 10 Bände. Berlin: Bruno Cassirer, 1921–23.

ILT Strauss, Leo. "Introduction to Mendelssohn's *Commentary on Moses Maimonides' 'Logical Terms.'*" Translated in the present volume.

IMH Strauss, Leo. "Introduction to Mendelssohn's *Morning Hours* and *To the Friends of Lessing.*" Translated in the present volume.

IP Strauss, Leo. "Introduction to Mendelssohn's *Phädon.*" Translated in the present volume.

IPM Strauss, Leo. "Introduction to Mendelssohn's *Pope a Metaphysician!*" Translated in the present volume.

IS Strauss, Leo. "Introduction to *The Soul.*" Translated in the present volume.

Ital. Italian

ITE Strauss, Leo. "Introduction to Mendelssohn's *Treatise on Evidence.*" Translated in the present volume.

JA Mendelssohn, Moses. *Gesammelte Schriften Jubiläumsausgabe.* Herausgegeben von F. Bamberger et al. Fortgesetzt von Alexander Altmann. 24 Bände in 32. Facsimile-Reprint, Stuttgart–Bad Cannstatt: Friedrich Frommann Verlag Günther Holzboog, 1972ff.

JPCM Strauss, Leo. *Jewish Philosophy and the Crisis of Modernity.* Edited by Kenneth Hart Green. Albany: SUNY Press, 1997.

Kau Nietzsche, Friedrich. *The Gay Science.* Translated by Walter Kaufmann. New York: Vintage Books, 1974.

KSA Nietzsche, Friedrich. *Sämtliche Werke. Kritische Studienausgabe in 15 Bänden.* Herausgegeben von Giorgio Colli und Mazzino Montinari. Neuausgabe. Berlin und New York: de Gruyter, 1999.

LAM Strauss, Leo. *Liberalism Ancient and Modern.* New York: Basic Books, 1968.

Lat. Latin

Lau Rousseau, Jean Jacques. *Émile, ou de l'éducation.* Présentation par Michel Launay. Paris: Garnier-Flammarion, 1966.

Lavater Mendelssohn, Moses. "Schreiben an den Herrn Diaconus Lavater zu Zürich," JA VII 5–17

LDW Bell, Ernest, ed. *The Dramatic Works of G. E. Lessing.* Bohn's Standard Library. 2 vols. London: George Bell & Sons, 1878.

Lit. literally

LM Lessing, Gotthold Ephraim. *Sämtliche Schriften.* Herausgegeben von Karl Lachmann. Durchgelesen und vermehrt von Franz Muncker. 23 Bände. Stuttgart: G. J. Göschen, 1895.

Logik	Mendelssohn, Moses. *Kommentar zu den 'Termini der Logik' des Mose ben Maimon*, JA II 197–230
LPW	Bell, Ernest, ed. *Selected Prose Works of G. E. Lessing*. Bohn's Standard Library. Rev. ed. London: George Bell & Sons, 1890.
LS	Leo Strauss
LSEW	*Leo Strauss: The Early Writings, 1921–1932*. Translated and edited by Michael Zank. Albany: SUNY Press, 2002.
LSGS II	Strauss, Leo. *Gesammelte Schriften, Band II: Philosophie und Gesetz— Frühe Schriften*. Herausgegeben von Heinrich Meier. Stuttgart und Weimar: J. B. Metzler Verlag, 1997.
LSGS III	Strauss, Leo. *Gesammelte Schriften, Band III: Hobbes' politische Wissenschaft und zugehörige Schriften — Briefe*. Herausgegeben von Heinrich und Wiebke Meier. Stuttgart und Weimar: J. B. Metzler Verlag, 2001.
Mas	Rousseau, Jean Jacques. *The First and Second Discourses*. Edited by Roger D. Masters. Translated by Roger D. and Judith Masters. New York: St. Martin's Press, 1964.
Mei	Rousseau, Jean Jacques. *Diskurs über die Ungleichheit/Discours sur l'inégalité*. Herausgegeben von Heinich Meier. 5. Auflage. Paderborn: Schöningh, 2001.
MMBS	Altmann, Alexander. *Moses Mendelssohn: A Biographical Study*. University, AL: University of Alabama Press, 1973.
MMFM	Altmann, Alexander. *Moses Mendelssohns Frühschriften zur Metaphysik*. Tübingen: J. C. B. Mohr Paul Siebeck, 1969.
MMGS	Mendelssohn, Moses. *Gesammelte Schriften*. Herausgegeben von G. B. Mendelssohn. 7 Bände. Leipzig, 1843–45.
MMTA	Altmann, Alexander. *Die trostvolle Aufklärung: Studien zur Metaphysik und politischen Theorie Moses Mendelssohns*. Stuttgart–Bad Cannstatt: Friedrich Frommann Verlag Günther Holzboog, 1982.
MoE	Hobbes, Thomas. *English Works*. Edited by Willam Molesworth. 11 vols. London: John Bohn, 1839. Reprint, Aalen, Germany: Scientia Verlag, 1966.
MoL	Hobbes, Thomas. *Opera philosophica quae latine scripsit omnia*. Edited by Willam Molesworth. 5 vols. London: John Bohn, 1839. Reprint, Aalen, Germany: Scientia Verlag, 1966.
Morgenstunden	Mendelssohn, Moses. *Morgenstunden, oder Vorlesungen über das Daseyn Gottes*, JA III.2 1–175
MW	Strauss, Leo. *On Maimonides: The Complete Writings*. Chicago: University of Chicago Press, 2012.
Nid	Locke, John. *An Essay Concerning Human Understanding*. Edited by Peter H. Niddich. Oxford: Clarendon Press, 1975.

Nis   Lessing, Gotthold Ephraim. *Philosophical and Theological Writings*. Translated by H. B. Nisbet. Cambridge: Cambridge University Press, 2005.

Nob   Mendelssohn, Moses. *Phädon, or On the Immortality of the Soul*. Translated by Patricia Noble. Introduction by David Shavin. New York: Peter Lang, 2007.

NRH   Strauss, Leo. *Natural Right and History*. Chicago: University of Chicago Press, 1953.

Ontologia   Wolff, Christian. *Philosophia prima, sive Ontologia*. Frankfurt und Leipzig, 1730.

Orakel   Mendelssohn, Moses. "Orakel, die Bestimmung des Menschen betreffend," JA VI.1 19–23

PAW   Strauss, Leo. *Persecution and the Art of Writing*. Glencoe, IL: Free Press, 1953.

Phädon   Mendelssohn, Moses. *Phädon oder über die Unsterblichkeit der Seele*, JA III.1 5–128

Phädon 2   Mendelssohn, Moses. "Anhang zur 2. Auflage der *Phädon* 1768," JA III.2 129–40

Phädon 3   Mendelssohn, Moses. "Anhang zur 3. Auflage der *Phädon* 1769," JA III.2 141–59

PL   Strauss, Leo. *Philosophy and Law: Contributions to the Understanding of Maimonides and His Predecessors*. Translated with an introduction by Eve Adler. Albany: SUNY Press, 1995.

Pop   Bayle, Pierre. *Historical and Critical Dictionary: Selections*. Translated by Richard H. Popkin. Indianapolis: Hackett, 1991.

Pope!   Mendelssohn, Moses, and Gotthold Ephraim Lessing. *Pope ein Metaphysiker!*, JA II 43–80

PPH   Strauss, Leo. *The Political Philosophy of Hobbes: Its Basis and Genesis*. Oxford: Clarendon Press, 1936. Reissued with a new preface, Chicago: University of Chicago Press, 1962.

PPU   Wolff, Christian. *Philosophia practica universalis . . . methodo scientifica pertracta*. Frankfurt und Leipzig, 1738–39.

RCPR   *The Rebirth of Classical Political Rationalism: An Introduction to the Thought of Leo Strauss*. Edited by Thomas L. Pangle. Chicago: University of Chicago Press, 1989.

ReBe   Leibniz, Gotthold Wilhelm. *New Essays on Human Understanding*. Translated by Peter Remnant and Jonathan Bennett. Cambridge: Cambridge University Press, 1996.

RK   Jacobi, Friedrich Heinrich. *Werke*. Herausgegeben von C. J. F. Roth und J. F. Köppen. 6 Bände in 8. Leipzig: Gerhard Fleischer, 1812–25.

Ros   Saadia Gaon. *The Book of Beliefs and Opinions*. Translated by Samuel Rosenblatt. New Haven: Yale University Press, 1948.

Roy Cudworth, Ralph. *The True Intellectual System of the Universe*. 2 vols. London: Richard Royston, 1678. Reprint, New York: Garland Publishing, 1978.

Sache Gottes Mendelssohn, Moses. *Sache Gottes oder die gerettete Vorsehung*, JA III.2 219–60.

Sam Samuels, M[aurice]. *Memoirs of Moses Mendelssohn, the Jewish Philosopher; including the Celebrated Correspondence on the Christian Religion with J. C. Lavater, Minister of Zurich*. London: Longman, Hurst, Rees, Orme, Brown, and Green, 1825.

Sch Leibniz, Gottfried Wilhelm von. *Monadology, and Other Philosophical Essays*. Translated by Paul Schrecker and Anne Martin Schrecker. Indianapolis: Bobbs-Merrill, 1965.

Scholz Scholz, Heinrich, ed. *Die Hauptschriften zum Pantheismusstreit zwischen Jacobi und Mendelssohn*. Berlin: Reuther & Reichard, 1916.

Schriften Mendelssohn, Moses. *Philosophische Schriften*, JA I 1–226 (1. Aufgabe, 1761), 227–535 (2. Aufgabe, 1771)

SCR Strauss, Leo. *Spinoza's Critique of Religion*. New York: Schocken Books, 1965.

Seele Mendelssohn, Moses. *Die Seele [aus dem Hebräischen übersetzt]*, JA III.1 201–33

Sendschreiben Mendelssohn, Moses. "Sendschreiben an den Herrn Magister Lessing in Leipzig," JA II 81–109

Sh Spinoza, Benedict. *The Letters*. Translated by Samuel Shirley. Introduction and notes by Steven Barbone, Lee Rice, and Jacob Adler. Indianapolis: Hackett, 1995.

Sno Jacobi, Friedrich Heinrich. "Something That Lessing Said." Translated by Dale E. Snow. In *What Is Enlightenment? Eighteenth-Century Answers and Twentieth-Century Questions*. Edited by James Schmidt. Berkeley: University of California Press, 1991. Pp. 191–211.

SPPP Strauss, Leo. *Studies in Platonic Political Philosophy*. Chicago: University of Chicago Press, 1983.

TM Strauss, Leo. *Thoughts on Machiavelli*. Glencoe, IL: Free Press, 1958. Seattle, WA: University of Washington Press, 1969. Chicago: University of Chicago Press, 1978.

TN Wolff, Christian. *Theologia naturalis methodo scientifica pertracta*. Frankfurt und Leipzig, 1736–37.

TWM Strauss, Leo. "The Three Waves of Modernity." In *An Introduction to Political Philosophy: Ten Essays by Leo Strauss*. Edited by Hilail Gildin. Detroit: Wayne State University Press, 1989.

Unkörperlichkeit *Abhandlung von der Unkörperlichkeit der menschlichen Seele*, JA III.1 161–88

Val   Vallée, Gérard, ed. *The Spinoza Conversations between Lessing and Jacobi: Text with Excerpts from the Ensuing Controversy*. Translated by Gérard Vallée, J. B. Lawson, and C. G. Chapple. Lanham, MD: University Press of America, 1988.

VGGM   Wolff, Christian. *Vernünfftige Gedancken von Gott, der Welt und der Seele des Menschen*. Halle, 1751.

VGMT   Wolff, Christian. *Vernünfftige Gedancken von der Menschen Thun und Lassen*. Halle, 1723.

Vos   Descartes, René. *The Passions of the Soul*. Translated by Stephen H. Voss. Indianapolis: Hackett, 1989.

Wal   Kant, Immanuel. *Theoretical Philosophy, 1755–1770*. Translated by David Walford, with Ralf Meerbote. Cambridge: Cambridge University Press, 1992.

Walch   Walch, Johann Georg. *Philosophisches Lexicon*. 3 Bände. 2. Aufgabe. Leipzig: Verlegts Joh. Friedrich Gleditschens seel. Sohn, 1733.

Wer   Spinoza, Benedictus de. *The Political Works: The "Tractatus theologico-politicus" in Part, and the "Tractatus politicus" in Full*. Edited and translated by A. G. Wernham. Oxford: Clarendon Press, 1958.

WhSt   Spinoza, Benedict de. *Ethics*. Edited by James Gutmann. Translated by William Hale White; revised by Amelia Hutchinson Stirling. Introduction by Don Garrett. Ware, UK: Wordsworth Classics, 2001.

Wie   Wiener, Philip, ed. *Leibniz: Selections*. New York: Scribner's, 1951.

Woo   Voltaire. *Candide, and Related Texts*. Translated by David Wooten. Indianapolis: Hackett, 2000.

WPP   *What Is Political Philosophy? and Other Studies*. Glencoe, IL: Free Press, 1959.

Zweifel   Thomas Abbt, "Zweifel über die Bestimmung des Menschen," JA VI.1 9–18

PART I

Leo Strauss's Introductions to Ten Writings of Moses Mendelssohn

Preliminary Remark[1]

ALEXANDER ALTMANN

The present volume already existed in proof pages when its esteemed editor, Professor Leo Strauss, passed away on October 18, 1973, at the age of seventy-four in Annapolis, Maryland (USA). A severe illness had made it impossible for him to read more than the proofs of the introductions. At his wish, I had undertaken to attend to the editing of the manuscript in every respect. It is deeply regrettable that he was not permitted to live to see the appearance of this work, which was so close to his heart. He had already completed the work on it in 1937, and as the chaos of that time prevented the continuance of the Moses Mendelssohn Jubilee Edition, he had taken the manuscript with him to the United States of America, where he found a new home and undreamed-of opportunities. Already highly respected in Europe as a scholar and thinker, he would now become a celebrity as a teacher of political science and author of prominent works in his own field as well as in the history of Jewish thought, for which he had a noble respect all his life.

One part of the manuscript designated for Volume III, Part 2, of the Jubilee Edition, to wit, the introduction to *Sache Gottes oder die gerettete Vorsehung* (pp. xcvi–cx of this volume),[2] Strauss published as a contribution to *Einsichten: Gerhard Krüger zum 60. Geburtstag* (Frankfurt am Main: Vittorio Klostermann, 1962). He was pained to see his essay designated in a publisher's notice as having already appeared in 1936 as part of the introduction to Volume IIIb of the Jubilee Edition of Mendelssohn's works.[3] The tragedy

---

1. JA III.2 vii–ix.
2. I.e., of JA III.2. See "Introduction to *God's Cause, or Providence Vindicated*," pp. 146–61, below.
3. Heinrich Meier's editorial note to LS's introduction to *Sache Gottes* as reprinted in LSGS II 624–25. reads in part as follows: "In a letter, a copy of which he enclosed with the offprints of his essay, Strauss writes to Klostermann Verlag on August 16, 1962: 'Dear Sir: I received just now the twenty-five reprints of my contribution to the Krüger Festschrift. You surely recall that we agreed that there should be a note at the beginning of my article to this effect: that the article was written in 1936 and meant to be used as part of the introduction to volume 3b of the Jubilee edition of the works of Mendelssohn, but that that volume could no longer be published for reasons which are well known. I deplore that you saw fit to deviate from the statement on which we had agreed. As a consequence I now appear to make the untrue statement that the article in question has already been published. This is particularly regrettable because in my opinion it is

of the historical reality appeared to him somehow denied by this mistaken announcement.

When, at the invitation of Friedrich Frommann Verlag Günther Holzboog, I took in hand the continuation of the Mendelssohn Jubilee Edition, Professor Strauss let me have the manuscript of his precious volume, which had been preserved for over three decades, as well as the first editions of the works of Mendelssohn's that were being edited, introduced, and commented on in it. I was busy at the time with the draft of a Mendelssohn biography—which has since appeared[4]—as well as with a few related articles on the Pantheism Controversy, the {VIII} main theme of Strauss's volume.[5] My view of the controversy differed from his in many respects, which I communicated with him about. It seems to me to be of objective interest to document his own attitude toward the presentation of the controversy, which he conceived in 1937. On May 28, 1971, he wrote to me:[6]

Dear Mr. Altmann:
Your friendly words about my work on *Morning Hours*, etc., have pleased me very much. They would have done so at any time, but never so much as now, as I am old and weak, and need a bit of encouragement. I am not in a position to say how I would state the controversy today, even how I would see it. The work was already concluded in 1937. I am eager to see how you will present the controversy in your Mendelssohn biography. I read your offprint[7] with great interest as soon as I received it. We seem to be at one about the *problem*, the existence of an esoteric doctrine of Lessing's; the question is only what this doctrine "contains." In 1937 I had meant to present, either in a concluding part of the introduction or in a separate article (under the title "Taking Leave of Germany"),[8] the center of Lessing's thoughts *de*

---

not proper to contribute to a Festschrift an article one has already published. Sincerely yours, Leo Strauss.'" (The letter is written in English.)

4. Altmann, *Moses Mendelssohn: A Biographical Study* (University, AL: University of Alabama Press, 1973); henceforth MMBS.

5. See the essays collected in Altmann, *Die trostvolle Aufklärung: Studien zur Metaphysik und politischen Theorie Moses Mendelssohns* (Stuttgart: Friedrich Frommann Verlag Günther Holzboog, 1982); henceforth MMTA.

6. Altmann quotes Strauss's letter of May 8, 1971, in its original German. The sentences from Strauss's letters of September 9 and 15, 1973, that Altmann quotes below are in their original English.

7. "Lessing und Jacobi: Das Gespräch über den Spinozismus," *Lessing Yearbook* 3 (1971): 25–70 [reprinted in AATA 50–83]. {AA}

8. Cf. LS's "Vorbemerkung" (Preliminary remark) to his projected *Eine Erinnerung an Lessing* [A Reminder of Lessing] (1937), translated in appendix 1, below.

Deo et mundo.⁹ The decisive points are still as clear to me now as they were then. But "Many a plan. . . ." The only thing I could do was refer my better students strongly to Lessing and say at a fitting opportunity what I owe to Lessing. (See *The College*, April 1970, which I have to send you under separate cover.)¹⁰

I am therefore looking forward with some excitement to the *fatum*¹¹ of JA III.2.

After the appearance of my Mendelssohn biography, he wrote me on September 9, 1973: "If I were not ill, I might *conceivably* change my final judgment on the controversy in the light of what you say about Reichardt¹² but as things are I must leave them more or less as I wrote them in 1936–37."¹³ At my request that he express himself more fully on this point, he replied on September 15, 1973—about a month before his death—but in all brevity: "I {IX} reckon now with the possibility that I put a greater faith in Reichardt's judgment than I would have done if I had read your interpretation; this applies especially to what Mendelssohn is said to have said to Reichardt about the point d'honneur."¹⁴

Wherever the final truth concerning the Mendelssohn-Jacobi controversy may lie, Strauss's ingenious, profound analysis is certain to win a place of honor in Mendelssohn scholarship and beyond.

January 14, 1974
Alexander Altmann

9. Lat.: about God and the world.
10. Reprinted in JPCM 457–66.
11. Lat.: fate.
12. See MMBS 270, 732–39, 745–46.
13. See IMH LIVn240 and LVIn247, below.
14. Fr.: point of honor. *Ibid.*, LVII.

1

[1931]

Introduction to Mendelssohn's *Pope a Metaphysician!*[1]

The pamphlet *Pope a Metaphysician!* was composed by Lessing and Mendelssohn jointly. The occasion for its emergence was the Berlin Academy's prize competition, set in 1753 for 1755, which called for the comparison of the Popeian principle "All is good"[2] with the (Leibnizian) system of Optimism[3] and for the examination of the "Popeian system" for its soundness. To the end—the entries had to be sent in by January 1, 1755[4]—the authors intended to participate in the call for entries; that is probably why the working out of the writing[5] was completed by and large at the end of 1754. Even before Mendelssohn's "refusal to add his name to it," however, Lessing determined that they would forgo submitting the writing as an entry[6] and would publish it as a pamphlet. It is not to be ruled out that Lessing, once he had so decided, added to the writing a few scathing statements against the Academy, which would have been out of place in an entry. The writing appeared anonymously in the late autumn of 1755.[7] Nothing was known initially of Mendelssohn's collaboration: Lessing passed as the sole {xvi} author.[8]

While the prize question itself does not have a prehistory, Lessing-

---

1. JA II xv–xx; LSGS II 467–72. LS cites "Pope ein Metaphysiker!" in JA II 47–80; henceforth, *Pope!* followed by page and line numbers. Interpolations inside square brackets in quotations in LS's text are LS's; those in LS's annotations are the translator's. Unless otherwise noted, emphases in LS's quotations are LS's.

2. Cf. IPM xviii9, below.

3. Cf. IPM xviii15, below.

4. See Formey, *Nouvelle Bibliothèque Germanique, ou Histoire Littéraire* 12 (Amsterdam, 1753), 458. {LS}

5. Ger.: *Schrift*. In the first sentence, above (and at IPM xvi and xviii15, below), "pamphlet" is *Streitschrift*—though in the sentence immediately following this one, it is *Pamphlet*. LS refrains from calling this or any other writing of Mendelssohn's a "book" (*Buch*), except for *Morning Hours*—and even then, mainly in reference to its emergence rather than its content (see IMH xlv–xlvii, xlix, lxxiv, lxxvii; cf. xxxi, liv–lv, lxxiv). On the other hand, he speaks of the three "books" of Plato's *Republic* that Mendelssohn translated, and of the inability or unwillingness of Mendelssohn's Jewish contemporaries to read "books" written in German (IP xv; IS xl).

6. Letter from Lessing of February 18, 1755 [JA XI 14]. {LS}

7. Letter to Lessing of November 19, 1755 [JA XI 21]. {LS; JA II xv has "February 19."}

8. Letter to Lessing of December 26, 1755 [JA XI 27–28]; *Mélanges Littéraires et Philosophiques* 1755, *Nouvelles Littéraires*, no. 3.7; Hamann to Lindner, see Heinrich Weber, *Neue Hamanniana* (Munich, 1905), 38–40. {LS}

Mendelssohn's response to it has the following one. *An Essay on Man*, the didactic poem of Alexander Pope in which the principle posed for discussion by the Academy, "*All is right*,"[9] is articulated and justified, had been attacked right after its appearance—it appeared in 1733–34—by the mathematician and philosopher Jean Pierre de Crousaz[10] of Lausanne on account of the "dangerous" doctrines stated in it, above all on account of the Determinism purportedly taken over from Leibniz. The Pope interpreter William Warburton[11] defended the poet against this attack by, among other things, contesting any dependence of Pope's on Leibniz. The recollection of this controversy had no influence, so it appears, on the setting up of the prize competition; Prémontval,[12] at least, gives assurances that he had been made aware of Crousaz's polemic against Pope and Leibniz only by Gottsched's pamphlet directed against the prize competition.[13] On the other hand, Lessing and Mendelssohn, perhaps first alerted to the earlier controversy by Gottsched as well, saw themselves prompted to take their stance. They could not pass up Gottsched's own thesis either. This Leibnizian had made the assertion—patent in light of the Academy's hostility toward Leibniz, accepted by our authors, and today generally recognized as correct—that with its prize competition the Academy wanted to promote a contesting of

---

9. Here LS quotes Pope in English, whereas the Berlin Academy's own way of stating the principle at issue in its announcement of the contest was "All is good" (as LS reports in the second sentence of the previous paragraph). Lessing and Mendelssohn begin *Pope a Metaphysician!* by quoting (in German) the beginning of the Academy's announcement as follows: "The Academy is asking for an investigation of the *Popeian system* that is contained in the principle *All is good*" (*Pope!* 47.1–2; the emphases are in the original). For the Academy's fuller announcement in its original French, see appendix 2, supplement to IPM xviii16. Lessing and Mendelssohn go on to criticize, among other things, the Academy's failure to take into account the difference between "right" and "good" (*Pope!* 60.10ff.).

10. On Crousaz, see the following note.

11. In letters to the editor of the journal *History of the Works of the Learned* that were first published in that journal in 1738 and appeared soon afterwards collected under the title *A Vindication of Mr. Pope's "Essay on Man" from the Misinterpretations of Mr. de Crousaz* . . . , William Warburton (1698–1779), bishop of Gloucester from 1759 on and famous as author of *The Divine Legation of Moses* [4 vols. (London, 1738–65; reprint, New York: Garland, 1978)], defended Pope against the accusation raised by Jean Pierre de Crousaz (1663–1750), professor of philosophy and mathematics in Lausanne at the time, in his *Examen de l'Essai de Herr Pope sur l'homme* (Lausanne, 1737) that Pope appropriated Leibnizian determinism and other "dangerous" doctrines. A German translation of Warburton's defense was added to Brocke's translation of Pope's *Essay*. . . . (B. H. Brockes . . . *Aus dem Englischen übersetzter Versuch vom Menschen, des Herrn Alexander Pope, . . . nebst einer Vorrede und einem Anhange von Briefen, worinn die Einwürfe des Hrn. C(rousaz) wider den 'Essay on Man' beantwortet werden, aus der* History of the Works of the Learned *übersetzet von B. J. Zinck* [Hamburg, 1740]). . . . {from LS's editorial annotations to *Pope!* 62.4–6 and 53.12–14 (JA II 383–84)}

12. On Prémontval (1716–64), see Bruno Strauss's editorial annotation at JA XI 391, in appendix 2, supplement to IPM xviii12.

13. *Vues philosophiques* (Berlin, 1761), II, 139–40. {LS}

the Leibniz-Wolffian philosophy. A presupposition for this assertion was that Pope's doctrine is essentially identical with Leibniz's doctrine, or at least could be considered by the Berlin Academy as being identical with it. In fact, the Leibnizian Gottsched doubted this identity as little as did the anti-Leibnizian Crousaz. But Warburton's polemic against Crousaz showed that the identity was not self-evident. That is why the first task for Lessing and Mendelssohn was the investigation of the relationship of Pope and Leibniz. In this way, *Pope a Metaphysician!* is already distinguished from {xvii} all other statements prompted by the prize competition for 1755—if one disregards the few remarks of Kant's on this point, which do not go beyond suggestions occasioned by the prize question that are found in his unpublished writings:[14] Lessing and Mendelssohn see in the relationship of Pope's doctrine to Leibniz's a *problem*. Whereas for all the others it was just a matter of whether "Optimism" (the doctrine that the actual world is the best of all possible worlds)[15] is true or false, and whereas the adherents as well as the opponents of Leibniz who participated in the controversy had no doubt about the identity of the two doctrines, Lessing and Mendelssohn put that very identity into question. Still, this did not amount to a substantive criticism of the Berlin Academy's prize competition; for, in the first place, the prize competition explicitly called for the assessment of the relationship and the *distinction* between the Popeian and the Leibnizian doctrines,[16] and, in the second place, Maupertuis[17] was in any case actually convinced that an essential distinction *did* exist between these two doctrines.[18] The authors are not satisfied with indicating particular distinctions as regards the content, however; nor do they limit themselves—as the Leibnizians that they are—to defending Leibniz by attempting to demonstrate that those principles of Pope's that supposedly or actually disagree with his system are untenable; in all this, they would respond to the Academy's question and thereby accept it as meaningful. Nonetheless, the real aim of their writing is to reject the Academy's question as fundamentally

---

14. See "Abriss des Optimismus," in Rudolf Reicke, ed., *Lose Blätter aus Kants Nachlass* (Königsberg, 1889), I, 293ff. [Wal 78–83]. {LS}

15. On "Optimism," see LS's annotations to *Pope!* 46.8 and 47.7–10, in appendix appendix 2, supplement to IPM xviiin15.

16. See annotation to *Pope!* 46.3ff. {LS}
For LS's editorial annotation to *Pope!* 46.3ff., see appendix 2, supplement to IPM xviiin16.

17. On Pierre Louis Moreau de Maupertuis (1698–1759), see Bruno Strauss's editorial annotation at JA XI 392, in appendix 2, supplements to IPM xviiin17, xviiin18, and xixn34, and ITE xlviin26.

18. See annotation to *Pope!* 64.10–38. {LS}
For LS's editorial annotation to *Pope!* 64.10–38, see appendix 2, supplement to IPM xviiin18.

flawed. The pointing out of particular distinctions between the two doctrines is guided by the fundamental insight into the *necessity* of such distinctions. The doctrines of both men necessarily differ because Leibniz is a philosopher and Pope is a poet: what makes a philosophical doctrine a *philosophical* doctrine, namely, its *systematic* form, precludes its poetic, i.e., *sensuous*[19] presentation, and vice versa. Since that is so, Pope's and Leibniz's doctrines are not only necessarily distinct, but also fundamentally not comparable; and so the Academy's prize competition is fundamentally flawed. Careful attention must be paid to the limit of Lessing-Mendelssohn's assertion, {xviii} lest one find in the Pope writing, in obvious contradiction to the explicit opinion of the authors, who recognize Pope as a "philosophical poet" through and through,[20] a "peremptory rule of the separation of the philosopher from the poet."[21] In truth, the authors deny only the compatibility of philosophy as a "system of metaphysical truths"[22] with poetry; they do *not* deny, instead they assert, the compatibility of doctrine in general with poetry; not only do they not deny the possibility of didactic poetry in general, they show instead *how* didactic poetry is possible: didactic poetry is possible insofar as there are doctrines that are convincing not just by force of their systematic justification; of such a type are the "*specific moral principles*" on whose recognition "all philosophers[23] agree, however distinct their fundamental principles may also be." And Pope meant his *Essay on Man* to be a *moral* poem: it "was to be no unfruitful association of truths." *That*

19. Cf. IMH LXIVn289.
20. See *Pope!* 50.31–32 [Gal 48]. {LS}
21. See Adolf von Harnack, *Geschichte der Königliche Preußische Akademie der Wissenschaft* (3 vols. in 4; Berlin: Reichsdruckerei, 1900), I, 1, 406. {LS}
22. See *Pope!* 49.20 [Gal 47].
23. Lessing and Mendelssohn's German word here is, in the singular, *Weltweise* (more or less literally, "worldly-wise")—rather than *Philosoph* ("philosopher"), which has been in use exclusively up until now in LS's introduction. When speaking in his own name, LS uses *Weltweise* only when referring to "a philosopher in the style of the eighteenth century" (IGC CII; cf. IMH XXII), i.e., as the equivalent of the French *philosophe* in its eighteenth-century usage. Since there does not seem to be any strict equivalent for this word in English, I will indicate by a footnote whenever "philosopher" is *Weltweise* (or *Weltweiser*) rather than *Philosoph*.

Similarly, I will also indicate where "philosophy" is *Weltweisheit* rather than *Philosophie*. According to J. C. Adelung's authoritative *Grammatisch-kritisches Wörterbuch der hochdeutschen Mundart, mit beständiger Vergleichung der übrigen Mundarten, besonders aber der Oberdeutschen* (1811), *Weltweisheit* is "an expression that had been introduced a long time ago by now in preference to the foreign expression *Philosophie*" (s.v. *Weltweisheit*). Adelung defines *Weltweisheit* as "the knowledge of natural things in the world, how and why they are, and the sum of the truths of reason belonging to it" (*ibid.*). *Weltweisheit* is thus identified with modern natural science and the metaphysical arguments in support of it. In his Mendelssohn introductions, LS is careful to distinguish *Weltweisheit* from *Philosophie*—notably when calling attention to Leibniz's observation concerning the prevalence of "system" or "demonstration" which differentiates modern from premodern philosophy (IMH LXVI; cf. IPM xxff.).

is why he sought "a lively impression rather than a deep conviction"; *that is why* he wrote in verse, not in prose.[24] The distinction between poetry as sensuous language and philosophy as a system of abstract principles does not convey its real sense in itself; it points back to the distinction between theoretical and practical, between demonstrative and living, between clear and effective knowledge[25]—and, therefore, doctrine—, between knowledge and "the knowledge's life," therefore to a distinction without which Mendelssohn's *Treatise on Evidence*[26] and Lessing's *Treatise on Fables*[27] would be unintelligible.[28] About the significance this distinction has for Mendelssohn, the "Introduction to the *Treatise on Evidence*" has more to say.[29] What significance it has for the aforementioned treatise of Lessing's results from the principles that come to the fore in it: that anyone "who lets himself succumb to presenting anything other than an *ethical doctrine* in" the fable "abuses it";[30] that "fable has as its aim our clear and *living* knowledge of a *moral* principle";[31] that he (Lessing) in his own fables "always [had]" his "focus only on this or that *ethical doctrine*, which {xix} I was eager to examine in *specific*[32] cases mostly for my own edification."[33]

The most important *presupposition* of the Pope writing is therefore common to Lessing and Mendelssohn. Judged by its initial *purpose*, however, the writing seems to belong to Mendelssohn rather than to Lessing. For this purpose is manifestly the defense of Leibniz against an attack by the Berlin Academy, the same purpose, therefore, to which a part of the *Philosophical Dialogues* is devoted.[34] In any case, the aim of defending Leibnizian philosophy was less important to Lessing than to Mendelssohn. Meanwhile, both

---

24. *Pope!* 51 and 60 [cf. Gal 48, 52], as well as annotations *ad loc.* {LS}
For LS's editorial annotations to *Pope!* 51, see appendix 2, supplement to IPM xviiin24. There are no editorial annotations to *Pope!* 60.

25. Or: cognition. LS's German word throughout this discussion is *Erkenntnis*. See IMH xiin13. Earlier in LS's sentence, "sense" is *Sinn*, which elsewhere is either "sense" or "meaning" or "mind," depending on the context.

26. See *Evidenz* 313 and 325–28 [Dah 293, 303–306]. {LS}

27. *Abhandlung über die Fabeln* (1759), LM VII 415–79.

28. Lit.: unthinkable.

29. See especially ITE l–liii.

30. LM VII 427. The emphasis is Lessing's. It is worth noting that the German *Fabel* (like the Greek *muthos*) also means "plot." Cf. IMH lxxxvii–lxxxix.

31. LM VII 454. The emphases are LS's.

32. Or perhaps: *special*.

33. LM VII 472. The emphases are LS's.

34. Cf. JA I xx. {LS}
LS is citing Fritz Bamberger's brief historical account of the Berlin Academy's anti-Leibnizianism in the latter's editorial introduction to JA I (which contains Mendelssohn's *Philosophische Gespräche*). For Bamberger's account, see appendix 2, supplement to IPM xixn34.

authors were at one in the protest against the national arrogance of the countries to the west,[35] which they believed they recognized in the overrating of Pope by the English and the underrating of Leibniz by the French; and besides, the author of several "Vindications"[36] had a more general reason for protesting against an unjust and veiled attack. So *Pope a Metaphysician!* is well classified as both Lessing's and Mendelssohn's writing equally. If one now attempts to determine the share of each of the two authors in working out the writing, then in the absence of direct attestations one must proceed, so it seems offhand, from the general impression that can be gained of Lessing's and Mendelssohn's style, interests, and expertises from their other writings in this period of their literary activity. With the support of this impression, it is generally asserted that the real investigation (the establishing of Pope's doctrine, the comparing of this doctrine with the doctrine of Leibniz's, the critique of particular principles of Pope's)[37] goes back to Mendelssohn, whereas the introduction (the "Preamble" and the "Precursory Investigation of Whether a Poet as Poet could Have a System"),[38] the conclusion[39] and the editing of the whole are ascribed to Lessing. Closer investigation confirms the dominant view. On the one hand, it is shown that the "Preamble" agrees with Lessing's letter to Mendelssohn of February 18, 1755,[40] and the "Precursory Investigation" agrees with corresponding passages from Lessing's "Vindications of Horace" (1754), that therefore these parts of the Pope writing agree, in part literally, with approximately contemporaneous statements of Lessing's.[41] On the other hand, the thesis that characterizes the Pope investigation {xx} and Pope critique is, in substance, contradicted most incisively by Lessing in his fragment "The Christianity of Reason" (1753), which is also only a little older than the Pope writing: especially in §17 of this fragment, Lessing appropriates the doctrine of the hierarchical ordering of being, which in the Pope writing is oddly contested as *the* un-Leibnizian and absurd doctrine of Pope's. It is very unlikely

---

35. Lit.: the western peoples.
36. I.e., Lessing. See his "Rettungen des Horaz" [Vindications of Horace] (LM V 272–309), "Rettung des Cardanus" [Vindication of Cardanus] (LM V 310–33), "Rettung des *Inepti Religiosi*" [Vindication of the "Pious Fool"] (LM V 334–52), and "Rettung des Cochläus aber nur in einer Kleinigkeit" [Vindication of Cochläus, but Only on a Small Point] (LM V 353–67).
37. *Pope!* 52–72 [Gal 48–57].
38. *Pope!* 47–52 [Gal 46–48].
39. *Pope!* 72–80 [Gal 57–59].
40. JA XI 14.
41. See annotations to *Pope!* 45.18 and 51.27–36. {LS}
   For LS's editorial annotation to *Pope!* 45.18, see appendix 2, supplement to IPM xixn41.
   For LS's editorial annotations to *Pope!* 51.27–36, see appendix 2, supplement to IPM xviiin24.

that the author of "Christianity of Reason" wrote the Pope critique in *Pope a Metaphysician!*;[42] and in view of the central passage that takes up the aforementioned critique in the context of the investigation concerning Pope and Leibniz,[43] the received assigning of this investigation to Mendelssohn is thereby justified. It can be objected that Lessing "was put off at once" from the theses of "Christianity of Reason" right after writing it by Mendelssohn's critique.[44] Nevertheless, as comes out in Mendelssohn's letter to Lessing of February 1, 1774,[45] this critique is directed only against Lessing's speculations about the Trinity that are found in the aforementioned fragment; and besides, "being put off" means only that Lessing gave up his preoccupation with the theses of the fragment for the time being—in §73 of "The Education of the Human Race"[46] he again takes up his thoughts on the Trinity—, it does not mean that he would have rejected these theses as absurd on the basis of Mendelssohn's critique and would have asserted their contrary, even if only initially.

---

42. Cf. especially *Pope!* 67.11–28 and annotation *ad loc.* {LS}
For LS's editorial annotations to *Pope!* 67.11–28, see appendix 2, supplement to IPM xxn42.
43. I.e., *Pope!* 67.11–28. For this passage, see the translator's footnote to appendix 2, supplement to IPM xxn42.
44. See his letter to Mendelssohn of May 1, 1774 [JA XII.2 47]. {LS}
45. JA XII.2 40–41.
46. LM XIII 430–31; cf. Cha 94–95; cf. Nis 234–35. For my own translation of this passage, see appendix 4.

2
[1931]

Introduction to Mendelssohn's "Epistle to Mr. Lessing in Leipzig"[1]

The "Epistle to Mr. Lessing in Leipzig," which Mendelssohn wrote in the last months of 1755 and at the beginning of 1756 as an appendix to his translation of Rousseau's *Discours sur cette question proposée par l'Académie de Dijon: Quelle est l'origine de l'inégalité parmi les hommes, et si elle est autorisée par la loi naturelle* (1753),[2] also owes its emergence to the friendly {xxi} association with Lessing, as the title already indicates. On July 10, 1755, announcing Rousseau's *Discours*, Lessing gave notice of the German translation of this work in the *Berlinische priviligierte Zeitung* with the following words:

> It is a man of insight and taste who has undertaken it [the translation], and we are certain that he will show both, in a line of work in which most are apt to show only expertise in languages.[3]

Before Lessing's departure for Leipzig,[4] Mendelssohn had "promised" him to "put into German" Rousseau's *Discours* and to append "to the translation my thoughts about the strange opinion of this philosopher."[5] Like other writings of this early period, the "Epistle" also preserves traces of oral controversies with Lessing; at the beginning of the discussion about the origin of languages, Mendelssohn says explicitly: "We have talked very often about these difficult matters, and I believe that it would not be unpleasant for you to read everything written here that we have dealt with orally in our talks about it."[6]

---

1. JA II xx–xxiii; LSGS II 473–75. LS cites "Sendschreiben an den Herrn Magister Lessing in Leipzig," JA II 81–109; henceforth, *Sendschreiben* followed by page-numbers. Interpolations inside square brackets in quotations in LS's text are LS's; those in LS's annotations are the translator's. Unless otherwise noted, emphases in LS's quotations are LS's.

2. Fr.: *Discourse on the question proposed by the Academy of Dijon: What is the origin of inequality among men, and whether it is authorized by the natural law.* Mendelssohn's translation may be found in JA VI.2 61–194.

3. LM VII 38. {LS}

4. Lessing left Berlin for Leipzig in October 1755.

5. See *Sendschreiben* 83. {LS}
Mendelssohn's word for "philosopher" here is *Weltweise*. See IPM xviiin23.

6. *Sendschreiben* 104. {LS}

The "Epistle" sets for itself the task of challenging Rousseau's paradoxical thesis: man became evil in that he became social; the state of unsocial life, of savagery, is the happiest. In a few passages, one discerns the indignation with which Mendelssohn responded to Rousseau's doctrine at first acquaintance with the *Discours*: this doctrine seemed to him "to run diametrically against all morality."[7] His concluding judgment[8] shows how much he valued Rousseau nevertheless, how much and on what ground he felt himself in accord with him:

> I can be at odds with Rousseau *in very few places*;[9] and nothing can annoy me more than if I see being proved in a philosophical account of politics that everything has had to be according to reason as it is among us. If only Rousseau had not refused morality to civilized man! This is what gets me so exercised.

Mendelssohn therefore saw the nerve of the Rousseauian writing in the critique of society in the narrower sense, in the critique of "how it is among us,"[10] of the state of present society; and this critique he makes entirely his own: he approves of Rousseau's critique as a critique of "certain abuses that have crept into our political constitution."[11] {xxii} He declines to follow him further in that direction; he contests the view° that the obvious evils that are given with social life give a right to the rejection of sociality as such. In his opinion, Rousseau commits the mistake of all those "odd minds" who, "if they have brought to light only a single truth," would "rather erect a whole strange system than present this truth naked"—the mistake of exaggerating and of "not presenting" the truth "cautiously enough."[12] Truth is *not* paradoxical, and every philosophers' quarrel ultimately goes back to a quarrel over words, to a difference in "presentation"—this is established from the beginning for the later philosopher of sound commonsense. — Mendelssohn contests the "strange opinion" of Rousseau's that sociality is not natural to man, that it is connected with a corruption of human nature, by above all exposing the contradictions of which Rousseau can be

---

7. *Sendschreiben* 83. {LS}
8. In the letter to Lessing of December 26, 1755 [JA XI 27]. {LS}
9. The emphasis is LS's.
10. LS is repeating the German expression *wie es bey uns ist*, which concludes Mendelssohn's first sentence in the immediately preceding quotation: depending on the grammatical context, *wie* in German means either "as" or "how."
11. *Sendschreiben* 98. {LS}
12. *Sendschreiben* 101. {LS}

accused. Thus he indicates that, in ascribing *"perfectibilité"*[13] to natural man as his specific difference vis-à-vis the animals, Rousseau thereby accepts that the perfecting of the natural faculties, i.e., social, moral life, is grounded in nature.[14] Thus he asks: if Rousseau "believes he sees all his *schwärmerisch*[15] wishes fulfilled in our world in the republic of Geneva, what right does he have to keep complaining about the state of sociality?"[16] He thereby points to the difficulties that characterize Rousseau's position. For all that, however, the point of contention escapes him: he does not know why Rousseau casts doubt on sociality as such, holds the state of savagery, of unsocial life, to be the best. Rousseau says it clearly enough:

> . . . le sauvage vit en lui-même; l'homme sociable, toujours hors de lui, ne sait que vivre dans l'opinion des autres, et c'est pour ainsi dire de leur seul jugement qu'il tire le sentiment de sa propre existence.[17]

The struggle against the passions, which is grounded in the will to freedom, to autarchy, becomes the struggle against sociality as the element of all passions: only on the ground of sociality is comparing oneself with another, measuring oneself by another, is interest in rank and privilege, is vanity, possible. That Rousseau sees passion essentially in vanity and not, say, in sensuality—this {xxiii} is grounded in his concept of man: he contests the view° that the understanding is man's specific difference; the specific difference of man is freedom:

> Ce n'est donc pas tant l'entendement qui fait parmi les animaux la distinction spécifique de l'homme que sa qualité d'agent libre.[18]

---

13. Fr.: "perfectibility." (See Mei 102, 126, 166; Mas 115, 124, 140.)
14. *Sendschreiben* 88–89. {LS}
15. Mendelssohn equates the noun *Schwärmer* with a variety of synonyms in his "Enthusiast, Visionair, Fanatiker" [Enthusiast, visionary, fanatic] (JA III.1 315–17; see 316). Here and elsewhere in LS's introductions, *schwärmerisch*, *Schwärmer*, and *Schwärmerey* (Mendelssohn's spelling for *Schwärmerei*) have been left untranslated, since it is hard to find simple English equivalents that convey their full range of meaning. In the present instance, an appropriate rendering might be "obsessive," were it not that this word has been coopted by twentieth-century psychoanalytical jargon. For the range of meanings as understood by Mendelssohn's contemporaries and near-contemporaries, see J. C. Adelung's *Philosophisches Wörterbuch* (1811), s.v. *Schwärmerey*, in the translator's note at IMH LXIVn297.
16. *Sendschreiben* 85. {LS}
17. Fr.: ". . . the savage lives within himself; social man, always outside himself, knows only how to live in the opinion of others, and it is, so to speak, from their judgment alone that he draws the sentiment of his own existence" (Mei 268; cf. Mas 179).
18. Fr.: "It is then not so much the understanding which constitutes the specific difference of man among the animals as his quality of a free agent" (Mei 100; cf. Mas 114). This English

Mendelssohn strikes at this basic antithesis without recognizing it in its significance and making it the pivot of his critique. He remarks on Rousseau's question of "whether man does not debase his own nature, whether he does not make himself the slave of blind instinct, like the animals, and insults the author of his existence when he renounces the noblest gift of heaven":[19]

> Oh what an impression these words make in the mouth of a Rousseau! He says them about freedom; but how much more naturally can they be applied to the use of reason![20]

It is telling that Mendelssohn does not make this remark on the aforecited central passage,[21] in which Rousseau opposes his concept of man as a free being to the traditional definition of man as *animal rationale*;[22] this central passage has escaped him. In a certain manner he makes up for what was missed, or° at least he indicates the correct viewpoint for a radical confrontation with Rousseau, by expressing the following suspicion about the historical provenance of Rousseau's critique of civilization:

> I believe a multitude of gloomy enthusiasts has laid the ground for this marvelous sort of thinking. They have gone out of their way to paint this world with odious colors. They have called it a prison, a vale of sorrows, so that by darkening it they might raise the splendor of a glorious future all the more in our eyes.[23]

---

translation of Rousseau's statement is LS's; see NRH 265. In Mendelssohn's German rendering (JA VI.2 102), the statement reads: "Dasjenige also, wovon sich Menschen von Thieren unterscheiden, muss mehr in der Freiheit zu handeln, als in dem Verstande liegen" [That by which men are distinguished from animals must have to do more with freedom, therefore, than with being located in the understanding].

19. JA VI.2 145; cf, Mei 236, Mas 167.
20. *Sendschreiben* 98. {LS}
21. I.e., the passage from Rousseau quoted in LS's text at IEL xxiiin18, above.
22. Lat. or Fr.: rational animal.
23. *Sendschreiben* 102. {LS}

3
[1931]

Introduction to Mendelssohn's *Commentary on Moses Maimonides' "Logical Terms"*[1]

Of the *Commentary on Moses Maimonides' "Logical Terms,"* which was written in Hebrew and is being published in its entirety among the Hebrew writings[2] with an in-depth introduction,[3] we bring into this volume a selection in German translation.[4] Selected are the preface, chapter 7 containing the doctrine of syllogisms, and parts of chapters 4 and 11.[5] The preface is interesting as a counterpart to *Jerusalem*: whereas in *Jerusalem* the justification of Judaism is undertaken before the forum of philosophy, this preface has the task of justifying philosophy, especially logic, before the forum of Judaism. In Mendelssohn's own judgment, in his commentary on the Maimonidean logic the doctrine of syllogisms is "treated with a clarity and brevity that one will seldom find in other Logics."[6] Mendelssohn refers to the parts of chapters 4 and 11 that have been translated by us, in the Hebrew writing *The Soul*,[7] whose German translation should be available with the printing of the next volume of this edition.[8]

---

1. JA II xli; LSGS II 476. See also ILT xlin2 and xlin4.
2. ביאור מלות ההגיון, JA XIV 23–119.
3. Cf. JA XX.1 xxxvii–xlvii. For the reasons touched on in part by Alexander Altmann in his preliminary remark to JA III.2 (translated in the present volume, above) and more fully in his foreword at JA I v–viii (see IMH xxxviii150), the promised introduction appeared only in 2004. It is by Heinrich Simon and introduces a fresh German translation of the entire *Commentary* by Reuven Michael, JA XX.1 33–175; see also Michael's remarks, JA XX.1 xlix–xlx.
4. Mendelssohn, *Kommentar an den "Termini der Logik" des Mose ben Maimon [In Auswahl aus dem Hebräischen übersezt]*, JA II 197–230. An English rendering of LS's German translation may be found at www.press.uchicago.edu/sites/strauss/.
5. For the Hebrew, see JA XIV 25–31 (preface), 45–46 (the excerpt from chapter 4), 51–66 (chapter 7), and 101–2 (the excerpt from chapter 11).
6. Letter to Moses Fischer of March 6, 1784 [JA XVI 290 in Mendelssohn's original Yiddish, JA XX.2 439 in German translation]. {LS}
7. *HaNefesh* 128.18–19 and 124.5–6, respectively; *Seele* 210.1–13 and 204.16–19, respectively.
8. See JA III.1 201–33. See also ILT xlin3 and xlin4, above.

4
[1932]

Introduction to Mendelssohn's *Treatise on Evidence*[1]

The *Treatise on Evidence in Metaphysical Sciences* was prompted by the prize question that had been set by the Berlin Academy's Classe de Philosophie spéculative[2] in 1761 for 1763. The question concerned

> whether metaphysical truths in general, and in particular the first principles of natural theology and morals, are capable of the same evidence[3] as mathematical truths, and in case they are not capable of it, what the nature of their {XLVI} certainty is, to what level it can reach, and whether this level is enough for conviction.[4]

Mendelssohn seized the opportunity to confront, fundamentally and thoroughly, the anti-metaphysical efforts whose center in Germany until recently had been the Berlin Academy. In the summer of 1762, the first three sections of the *Treatise* were "already drafted"; the fourth section was "prepared in the first honeymoon weeks after my wedding, among a thousand distractions, which never let me pay attention to myself."[5] Mendelssohn at first had the intention of having the *Treatise* translated into Latin, but then abandoned it on Abbt's advice.[6] Taking part in the competition, besides Mendelssohn et al., was Kant. Abbt too worked out an entry; but he began

---

1. JA II XLV–LIII; LSGS II 477–84. LS cites Mendelssohn's *Abhandlung über die Evidenz in metaphysischen Wissenschaften* as found in JA II 267–330; henceforth, *Evidenz* followed by page-numbers. Interpolations inside square brackets in quotations in LS's text are LS's; those in LS's annotations are the translator's. Unless otherwise noted, emphases in LS's quotations are LS's.
2. Fr.: Speculative Philosophy Class.
3. Or perhaps: evidentness. I.e., "certainty" and "perspicuity" combined. Likewise throughout. See ITE XLIX–L and LII, below.
4. I.e., enough to carry the force of conviction. LS's editorial annotation to *Evidenz* 271.20–22 (JA II 417) quotes the original French: "... '*On demande, si les vérités métaphysiques en général et en particulier les premiers principes de la Théologie naturelle et de la Morale sont susceptibles de la même évidence que les vérités mathématiques, et au cas qu'elles n'en soient pas susceptibles, quelle est la nature de leur certitude, à quel degré elle peut parvenir, et si ce degré suffit pour la conviction?* (According to GAW II, 306–7)."
5. To Lessing, May 1763 [JA XII.1 9]. {LS}
6. To Abbt, July 4, 1762; from Abbt, July 21, 1762 [JA XI 347, 352]. {LS}
   On Thomas Abbt (1738–66), see Bruno Strauss's editorial annotation at JA XI 456, in appendix 2, supplement to IP XVII.29.

so late with it that he could no longer, so it appears, submit it at the prescribed time.[7] In the Classe de Philosophie spéculative session of May 26, 1763, after some vacillation the prize was awarded to Mendelssohn's *Treatise*. The session's minutes read:[8]

> Les deux pieces No. XX [*sc.*, Mendelssohn's *Treatise*] et No. XXVIII [*sc.*, Kant's "Inquiry into the Distinctness of the Basic Principles of Natural Theology and Morals"][9] ont balancé quelque tems les suffrages qui se sont enfin réunis en faveur de No. XX mais avec la clause qu'on déclaroit dans l'Assemblée publique que le No. XXVIII en approchoit autant qu'il étoit possible, et méritoit les plus grands éloges.[10]

The announcement of the results and the recording of the name of the prizewinner by Formey,[11] the secretary of the Academy, took place at the Academy's full public session of June 2; afterward Merian[12] read out an abstract composed by him "de la Pièce victorieuse de Herr Moses"[13]—which was later published together with the entry.[14] The entries were published by the Academy the following year. Mendelssohn had the intention of enlarging his *Treatise* for this occasion with an appendix, in which he wanted to consider the remarks of Abbt's that had been requested by him;[15] it is not to be ruled out that only then did the *Treatise*'s conclusion emerge—for reasons unknown, it is missing from the edition in the {XLVII} *Gesammelte Schriften*,[16] for which a manuscript of Mendelssohn's was perhaps to blame. Several years later, Mendelssohn was occupied with the thought of incorporating an emended *Treatise* into the second edition of the *Philosophische Schriften*;[17]

---

7. To Abbt, January 3, 1763 [JA XIII.1 4]; Abbt to Nicolai, December 26, 1762. {LS} On Friedrich Nicolai, see MMBS 65ff., 103ff.
8. *Akten der Königliche Preußische Akademie der Wissenschaf,*. I, IV, 31. {LS}
9. *Untersuchung über die Deutlichkeit der Grundsätze der natürlichen Theologie und der Moral*, IKW II 173–202; Wal 243–86.
10. Fr.: "The two pieces, no. 20 ... and no. 28 ... kept splitting the votes, which finally converged in favor of no. 20, but with the proviso that it would be declared in the public assembly that no. 28 came as close as possible and deserved the greatest praises."
11. On Jean Henri Samuel Formey (1711–97), see appendix 2, supplement to ITE XLIXn39.
12. On Johann Bernhard Merian (1723–1807), see Bruno Strauss's editorial annotation to Mendelssohn's letter to Lessing at the end of October 1755, in appendix 2, supplement to ITE XLVIn12.
13. Fr.: "of Mr. Moses's winning piece."
14. *Loc. cit.* [ITE XLVIn8, above]. {LS}
15. Letter to Abbt of February 9, 1764 [JA XII.1 33]. {LS}
16. The omission is rectified at JA II 328.36–330.7 (see LS's editorial remark *ad loc.*, JA II 360). Cf. ITE LIIIn62, below.
17. Karl Lessing to Lessing, April 17, 1770 [LM IX 352]. {LS}

this plan was not carried out. The second edition,[18] which appeared in 1786, is in essence a copy of the first. — Mendelssohn did not let his success cloud his judgment about the value of his *Treatise*. "Don't ever believe," he wrote to Abbt on November 20, 1763, "that because the Academy awarded me the prize, I imagine that I won. I know very well that in war not seldom does the weaker general pull off the victory."[19] And when in the following year he learned of Lambert's *New Organon*,[20] he avowed:[21] "Had I read Mr. Lambert's *New Organon* a few years earlier, my entry would certainly have remained on the desk, or maybe felt the wrath of Vulcan."[22] He was from the beginning especially dissatisfied with the fourth section.[23]

Having emerged as the answer to a prize question of the Berlin Academy, the *Treatise on Evidence* is directed against the thesis of a leading academic. Maupertuis[24]—president of the Academy until 1756—had asserted in his "Examen philosophique de la preuve de l'existence de Dieu employée dans *l'Essai de Cosmologie*"[25] that there are evidence and agreement of opinions only in the mathematical sciences;[26] he had deduced this superiority of mathematics from the fact that only *its* objects, numbers and extension, are capable of more or less: only numbers and geometrical images can be added and subtracted as such; qualities cannot be calculated as these can, except in that the effects that follow from them are connected with numbers or extension. Mendelssohn on the contrary asserts, to begin with, that the basis of mathematical certainty is the principle of contradiction; {XLVIII} proceeding from Wolff's definition of quality and quantity, and from the

18. I.e., of the *Treatise*.
19. JA XII.1 26–27.
20. Johann Heinrich Lambert, *Neues Organon, oder Gedanken über die Erforschung und Bezeichnung des Wahren und dessen Entscheidung vom Irrthum und Schein* [New Organon, or Thoughts on the Investigation and Characterization of the True and Its Distinction from Error and Appearance] (3 vols.; Leipzig: Johann Wendler, 1764; reprint, Berlin: Akademie-Verlag, 1990). Mendelssohn's review of Lambert's book appeared in *Allgemeine deutsche Bibliothek* 3.1 (1766) and 4.2 (1767); see JA V.2 31–45 and 45–64.
21. To Abbt, July 12, 1764 [JA XII.1 49]. {LS}
22. I.e., been thrown into the fireplace.
23. Cf. the letter to Lessing of May 1763 [JA XII.1 9]. These judgments admittedly relate much more to the exposition of the thoughts in the *Treatise on Evidence* than to the thoughts themselves, which Mendelssohn still professed in toto even in *Morning Hours*. {LS}
24. On Maupertuis, see IPM XVII, with appendix 2, supplements to IPM XVIIn17, XVIIn18, XIXn34, and ITE XLVIIn26.
25. Fr.: "Philosophical Examination of the Proof of the Existence of God Employed in the *Essay on Cosmology*."
26. It appeared in *Histoire de l'Académie Royal des Sciences et Belles-Lettres, Année 1756* (Berlin, 1758). {LS}
On David Hume's (1711–76) formulation of this view, see LS's editorial annotation to *Evidenz* 271.15–19 (JA II 416–17), in appendix 2, supplement to ITE XLVIIn26.

correlation of quality and quantity posited with this definition, he then infers "the precise kinship and reciprocal bond between philosophy[27] and mathematics";[28] for philosophy is (by the Wolffian Baumgarten's definition) the *scientia qualitatum*.[29] This correlation acquires a concrete meaning only in terms of the infinitesimal calculus and its application, as Mendelssohn strongly emphasizes. Mendelssohn therefore rebuts Maupertuis's critique of metaphysics on the basis of Leibniz-Wolffian philosophy.

However things now stood with the *justification* that Maupertuis had given for his critique of metaphysics, a historical *experience* spoke immediately in favor of this critique, namely, the experience that "in every century new systems rise up, glimmer, and again pass away."[30] Especially "in our century," the attempt "to place the first principles of metaphysics on a footing as unalterable as the first principles of mathematics by means of infallible proofs" had failed:

> Even those who consider metaphysical concepts to be convincing and irrefutable must nevertheless ultimately concede that so far these have not been given the evidence of mathematical proofs; otherwise it would have been impossible for them to find such a welter of contradiction.[31]

This experience, to which especially Condillac,[32] Voltaire,[33] and d'Alembert[34] were appealing besides and before Maupertuis, Mendelssohn confronts in the *Treatise on Evidence*. Meanwhile he continues to hold firmly to Wolffian metaphysics, which is assumed root and branch. In carrying out the confrontation with the critique of metaphysics in general, however, he gives to (traditional) metaphysics a meaning it does not have in its own terms. With this interpretation of metaphysics he distances himself, without explicitly

---

27. Ger.: *Weltweisheit*. Likewise later in this sentence. In the last sentence of this paragraph, however, "philosophy" is *Philosophie*. Cf. IPM XVIIIn23.

28. *Evidenz* 286 [Dah 271]. {LS}

29. Lat.: science of qualities. For this definition of philosophy in Alexander Baumgarten (1714–62) and, derivatively, Immanuel Kant (1724–1804) and Thomas Abbt (1738–66)—and the corresponding definition of "science" in Christian Wolff (1679–1754)—see LS's editorial annotations to *Evidenz* 286.27–28 and 286.29 (JA II 419), in appendix 2, supplement to ITE XLVIIIn29.

30. *Evidenz* 269 [cf. Dah 253]. {LS}

31. *Evidenz* 271 [cf. Dah 255]. {LS}

32. See Étienne Bonnot, Abbé of Condillac (1715–80), *Traité des systèmes* (1746); *A Treatise on Systems*, in *Philosophical Writings of Etienne Bonnot, Abbé de Condillac*, trans. Franklin Philip, with Harlan Lane (Hillsdale, NJ: Erlbaum, 1982), 1–153, esp. 9ff.

33. For Voltaire's (1694–1778) pithy critique of metaphysics, see LS's editorial annotation to *Evidenz* 269.3–6, in appendix 2, supplement to ITE XLVIIIn33.

34. On Jean Lerond d'Alembert (1717–83), see LS's editorial annotations to *Unkörperlichkeit* 176.9 and 176.13–20, in appendix 2, supplement to ITE XLVIIIn34.

giving an account of it, from the metaphysics being interpreted in that way. In this interpretation lies the significance of the *Treatise on Evidence.*

To recognize this significance, one can hardly confine oneself to the initial answer that Mendelssohn gives to the question pressed on him by the historical experience; for this answer is less a response to the question than a denial of it. {XLIX} Namely, Mendelssohn answers: "metaphysical truths are capable of the same certainty as geometrical truths, of course, but not the same perspicuity."[35] In saying this, he understands "perspicuity" as in the following example: "The first principles of the differential calculus are just as undeniable as geometrical truths, but they are not as illuminating or perspicuous."[36] The problem, however, was just "that many discerning minds who have given sufficient proof of their competence also reject the first principles of metaphysics."[37] Mendelssohn sees himself also forced to recognize in fact, besides the reasons inherent "in the thing itself" that interfere with the perspicuity of metaphysics, "important difficulties" that exist "subjectively, or with regard to the human beings who are to be convinced[38] by the philosophical truths."[39] These difficulties are given with the special significance that the themes of metaphysics have for life and in life. In the first place, the doctrines of metaphysics have

> an influence so immediate on our way of life, happiness, and opinions, that everyone chooses a side in advance and, on the basis of preconceived opinions, builds a system of his own that accords very well with his weaknesses;

that is why metaphysics finds "hearers not only ignorant, but prone to be at odds with themselves, who do not *want* to be convinced."[40] And in the second place, "the main concepts that come up in philosophy"[41] have "gone into everyone's ear so often in common life that everyone° believes he is fa-

---

35. *Evidenz* 272 [cf. Dah 255]. {LS}
36. *Evidenz* 271 [cf. Dah 255]. {LS}
Mendelssohn's word for "differential calculus" here is *Fluxional-Rechnung*; at ITE XLVIII, above, Strauss uses *Infinitesimal-Rechnung*.
37. *Ibid.* [cf. Dah 255]. {LS}
38. Lit.: "with regard to the subject, or the human beings who are to be convinced..."
39. *Evidenz* 295 [cf. Dah 276]. {LS}
For Formey's further assessment of why there are controversies in metaphysics, see LS's editorial annotation to *Evidenz* 295.11ff., in appendix 2, supplement to ITE XLIXn39.
40. *Ibid.* [cf. Dah 277]. {LS; the emphasis is LS's}
41. Ger.: *Weltweisheit*. Likewise in the Mendelssohn quotations later in this sentence and in the third sentence of the next paragraph. See IPM XVIIIn23.

miliar enough with them"; that is why "in philosophy, in ethics, in politics, each man's vision" is "brazen enough to assume the office of judge."[42] The *importance* of and *familiarity* with what metaphysics is about is the reason—indeed, according to Mendelssohn's explicit opinion there is only *one* reason besides the difficulties inherent "in the thing itself"—that the fate of metaphysics is other than that of mathematics.

For the correct understanding of Mendelssohn's initial answer, thus "supplemented," one must take into consideration the consequences that this answer carries with it, even if one disregards the foregoing "supplement." The consequence is *not* that, in order to obtain for metaphysics the force of conviction that has so far been missing, a *reform* of metaphysics must be attempted: {L} during his whole life, Mendelssohn held metaphysics to be essentially complete. To be sure, he does not deny that the fate[43] of metaphysics has causes that are partly accidental, i.e., to be removed in future—as a cause of this sort, he mentions that "*up till now* philosophy *still* lacks the aid of essential signs"[44]—; "greater difficulties"[45] belong to metaphysics *essentially*, however, so that this science cannot attain the evidence of mathematics by any future improvement. Under these circumstances, it cannot fulfill the function of the *guidance of life*; life, action, is then given over to the directives that furnish it with commands without any metaphysics, *prior to* any metaphysics. *That* such directives furnish us with commands, that there is a "practical conviction" that is distinguished from and independent of the "theoretical," then, is Mendelssohn's assertion also. In this connection he must distance himself from Wolff: he understands the concept of "living knowledge"[46] (*cognitio viva*), which has been assumed from Wolff, and correspondingly the concept of certainty, otherwise than Wolff. As Wolff defines it:[47]

> Cognitio viva dicitur, quae fit motivum voluntatis vel noluntatis. Ast mortua vocatur cognitio, quae non fit motivum voluntatis vel noluntatis.[48]

---

42. *Evidenz* 296 [cf. Dah 277–78]. {LS}
43. Ger.: *Schicksal*. In the last sentence of the previous paragraph, "fate" is *Geschick*. At ITE LIII, below, it is again *Schicksal*, as at IP XXI and IMH XXIII. Cf. IMH LXXXVIIIn424.
44. *Evidenz* 290 [cf. Dah 272]. {LS; the emphasis is LS's}
45. *Evidenz* 291 [Dah 273]. {LS}
46. Ger,: *Erkenntnis*. Elsewhere: cognition. Likewise in the following. See IMH XIIIn13.
47. PPU II §244. {LS}
48. Lat.: "Knowledge is said to be 'living' that becomes a motor of the will or of forbearance. And knowledge is said to be 'dead' that does not become a motor of the will or of forbearance."

Only a *certain* knowledge, however, can become a motor of the will (*certitudo cognitionem vivam efficit*),[49] which is to say, for Wolff: a knowledge having the certainty characteristic of mathematics. That is why whoever wants to acquire a living knowledge must make himself familiar with the *proofs* for what he knows; in the interest of the liveliness of knowledge, ethics in particular must be transmitted as a demonstrative science. Since, however, conviction on the part of the "higher faculties" is not enough, since for that reason care must be taken "that the lower faculties agree with the higher ones," the prescriptions of morals that are proved a priori must be strengthened by an a posteriori knowledge—preferably by examples that point to the realizability of the moral prescriptions.[50] According to Wolff, therefore, "practical conviction" is identical with complete theoretical conviction, a priori as well as a posteriori; Mendelssohn asserts, on the contrary:

> Here practical conviction departs from the merely theoretical. The latter is satisfied with the driest {LI} demonstration, with merely distinct knowledge; the former, however, does not explicitly demand distinctness and certainty, but mainly a living, effective knowledge, a strong and lively impression on the mind, by which we are driven to direct our acting and forbearing commensurately with this knowledge.[51]

To be sure, in *Rational Thoughts on Men's Acting and Forbearing*,[52] his German ethics, Wolff lets the knowledge resting only on "persuasion," not only that resting on "conviction," count as living knowledge: knowledge we are not certain of, but only "suppose to be certain," can also become a motor of the will. But since in the case of the knowledge resting only on "persuasion,"

> the man can know that he is not yet converted, from then on this knowledge also ceases to be a motor of the will, and then it no longer remains living. On the other hand, since where there's a conversion one needn't worry that the man is brought into doubt of that sort, in this case the knowledge also continues to remain living. And it is in fact genuinely living knowledge, whereas the other has *only the appearance* of it.[53]

---

49. Lat.: "certainty makes knowledge 'living.'"
50. PPU II §§245ff. and 270ff. {LS}
51. *Evidenz* 311 [cf. Dah 291–92]. {LS}
52. *Vernünftigen Gedanken von der Menschen Thun und Lassen*; henceforth VGMT.
53. VGMT §169; cf. also §683. {LS; the emphasis is LS's}

In this interpretation of "living knowledge," nothing is altered by Wolff's granting that "a simple man," who "does not investigate all the reasons by which something is proved as carefully as an acute one," could be completely certain

> where the latter still has many doubts left. And thus he can have more certainty in his indistinct knowledge than the other has in his distinct knowledge, and consequently also love God more ardently than the other;[54]

for here Wolff is comparing the two possibilities of inadequate knowledge which are being distinguished, by measuring them by the standard of the completely certain knowledge that is, as such, alone genuinely living. — A corresponding deviation may be pointed out with respect to the concept of conscience. According to Wolff, conscience is "the judgment about whether our actions are good or evil."[55] From this concept of conscience, it results that

> It is admittedly true that no man turns out to be capable of judging what is good or evil in all cases, particularly under specific circumstances, but he must meanwhile be content with only a probable judgment: but then it will also be recognized that at the {LII} time no one would ever have a correct conscience[56] in this material.... Since, however, it quite often comes down to probability when one has to judge of men's actions, especially under specific circumstances, one sees from this how conducive it would be to the satisfying of conscience for the art of reasoning about the probable to be brought into good shape.[57]

---

54. VGMT §681. {LS}
55. VGMT §73. {LS}
56. Cf. Altmann, MMBS 125: "In his *Essay Concerning Human Understanding* [IV.iii.18, with III.ix.16–17], Locke had declared that morality was capable of the same degree of demonstration as mathematics, and the Wolffian school had adopted this view. It had gone beyond Locke in considering the conviction obtained by demonstrating moral truths as essential for acquiring a 'correct and certain' conscience. Baumgarten defined the correct conscience (*conscientia recta*) as one that reasoned correctly, and the certain conscience (*conscientia certa*) as one that was sure of the correctness of its reasoning. The only difference between Wolff and Baumgarten was this: according to Wolff, conscience was the ability to judge the result of our actions, since it was the result of our actions that was the criterion of morality; according to Baumgarten, conscience was the ability to judge our actions in the light of the moral law." (For the pertinent sources, Altmann in MMBS 782n62 refers his reader to MMFM 341ff., which cites, inter alia: VGMT §§23–29, 73–75, 93–95, 100–103, 169, 288, 293; PPU II §598; EP §§177, 189.)
57. VGMT §97. {LS}

In contrast to this, Mendelssohn explicitly distinguishes conscience from reason: conscience, as "a skill at distinguishing good from evil correctly by means of indistinct inferences," must "take the place of reason in most situations, where we should not have the opportunity to be stiff-necked before we make use of the latter." "This inner feeling," based on indistinct knowledge, works on the faculty of desire "far more intensely and vividly"[58] than do the "most distinct inferences of reason."[59]

In that the force of conviction of metaphysics becomes doubtful for Mendelssohn, he must attribute a much higher significance than Wolff does to the indistinct but yet not for that reason un-living—rather, precisely genuinely living—knowledge that is distinguished from metaphysics. More precisely: *since* he sees the possibility of such a knowledge as is non-demonstrative, adequate for the guidance of life, and much more effectively convincing to human beings than demonstrations, he can grant the inferior "perspicuity" of metaphysics without for that reason straying from the Wolffian metaphysics he holds firmly to and having to ponder a fundamental reform of metaphysics. If he now holds firmly to that complete[60] metaphysics as the true metaphysics, then under the altered presupposition he must give it another meaning: metaphysics now receives the function of the *defense* of the knowledge that is available and reliable for human beings independently of metaphysics:

> Demonstrative proofs are like the *fortresses* that *protect* a land *against enemy attacks* but are dwelling places that are neither the most comfortable nor the most charming for peaceful inhabitants. Whoever has no *opponents to contest*, no hairsplitting *doubt to contest*,

does not need metaphysical demonstrations.[61]

> Either type of knowledge [*sc.*, the demonstrative or the living] has its value. Where there are *doubts to remove*, *opponents to contest*, theoretical *enemies* of virtue {LIII} to *shame*, there remains no other means but to take refuge in the strictest proofs.[62]

---

58. Or: "... and in a far° livelier way."
59. *Evidenz* 325 [cf. Dah 303]. {LS}
60. See ITE XLVIIIff., above.
61. *Evidenz* 313 [cf. Dah 293]. {LS; the emphases are LS's}
62. *Evidenz* 328–29 {LS; the emphases are LS's}
  This passage is omitted in Dah, which is based on the German text as originally published by Mendelssohn himself, rather than on the critical text in JA II 267–330 (cf. Dah ix, xxxvi–xxxvii).

Metaphysics therefore receives the task of subsequently securing the originally familiar truth *insofar as* being convinced of it is threatened.

From where can this being convinced be threatened, however? Mendelssohn does not answer this question explicitly in the *Treatise on Evidence*. To arrive at his implicitly given answer, we recall his remark about the *resistance* that metaphysics meets up with. Now if the truths that metaphysics undertakes to prove "are just as brightly illuminating, just as unassailably certain to incorrupt, non-misled commonsense as any proposition in geometry,"[63] then the resistance that metaphysics meets up with will already be active over against "sound commonsense's" original state of being convinced. The same reasons for which human beings do not *want* to be convinced by metaphysics will already prompt them into a doubting of the original conviction; these reasons will propel the doubt that metaphysics becomes necessary for combating. Then metaphysics may still have its peculiar difficulties, so that it can never attain the evidence of mathematics for that reason alone as well: in any case, these difficulties are then *secondary* as opposed to the resistance that already threatens the original conviction; this resistance, and not mere perspicuity, is then the *ultimate* reason for the peculiar fate of metaphysics, so very much distinguished as it is from that of mathematics. Notwithstanding all skepticism vis-à-vis the perspicuity of metaphysics, the unbroken conviction about the certainty of metaphysics, about natural religion's noblest truths having been demonstrated by Leibniz and Wolff, is the reason that Mendelssohn has not drawn this consequence explicitly.

Unfortunately, the originally published text is inadvertently incomplete, as LS has pointed out at ITE XLVIf., as well as in his list of variant readings for *Evidenz* (see JA II 360 *ad loc.*). Dah does not seem to be aware of the omission.

63. *Freunde* 198.1–2 [cf. Got 163]. {LS}

5 Introduction to Mendelssohn's *Phädon*[1]

[1932]

The *Phädon* came about from the study of the Platonic dialogues, from admiration for Plato's "conquering eloquence,"[2] from veneration as well for the person of Socrates as the exemplar of an unpedantic, unprejudiced, pious "philosophy"[3] that prudently and courageously combats superstition and "sophistry," and not, at first, from the aim of treating the question of immortality. Mendelssohn had begun learning Greek in the second half of 1757,[4] having done so from the outset "in order to read Plato," by whom he was "extremely taken, even in translation." He read all the Platonic dialogues in the original language the next year—as Nicolai, whom we follow here, reports further in his essay "Something about the Late Rector Damm and Moses Mendelssohn."[5] In the summer of 1760, he reviews Hamann's *Socratic Memorabilia*, Wegelin's *Last Dialogues of Socrates and his Friends*, and Diderot's "Plan for a Tragedy about the Death of Socrates" in the *Literaturbriefe*;[6] in the context of these reviews, in which he announces the introduction to the *Phädon* ("Life and Character of Socrates"),[7] he translates several passages from the Platonic dialogues, including three short passages from the *Phaedo* and a longer one from the *Crito*; later he takes up the translation of the *Crito*

---

1. JA III.1 XIII–XXXIII; LSGS II 485–504. LS cites Mendelssohn's *Phädon oder über die Unsterblichkeit der Seele*, JA III.1 5–159; henceforth *Phädon* followed by page and line numbers. Interpolations inside square brackets in quotations in LS's text are LS's; those in LS's annotations are the translator's. Unless otherwise noted, emphases in LS's quotations are LS's.
2. See IP xxn53, below.
3. Ger.: *"Weltweisheit"* (the quotation marks are LS's). See IPM xvIIIn23.
4. JA XI 103, 130–31, 168, and 441. {LS}
5. ["Etwas über den verstorbenen Rektor Damm und Moses Mendelssohn,"] *Neue Berlinische Monatsschrift* III (1800), 338–63. {LS}
6. The *Literaturbriefe*, or *Briefe, die neueste Literatur betreffend* [Letters apropos the Latest Literature], was the book-review quarterly founded by Lessing, Mendelssohn, and Friedrich Nicolai in 1759. It appeared regularly until 1765. Mendelssohn's numerous "Letters" (articles) in it are reproduced in JA V.1, including those mentioned here by LS: review of Johann Georg Hamann, *Sokratische Denkwürdigkeiten für die lange Weile des Publikums* [*Socratic Memorabilia for the Boredom of the Public*] (Amsterdam, 1759), *Literaturbrief* #113, JA V.1 200–206; review of Jakob Wegelin, *Die letzten Gespräche des Sokrates und seiner Freunde* (Zürich, 1760), *Literaturbrief* #115, JA V.1 207–10; review of Denis Diderot, "Plan zu einer Trauerspiel über den Tod des Sokrates," *Literaturbrief* #119, JA V.1 225–34.
7. *Phädon* 11–36; Cul ix–lx.; Nob 45–65.

passage, with minor alterations, {xiv} into the introduction to the *Phädon*;[8] probably, therefore, it is the earliest part of the *Phädon*. Around this time, he decides "to recast and publish the [*sc.*, Platonic][9] *Phaedo*." On December 19, 1760, he writes to Lessing, who had left Berlin a few weeks earlier:

> I keep thinking about my *Phädon*. As soon as the *Letters* [*sc.*, the *Literaturbriefe*] stop weighing me down, I shall first arrange the second edition of my lesser writings[10] and then apply myself to working out this treatise.[11]

From the beginning, it was firmly established for Mendelssohn that his task would not be a translation of the Platonic dialogue, but only a reworking that took advantage of the "progress" of philosophy in the recent centuries. From the beginning, he wanted "to borrow . . . nothing from Plato really except the arrangement, which in fact is excellent."[12] But since his decision to write the *Phädon* had been prompted by the impression that Plato's art had made on him rather than by interest in a treatment of the question of immortality in general, he thus believed initially that, even if it involved a most thoroughgoing reworking of Plato's particular proofs, he could still make do by and large with just a reworking of the particular proofs. A "Draft for the *Phädon*," which has recently been discovered in the Campe Collection of the Hamburg State and University Library, informs us about his original plan.[13] This draft sketches in extensive detail two proofs for immortality, which, as the conclusion indicates, further proofs were to have followed. Despite its obvious incompleteness, it makes possible a secure judgment about the characteristic difference between the original plan and the completed work. The first proof of the draft agrees by and large with the proof of the First Dialogue of the *Phädon*;[14] in keeping with Mendelssohn's aim, it corresponds to the proof set forth in the 15th and

---

8. See *Phädon* 35.5–36.29 [Cul lvi–lx; Nob 62–65]. {LS}
9. LS's interpolation is owing to the fact that the titles of Plato's and Mendelssohn's books are indistinguishable in Mendelssohn's German. (Cf. my own interpolation at IP xx, below.) When referring to Plato's book separately, LS uses the transliterated Greek title, *Phaidon*.
10. I.e., his *Philosophische Schriften*, JA I 1–226 (1st ed., 1761), 227–535 (2nd ed., 1771; Dah translates this edition, though cf. ITE LIII n62). "Second edition" actually refers to the first edition of the *Philosophische Schriften* as such, which includes his previously published *Philosophical Dialogues, On the Sentiments, Thoughts on Probability, Treatise on Evidence*, etc.
11. JA XI 190.
12. To Iselin, July 5, 1763 [JA XII.1 15]. {LS}
13. See *Phädon (Entwurf)*, JA III.1 3–4.
14. The three "Dialogues" that make up Mendelssohn's *Phädon* correspond more or less to Plato's *Phaedo* 57a–84b, 84b–95c, and 95c–118, respectively.

16th chapters of the *Phaedo*.¹⁵ Following the model and explicitly citing its 17th chapter,¹⁶ the draft concludes the first proof with an argument that has altogether vanished in the *Phädon*. The draft follows Plato further in that it sets forth the second proof by means of the doctrine of learning as recollection (reinterpreted, however, in Leibniz's sense);¹⁷ any trace of this proof is also missing in the *Phädon*. {xv} The proof for the simplicity of the soul (cf. *Phaedo*, ch. 27ff.)¹⁸ was to have followed this proof; in keeping with Mendelssohn's aim, the soul's ability to represent to itself realities without their limitations¹⁹ was to assume the function that knowledge of the invisible ideas that always behave in the selfsame way has in Plato; this proof is also missing in the *Phädon*. Comparison of the draft with the completed work therefore documents that Mendelssohn originally wanted to stay much closer to his model than he did in working it out.

Mendelssohn wrote the first part of the *Phädon* in the years 1761–63. On July 5, 1763, he puts it in a letter to Isaak Iselin, the Basel city clerk, as an entry at the disposal of the "Patriotic Society" founded by a few Swiss, together, significantly, with a translation of three books of Plato's *Republic*, which must have emerged at the time of the *Phädon*'s conception or at the time of the working out of its first part.²⁰ On November 16 of the same year, he sends off the manuscript of the first part of the *Phädon* to Iselin, asking him in the cover letter for his judgment: "Your evaluation will decide whether the work deserves to be continued, and I have the confidence in your friendship that you will be candid with me."²¹ As to whether and how Iselin replied, nothing is known to date.

What is to be understood, though, by the "first part"²² of the *Phädon*, which Mendelssohn had completed in 1763? The letter to Iselin of July 5, 1763, reads:

> The first half of this plan, in which the proofs for the immutability of the soul are presented, is finished. Those for immortality are to follow in a second part.²³

---

15. I.e., *Phaedo* 70c–72a.
16. I.e., *Phaedo* 72a–e.
17. Cf. IP xv, xx–xxi, xxv–xxvii, below.
18. I.e., *Phaedo* 79c ff.
19. Cf. Leibniz, *Monadologie* §30 (Ger VI 612; Wie 539 or Sch 152 or FrWo 272).
20. JA XII.1 15. On Isaak Iselin (1728–82), see also *Jerusalem* 146–47n (Ark 78–79n).
21. JA XII.1 22.
22. *Ibid.*
23. JA XII.1 15.

Immortality differs from immutability (or imperishability)—according to Leibniz,[24] whom Wolff and his disciples follow[25]—in that wakefulness, the awareness of present circumstances and recollection of past ones, belongs to immortality over and above immutability, the latter being the mere persistence of the soul-substance. Since immortality, so understood, is proved in the Third Dialogue of the *Phädon*, and immutability in the First and Second, {XVI} it seems to result from the letter cited that the content of the manuscript sent to Iselin was the First and Second Dialogues of the *Phädon*. But now Mendelssohn writes to Iselin on May 7, 1767, shortly after the appearance of the *Phädon*: "I am taking the liberty of sending you a copy of the *Phädon*, the First Dialogue of which you were kind enough to read in manuscript."[26] Had Mendelssohn in 1763 therefore completed only the First Dialogue of the *Phädon*? Was the Second Dialogue moreover written only after 1763? But how can Mendelssohn then write, in the letter to Iselin of July 5, 1763, already cited,[27] that the proofs for the immutability of the soul are presented in the now-finished first part of the work? For it was clear to him from the beginning that, in order to be conclusive, the proof for immutability set forth in the First Dialogue presupposes the proof for the simplicity of the soul set forth only in the Second Dialogue: the draft already points to a proof for the simplicity of the soul. We must therefore leave unanswered the question of what point the working out of the *Phädon* had arrived at in 1763.

The completion of the *Phädon*, i.e., the working out of the Third Dialogue in any case and at minimum, happens in the summer of 1766. That Mendelssohn did not in general work on the *Phädon* the whole time between 1763 and 1766, perhaps waiting to no avail for Iselin's encouraging judgment, can be supposed, but not said with certainty; in any case, as he reports in the preface to the *Phädon*, he "put aside" for a while "the work begun a few years earlier."[28] A suggestion that came from his friend Thomas Abbt[29] prompted him to take up the work again. He writes to Abbt on July 22, 1766:

> Your questions have encouraged me to complete the working out of a treatise on the immortality of the soul that I started many years ago. I am

---

24. *Théodicée* §89 [Ger VI 149; Hug 171–72]. {LS}
25. See, e.g., Wolff, VGGM §§926–27, and Bilfinger, *Dilucidationes* §359; cf. also letter to Nicolai of February 1768 [JA XII.1 156]. {LS}
26. JA XII.1 131.
27. See IP XVn23, above.
28. *Phädon* 7.4–5 [cf. Nob 41].
29. On Abbt, see ITE XLVIII, and Bruno Strauss's editorial annotation at JA XI 456, in appendix 2, supplement to IP XVIn29.

putting my arguments into Socrates' mouth.... These are the eggs I have begun to hatch this summer and, for this reason, must not abandon.[30]

Abbt's questions were doubts about the answer that the Berlin Prior Johann Joachim Spalding (in his *The Destiny*[31] *of Man*)[32] had given to the question of the destiny of man; they had been offered in an article, "Doubt Concerning the Destiny of Man,"[33] which was the basis for the later epistolary controversy {xvii} that appeared in the *Literaturbriefe* in the summer of 1764, together with Mendelssohn's reply, "Oracle apropos the Destiny of Man."[34] The Spalding writing agrees in doctrine and conviction with the corresponding parts of the *Phädon* (above all, therefore, with the Third Dialogue); this doctrine and this conviction were the common coin of the German Enlightenment, standing as it did on the soil of Leibniz-Wolffian philosophy. Defending Spalding's theses against Abbt's doubt, Mendelssohn explicitly invoked the "spirit of the great Leibniz" against Bayle, who is cited by Abbt as "an enemy to systems."[35] At the very° latest in this controversy with Abbt, which in fact repeats the controversy between Leibniz and Bayle though on a narrower basis,[36] Mendelssohn must have known that the task of his *Phädon* would have to be the defense of the rational doctrine of immortality against the dangers that threatened it from skepticism grounded in faith, though above all from the unbelief powerfully advancing at that time from the west.[37] This knowledge determined the style and manner in which Mendelssohn, distancing himself from the plan of the Hamburg draft, worked out the *Phädon*. Thus Abbt's suggestion was not only the occasion for Mendelssohn's taking up the work on the *Phädon* again at all; it was in addition an influence on the direction in which this work was continued and completed, even if only a concurrent influence, perhaps even just an incidentally corroborating one.

Admiration for Plato's art and veneration for the person of Socrates, which have been indicated as being the initial causes of the emergence of the *Phädon*, have their common root in the opposition to scholastic philosophy,

---

30. JA XII.1 118.
31. Or: *Vocation*. Likewise throughout.
32. On Johann Joachim Spalding (1714–1804), see LS's editorial annotation to *Phädon* 7.8–9, in appendix 2, supplement to IP xvიn32.
33. "Zweifel über die Bestimmung des Menschen" (JA VI.1 9–18; henceforth *Zweifel*).
34. "Orakel, die Bestimmung des Menschen betreffend" (JA VI.1 19–25; henceforth *Orakel*).
35. *Zweifel* 10.13–14; *Orakel* 21.27.
36. On Bayle, cf. IMH xxxiiif., lxx–lxxi, lxxxviii, xciii–xciv; IGC cv–cix.
37. I.e., especially from France. Cf. IMH lxx–lxxi, with IPM xix, IGC ci–cii.

to its dogmatism and pedantry; they are at the same time, therefore, expressions of the sentiment that expresses itself in general in the philosophy of the Enlightenment. Accordingly, they occur in the broader context that is characterized by the struggle not only against the scholastic tradition, but against tradition simply, against "prejudices" simply, especially against the traditions of the revealed religions. For this context, Socrates and Plato become interesting not only as non-pedants, but also as "philosophers"[38] who do not believe in revelation, as rational "pagans." Mendelssohn {xviii} spells it out:[39]

> I am putting my reasons into Socrates' mouth.... I need a pagan so as not to have to get involved with revelation.[40]

The *Phädon* is written as a document of a° merely rational religion, not guided by revelation: it shows what reason not guided by revelation can know, by its own powers, with respect to the immortality of the soul.[41]

Rational religion, and therefore also the doctrine of immortality in particular, is for Mendelssohn and those who share his sentiment not simply a product of reason trained in science, but "just as illuminating, just as irrefutably certain to incorrupt, non-misguided commonsense, as any proposition in geometry"; it needs detailed proofs only because "superstition, priestcraft, a contrarian spirit, and sophistry have, through so much hairsplitting and sleight-of-hand, distorted our purview and brought sound commonsense into confusion."[42] The proofs are therefore not the first word, and not the last, in support of the doctrine of immortality; they appeal to an original conviction of "sound commonsense" that precedes and underlies all scientific endeavor. "When I raise doubt about the immortality of the soul"—Mendelssohn has Simmias, the first to contest the proof of immortality in the *Phädon*, recall—

> it is not about the truth of this divine doctrine, but about its rational demonstrability, or rather about the way that you, Socrates, have chosen to convince us of it through reason. In other respects, I accept this consol-

---

38. Ger.: *"Weltweise"* (the quotation marks are LS's). Two sentences earlier in IP xvii, "philosophy" (without quotation marks) is *Philosophie*. See IPM xviiin23.
39. In his letter to Abbt of July 22, 1766 [JA XII.1 118]. {LS}
40. [Marginalia in LS's handwriting:] Simone Luzzatto (1580–1663), *Socrate*. {LSGS II ad loc.}
41. Cf. also IS xl. {LS}
42. *Freunde* 198 [Scholz 308; cf. Val 139; cf. Got 164]. {LS}

> ing doctrine wholeheartedly, not only as you have presented it to us, but as it has been *handed down* to us *from the most ancient sages*....[43]

The proofs were to succeed in nothing else but the *defense* of a doctrine that is originally a familiar one, familiar through tradition from time immemorial, against "sophistry."[44]

The doctrine of immortality is originally familiar to sound commonsense because it is urgently indispensable for our happiness: "... man robbed {xix} of the hope of immortality is the most pitiful beast on earth, who, to his misfortune, must reflect on his condition, fear death, and despair."[45] But what is indispensable for our happiness stands at our disposal: "According to the concepts of true Judaism," which in Mendelssohn's view coincide completely with the concepts of rational religion,

> all the inhabitants of the earth are called to happiness, and the means toward it are as widespread as humanity itself, as softly dispensed as the means for warding off hunger and other natural needs.[46]

We are destined for happiness, we have all the means for happiness at our disposal, because "an all-benevolent and all-wise being has brought us forth,"[47] because we "are loved most tenderly ... by that holiest being of all, which has brought us forth."[48] Here we confront the presupposition of the doctrine of immortality which is at the root of Mendelssohn's orientation as such;[49] this presupposition is the belief in God as a God that is only benevolent, only "tenderly loving," "softly dispensing" the means for happiness.

The entire Enlightenment, insofar as it maintains the connection explicitly or implicitly with the tradition founded in the Bible, is characterized by its combating the traditional doctrines and sentiments that it combats by recourse to God's benevolence.[50] More exactly: the unequivocal elevation of God's benevolence over His power, His glory, and His punitive anger is peculiar to the Enlightenment; for the Enlightenment, God is above all not

---

43. *Phädon* 79.5–13 [cf, Cul 93–94; cf. Nob 104]. {LS; the emphasis is LS's}
44. *Phädon 3* 149.24–36 [Nob 152]{LS}
45. *Phädon* 80.4–7 [cf. Cul 96; cf. Nob 104]. {LS}
46. *Jerusalem* 160 [cf. Ark 94; cf. Got 85]. {LS}
47. *Morgenstunden* 70. {LS}
48. *Phädon* 102.15–17 [cf. Cul 152; cf. Nob 125]. {LS}
49. Lit.: which is in Mendelssohn's orientation itself radical. Cf. IEL xxiii, IMH lxxi, IGC cvff.
50. Cf. IMH lxi–lxii, lxiv, lxxiii–lxxv, IGC ciii–cix. See also, Strauss, *Die Religionskritik des Hobbes*, LSGS III 68–69; HCR 67–69.

a demanding, summoning God, but a benevolent one. This conception had emerged in the struggle against the Christian Church, especially against Calvinism;[51] and initially it is characteristic of the Enlightenment only in relationship to Church doctrine. That it also goes beyond this, however, that it is characteristic of the Enlightenment simply, the comparison of the *Phädon* with its Platonic model documents ever so perfectly. Just because, for reasons that are patent, the comparison of the theological presuppositions of the *Phädon* with those of the Platonic dialogue is very difficult at best, we must limit ourselves to the anthropological side of the relationship. {xx} The anthropological meaning of the elevation of God's benevolence over His power, His glory, and His punitive anger comes out in the following fact: Mendelssohn can describe the knowledge that the God of power is at the same time the God of love, that God's glory is nothing else but His benevolence, as a "*refinement.*"[52] Basically, the manner in which Mendelssohn has recast the Platonic *Phaedo* may be characterized as a "refinement," i.e., as a *softening* of the Platonic sternness.

The Platonic assertion of immortality is not to be separated from the philosopher's reflection on his philosophizing. In the implementation of his philosophizing, the philosopher experiences that he can reach his goal, Being, Truth, only if he has freed himself from the body, that he reaches Truth more, the more he frees himself from the body: the freeing of the soul from the body, dying, is the ideal condition of philosophizing as disclosed in philosophizing itself. Mendelssohn does away with this connection explicitly:

> The long and weighty declamation against the human body and its needs, which Plato seems to have written more in the spirit of Pythagoras than of his own teacher, must, according to our better concepts of the value of this divine creature, be very much *softened*; and yet it will ring strange in the ear of many a reader nowadays. I confess that I have retained this passage merely out of a liking for Plato's conquering eloquence.[53]

Here he is already making it known that his hope for immortality is fundamentally different from that of the Platonic Socrates. Further: for Plato, too, the thought of immortality is a basis for confidence for the dying; but—wholly disregarding the fact° that, in this, Plato always has the dy-

---

51. Cf. the critique of the doctrine of eternal punishments in hell by recourse to God's benevolence, *Phädon* 102 [Cul 151–52; Nob 125]. {LS}
52. *Jerusalem* 186 [Ark 121; Got 108]. {LS; the emphasis is LS's}
53. *Phädon* 8.23–30 [cf. Nob 42]. {LS; the emphasis is LS's}

ing *philosopher* before his eyes (cf., above all, *Phaedo* 82a–c)—he is far from asserting that, without faith in survival after death throughout "the bitter reminder of death,"[54] the difference between the right life and the perverted life loses its meaning.[55] Were the soul to die with the body, death would be a victory for the wicked because in dying they would then lose their wickedness—this principle of Plato's (107c) cannot be confused with Mendelssohn's assertion {xxi} that, were our soul mortal, it would make no difference "whether I was an ornament or a scandal of creation,"[56] that therefore without immortality there would be no reason for being good. Finally: because for Plato the main thing is philosophizing, for that very reason the solace of the thought of immortality can be for him no argument for immortality. In his interest in his own immortality, the Platonic Socrates sees at once a danger for the philosophical discussion of the question of immortality; he believes, just *because* he is so interested, that he is not behaving philosophically; he warns his friends about himself in that regard (91a–c). Mendelssohn, if he wanted to remain true to himself, could not transfer this passage into his *Phädon* without also essentially "softening" it. He has his Socrates explain in this context:

> I meanwhile please myself in the thought that everything that would bring true consolation and advantage to the entire human race, if it were true, on just that account would have a great deal of plausibility in itself of being true. . . . Think up a doctrine that is as indispensable to human society [*sc.*, as the doctrine of immortality is], and I wager that it is true.[57]

The different sentiment demands a different tone. The tone of the *Phädon* is censured by a contemporary critic with expressions like "sweet," "Frenchifying," "courtly," "*refined.*"[58] The striving for "refinement," for softening, which determines Mendelssohn's thought generally, therefore shows up even in the tone. Led by the striving for a "softening" of the Platonic sternness, Mendelssohn recast in particular the "framework" of the dialogue, i.e., the depicting of the situation in which the question of the future fate of

---

54. *Phädon* 80.12 [cf. Cul 96; cf. Nob 104]. {LS}
55. *Phädon* 79–80 [cf. Cul 94ff.; cf. Nob 104ff.]. {LS}
56. *Phädon* 79.30–31 [cf. Cul 93; Nob 104]. {LS}
57. *Phädon* 88.16–25 [cf. Cul 115–16; cf. Nob 111–12]. {LS}
58. See annotations to *Phädon* 39.14–17 and 40.2. {LS}

For LS's editorial annotations to *Phädon* 39.14–17 and 40.2, see appendix 2, supplement to IP xxin58.

the soul is without any doubt the "appropriate thing" (70c). Socrates' dying becomes, contrary to Plato's explicit meaning, in Mendelssohn a poignant spectacle. To be sure, he translates the corresponding sentences of Plato's; but by the style in which he translates, he destroys the latter's purpose. A few examples chosen above all from the first pages of the Greek *Phaedo°* and the German *Phädon* may serve as illustration: {XXII}

PLATO[59]	MENDELSSOHN[60]
to remember Socrates [58d]	to remember *my* Socrates (3rd ed.)
no pity overcame me as one who is present at the death of a man befriended [58e]	I *felt* no pity, no *such uneasiness* as we are used to feeling when a friend *fades in our arms*.
he died . . . so fearlessly [58e]	so quiet was his behavior *in the hour of death*
to go to Hades [58e]	*to change* into the shades of Orkus *below*
. . . an unaccustomed mixture of pleasure and sorrow together, when I thought that he was to die presently [59a]	a . . . mixture of pleasure and bitterness never felt before; for the pleasure was constantly interrupted by the *gnawing feeling:* "Soon we will lose him forever."
sometimes laughing, sometimes crying [59a]	We were seen now laughing, now *pouring tears, and often a smile showed up on the lips and called tears to the eyes*
He [Apollodorus] quite especially behaved that way now; but I myself was as agitated as the others. [59a–b]	He made *strange movements. He felt everything quite ardently, was delighted when we smiled, and where our eyes were bedewed, he swam in tears. We became almost more moved by him than by our dying friend.* {XXIII}
Xanthippe with her child and sitting beside him [60a]	Xanthippe . . . sat beside him *in silent sorrow*, and held her child *to her womb*.
When Xanthippe saw us, she cried aloud and said, as women customarily do: "Socrates, your friends are now speaking with you and you with them for the last time." [60a]	When she espied us, she began, in the women's manner, to wail out loud. *Oh!* Socrates! you are seeing your friends today, and they are seeing you today for the last time! *and a stream of tears followed these words.*
Socrates sat up in the bed . . . [60b]	We stood thus bedewed. Finally, Socrates straightened himself up in the bed . . .
You men! [60b]	*O my friends!*
I hope [63c]	. . . I have the *all-consoling* hopes
do you mean to keep this opinion to yourself and so depart, or might you also share it with us? [63c]	Will you be taking with you this *wholesome assurance locked in your innermost soul*, or will you also favor us with a *doctrine that is so consoling?*

59. The Stephanus page references to Plato's *Phaedo* in the square brackets below are not in LS's German original.
60. The quotations of Mendelssohn's *Phädon* listed below are all found in JA III.1 41ff. and 362; cf. Cul 4ff.; cf. Nob 70ff. The emphases are LS's.

A philosopher who dies as Mendelssohn's Socrates does cannot believe, as Plato's does, that all who grasp philosophy in the correct manner care for nothing else but dying and being dead (64a); he must rather opine "that one who genuinely gives himself over to the love for wisdom applies his whole lifetime to becoming more familiar with death, to learning how to die."[61] He does not devote himself to contemplating something (66d), but he "makes himself ready to *embrace* the truth."[62]

That Mendelssohn much more than Plato, nay, against the spirit and the letter of Plato,[63] presses for proof and doctrine seems at first glance to be in contrast with the striving so displayed toward a softening of the Platonic sternness. The Mendelssohnian Cebes {XXIV} is not satisfied, as the Platonic one is, with having heard something from Philolaus (61e), but Philolaus "*enjoined*" it on him;[64] he does not ask, as in Plato, "Why do they say that it is not right to kill oneself?" but "How do they *prove* that suicide is not allowed?"[65] The Mendelssohnian Socrates does not opine, as the Platonic one does, that his proof "still permits many misgivings and objections" (84c), but that "various things still lack complete distinctness."[66] The Mendelssohnian Simmias does not at all wish to hear what Socrates answers to his objection (84d), but he wishes "to hear" his "*refutation*."[67] Most significantly: Mendelssohn translates, "Our *teacher* had had his say,"[68] where Plato says only that Socrates had spoken (84c). This pressure for doctrine, this prevalence of proof seeking, which in view of the emphatically *popular*, "exoteric" character of the *Phädon* cannot possibly be explained in terms of an intensifying of the will to strict knowledge,[69] needs clarifying; in other words, it needs clarifying why for Mendelssohn it is a matter of popularity and proof at the same time.[70]

It has already been indicated that for Mendelssohn the immortality of

---

61. *Phädon* 50.9–12 [cf. Cul 25; cf. Nob 78].
62. *Phädon* 56.9 [cf. Cul 39; cf. Nob 83]. The emphases here and in the following quotations are LS's.
63. Lit.: against Plato's spirit and word.
64. *Phädon* 45.35 [cf. Cul 16; cf. Nob 74].
65. *Phaedo* 61e, with *Phädon* 45.33–34 [cf. Cul 16; cf. Nob 74].
66. *Phädon* 78.8 [cf. Cul 91; cf. Nob 103].
67. *Phädon* 78.16 [cf. Cul 91; cf. Nob 103].
68. *Phädon* 78.2 [cf. Cul 91; cf. Nob 103]. In LS's German, the italicized word, *Lehrer*, is akin to *Lehre*, translated in LS's next sentence (and elsewhere) as "doctrine."
69. Lit.: to strict science. LS's adjective *strenger* is akin to the noun *Strenge*, translated throughout as "sternness."
70. [Marginalia in LS's handwriting:] This is so from the outset in the 17th century: philosophy is "more mathematical" *and* more popular than the ancient—*la mathématique* et les femmes [Fr.: mathematics *and women*] characterize the *esprit classique* [Fr.: classical spirit]. {LSGS II 495n; the emphasis on the conjunction is LS's}

the soul, like all other doctrines of natural religion, is established *prior to* all proofs. The proofs, so it appears initially, have no more to accomplish than to defend the originally familiar doctrine from the sophistical challenge. The original conviction is not groundless; but its grounds do not have the character of "demonstrative," "speculative," "mathematical" certainty; they are, as far as their theoretical dignity goes, merely probable; but they nevertheless act "quite often more intensely and vividly[71] on the mind"—i.e., on our faculty of desire—"than speculative reasonings"; their yield is "practical conviction." In the sense of this interpretation of the relationship of the theoretical and the practical "mode of knowledge" which is developed in the *Treatise on Evidence*,[72] Mendelssohn in the *Phädon* has Simmias, before laying out his objections to the proof of immortality presented by Socrates, initially declare explicitly that he is not directing his doubt against the doctrine of immortality itself[73] and then enumerate a series of reasons for immortality, {xxv} of which, "taken singly, perhaps none carries with it the highest degree of certainty," but which, "taken together, yet [convince] us with such a conquering power that they completely calm us and beat all our doubts from the field."[74] But why are "speculative reasonings" nonetheless needed? The Mendelssohnian Simmias says, immediately after the words of his just cited:

> The only difficulty . . . is to have all these reasons present with their inherent liveliness whenever we wish. . . . Whenever we represent to ourselves a part of the truth either not at all or without the requisite liveliness, it loses its force, and *our peace of soul is in danger*. But if the way that you are taking, Socrates, leads us to the truth through a simple series of

---

If "*esprit classique*" is Strauss's slip of the pen—or else an editorial misconstrual of Strauss's handwriting—for "*esprit critique*," then the French expression should be rendered "critical spirit"; cf. ITE xlviiin30 on Voltaire, with Strauss, "Cohen und Maimuni," LSGS II 402: "*Kritik ist das Element der Aufklärung, die sich selbst in ihrem berühmsten Vertreter [sc., Voltaire] als esprit de discussion et de critique bezeichnete*"; "Cohen and Maimonides," trans. Martin D. Yaffe and Ian Moore, in MW: "Critique is the element of the Enlightenment, which itself is described by its most famous representative as 'the spirit of discussion and critique.'" Cf. also SCR 190n248.

71. Ger.: *lebhafter*. More or less lit.: in a livelier way°. Cf. the corresponding noun "liveliness" (*Lebhaftigkeit*) in the block quotation later in this paragraph, as well as IPM xviii, ITE Lff. and IP xxv.

72. *Evidenz* 313 and 328–29 [Dah 293; Dah unfortunately omits JA II 328–29—see ITE lii–liiin61]. {LS}

73. *Phädon* 79.5–7 [Cul 93; Nob 104]. {LS}

74. *Phädon* 80.37–81.3 [cf. Cul 98; cf. Nob 105]. {LS}

unshakeable reasons, then we can hope to assure ourselves of the proof for ourselves and *remember it at all times*.[75]

Our peace of soul, our happiness demands not only the original practical certainty about immortality, but the ultimate securing of it through a "chain of distinct inferences" easily remembered at any time.[76] For this reason, therefore, it is for Mendelssohn a matter of a *proof* as certain as possible, as simple as possible, with as few presuppositions as possible, as *popular* as possible; he wants to set forth the proof on the broadest foundation, so that sound commonsense gains the easiest access to the consoling certainty. He himself was, to be sure, a Leibnizian; but since it was important to him "not to confuse the very intricate question of immortality with too many side issues," Leibniz's metaphysics did not seem to him to be the appropriate basis for the proof of immortality. He decided in the *Phädon* to philosophize "exoterically," to employ "mere *bon sens*."[77] He looked around among the traditional proofs from this point of view.

The structure of the whole connection among the proofs was adumbrated *in the first place* by the related thesis, tracing back to antiquity, of Plato's for the proof of immortality in the *Phaedo* (78b ff.) that only the composite is perishable whereas the non-composite is imperishable; this thesis had to be proved as the major premise {xxvi} (First Dialogue), and then that the soul is non-composite, simple, had to be proved as the minor premise (Second Dialogue); from these premises, it then follows that the soul is imperishable. The structure of the whole was adumbrated *in the second place* by the difference tracing back to Leibniz, being grounded in his concept of monads, between imperishability and immortality;[78] the proof for imperishability set forth in the first two dialogues therefore demanded as a supplement the proof for immortality set forth in the Third Dialogue.

About the sources for his proofs, Mendelssohn expressed himself in detail in the appendix added to the *Phädon* in the second edition; reference will be made here to this appendix and our annotations on it.[79] Only whether

---

75. *Phädon* 81.3–18 [cf. Cul 98–99; cf. Nob 105]. {LS; the emphases are LS's}
76. *Phädon* 81.18–21 [cf. Cul 99; cf. Nob 105]. {LS}
77. [Fr.: sound commonsense.] See the letters to Raphael Levi at the end of 1767, to von Platen of April 7, 1769, and to Herder of May 2, 1769 [JA XII.1 149, 170ff., 182ff.]. {LS}
78. See above, IP xv. {LS}
79. LS's editorial annotations on *Phädon* 2 are included in those on *Phädon* 3 at JA III.2 408–20. See IP xxviin84, xxviin85, xxxn96, xxxiiin103, and xxxiiin105, below.

and in what sense Mendelssohn has remodeled the traditional proofs is to be discussed here.

Kant in the second edition of the *Critique of Pure Reason*[80] thought the proof of the First Dialogue worthy of an explicit refutation. Kant presents it as if Mendelssohn, "in the usual argument by which it is to be proved that the soul ... cannot cease to be through *dissolution*," noticed "a lack of support for the aim of securing for it the necessary continuance" and for that reason drew into consideration "a ceasing of its existence through *vanishing*." That sort of doubt of the usual argument does not occur to Mendelssohn at all, however. He simply starts out from the impossibility of the vanishing, the sudden ceasing of the soul, and then shows that the putatively gradual ceasing of the soul, dissolution, in truth would likewise be a sudden ceasing and is therefore likewise impossible:

> the last step, no matter how long one may put it off, would still always be a leap from existence to nothingness, which cannot be grounded either in the essence of an individual thing or in the entire system.[81]

Admittedly, Mendelssohn believed that in the *Phädon* he had to prove explicitly the principle that in nature nothing vanishes; but not because he held it to be doubtful, but because he presupposed readers

> who are no metaphysicians, but possess sound commonsense and wish to reflect; {xxvii} these I have had to acquaint with metaphysical concepts bit by bit in the First Dialogue. The thing most needed was to make distinct the law of stability and that no leap occurs in nature.[82]

Mendelssohn's apparent deviation from the usual argument, therefore, has at bottom nothing else as its aim but to set forth a proof that is as universally intelligible as possible and presupposes as little as possible.

As for the proof for the simplicity of the soul, Mendelssohn had two possibilities for setting it out.[83] Initially, a modern one that he traced back with only limited justification to Descartes and his students. The "Cartesian" proof infers the presence of an immaterial substance underlying mental

---

80. B413ff., "Refutation of the Mendelssohnian Proof of the Permanence of the Soul." {LS; the emphases in the Kant quotations that follow are Kant's}

81. *Phädon* 73.4–7 [cf. Cul 73; cf. Nob 98]. {LS}

82. To Raphael Levi [JA XII.1 149]. {LS}

83. See *Phädon 3* 152.8ff. [Nob 154ff.] {LS}

processes from the impossibility of explaining mental processes by material ones.[84] Although he held it to be "convincing," Mendelssohn rejected it because he needed a proof that "could be treated in keeping with Socratic method"—here this means: popularly—"with fewer difficulties." As such, a proof tracing back to Plotinus offered itself that inferred the immateriality of the soul from the simplicity, and therefore the indivisibility, of both thinking and thought, in the light of the divisibility of everything material.[85] The Plotinian proof differs from the "Cartesian" one in that the latter does not have to do with the unity of thinking, but only with its immateriality, or rather non-extendedness. To the Plotinian proof, which Mendelssohn favored in general as the *Treatise on the Incorporeality of the Human Soul* shows,[86] he now gives a suggestive turn in the *Phädon* via the Platonic model. Through Simmias, Plato has an objection brought up against immortality that needed only to be followed out further by Mendelssohn in order to coincide fully with the argument of contemporary materialism: namely, the objection that the soul is indeed manifestly different from the body; but this manifest, phenomenal difference does not exclude the soul's being a mixture and harmony of corporeal elements, bound in its existence to the existence of the body. Plato introduces his objection with the question: can a composite behave otherwise, do or suffer anything other than that out of which it {xxvIII} is composed? (92e–93a) Mendelssohn focuses on this question. Admittedly, he is unable to answer it in the negative as simply as Plato can, which is only partly based on his having conceived it from the outset not quite in Plato's sense; he must object against Plato and his followers:

> But why is it that a rule-governed whole can be composed out of non-rule-governed parts, a harmonious concert out of disharmonious tones, a powerful state out of powerless members?[87]

He must make this objection because "in keeping with the system of that school to which I supposedly adhere too much"—namely, the Leibniz-Wolffian—"movement is to arise from such forces as are not movement, and extension from properties of substances that are something quite other

---

84. On the difference between Descartes's proof and Mendelssohn's version of it, see LS's editorial annotation to *Phädon 3* 152.9–18, in appendix 2, supplement to IP xxvIIn84.
85. On Mendelssohn's debt to Ralph Cudworth (1617–88) for alerting him to the Plotinian proofs, see *Phädon 3* 152.30–153.18ff. [Nob 156–57] with LS's editorial annotations *ad loc.*, in appendix 2, supplement to IP xxvIIn85.
86. See *Unkörperlichkeit* 164.12–165.5.
87. *Phädon 3* 153.21–24 (cf. Nob 155). Cf. *Phädon* 90.33–35 (Cul 121–22; Nob 114) and context.

than extension."[88] He must therefore ask: under what condition, on what basis can a composite behave otherwise, do or suffer otherwise than its parts? And in keeping with Leibniz's system he must answer: on the basis of the thinking that collects the parts into a whole, on the basis of the thinking to which the collected elements *appear* other than isolated. This, therefore, is how Mendelssohn's argument for the simplicity of the soul runs: the soul, which, as is granted on all sides, is distinguished phenomenally from everything material, cannot be the *consequence* of a compositing of material elements, for the reason that its activity is already a *condition* of a composite's appearing otherwise than its component parts. Nowhere else has the editor[89] met up with an argument for the simplicity of the soul with this precision. Since, given the unsurveyability of the literature on immortality—in German and other languages—it is not to be ruled out that the editor has not come to learn of this or that writing that is important for the assessment of the *Phädon*, let the judgment of one of Mendelssohn's contemporaries who is doubtless familiar with the status of the immortality discussion fill the generally unavoidable gap. Garve writes about the proof of the Second Dialogue in his review of the *Phädon* in the *Neue Bibliothek der schönen Wissenschaften und der freyen Künste*:[90]

> The Second Dialogue is, in our consideration, the most beautiful on account of the conciseness of the reasons, their clarity, and their arrangement, and on account of the felicitous use of a few of Plato's merely scattered thoughts.... Plato presents merely in passing the thought {xxix} "that the composite cannot act and suffer otherwise than the component parts so allow," in other words, that the action of the whole cannot be an action other than the action of the parts, but merely the sum of these actions, except for those that are destroyed by one another; Mr. Moses builds on this.... In our author, the removal of Simmias' objection and the proof of the simplicity of the soul are a masterpiece.

The innovation that Mendelssohn undertook in the proof for the simplicity of the soul is admittedly limited wholly to the form; his argument

---

88. *Phädon 3* 153.25–27 (cf. Nob 155).
89. I.e., LS himself, as editor of the JA III.1 text of the *Phädon* (and author of IP).
90. VI, 325ff. {LS}
For LS's editorial annotation on Christian Garve's review and Alexander Altmann's editorial annotation to Garve's letter to Mendelssohn of May or October, 1769, see appendix 2, supplement to IP xxviiin90.

says essentially the same as what the received argument says. That is why he could employ the proof in its traditional form later on, in his *Treatise on the Incorporeality of the Human Soul*, for its being "very convincing," "completely decisive in favor of spirituality."[91] The reason for the deviation from the usual argument in the *Phädon* had to be that Mendelssohn here was intent on a refutation of materialism that as much as possible would be an inner critique of this position, which in just that way would prove the universal intelligibility of the refutation, its independence from the special presuppositions of the author's school. The proof under discussion sets forth an inner critique of materialism insofar as it reminds the latter, which must distinguish between being and appearance, between primary and secondary qualities, of the difficulty that clings to this distinction under the materialist presupposition.[92]

The same goes for the argument of the Third Dialogue, which Mendelssohn himself points to as being an innovation.[93] This argument says: if the soul were mortal, then "the present existence" would be "the highest good"; now, the fatherland can demand, with right, that a citizen sacrifice his life; but if life is his highest good, this citizen has the right to defend his life by any means against anyone, therefore even by rebellion against his fatherland; therefore, there would then be a "war that is right on both sides," "a right equal to its opposite"—which is absurd. In particular, if life is the highest good, the criminal rightfully condemned to death would have the right "to confound the state with fire and sword if he can save his life by doing so"; this right, which he did not have before, {xxx} he would have won through the crime committed by him—which no one understands himself to be advocating.[94] This argument, too, tries to refute materialism on its own soil; starting out from materialism's accepting the right of capital punishment, it reminds it of the difficulty that clings to the justification of the right of capital punishment under the materialist presupposition.

In general, it will have to be said that in no other writing were the proofs of immortality that were possible under the presuppositions of the eighteenth century so prudently, so thoroughly, and so clearly presented as in

---

91. See *Unkörperlichkeit* 165.27–167.2, with LS's editorial annotation *ad loc.*, in appendix 2, supplement to IP xxixn91.
92. [Marginalia in LS's handwriting:] But only when the subjectivity of secondary qualities is asserted. (Cf. Fr. Brandt's Hobbes book on this point.) {LSGS II *ad loc.*}
    LS refers to Frithiof Brandt, *Thomas Hobbes' Mechanical Conception of Nature*, trans. from the Danish by Vaughan Maxwell and Annie I. Fausbøll (Copenhagen: Levin & Munksgaard, 1928).
93. *Phädon* 9.26–27. {LS}
94. *Phädon* 116–19 [cf. Cul 184–92; cf. Nob 137–39; cf. Got 243–44 (= *Phädon* 116–18)]. {LS}

the *Phädon*. This preeminence is based not on Mendelssohn's new insights but on Mendelssohn's being the best writer, at least among German literary authors who made the question of immortality the subject of a particular work. So the *Phädon* really owes the applause that it found—the first edition was out of print after four months, the second and third edition followed in the interval of but a year, to say nothing at all of the reprints and translations that appeared at once and later—not to its scholarly[95] significance but, aside from the sentiment to which it gave expression, to the art with which it was written. One who compares the work with its model—following as it were the invitation of the *Phädon* itself—will not recognize this art. But whoever casts a glance at the other German literature on immortality of the eighteenth century will perhaps judge more appreciatively; to him, the applause of contemporaries will not seem altogether unwarranted.[96]

Of all the men of the time who had an effect beyond that time, none occupied himself so thoroughly with the *Phädon* as did Herder. "No man in the world can have read Moses' *Phädon* with closer concentration, with heart and soul, than I," he wrote to Nicolai on January 10, 1769. He initially thought about "dressing up [his] doubt in a Fourth Socratic Dialogue," in which Mendelssohn would then answer as Socrates. The plan fell through; Herder limited himself to presenting his objections to Mendelssohn in a letter. That the soul is "a simple, indestructible substance"—about this, he was of one opinion with Mendelssohn against materialism. The quarrel began for him with the question {xxxi} of *how* the soul, more exactly, how the man, remains after death, whether—what the *Phädon* seemed to assert—without body, or—what Herder asserts—with body. Man, objects Herder, is a "mixed being," consisting of soul and body; he would cease to be a man if he survived only as a spiritual being. Focusing on Mendelssohn's polemic against Plato's "declamation against the human body and its needs," Herder demands that this anti-Platonic tendency be followed through resolutely. Mendelssohn in his answer gives Herder his due: "a soul freed from all sensuality" seems to him to be "a chimera in that life as well as in this"; in the *Phädon*, he wished only to "leave the matter undecided, so as not to confuse the very intricate question of immortality with too many side issues"; thus he seems in fact "to agree so much" with Herder "that we need only to understand each other in the *basic principles* in order to be in agreement in the

---

95. Lit.: scientific. Cf. IP xxivn68, above.
96. LS quotes some examples in his editorial annotation to *Phädon 3* 143.17–20; see appendix 2, supplement to IP xxxn96.

consequences too."⁹⁷ The disagreement with respect to the "consequences" had to do above all with Mendelssohn's proof for immortality in the narrower sense, for the continuation of the individual aware of his own self (and his past) after death, and, moreover, with the thesis to be proved as well as the proof. The proof opened up the destiny of man to unceasing perfecting, to eternal progress "even in that life," on the presupposition of divine providence, from the fact that "striving" knows "no limits in human life," that life is a constant "increase in inner excellence." Against this, Herder objects: any perfecting of one power is necessarily bought at the price of the deterioration of another power; that is why this perfecting cannot be looked at simply as a progress; that is why "in no human creature" is there "a rising *up*," but there is a "sort of *cycle*," and all stages are of equal perfection; that is why *this* life does not point beyond itself: "perfecting and developing *in this life, that* is the purpose, *that* is the destiny"; "The five acts are in *this* life"; this life must "already make up a whole unto itself." That is why "the goal of speculative reason and perhaps even of human *wish*" is not immortality qua continuation of the individual aware of his own self, but "an indestructible {xxxii} duration and at most a human palingenesis."⁹⁸ These theses of Herder's let it be clearly known that his controversy with Mendelssohn was in no way merely a matter of "consequences," as the latter opined: the basic principles, indeed, even the "wishes" were different on both sides. Herder's opinion was based on the belief, coming into dominance for more than a century by now, in the eternity of life as *"this"* life, *in* which death acts as a moment of life itself, whereas Mendelssohn is still totally dominated by the original despair in light of the possibility that a man passes away as a person: Herder puts the "old, dualistic concept of death and immortality out of power . . . through the 'die and come-to-be'⁹⁹ born out of the live sense¹⁰⁰ of an immanent view of God and the world."¹⁰¹ That is why, first and last, Mendelssohn had an interest only in proving *that* the person endured beyond death; that is why it was altogether possible

---

97. In these quotations from Mendelssohn, the emphases are LS's; in the quotations from Johann Gottfried Herder (1744–1803) that follow, the emphases are Herder's own. Cf. the Herder quotations also with NRH 15n6.

98. Herder to Mendelssohn, April 1769; Mendelssohn to Herder, May 2, 1769 [JA XII.1 174–81, 182–87]. {LS}

99. Ger.: *Stirb und Werde*. See the last stanza of Goethe's poem "Selige Sehnsucht" [Blissful Longing] (Goe II 26).

100. Ger.: *Lebensgefühl*. More or less lit.: feeling of life.

101. Rudolf Unger, *Herder, Novalis und Kleist* (Frankfurt am Main: M. Diesterweg, 1922), 6; cf. also 11. {LS}

for him to forgo treating the question of *how* the soul remains after death, whether with or without the body—this possibility he then made use of on the methodological ground claimed by him. With respect to the fundamental antithesis, more appropriate than Mendelssohn's conciliatory opinion that there existed an agreement between him and Herder on the basic principles, seems the concluding judgment of Herder's in his letter to Nicolai of November 30, 1769: "we [*sc.*, Mendelssohn and Herder] have understood ourselves too little!"—

The criticism that the *Phädon* experienced with respect to proofs, method, and literary style gave Mendelssohn an opportunity, in the second and third editions, to undertake a series of alterations and additions. The most important addition is the "Appendix Apropos a Few Objections That Have Been Made to the Author," which was added to the second edition and, enlarged by perhaps half, to the third;[102] this appendix serves as the refutation, above all, of the objections that had been raised by Riedel in *Klotzens Deutsche Bibliothek*,[103] by Garve in *Neue Bibliothek der schönen Wissenschaften und der freyen Künste*,[104] and by Resewitz in *Allgemeine Deutsche Bibliothek*.[105] {XXXIII} From 1769 on, Mendelssohn altered nothing more in the *Phädon*; the fourth edition, which appeared in 1776, is essentially an unaltered copy of the third. The epistolary controversy with Herder occurred at the time when the third edition had just gone to press. Nicolai, in order to give the third edition "a preeminence over the previous one ... on account of the double reprinting," "had come to the thought of appending [Herder's] letter and [Mendelssohn's] answer ... to the new edition";[106] but he abandoned it at the request of Herder,[107] who had not yet been satisfied by Mendelssohn's answer. Apparently, the wish to give satisfaction to Herder's considerations was the reason why Mendelssohn for a while was plan-

---

102. I.e., *Phädon* 2 129–40 and *Phädon 3* 141–59 [Nob 147–60], respectively.

103. See LS's editorial annotation on *Phädon* 143.7, in appendix 2, supplement to IP XXIIn103.

For excerpts from Riedel's review, see LS's editorial annotations to *Phädon* 39.14–17 (in appendix 2, supplement to IP XXIn58), 40.2 (*ibid.*), 40.35–41.5 and 64.29ff., and to *Phädon 3* 143.17–20 (in appendix 2, supplement to IP XXIXn91), 143.23–31, 144.3–7, 144.12–145.14, 148.7–11 and 149.3–5.

104. See IP XXVIIIn90, above.

105. *Allgemeine Deutsche Bibliothek* (1769), 128–38. (The author is [Friedrich Gabriel] Resewitz [1729–1806], as it turns out from his correspondence with Nicolai [Nicolai-*Nachlass* of the Prussian State Library, no. 60; cf, above all Resewitz's letter of September 8, 1768].) {LS's bibliographical annotation to Friedrich Gabriel Resewitz's review at JA III.1 409, item 9}

For excerpts from Resewitz's review, see LS's editorial annotations to *Phädon 3* 144.3–7 and 149.37–152.7 (JA III.1 144 and 415).

106. Nicolai to Herder, May 19, 1769. {LS}

107. In his letter to Nicolai of August 5, 1769. {LS}

ning to rework the Third Dialogue; for Herder's critique was certainly directed against this Dialogue above all. On September 11, 1770, Marcus Herz writes to Kant: "In a short while, there will come out from Mendelssohn . . . his *Phädon*, in which the Third Dialogue is much altered."[108] Perhaps Mendelssohn was kept from following out this plan by the illness that meanwhile made any literary activity in the next years impossible for him.[109] Mendelssohn had to have had in mind the refutation of Herder's objections against the Third Dialogue simply because these objections were identical at least in part with Abbt's objections against Spalding's *Destiny of Man*[110] and Mendelssohn from the outset had assigned to the Third Dialogue the task of invalidating just these objections.[111] In any case, he published the material that he wanted to work into the Third Dialogue in his "Annotations to Abbt's Friendly Correspondence."[112] In the "Foreword" to these annotations, in the autumn of 1781, he says:

> These annotations . . . appear here . . . too soon for me, who no longer have either the time or the strength to follow them out properly and bring them into the form in which the important part of them, which concerns the destiny of man,[113] should have been used for the second part of the *Phädon*.

108. Cf. also IS XL. {LS}
109. See IMH xxxn114.
110. See above, IP XVI–XVII.
111. Cf. the letter to Abbt of July 22, 1766 [JA XII.1 118–19]. {LS}
112. "Anmerkungen zu Abbts freundschaftlicher Correspondenz," JA VI.1 27–65. The quotation that concludes the text of IP is from JA VI.1 29.
113. Or perhaps: *The Destiny of Man*.

6
[1932]

Introduction to Mendelssohn's *Treatise on the Incorporeality of the Human Soul*[1]

As a consequence of the publication of the *Phädon*, a series of men turned to Mendelssohn with questions and doubts concerning the immortality of the soul. Probably the *Treatise on the Incorporeality of the Soul* emerged in the controversies that attended the *Phädon*.

The *Treatise* was published not by Mendelssohn himself but by Joseph Grossinger, a Viennese admirer of Mendelssohn's who translated it into Latin, in 1784 in translation and in 1785 in the original with the omission of its "Entrance," so named by Grossinger. Mendelssohn himself published only the second essay of the *Treatise* ("Hylas and Philonous") and, to be sure, after he had made considerable stylistic alterations to the original version. The title stems from Grossinger; we retain it because the writing has become known only by it; admittedly it is not quite suitable. The writing begins with an articulation of the "question of the *immortality* of the soul";[2] regarding the third essay, Grossinger himself remarks: *Quaestio haec immediate Immortalitatem potius, quam Immaterialitatem eiusdem concernit.*[3] Above all, however, if one considers the whole as it has been transmitted to us in a copy belonging° to Countess Marie of Schaumburg-Lippe, the description "treatise" is misapplied. The "Entrance" omitted by Grossinger, which has never been published till now, contains the articulation of the question of immortality (in the broader sense) and the beginning of a treatment of the first part of the question; it breaks off in the middle of the controversy, in the middle of a sentence. The first part of the question has to do with the incorporeality of the soul; this question is articulated in two sub-questions, which are the explicit subject of the first two essays of the *Treatise* published by Grossinger. It could therefore be assumed that the *Treatise* was the implementation of the draft set forth in the "Entrance." Speaking

---

1. JA III.1 xxxiv–xxxviii; LSGS II 505–509. LS cites Mendelssohn's *Abhandlung von der Unkörperlichkeit der menschlichen Seele*, JA III.1 161–88; henceforth *Unkörperlichkeit* with page and line numbers. Interpolations inside square brackets in quotations in LS's text are LS's; those in LS's annotations are the translator's.
2. *Unkörperlichkeit* 163.1; the emphasis is LS's. Likewise in the quotations in IIS xxxv, below.
3. Lat.: "This question directly concerns its Immortality rather than its Immateriality."

in favor of this is that the part of the question cited in a second passage in the "Entrance" (concerning the imperishability of the soul) is treated in the third essay; speaking decidedly against it is that the "Entrance" does not contain a mere draft at all, {xxxv} but, undeniably, an implementation as well, if only a fragmentary implementation. In any case, the "Entrance" is therefore a self-standing piece, a fragment on the immortality question. But even the main part published by Grossinger, taken by itself, is no treatise, no whole. To begin with, the fourth essay, a critique of d'Alembert's arguments against incorporeality, is, to be sure, bound up with the foregoing thematically and by explicit refutations,[4] but compositionally it is a piece by itself. The fourth essay already falls outside the framework in that it is titled "Fourth *Consideration*," whereas the preceding essays bear the title "First (Second) *Question*." In Countess Marie's copy, the title of the third essay also reads "Third *Consideration*," whereas the edition seen to by Grossinger reads "Third *Question*"; it is likely that the printed reading rests on an emendation of Grossinger's, who in this way wanted to manufacture a nonexistent uniformity and unity. Not only the title of the third essay, however, but all the titles are dubious. A lost copy, so it seems, had as titles only Roman numerals;[5] "Question" or "Consideration" seems to have been entirely missing in it. We have no basis for assuming that what is missing in this copy does not stem from Mendelssohn himself. Perhaps, however, this variant reading allows the suspicion that what is to be read as Mendelssohn's meaning[6] is not "First Question," etc., but "Question at First [if not Question One]," from which the question would have to follow. In fact, Countess Marie's copy has as the title of the second essay, "Question II." It is very likely that the titles that counterfeit a closer connection in the printed version, and in part also in Countess Marie's copy, rest on faulty readings or emendations of Countess Marie's and Grossinger's. However it stands with this warranted suspicion, the *Treatise* is in any case no more than a collection consisting of one fragment and four essays, whose individual pieces are, to be sure, bound together by theme, but not compositionally: at most, the first three essays[7] can be described as part *of a* treatise. Mendelssohn himself obviously considered the collection not ready for publication, not a treatise. {xxxvi}

The "*Treatise*," which therefore may continue to carry this designation, differs from the *Phädon* above all in that it deals only with the question of

4. *Unkörperlichkeit* 177.13 and 29; 179.3. {LS}
5. See "Variant Readings" at *Unkörperlichkeit* 165.18 [JA III.1 376]. {LS}
6. Lit.: in Mendelssohn's sense.
7. *Unkörperlichkeit* 165.18–176.3. {LS}

imperishability, to which the question of incorporeality does, of course, belong; in general, it serves as the confrontation with materialism more exclusively than does the *Phädon*. This would have to be connected with the fact° that the moderate Enlightenment's doctrine of immortality was threatened most strongly and most obviously by materialism; it is for this reason that the question of immortality steps back into significance.

The time of the emergence of the *Treatise* is usually given as about 1760.[8] This dating goes back in the first instance to the suspicion of a reviewer in the "Supplementen zur Allgemeine Literatur-Zeitung vom Jahre 1785":[9] "It looks to this reviewer as if this small writing must have been an early attempt by the esteemed gentleman." How little this reviewer is to be relied on is shown in his assertion: "Mendelssohn worked this writing out in Latin, and it was first published in this language by someone unknown; now this unknown has translated the writing and published it in German." Sitting there in the "Editor's Preface" to the edition indicated by the reviewer is:

> Now that I have already published this writing in Latin, and the author through his friend R** has assured me that *my* translation has not displeased him, I am taking for myself the liberty of having it printed also in the *German original*.[10]

The erroneous and arbitrary assertions of this reviewer were then taken over, unexamined, by *Jördens' Lexikon deutscher Dichter und Prosaisten*.[11] The received dating goes back in the second instance to an error of David Friedländer's.[12] Friedländer says in his introduction to the fifth edition of the *Phädon*,

> Even earlier, perhaps around 1760, M.M. wrote the treatise that is very relevant these days, *On the Incorporeality of the Human Soul, in Four Questions or Considerations*. The author never allowed it to be published, but perhaps he shared it with a few friends in manuscript.... The whole was

---

8. Cf., e.g., Karl Goedeke, *Grundriß zur Geschichte der deutschen Dichtung aus den Quellen* (3rd ed.), vol. IV, pt. 1 [Dresden: L. Ehlermann, 1916; reprint, Berlin: Akademie Verlag, 1955], 490 {LS}

9. [In *Allgemeine Literatur-Zeitung. Ergänzungsblätter* (Halle und Leipzig: Expedition dieser Zeitung, 1838–43),] 209–10. {LS}

10. The emphases are LS's.

11. (Leipzig, 1808), III, 541–42. {LS}

12. Incidentally, the review in *Allgemeine Deutsche Bibliothek*, vol. 102 (1791), 426, also commits the same error. {LS}

first published three years after his death, in the collection that bears the title *Moses Mendelssohns* {xxxvii} *kleine philosophische Schriften* (Berlin, 1789), 171–230.

In a footnote *ad loc.*, Friedländer remarks further: "The editor of this collection, Professor Müchler, says in the preface that 'he received the essays from the author over thirty years ago.'" From this misleading note of Müchler's, which, as the context already shows, cannot refer to the *Treatise*, Friedländer concluded that the dating was "around 1760." How little Friedländer was otherwise informed about the history of the *Treatise* in general comes out in his obviously having known nothing at all about the edition prepared by Grossinger, which appeared in 1785—this edition, not the manuscript, was the basis for the printing in Müchler's collection of 1789.

The received dating, which proves in the first place to be unwarranted, is moreover impossible. A "Meditation" "About the Thoughts of Mr. d'Allembert [*sic*] apropos the Spirituality of the Soul" takes up a good half of the *Treatise*. These "Thoughts" of d'Alembert's are found in the fifth volume of *Mélanges de Littérature, d'Histoire et de Philosophie*, titled "Éclaircissements sur différens endroits des éléments de philosophie," which appeared in the first edition of 1767 and the second edition of 1768.[13] Mendelssohn, as it appears, used the second edition, not the first in any case.[14] The *Treatise*—or, to be entirely circumspect, the second half of the *Treatise*—therefore cannot have emerged before 1768, i.e., not before the *Phädon*; this very important datum is therefore secured beyond any doubt. On the other hand, the *Treatise* cannot have emerged after 1774; for in this year Mendelssohn sent it to Count Wilhelm of Schaumburg-Lippe,[15] whose wife, Countess Marie, copied it out in order to make "a most valuable gift" for the Count. On the title page of another copy was: "A Manuscript by Mr. Moses Mendelssohn. Berlin 1774."[16] In any case, the *Treatise* therefore emerged between 1768 and 1774. Since nothing {xxxviii} attests to it before 1774, barring any strange error we would have to give as the date for its emergence: 1774.

Speaking in favor of a somewhat earlier dating are two vague indicators, which are communicated because they are perhaps of use for further inves-

---

13. Hence the allegation by G. Misch, "Zur Entstehung des französischen Positivismus" (*Archiv für die Geschichte der Philosophie* XIV, 12n), that the "Éclairicissements" first appeared in 1770, needs correcting; incidentally, cf. also d'Alembert's letter to Friedrich the Great of December 12, 1766 (*Oeuvres de Frédéric le Grand*, ed. J. D. E. Preuss [31 vols.; Berlin, 1846–57], XXIV, 414). {LS}
14. Cf. variant reading to *Unkörperlichkeit* 176.13 [JA III.1 378]. {LS}
15. See the letter to Count Wilhelm of February 11, 1775 [JA XXII.2 60]. {LS}
16. See JA III.1 371. {LS}

tigations. The first editor of the *Treatise*, Grossinger, remarks in his "Preface": "We owe the source of this writing to a Prussian Royal Highness." The result of our search that was occasioned by this remark was no more than a suspicion. The sister of Friedrich the Great, the Queen-Widow Luise Ulrike of Sweden, spent a fairly long time in Berlin at the end of 1771 and got to know Mendelssohn there. She had a fairly long conversation with him around New Year's of 1772, probably about philosophical subjects.[17] Perhaps she was the "Prussian Royal Highness" to whom "We owe the source of this writing."[18] Were this the case, then the "1772" dating would make sense. In 1772 Mendelssohn, as his physician Marcus Eliezer Bloch reports,[19] "produced three different learned works at the same time."

    17. Cf. Fritz Arnheim, "Moses Mendelssohn und Luise Ulrike von Schweden," *Zeitschrift für die Geschichte der Juden in Deutschland* III, 283–84. {LS}
    18. Subsequent investigations in the University Library in Uppsala and in the Stockholm National Archives have remained without results. {LS}
    19. *Medicinische Bemerkungen* (Berlin, 1774), 61 and 69. {LS}

7

[1932]

Introduction to Mendelssohn's "On a Handwritten Essay of Mr. de Luc's"[1]

On May 12, 1778, Mendelssohn writes to Zimmermann: "I have just now received the manuscript of Mr. de Luc's, together with your cover letter."[2] The Geneva-born physicist Jean André de Luc, who was then living as a lecturer at the English court, had for that reason asked Zimmermann to make handwritten remarks on the sketch of a *Traité sur le matérialisme*[3] being planned by him, which he wanted to send him, and to forward the same request to Mendelssohn and Sulzer.[4] Mendelssohn granted de Luc's wish immediately. De {xxxix} Luc just at this time was making a study trip through northwest Germany to gather material for the geological part of his work, *Lettres physiques et morales sur l'histoire de la terre et de l'homme*.[5] For this reason above all, only in the autumn of 1778 did he come into possession of the remarks that Mendelssohn had sent to Zimmerman. Initially he let them lie "for some time."[6] Almost a year later, when he wanted to use them as an annotation in the first volume of the aforementioned *Lettres*, he turned to Mendelssohn, this time without Zimmermann's involvement, with the request to revise the annotation.[7] The annotation, which was printed in the first volume of the *Lettres*,[8] renders the second half of Mendelssohn's remarks in a very free French translation. In the meantime, de Luc had obvi-

---

1. JA III.1 xxxviii–xxxix; LSGS II 510–11. LS cites "Über einen schriftlichen Aufsatz des Herrn de Luc" in JA III.1 195–99; henceforth "de Luc" followed by page and line numbers. Interpolations in square brackets in quotations in LS's text are LS's.
2. JA XII.2 125.
3. Fr.: *Treatise on Materialism*.
4. De Luc to Zimmermann, April 10, 1778; de Luc's letters to Zimmermann are found under Number A II 58 in the Zimmermann Papers of the former Royal Library of Hanover. {LS}

   Johann Georg Sulzer (1720–79), a Swiss mathematician and a pioneer in the discovery of electrodes, was a Leibniz-Wolffian. As director of the *Classe de philosophie spéculative* of the Royal Academy of Sciences in Berlin, Sulzer proposed in 1771 that "*le juif*" Mendelssohn be made a member. The Academy's vote in favor of Mendelssohn's membership did not receive the necessary subsequent endorsement of the Academy's royal patron, Friedrich II, however. (See Altmann, MMBS 264–65)
5. [Writings in Physics and Morality on the History of the Earth and of Man] (The Hague and Paris, 1779). {LS}
6. De Luc to Zimmermann, September 9 and October 30, 1778. {LS}
7. Cf. Mendelssohn's answer to de Luc of September/October 1779 [JA XII.2 167–68] and de Luc's letter to Zimmermann of January 21, 1780. {LS}
8. See *Lettres*, 236–37. {LS}

ously decided to work out the originally planned *Traité sur le matérialisme* as part of the *Lettres*. Thus he could introduce Mendelssohn's remarks as "des remarques qu'il [*sc.*, Mendelssohn] a eu la bonté de faire sur l'esquisse de ce Discours, que je lui avois envoyée."[9] In any case, the "handwritten essay" remitted to Mendelssohn must have been sketched apart from "ce *Discours*,"[10] i.e., apart from the twelfth *Discours* of the *Lettres*, in which Mendelssohn's remarks were published by de Luc, and also apart from the tenth and eleventh *Discours*.[11]

9. [Fr.: "remarks that he ... was good enough to make on the sketch of this 'discourse' that I had sent him"]. *Lettres*, I, 236. {LS}
10. Fr.: "*this* 'discourse'" (the emphasis is LS's).
11. Cf. annotations to de Luc 197.7–8 and 30–32. {LS}
LS's editorial annotation to de Luc 197.7–8 ("Mr. de Luc polemicizes against the subtlety of metaphysics with the subtlest metaphysical reasons") reads: "A thoroughgoing polemic against 'subtle' metaphysics is found in the tenth *Discours* (*Lettres*, 167–79), which had perhaps already been sketched in the draft. Cf. especially also *Lettres*, 246–47."
LS's editorial annotation to de Luc 197.30–32 ("According to his basic principles, movement, elasticity, and density do not belong to the properties of matter") reads: "Cf., on this, the eleventh *Discours*."

8 Introduction to Mendelssohn's *The Soul*[1]

[1932]

This writing, which will be printed among Mendelssohn's° Hebrew writings in the Hebrew original[2] with in-depth introduction,[3] was put together after Mendelssohn's death from the two completely self-standing treatises of which it consists and published (in the year 1787) by David Friedländer. The two treatises belong together, since each of them treats a theme of rational psychology—the first treats the problem of immortality, the second treats the psycho-physical problem. {XL}

The first treatise undoubtedly emerged later than the *Phädon*.[4] As Mendelssohn reports in a letter written to Hartwig Wessely in the autumn of 1768, he originally had the aim of treating the problem of immortality in the Hebrew language and in connection with Jewish tradition and, in that way, of renouncing any dependence on the Platonic *Phaedo*: "for what do we, the adherents of the true religion, have to do with the son of Sophroniscus?"[5] But after he had decided to write the *Phädon*—and, to be sure, especially so as "not to have to get involved with revelation"[6]—and had carried out this decision, it might have appeared advisable to him to make the content of this writing accessible also *to* Jews who could not or would not read a book composed in the German language. Convinced that the doctrines of Judaism coincide completely with the doctrines of natural religion, he could say to himself that by composing the *Phädon* he had satisfied an important concern of Judaism also[7] and that the edification he supplied for the numerous readers of his *Phädon* hardly had to be denied to his coreligionists. The

---

1. JA III.1 XXXIX–XLI; LSGS II 512–13. LS cites *Die Seele [aus dem Hebräische übersetzt]* as found in JA III.1 201–33; henceforth *Seele* followed by page- and line-numbers. For an English translation of LS's German version of Mendelssohn's original Hebrew (*HaNefesh*), see www.press.uchicago.edu/sites/strauss/.
2. JA XIV 121–44.
3. The promised in-depth introduction never appeared. Cf. Altmann's *"Geleitwort"* (JA I v–VIII) on the political difficulties impeding the emergence of JA as originally planned, during the Germany of the 1930s.
4. See the reference at *Seele* 212.26–27. {LS}
5. See letter #98 (Hebrew), JA XVI 119 (German trans. by R. Michael, JA XX.2 160).
6. See IP XVIII. {LS}
7. Cf. *Seele* 203.6–7. {LS}

Hebrew treatise renders the thoughts of the *Phädon* in a more traditional and more scholarly manner. It is distinguished from the earlier and more significant writing in addition by the manner in which it treats the question of immortality in the narrower[8] sense.[9] This deviation is further testimony to Mendelssohn's aim of revising the Third Dialogue of the *Phädon*.

The second treatise already deserves acceptance into the corpus of philosophical writings for its containing Mendelssohn's only detailed statement on the problem of the synthesis of soul and body. The expositions relevant to this problem admittedly do not deviate in any way from the doctrine of the Leibniz-Wolffian school. It is otherwise with the remarks on reward and punishment,[10] whose relation to Leibniz's doctrine will be discussed in the "Introduction to Mendelssohn's *God's Cause, or Providence Vindicated*."[11]

Both treatises were translated into German soon after their appearance. {XLI} It appeared impossible for us to accept the very defective translations into our edition.[12] In our translation we have been guided, so far as it was possible for us, by the usage and terminology of Mendelssohn's German writings.

---

8. See IP xv. {LS}

9. See above all *Seele* 211.30–213.3 and annotations. {LS}

LS's annotations to *Seele* 211.30–213.3 may be found in www.press.uchicago.edu/sites/strauss/.

10. *Seele* 231.33ff. {LS}

11. The remainder of LS's sentence in the original German reads: "(in the next volume of this edition)." LS's reference is to IGC xcvi–cx, especially cii–cx, in JA III.2. Concerning the delayed publication of JA III.2, see Altmann's remarks in his editorial introductions to JA I and JA III.2, as well as IMH xxxviii150.

12. See their titles below, JA III.1 381–82. {LS}

LS's reference is to his editorial annotation concerning Variant Readings of Mendelssohn's *Die Seele*, which is reproduced in note 1 of our English translation at www.press.uchicago.edu/sites/strauss/.

9

[1937/1974]

Introduction to Mendelssohn's *Morning Hours* and *To the Friends of Lessing*[1]

These two writings are so closely connected, both as regards the history of their emergence and in substance, that they cannot be considered separately: *To the Friends of Lessing* is, as may be said with a certain right, the second part of *Morning Hours*. {xii}

I. HISTORY OF THEIR EMERGENCE[2]

Morning Hours has two reasons for its emergence, each completely independent of the other, whose accidental unification brought it about that the work assumed its present form, and in particular had the consequence that *To the Friends of Lessing* could take the place of the second part.

The manifest reason for its emergence is to be sought in Mendelssohn's aim of presenting the proofs for the existence of God in a pleasing manner, as would appeal to contemporary taste. Already in his earliest period, "a few people" had wanted "to persuade [him] to treat all of metaphysics in keeping with [his] style."[3] About six years later, he developed the principles of natural theology in the *Treatise on Evidence*, but even so, not "in keeping with his style."[4] Besides, from the beginning he was not totally satisfied

---

1. JA III.2 xi–xcv; LSGS II 528–605. LS cites Mendelssohn's *Morgenstunden* and *An die Freunde Lessings* as found in JA III.2 1–157 and 177–218. Wherever possible, I have added cross-references to the page numbers in Scholz, and vice versa. Concerning LS's sources for Jacobi's texts, see IMH xviii n29, below. Interpolations inside square brackets in quotations in LS's text are LS's; those in LS's annotations are the translator's. Unless otherwise noted, emphases in LS's quotations are LS's.

2. For reasons of English idiom, I have had to split the single German word LS uses as the subtitle for part I of his two-part introduction, *Entstehungsgeschichte*, into its two lexical components and insert a possessive where none exists in the original. The same word, also translated idiomatically, has already occurred in adverbial form (*entstehungsgeschichtlich*) in LS's previous paragraph. It shows up frequently in IMH, sometimes in its plain meaning, sometimes in reference to part I of IMH as a whole, and sometimes in reference to the preface to *Morning Hours* (JA III.2 3–5), where Mendelssohn himself gives an account of the history (*Geschichte*) of his book's emergence (*Entstehung*). Similarly, "reason for its emergence" at the beginning of the second paragraph below (and in the plural at the beginning of the first paragraph below) is *Entstehungsgrund*.

3. To Lessing, January 10, 1756 [JA XI 32]. {LS}

4. The German word for "style," both here and in the previous sentence, is *Art*. Usually, however, *Art* is either "mode" or "sort," but sometimes it is "type" (as in *Gemütsart*, "type of

with that writing for other reasons.[5] The publication of the *Phädon* led to[6] two, more definite suggestions. Iselin expressed the "felicitous brainstorm of transforming the proof for the immateriality of the soul into a proof for the immateriality and unity of God." Mendelssohn considered "the implementation[7] possible and even very useful."[8] The traces of this suggestion are still recognizable in the Thirteenth and Sixteenth Lectures of *Morning Hours*.[9] The publication of the *Phädon* had the further consequence that the hereditary prince of Brunswick at the time expressed to Mendelssohn the wish "to see a similar tract worked out on the existence of God."[10] "A similar tract"—possibly that means: a dialogue.[11] *Morning Hours* is in fact composed at least partly in dialogue form.[12] These and similar suggestions might have prompted Mendelssohn, albeit gradually, to occupy himself in depth once more with the proofs for the existence of God. The pressure to do so grew in him—so he reports in the preface to *Morning Hours*—out of his obligation "to guide" his adolescent son Joseph "at an early age to the rational

---

temperament") or "cast" (as in *Geistesart*, "cast of mind") or even "variant" (as in *Lesarten*, "variant readings"). Later in IMH, "style" is *Stil*. I have saved "manner" for *Weise* (though for reasons of English idiom *Weise*, whether alone or in a compound, is sometimes "way").

5. See ITE XLVII. {LS}

6. The German idiom here (and at IMH XVII) is *hatte zur Folge*, which I have translated somewhat more literally in the previous paragraph as "had the consequence." The noun *Folge* occurs some twenty-two times in IMH, sometimes in its practical (or temporal) meaning, sometimes in its purely theoretical meaning (the three occurrences at IMH XCI are translated as "conclusion"; and "conclusion" at IMH XCIII is *Folgerung*), and sometimes in both meanings at once. Since the theme of IMH is how Mendelssohn is brought face to face with the "consequences"—both practical and theoretical—of the philosophical systems associated with Leibniz, Spinoza, et al. (see especially IMH XVIIff., LXIIff. and LXXVIII), I have tried to keep LS's frequent use of *Folge* in that connection visible to the reader. "To follow," which also occurs frequently in IMH, is *folgen*. As a noun, "follow-up" is *Anschluß* (as at IMH XIII and XXIII); as an adjective, it is *folgend* (as at IMH XXXIII). Cf. also *Seele* 214n98.

7. The German is *Ausführung*, which in the remainder of IMH is almost always "carrying out" or, in the plural, "details." (In IIS, as in the present instance, it is always "implementation.") Its cognates include *Ausführlichkeit* ("detail"), *ausführlich* ("detailed" or "in detail") and *ausführen* ("carry out" or "amplify"; or, as a passive participle, either "detailed" or "realized"). To judge by the various related contexts in which LS uses these cognate words, he may well have all their meanings in mind at once.

8. To Iselin, September 10, 1767 [JA XII.1 144–45]. {LS}

9. See *Morgenstunden* 111.25–113.6 [Scholz 13–15; DaDy 80–81] and 141.20–21 [DaDy 103], as well as the annotations. {LS}

For LS's editorial annotations to *Morgenstunden* 111.25–113.6 and 141.20–21, see appendix 2, supplement to IMH XIII9.

10. To the Present Duke of Brunswick, Autumn 1785 [JA XIII 311]. {LS}

11. Ger.: *Dialog*. LS uses *Gespräch* to mean either "dialogue" as a literary form or "conversation" in the plain meaning of the term; sometimes, moreover, it has both meanings at the same time. For "conversation" as opposed to "dialogue," he uses *Konversation*. In what follows, I have translated *Gespräch* as either "dialogue" or "conversation," depending on the context, and have used a footnote to indicate those few instances where "conversation" is *Konversation*.

12. Cf. especially the Fourth and Fifteenth Lectures. {LS}

knowledge[13] of God." As he recounts further in the same place, he {xiii} developed the truths of natural religion for his son and two other young people, partly in discussions, partly in related lectures, "in such a manner" as to ensure that *Morning Hours* would emerge. There are several further reports concerning this home instruction, of which the two most important may be cited here. Nicolai recounts in his obituary for Mendelssohn[14] that Mendelssohn "would explain the basic principles of his philosophical system orally" to his eldest son "and a few other promising people of his nation in a few morning hours." According to Joseph Mendelssohn's account in the introduction to the *Gesammelte Schriften*,[15] Mendelssohn

> in the hours from five to nine in the morning gave instruction in philosophical subjects to his son-in-law,[16] his eldest son,[17] and the latter's schoolmate Wessely,[18] eventually the Royal Music Director, and then [in the immediate follow-up to the individual instruction sessions, or at the conclusion of the entire instruction?] dictated that work [*sc.*, *Morning Hours*] for them to write down.

The reports are too indefinite for anyone to be able to gather from them in what year the instruction took place. The earliest possible date would have to be 1783. It is not to be ruled out, however, that the instruction began only toward the end of 1784, if indeed not at a still later point in time.[19] However that may be, the emergence of the much larger part of *Morning Hours*—the First through Twelfth and Sixteenth through Seventeenth Lectures—may in any case be loosely explained by the occasion of the home instruction or by Mendelssohn's aim of occupying himself in depth once more with natu-

---

13. Ger.: *Erkenntnis*. Unless otherwise noted (as here), this word is rendered as "cognition" in LS's quotations from Mendelssohn et al. and, for reasons of English idiom, as "knowledge" elsewhere. Inside LS's quotations, "knowledge" is normally *Wissen*. Whether inside or outside of them, the verb "know" is normally *wissen*, and *erkennen* is "cognize," "recognize," etc.

14. Which I cite following the excerpt in J. Heinemann, *Moses Mendelssohn* (Leipzig, 1831), 1–8. {LS}

15. MMGS I 32. {LS}

16. Mendelssohn's son-in-law Simon Veit (Witzenhausen), born May 23, 1754, the first husband of Brendel Mendelssohn, the later one of Dorothea Schlegel. {LS's editorial annotation to *Morgenstunden* 4.12 (JA III.1 278)}

17. Joseph Mendelssohn, born August 8, 1770. {LS's editorial annotation to *Morgenstunden* 3.28 (JA III.2 277)}

18. Bernhard Wessely, born September 1, 1768, the son of Aron Wessely. {LS's editorial annotation to *Morgenstunden* 4.13–14 (JA III.2 278)}

19. Cf. annotation to *Morgenstunden* 4.10–25. {LS}

For LS's editorial annotation to *Morgenstunden* 4.10–25, see appendix 2, supplement to IMH xiiin19.

ral theology. And not only that: a few indications of Mendelssohn's let it be known that, to a certain extent, the second part of the work being planned by him might have deserved the description *Lectures on the Existence of God*. Mendelssohn wanted in the "continuation of [his] *Morning Hours*" to deal with the popular mode of knowledge of the existence of God, i.e., especially the teleological proof of God.[20] {XIV} Accordingly, the plan of *Morning Hours*, insofar as it was to have been nothing more than lectures on the existence of God, must have been envisaged[21] such that the first part had been intended for treating the scientific proofs, and the second part, in contrast, for treating the popular proofs. In any case, the realized first part corresponds to this plan: the main portion of this part is titled "*Scientific* Axioms concerning the Existence of God."[22] The presumption with respect to the second part, which remained unrealized, is corroborated by the observation that Mendelssohn, who in the *Treatise on Evidence* had already thought the popular proofs of God worthy of a detailed mention,[23] had gone considerably further along the road from this writing to the *Morning Hours* of the philosophy of sound commonsense and, with that, to the preference for popular proofs; he therefore must have been incomparably more strongly interested by now in a detailed discussion of these proofs. — More cannot and need not be said about the emergence of *Morning Hours* as a tract on the existence of God. For *Morning Hours* would never have been published,[24] would never have been worked out, would never even have been conceived, if another, more urgent occasion had not forced Mendelssohn into it.

The hidden and real reason for the emergence of *Morning Hours* was a consequence of Mendelssohn's plan to write *Something about Lessing's Char-*

---

20. Cf. *Freunde* 199.6–7 [cf. Got 164] and 212.35ff. [Scholz 309, 316; Val 139, 144], as well as *Morgenstunden* 72.37–73.4 and 91.32–34 [DaDy 52 and 66], with *Evidenz* 311.21–313.33 [Dah 290–93]; cf. further the letter to Hennings of November 5, 1785 [JA XIII 323–24]; according to Nicolai's statement in the obituary to Mendelssohn, the second part of *Morning Hours* was indeed to have brought about the application of natural theology to natural right and ethical doctrine. {LS}

21. The verb *vorstellen* recurs as "envisage" at IMH XCI. Usually it is "represent," as is *repräsentieren*, which occurs twice at IMH LXXIX. At IMH XXXVI and LII, it is "set forth" (as is *aufstellen* at IMH XCI and *darlegen* at IMH XXXVII and XCIII). The corresponding noun is *Vorstellung*, which is almost always "representation" (meaning something conceived by the mind), but occasionally "notion." "Representative," however, is *Vertreter* (except at IMH LXXXIII, where it is *Repräsentant*). The corresponding verb, *vertreten*, is also, unavoidably, "represent"; it occurs three times at IMH LXXXIX (in a context where its meaning as *vertreten* rather than *vorstellen* is unmistakable).

22. The emphasis is LS's. "Wissenschaftliche Lehrbegriffe vom Daseyn Gottes" is the title of the Eighth through Seventeenth Lectures of *Morning Hours* (see the table of contents, *Morgenstunden* 6ff. [cf. DaDy xvii–xviii]).

23. See *Evidenz, loc. cit.* [Dah 290–93]. {LS}

24. See *Morgenstunden* 4.23–26 [DaDy xx] and the variant readings *ad loc*. {LS}

The variant readings *ad loc*. (JA III.2 266) quote a deleted passage in Mendelssohn's manuscript version of *Morgenstunden* that reads: "It was originally not intended for this use."

acter. This plan had surfaced right after Lessing's death, and Mendelssohn had the aim of carrying it out in the summer of 1781.[25] Mendelssohn did make a few preliminary sketches, but did not get as far as a working out of the writing: when Elise Reimarus, the daughter of the author of the "Wolfenbüttel Fragments"[26] and a friend of Lessing's, visited him in Berlin in March of 1783, he must have promised her "to keep my word regarding *Something about Lessing's Character*." Elise Reimarus's conversation with Mendelssohn, which should have propelled him to the working out of the Lessing writing, had the unforeseeable consequence that this writing never came about. {xv} Namely, Elise Reimarus thought it harmless to report to her friend Friedrich Heinrich Jacobi concerning her friend Moses Mendelssohn's plan. Then Jacobi seized the occasion to let Mendelssohn know through Elise Reimarus "that Lessing in his last days was a decided Spinozist." From this communication grew the most remarkable controversy of the German eighteenth century, which among other things had the consequence that the parts of *Morning Hours* dealing indirectly or directly with Lessing—the Thirteenth through Fifteenth Lectures—or, rather, *Morning Hours* as a whole and *To the Friends of Lessing*, took the place of the planned Lessing writing. Actually, the significance of these two writings consists chiefly in the fact° that they belong to the most important documents of that remarkable controversy—a controversy that from the beginning was animated and distorted by the prejudices of the two men involved.

It started with a distortion of Jacobi's. His letter to Elise Reimarus of July 21, 1783,[27] reads:

> I [wanted] to update you about something very important—about our friend Lessing's final sentiments . . . , so as to communicate it to Men-

25. To Herder, May 18, 1781 [JA XIII 19]. {LS}
26. In 1774, 1777, and 1778, under the title "Fragments of an Unnamed," Lessing [as librarian of the ducal library at Wolfenbüttel, Brunswick, and editor of its official publications] had published a part of the *Apologie oder Schutzschrift für die vernünftiger Verehrer Gottes* [Apology or Defense for the Rational Worshipers of God], whose author was Hermann Samuel Reimarus (1694–1768). Reimarus had been expounding the religion of reason, especially in his *Vornehmsten Wahrheiten der natürlichen Religion* [Noblest Truths of Natural Religion] (1754 and at other times). As concerns revelation, the "Second Fragment" asserted "the Impossibility of a Revelation that All Men can Believe in a Well-Founded Mode." To his edition of the "Fragments" Lessing had added "Counterpropositions," from which it turns out that he did not "adopt the entire sentiment" of the Fragmentist's in any case. On the other hand, Lessing had to defend the Fragmentist to Mendelssohn in particular (see his letter to Mendelssohn of January 9, 1771 [JA XII.2 2]). {LS's editorial annotation to *Morgenstunden* 125.27–126.2 [Scholz 30; Val 66; DaDy 9; Got 151] (JA III.2 304)}
27. Jacobi's letter is reproduced as an Appendix to Elise Reimarus's letter to Mendelssohn of August 4, 1783, in JA XIII 120ff. See also Scholz 67n (Val 79n).

delssohn, if you find it to the good. — Perhaps you know, and if you don't know I'll confide it to you here sub rosa in friendship, that Lessing in his last days was a decided Spinozist. It might be possible that Lessing expressed these sentiments to several people; and then it would be necessary for Mendelssohn, in the monument he wants to erect to him, either to avoid certain materials altogether or at least to treat them extremely cautiously. Perhaps Lessing expressed himself to his beloved Mendelssohn just as clearly as he did in my presence; or perhaps not, since he did not speak with him for a long period and wrote letters very reluctantly. It is here left to you, my confidante, whether you want to divulge something of this or not. I cannot write more specifically about the matter at this time, however.[28]

In this letter, one dishonesty follows another. Jacobi leaves it to Elise Reimarus's discretion whether or not to make his communication known to Mendelssohn; he indicates the importance and urgency of his communication so strongly, however, that in truth he leaves his correspondent no choice. {xvi} He treats the communication as a secret that he confides only sub rosa in friendship, and two years later he himself chafes to speak with Elise Reimarus in public about "the complete details [of] the friendly conversations" that he had had with Lessing about Spinozism. He gives Mendelssohn the friendly advice of either avoiding "certain materials" altogether or treating them only with extreme caution, and when Mendelssohn in *Morning Hours* follows exactly that advice, he reproaches him most severely for his "pious fraud":

> Evidently Mendelssohn did not want [the truth] to come to light. If something of it should ever leak out, it was now and forever to be hushed up, and any future rumor about it was to be headed off.[29]

---

28. See JA XIII 122.
29. Scholz LXXXIX. Re the Jacobi citations, cf. the "Preliminary Remark" to the annotations to *An die Freunde Lessings* [JA III.2 312]. {LS}
LS's "Preliminary Remark" reads: "I cite Jacobi's *Über die Lehre des Spinozas, in Briefen an den Herrn Moses Mendelssohn* [On Spinoza's Doctrine, in Letters to Mr. Moses Mendelssohn] and the second half of his *Wider Mendelssohns Beschuldigungen betreffend die Briefe über die Lehre des Spinozas* [Against Mendelssohn's Accusations apropos the Letters on Spinoza's Doctrine] according to the reprint in *Die Hauptschriften zum Pantheismusstreit zwischen Jacobi und Mendelssohn*, edited ... by Heinrich Scholz ... (Berlin: Reuther & Reichard, 1916) [reprint; intro. Wolfgang Erich Müller, Theologische Studien-Texte 17 (Waltrop: Hartmut Spenner, 2004)]. The first half of *Wider Mendelssohns Beschuldigungen*..., which was not republished by Scholz, I cite according to the reprint in Friedrich Heinrich Jacobi's *Werke* [ed. C. J. F. Roth and J. F. Köppen (6 vols. in 8; Leipzig: Gerhard Fleischer, 1812–25], IV 2..., 169–232 [abbreviated RK IV.2 169–232]...."

Jacobi pretends not to know whether Lessing had expressed himself to "his beloved Mendelssohn" quite as openly as he had to him; yet no fact was more vividly present to him than that Lessing had not so much as spoken with Mendelssohn about the subject at hand.[30] Jacobi in no way intimates that his communication must have been disagreeable to Mendelssohn, and yet he was convinced of nothing more than that it would exasperate Mendelssohn in the highest degree.[31] And finally, Jacobi cannot write more specifically about the matter at this time; for were he to do so, were he to lay out all at once the detailed report of his conversations with Lessing, then Mendelssohn from the outset would perhaps react accordingly and Jacobi would not succeed in his goal. Jacobi's communication is a trap, into which Mendelssohn has now walked in just the manner wished for by Jacobi.

But what was the goal that Jacobi was trying to reach by his devious communication to Mendelssohn? Having correctly foreseen that, with this communication, Mendelssohn could "begin" nothing, why did he not publish his conversations with Lessing on his own, without entering into contact with Mendelssohn? It will hardly do to assume that he feared the odium of the publication of confidential conversations: his *Something that Lessing Said*,[32] which had appeared a short time before, proves that {xvii} such considerations did not restrain him. It is far more probable that he wanted to pressure[33] Mendelssohn, who was holding back from any quarrel, into a controversy that sooner or later had to be brought into the public forum and in which, as he must have flattered himself, victory was assured him from the outset. But why did a public quarrel with Mendelssohn, a public humiliation of Mendelssohn, matter to him?

The communication to Elise Reimarus, intended as it was for Mendelssohn, has a longer prehistory that is far from being fully discernible, but yet just enough of it is known for sure to enable Jacobi's behavior to be grasped. Jacobi, being forty years old when he started the quarrel with Mendelssohn, therefore about fourteen years younger than Mendelssohn, had from 1773 on published a series of essays, mostly political in content, in

---

30. See *Freunde* 193.4ff. [Scholz 310; Val 134; Got 159]. {LS}

31. See *Freunde* 189.7–8 [Scholz 296; Val 130; Got 155] and annotation. {LS}

For LS's editorial annotation to *Freunde* 189.7–8, see appendix 2, supplement to IMH xviiin31.

32. *Etwas, das Lessing gesagt hat. Ein Kommentar zu den Reisen der Päpste nebst Betrachtungen von einem Dritten* [Something That Lessing Said: A Commentary on "Journeys of the Popes" along with Considerations by a Third Party] (Berlin: George Jacob Decker, 1782); RK II 325–88; cf. Sno 191–211. See IMH xviiin39, below.

33. Or: compel (as at IMH xviii, below).

Teutscher Merkur, as well as earlier versions of his novels *Allwill* and *Woldemar*.[34] In 1781 he had edited and unified a part of these works into a volume, *Miscellaneous Writings: First Part*;[35] he had presented a copy of this volume to Mendelssohn;[36] it is not to be ruled out that in the very same year there came about an exchange of opinions over it. In the following year, Jacobi published his treatise *Something that Lessing Said*,[37] which led to a controversy between Mendelssohn and Jacobi and which moreover prefigures in its content the theses of Jacobi's *Spinoza Letters*.[38] That is why a brief characterization of the aim and the form of thinking that show up in this treatise is indispensable for understanding the emergence of *Morning Hours*.

Focusing on a statement that Lessing had made to him orally,[39] and in the sense of this statement of the author *Emilia Galotti*,[40] Jacobi demanded that the critique of papal despotism be broadened into a critique of any despotism, i.e., especially princely despotism. This critique is sustained by the same political sentiment as was later called Liberalism; it is guided by the ideal of the constitutional state, in which {xviii} the sovereign is unconditionally bound by positive right, especially by the lawful regulation of property relations.[41] Jacobi justifies this ideal by recourse to the essence of religion and virtue, and ultimately by recourse to the rationality that constitutes the essence of man (whereby he nevertheless understands "reason" entirely in the sense of the Enlightenment, as the citations from Hobbes

---

34. *Teutscher Merkur* was a journal of which Jacobi was the chief founder (Gio 36, 52, with 13–16 *passim*). On *Allwill* and *Woldemar*, see Gio 117–51 and the translation of *Allwill* at Gio 379–96.

35. *Vermischte Schriften: Erster Theil* (Breslau: J. F. Korn, 1781).

36. See *Zeitschrift für die Geschichte der Juden*, ed. L. Geiger, IV, 304; Mendelssohn's acquaintance with *Allwill* is evidenced by his letter to Hennings of June 25, 1782 [JA XIII 66]. {LS}

37. RK II 325–88 [Sno 191–211]. {LS}

38. I.e., *On Spinoza's Doctrine, in Letters to Mr. Moses Mendelssohn*. See IMH xvin29, above.

39. The opening sentence of Jacobi's *Something that Lessing Said* reads: "This I heard Lessing say: the statements of Febronius and his followers were a shameless flattery of the princes; for all their arguments against the privileges of the pope were either groundless or applied with double and triple force to the princes themselves" (RK II 334; Sno 191). Sno's note *ad loc*. reads: "Justinius Febronius was the pseudonym of Johan Nicolaus von Hontheim, auxiliary bishop of Trier, theologian, and historian. He defended the limitation of papal powers in his *De statu ecclesiae et legitima potestate Romani Pontificis* (1763, 1765)" (Sno 209n2; cf. Gio 17). See also ET 58–59 (RCPR 70–71).

40. LM II 377–450 (trans. R. Dillon-Boylan, in LDW I 133–225). Cf. Gio 54n136: "[In] the play *Emilia Galotti*, . . . the false situation created by a despot leads to the killing of a daughter by her father. Odeardo kills the daughter Emilia with the sword with which she wanted to kill herself and that had been given to her by the [despot's] former mistress."

41. RK II 347 [cf. Sno 196]: "security of property in the broadest understanding of the term° and in absolutely the highest degree." {LS}

already prove by themselves):[42] true religion and true virtue are by their essence voluntary, not compulsory; man does not need "formal legislation," a "system of compulsion,"[43] insofar as he is guided by reason, but only insofar as he is subject to passions. It follows from this presupposition, therefore, not that the state would have to compel the multitude who are incapable of true virtue into virtuous behavior, but on the contrary that the state should have no other purpose than the purely "negative" one of "protection," i.e., to be each's shield in the free use of his powers and especially in the free play of his passions: in the state that would be erected according to Jacobi's principles, "the passions themselves of each individual member" would have "a far freer play than in other states; for here nothing would be prevented by force[44] except only what violated property." The presupposition of this astonishing consequence of the principle of the voluntariness of virtue is the assumption of the elementary rights of man, unconditional claims that would be the source and legitimate basis of the state and to which obligations would remain subservient: Jacobi's ideal is "a community that would be united solely and only for preserving the security of all rights, by the fulfillment of all obligations without which these rights could not exist or be valid."[45] The recognition of the rights of men[46] means the recognition of the equality of these rights, the denial of all privilege: all privileges, especially the privileges of an absolute monarch, are reduced by Jacobi critically to the will to be privileged, i.e., to vanity, self-centeredness. Although he speaks against despotism with a decisiveness reminiscent of Rousseau, he nevertheless declares himself to be of a mind to bestow a laurel wreath on the classic of despotism, Thomas Hobbes, {xix} and to "tear" it "from the brow of those who were deceivers, hypocrites, or shallow-pates"; for Hobbes is to be considered a "serious thinker," "since he himself believed only in passions and bodily drives," "being honest enough . . . for just that reason to have denied right and virtue, and not willing to derive them from things they do not follow from."[47] For Jacobi, therefore, the inner consis-

---

42. See RK II 342, 384–85 (Sno 194, 207). Cf. Strauss, LSGS I 130–34 (SCR 89–92), LSGS III 364–69 (HCR 109–14), PPH 80–81, 93, 130, 158–60, NRH 180, 186, 201–2, LAM 220, 240, with WPP 176–77n2, TWM 83, 84, 87, 90. 91; contrast PPH 145–50.
43. RK II 346 [Sno 195]. {LS}
44. Ger.: *mit Gewalt*. Lit.: with power. Earlier in LS's sentence, "powers" is *Kräfte*, more or less literally, "forces."
45. RK II 387 [cf. Sno 208]. {LS}
46. Cf. RK VI 365–68. {LS}
47. RK II 384–85 [cf. Sno 207]. {LS}

tency of the thought is more important than the accidental correctness of the result. Here too, and not only in the struggle against princely despotism, he knows himself to be of one mind[48] with Lessing.

"Mr. Mendelssohn ... had seen *Something that Lessing Said*," as Jacobi himself reports,[49]

> for he had drafted some remarks about it. . . . These remarks were communicated to me with Mendelssohn's approval. I combined with his objections those of another worthy gentleman and sent the essay to a common friend, who in line with my wish had it published with Mendelssohn's permission under the title chosen by him, "Thoughts of Various Men about a Remarkable Writing."[50]

Mendelssohn's remarks about Jacobi's treatise are directed both against its tendentiousness[51] and against the appeal to a saying of Lessing's. He reprimands the tendentiousness: he who is manifestly dominated by the original Enlightenment's mistrust of the *vulgus hominum*,[52] given over as they are to the delusion of the priests, and who for that reason is not willing to let the alliance between (enlightened) despotism and philosophy[53] totter, rebukes not only the putatively democratic tendency in Jacobi's writing, but also the shifting of the problem of "prince and pope" to "prince and people."[54] And as for the statement of Lessing's to which Jacobi had appealed, he saw in it a peculiarly Lessingian paradox, inasmuch as it was suitable for conversation,[55] to be sure, but not for instruction: the author who wants to instruct has to strive not for exaggeration, but for distinct and pure concepts. Mendelssohn had involuntarily let the critique of Jacobi pass over

---

48. Ger.: *einen Sinnes*. Lit.: of one sense. Cf. LS's use of this noun in first sentence of the present paragraph, as well as at IMH xx, below. Earlier, at IMH xviii–xix, "of a mind" is *willens*—more or less literally, "of a will," i.e., "disposed"; likewise in the Mendelssohnian passages LS quotes at IMH xxxix and li, below. The cognate verb *wollen*, rendered in context as "willing" in the quotation in the text at IMH xixn47 and also in the second sentence after the block quotation in the next paragraph, is elsewhere always "want."

49. RK IV.2 200 and note. {LS}

50. RK II 389–400.

51. Ger.: *Tendenz*. Or: tendency (as in the latter part of the next sentence, and at IP xxxi and IMH xlvi, along with IMH lxivn297; at IMH xlii, it is, again, "tendentiousness"; at IMH xxvn92, it is "bias").

52. Lat.: the common run of human beings.

53. Ger.: *Weltweisheit*. See IPM xviiin23.

54. His *Jerusalem*, with whose working out he was busied just then, treats "prince and pope" exclusively. {LS}

55. Ger.: *Konversation*. Likewise in the fifth sentence of the next paragraph. See IMH xiin11, above.

into a critique of Lessing, of Lessing's "theater logic";[56] he had involuntarily drawn the dividing line between the Berliners,[57] who were pressing for clear and distinct concepts, and the paradoxical Lessing. {xx}

Jacobi answered in his "Objections to 'Thoughts of Various Men about a Remarkable Writing.'"[58] He exposes the misunderstanding that believes it recognizes a democratic or papist tendency in his writing. His reply puts the strongest emphasis by far, however, on the explanation of the sense of Lessing's paradox. Again he appeals to a statement that Lessing had made to him orally in his presence;[59] again he knows himself to be of one mind with Lessing. The counterclaim that Jacobi raises against Mendelssohn concerning this decisive point can be rendered as follows: far from being a form of discourse inferior to instruction, conversation as an awakening to the search for truth would instead be the highest manner in which one human being can improve another.[60] It was a critique that was peaceful in form, cutting in substance, which a fairly unknown author was directing at the "German Plato" here. And it had been brought forward not in connection with the dialogues of Plato, whose thoughts were of only limited present-day relevance for Mendelssohn, but in connection with the dialogues[61] of Lessing.

In view of this victory of Jacobi's, it remains inexplicable initially how this first controversy with Mendelssohn can have left a sting in him. The observation that for Jacobi the controversy with Mendelssohn was incomparably more important than for the latter yields a clue to the solution of this riddle: it was Jacobi who, by the publishing of Mendelssohn's critique of *Something that Lessing Said*, had conferred a significance on this critique that it might well not have had at all for Mendelssohn himself and that, in that way, had at the same time created for him first of all the occasion for a public reply. Mendelssohn was much more indifferent than Jacobi. Was it not in the end this indifference that aroused Jacobi in the extreme, that ir-

---

56. See Lessing, " 2er Anti-Goeze" [Second anti-Goeze], LM XIII 151.
57. I.e., the Berlin Academy. Cf. IPM xv–xvii; ITE xlv–xlviii.
58. RK II 400–11. {LS}
59. The statement reads: "The logical order of our thoughts is not always the one in which we communicate them to others. But it is the one that the opponent must seek out before everything if his attack is to be fair." See RK II 402, with Lessing, "Axiomata" [Axioms], LM XIII 110 (cf. Nis 123).
60. Cf. RK II 404–5. {LS}
61. Cf. IMH xiiin11, above. In a posthumously published essay on Lessing written in English in 1939, LS remarks that "Lessing's dialogues ('Ernst und Falk' and Lessing's conversations with F. H. Jacobi) . . . probably come closer to the spirit of Platonic dialogues and their technique than any other modern work in the German language" (ET 57; reprinted in RCPR 69).

ritated his noblest and at the same time his most contemptible impulses in the highest degree?

Mendelssohn could have no inkling of how much Jacobi was prepared for Mendelssohn's unintended self-exposure in "Thoughts of Various Men," how exquisitely it fit into the image he had made for himself in many years of thinking about Mendelssohn, about the Enlightenment, about God and the world. For, to be sure, he knew {xxi} of Jacobi's "merits as an author; but [he] had never seen anything by him in the metaphysical department."[62] On the other hand, precisely through one of his metaphysical writings, Mendelssohn had without knowing it played a remarkable role for Jacobi at a decisive moment for his development. Jacobi had returned to Germany as a twenty-year-old after a long stay in Switzerland, just at the time when the Berlin Academy had set up the competition concerning evidence in the metaphysical sciences.[63] "No question," he later reported in his dialogue *David Hume on Belief, or Idealism and Realism*,

> could have attracted my attention to a greater degree. I awaited the publication of the treatises longingly.... The prizewinning writing [*sc.*, Mendelssohn's *Treatise on Evidence*] did not fulfill the expectations that the name of the philosophical author, who by that time was already very famous, had aroused in me. It had been especially striking to me to find in the prizewinning treatise how extensively the proof of the existence of God from the idea[64] was discussed and with what great assurance its validity was asserted.

Not that the ontological proof of God would have made more of an impression on Jacobi this time than earlier. He

> felt only the necessity of studying it now from the ground up, in order to be able to expose its mistake and make the force it had for others completely intelligible to me as well.... So I think you will grasp the state I found myself in as I read the critical passages of Mendelssohn's *Treatise*. ... I attacked the material without further ado by tirelessly pursuing the historical threads, as is my wont. And here is the time of my closer

---

62. *Freunde* 189.9–11 [Scholz 296; cf. Val 130; cf. Got 155]. {LS}
63. Cf. ITE XLV–XLVI.
64. I.e., of God. See *Evidenz* 297–11; Dah 279–91.

acquaintance with the writings of Spinoza. I had read in Leibniz that
Spinozism is exaggerated Cartesianism....[65]

The result to which Jacobi was led by his critical study of modern philosophy may be summarized as follows: the ontological proof of God is the most extreme expression of the tendency to prove everything, to take nothing for granted; if one follows this tendency forthrightly, i.e., without misgivings, then it leads to Spinozism, i.e., to atheism and fatalism; since Leibniz-Wolffian philosophy rests on the principle of {xxii} demonstration, of clear and distinct concepts, it is "no less fatalistic than the Spinozist one and leads the persevering investigator back to the basic principles of the latter";[66] since "each avenue of demonstration" ends up ". . . in fatalism" and atheism, and therefore leads to absurd consequences, one must hold firmly to the original, prescientific knowledge existing prior to and at the basis of all demonstration, the knowledge of sound commonsense,[67] one must risk the "*salto mortale*"[68] of "believing" the truth or, what is tantamount to the same thing, of "presupposing" it in the "knowledge of ignorance"; the source of the tendency to prove everything is man's will to be dependent on nothing outside himself, on no truth transcending him, is his will "not [to] obey the truth but [to] control it,"[69] is arrogance, self-centeredness. In the same sentiment in which Jacobi combats the claims to sovereignty of despots of whatever sort in the realm of the political—in that° same sentiment he contests the claim to sovereignty of demonstrative "reason": he recognizes dogmatism as despotism in the realm of thought itself. And just as he preferred the classic of political despotism, Hobbes, over all "shallow-pates" who in cowardly weakness were bringing Hobbes's doctrine to the marketplace, so he preferred the classic of metaphysical despotism, Spinoza, over the philosophers[70] of the German Enlightenment.

Jacobi's report about the remarkable, if indirect, suggestion that he owed to Mendelssohn requires a not wholly unimportant supplement. Through Mendelssohn, not only had the problematic of Cartesian-Leibnizian meta-

---

65. RK II 183–87 [cf. Gio 281–82]. {LS}
For Jacobi's source, see Leibniz, *Théodicée* §393 [Ger VI 350; Hug 359–60].
66. Scholz 177 [cf. Gio 234; cf. Got 137]. {LS}
67. RK II 415 and 469ff. {LS}
68. Ital.: summersault. More or less lit.: death-defying leap.
69. RK II 417. {LS}
LS quotes this last passage more fully at IMH xxix, below.
70. Ger.: *Weltweiser*. See IPM xviiin23.

physics been pressed upon him in a decisive moment for him. An earlier writing of Mendelssohn's, the *Philosophical Dialogues*,[71] had corroborated for him the thought (assuming that it did not bring him to this thought in the first place) that the kinship of Leibniz's philosophy with Spinozism is considerably greater than the dominant view at the time wanted to allow. He says in the earliest presentation of his principles,[72] right after the relationship of Leibniz and Spinoza has come up:

> Mendelssohn has clearly shown that the *harmonia praestabilita*[73] is in Spinoza. From this alone it already follows that Spinoza {xxiii} must contain even more of Leibniz's basic doctrines. . . .[74]

In any case, Jacobi had developed the more important part of the previously sketched reflections of his in confidential conversations with Lessing. He had followed Lessing's philosophical statements of the '70s with serious interest.[75] Perhaps Lessing's theological campaign, the struggle against Goeze's orthodox dogmatism,[76] had aroused him even more strongly than those statements.[77] It had not escaped him that Lessing had directed his attack not just against that particular dogmatism, but against any dogmatism. His "propitious fate granted" that Lessing wrote to him in 1779. Jacobi "replied that [he] was planning a trip for the following spring that should take [him] by Wolfenbüttel, where [he] longed to conjure up in him the spirits of several wise men whom [he] could not get to speak about certain things."[78] The discussions, stretching over several days, which came about in Wolfenbüttel, Brunswick, and Halberstadt in July and August of 1780, corroborated the impression that Jacobi had gained from reading Lessing's writings: Lessing had broken with the theism not only of the tradition but also of the Leibniz-Wolffian Enlightenment. As for Leibniz himself, Lessing

---

71. See *Gespräche* 6–12, 14–19; or *Schriften* 341–47, 349–55 (Dah 100–104, 106–11).
72. I.e., in his *Spinoza Letters*. See IMH XVIIn38 (with the corresponding text of IMH XVII), above, and xxiiin74, below.
73. Lat.: preestablished harmony.
74. Scholz 85 [cf. Gio 191; cf. Val 92; cf. Nis 248]. {LS}
75. Scholz 335–36 [Val 152] {LS}
76. Lessing's replies to Pastor Johann Melchior Goeze of Hamburg et al. during the controversy over Lessing's publication of the "Wolfenbüttel Fragments" include "Eine Parabel" [A Parable] (LM XIII 91–103; Nis 110–19), "Axiomata," LM 105–37 (Nis 120–47), "Anti-Goeze" (LM XIII 139–213) and "Der nöthigen Antwort auf eine sehr unnöthige Frage" [The Necessary Answer to a Very Unnecessary Question] (LM XIII 329–36; Cha 62–64; Nis 172–77). For a handy summary of these, see Nis 6–14.
77. Scholz 74 [Gio 184; Val 84; Nis 241; Got 131]. {LS}
78. *Ibid.* {LS}

admired him "for his grand style of thinking, and not for this or that opinion that he only appeared to have held or may even actually have held."[79] About Spinoza he expressed himself such that Jacobi could believe that Lessing was a decided Spinozist: "There is no philosophy other than the philosophy of Spinoza."[80] Lessing was visibly impressed by Jacobi's thorough understanding of Spinoza, by his philosophical resourcefulness: he recognized at once the originality of Jacobi's guiding thought; when Jacobi said in an immediate follow-up to his exposition of Spinoza's axiom, buoyed as it was by admiration, "my credo is not in Spinoza.... I believe in an intelligent personal cause of the world," Lessing replied, "Oh, so much the better. I must be about to hear something entirely new."[81] Jacobi's thought, which is "entirely new" in fact although in many respects prepared partly by Pascal,[82] partly by Bayle,[83] {xxiv} consists "in inferring immediately from fatalism against fatalism and against everything connected with it."[84] This thought, and the "*salto mortale*" essentially belonging to it, Lessing dismissed, playfully to be sure.[85] Perhaps most important in the present context is what Lessing said about Mendelssohn. As Jacobi recounts, he valued Mendelssohn

> most among his friends.... He was very eager for me to get to know him personally. In one discussion, I expressed my amazement that a man of such clear and accurate understanding as Mendelssohn could have endorsed the proof of the existence of God from the idea[86] as zealously as he had done in his *Treatise on Evidence*; and Lessing's excuses led me straight to the question of whether he had ever declared his own system to Mendelssohn. "Never," replied Lessing.... "Once I only said to him, more or less, just what struck you in 'The Education of the Human Race' (§73).[87] We never came to closure, and I left it at that."[88]

---

79. Scholz 84 [cf. Gio 190–91; cf. Val 90–91; cf. Nis 247]. {LS}
Lessing's (or Jacobi's) word for "style" here is *Art*; see IMH 59–60n4, above.
80. Scholz 78 [cf. Gio 187; cf. Val 86; cf. Nis 244; cf. Got 132]. {LS}
81. Scholz 80–81 [cf. Gio 189; cf. Val 88; cf. Nis 246; cf. Got 133]. Lessing's remark has an ironic overtone: according to its naked wording, Jacobi's thesis is identical with the opinion dominant for many centuries, therefore precisely "nothing new." {LS}
82. See Scholz 122, 185 (Gio 204. 237).
83. See Scholz 104 (Gio 201). Cf. IMH lxx, lxxxviii, and xciii, with IGC cv–cix.
84. Scholz 81 [cf. Gio 189; cf. Val 89; cf. Nis 246]. {LS}
85. Scholz 81 and 91 [Gio 189, 195; Val 88, 96; Nis 246–47, 251; Got 134–36]. {LS}
86. See IMH xxn60, above.
87. The parenthesis is Jacobi's interpolation. See LM XIII 430–31 (Cha 94–95; Nis 234–35). Lessing's "The Education of the Human Race" §§70–73 is also translated in appendix 4.
88. Scholz 68–69 [cf. Gio 182; cf. Val 80; cf. Got 128]. {LS}

The discussions with Lessing had therefore provided Jacobi with full clarity about having Lessing's authority on his side in his opposition to both (enlightened) despotism—recall *Something that Lessing Said*—and the dogmatism of the Leibniz-Wolffian Enlightenment, and especially also about an unbridgeable difference of opinion with respect to natural theology that existed between Lessing and Mendelssohn, notwithstanding all their friendship.

Mendelssohn had first drawn Jacobi's attention to himself as a defender of the ontological proof of God in 1763, and this first impression was so unforgettably connected with all Jacobi's further studies that he brought up the defense of the ontological proof in the *Treatise on Evidence* at this first and only meeting with Lessing seventeen years later: Mendelssohn had become for Jacobi, for quite accidental reasons, the representative of dogmatism. But how had he been able to satisfy himself with this impression? To be sure, Mendelssohn had declared himself in favor of the ontological proof of God, as he had in favor of the whole metaphysics of the Cartesian-Leibnizian stamp. But had he not, precisely in {xxv} the *Treatise on Evidence*, done justice to the popular proofs of God, illuminating as they are to sound commonsense?[89] And had his aesthetic investigations any other aim besides proving the priority (conditional though it may be) of "sensuously[90] perfect representation" over clear and distinct concepts?[91] Mendelssohn spells it out:

> Since Mr. Jacobi does not know me, I may have been described to him as a witling of the sort who concedes too much to reason and nothing at all to belief; who stands under the illusion that he could pull off anything with the help of metaphysical demonstrations, perhaps banishing spirits or counteracting the Secret Society with his quiddities.[92]

But this was indeed just what was so thoroughly unintelligible and consequently so thoroughly intolerable to Jacobi: in Jacobi's eyes the circumspection, the caution by virtue of which Mendelssohn was able, for example, to declare himself in favor of both the scientific and the popular

---

89. See *Evidenz* 311–15; Dah 291–94.
90. Ger.: *sinnlich*. Cf. IMH xlivn299, below.
91. *Schriften* 431 (cf. Dah 172). See also IMH lixn264 and lxivf., below.
92. *Freunde* 196.5 to 10 [Scholz 305; cf. Val 137; cf. Got 161–62]. {LS}
As regards Mendelssohn's reference to "the Secret Society," LS's editorial annotation to *Freunde* 196.10 (JA III.2 326) reads: "[Its] allegedly Jesuit bias. Jacobi had a controversy with Nicolai soon after Mendelssohn's death about the existence of such a secret society."

knowledge of God was nothing more than an abominable indecisiveness, an indifference toward the truth. Being strongly opposed to such a cautious, half dogmatism, he was ready to fight fully on the side of the open, radical, total dogmatism of Spinoza and recognized in radical dogmatism his ally in the struggle against lukewarmness, compromise, middlingness. Everything else comes down decisively to the characteristic shift of objective that takes place such as it does in Jacobi's mind. In keeping with his original aim he pits himself against despotism, whether of the political or of the metaphysical sort, rooted as it is in self-centeredness; he pits himself especially against the classic of dogmatism, against Spinoza. But suddenly his struggle is no longer directed solely against that dogmatism itself, but also against its ambivalent enablers, who try to manufacture a compromise between political despotism and political freedom, between fatalism and metaphysical freedom. Ultimately the real objective is almost lost from sight, and the struggle is directed almost exclusively against the sort of man who can let himself be satisfied with compromises. And now it is the attitude of this sort of man, rather than the radical dogmatism itself, which is branded as the outgrowth of {xxvi} self-centeredness, of the vain wish to be a know-it-all. If Lessing is Jacobi's model in anything, it is in the sort of polemical thinking to which there belongs an, as it were, constant switching of sides, partly actual, partly apparent: thirty years later, he still compares his siding with the Spinoza repudiated by him because of his doctrine but admired because of his decisiveness, against a Leibniz-Wolffian Enlightenment that is "thoroughly muddled about itself," with Lessing's siding with "the old, inflexible but consistent orthodoxy" against "a very flexible but thoroughly inconsistent new one."[93] One might add that Lessing had pitted himself not merely against the half orthodoxy of Goeze,[94] but just as vigorously against "rational Christianity" (where "one doesn't really know either where reason comes in or where Christianity comes in")[95] and against Eberhard's (an adherent of Mendelssohn's) attempt in an *Apology of Socrates* to deny the eternity of punishments in hell,[96] and one grasps that Jacobi's

---

93. RK II 116–17 [cf. Gio 587]. {LS}
94. See IMH xxiiin76, above.
95. Lessing, "Von Duldung der Deisten: Fragment eines Ungenannten" [On Tolerance of the Deists: Fragment of an Unnamed], LM XII 271. Cf. Lessing's letter to his brother Karl, February 2, 1774 (LM IX 596–97; quoted in All 84).
96. Johann August Eberhard, *Neue Apologie des Sokrates, oder Untersuchung der Lehre von der Seligkeit der Heiden* [New *Apology of Socrates*, or Investigation of the Doctrine of the Blessedness of the Heathens] (1772–). See Lessing, "Leibniz von den ewigen Strafen" [Leibniz on Eternal Punishments], LM XI 461–87, esp. 469–85 (cf. Nis 37–60, esp. 45–59).

76 CHAPTER NINE

struggle was against a moderate Enlightenment that served two masters,[97] that his later struggle against Mendelssohn's conception of a "purified" Pantheism was entirely in Lessing's sense. If one pays more attention to the how than to the what—and the grand *style* of thinking was for Jacobi, just as for Lessing, more important than the accepting of this or that opinion—then one will be inclined to consider the possibility that Jacobi was the most understanding adherent that Lessing found among his contemporaries.[98]

Nevertheless—Mendelssohn's caution allows for a kinder interpretation, which is, just for that reason, perhaps the more correct one. Jacobi transmitted a further statement of Lessing's about Mendelssohn, whose exact wording admittedly cannot be drawn from his report.

> Mendelssohn had thoroughly immersed himself in Leibniz-Wolffian philosophy only; and he had become steeped in it. With that, Lessing also exonerated him with respect to the tautological [*sc.*, ontological] proof of the existence of God—he exonerated him with what he had already admitted to me just now, and no doubt from word one, that Mendelssohn was, to be sure, a bright, accurate, superior mind, but no metaphysical one. Mendelssohn needed philosophy, found what he needed in the dominant doctrine of his time, and clung to it. For investigating other systems, soaking them in, {xxvii} and transforming them into blood in the veins,[99] he had neither calling nor desire. He lacked the philosophical resourcefulness that was precisely Lessing's outstanding character trait°.[100]

It is idle to quarrel over whether Jacobi might have contented himself with this kinder interpretation and might therefore have left Lessing's oldest and closest friend in peace, had Mendelssohn kept within the limits indicated by this interpretation. For with Jacobi's boundless irritability, it was impossible for Mendelssohn not to say or do some things by which he did not, in Jacobi's opinion, overstep his bounds.

These private causes of the quarrel between Mendelssohn and Jacobi cannot be disregarded. Jacobi was sensitive. As a sensitive-emotional nature, of no common intellectual passion, he was inclined to mistake indifference toward him personally for indifference toward the truth that his

97. Scholz 190–91 [cf. Gio 281]. {LS}
98. Cf. also Scholz 337n. {LS}
99. Lit.: into sap and blood.
100. RK IV.2 211. {LS}

soul sought. His critique of Mendelssohn's cast of mind might be fully warranted: it was bound up in an indefensible way with his critique of Mendelssohn's behavior toward him, one that, taken by itself, might be equally warranted. Dogmatism of every sort, and especially the half dogmatism of the Berlin Academy, so decisive in its assertions, so indecisive in its presuppositions, he had critically reduced to self-centeredness: it was only a short step for him to judge the dogmatist Mendelssohn's behavior toward him as pretentious, once that behavior hurt his self-esteem.[101]

Jacobi felt himself, not entirely without grounds, to be Lessing's legitimate heir, the heir to Lessing's radical, i.e., undogmatic style of thinking. This legacy was already bringing him into an unbridgeable opposition to Lessing's best friend. But this substantive opposition did not need, so it seems offhand, to lead to a personal spat: could not friendship with Mendelssohn be a Lessingian legacy as well? It is not known whether Jacobi did not solicit Mendelssohn's friendship—perhaps in the spirit of Herder's letter to Mendelssohn of February 21, 1781[102]—and whether Mendelssohn did not behave somewhat dismissively toward such a solicitation. The fact is, Jacobi already approached Mendelssohn in {xxviii} the last year of Lessing's life. Besides, in his letter to Mendelssohn of November 4, 1783,[103] he attempted to bring Mendelssohn "into a somewhat closer acquaintance" with him by a two-page self-characterization. And if after Mendelssohn's death he remarked, against "the outcry in all the newspapers about [his]

---

101. Ger.: *Eigenliebe*. This word has both an honorific and a pejorative meaning. Cf. Adelung, s.v.: ". . . love toward oneself; both (1) in the good sense, since *Eigenliebe* consists in being happy in respect of the natural impulse that is the basis of the entirety of physical and moral life. In this sense the word is usual only among a few, whereas others, with more right, call this impulse self-love [*Selbstliebe*]. The word *Eigenliebe* . . . is used . . . most frequently (2) of inordinate self-love, which exceeds the rational goal of one's efforts and considers only oneself as the ultimate goal. In the common and narrower meaning, *Eigenliebe* is the ungovernable enjoyment that is felt in imagined perfections and the impulse to convey these. A man has much *Eigenliebe* if he hardly stops praising himself, preens himself in some vain manner, cares for his comfort in an excessive manner, etc."

LS mentions Mendelssohn's *Eigenliebe* below at IMH LIII, and Jacobi's again at IMH LVII (twice). In the latter context, he identifies it with Rousseau's *amour-propre*; see, e.g., Rousseau, *Discours sur l'origine et les fondements de l'inégalité parmi les hommes*, Remarque XV; cf. *Discourse on the Origin and Foundations of Inequality among Men*, annotation (o)—Mas 221–22, where it is rendered as "vanity"; but consider the translators' subsequent second-thought in Roger D. Masters, *The Political Philosophy of Rousseau* (Princeton: Princeton University Press, 1968), 40n187: "In our translation of the *Discourses* . . . , *amour-propre* was rendered as 'vanity'; this is imprecise since Rousseau speaks of *vanité* and *orgueil* ['vanity' and 'pride'] as two different forms of *amour-propre* (*Émile*, IV . . . [Lau 278; Blm 215])." In *Émile*, Rousseau also pairs *amour-propre* with *estime de soi-même* (Lau 342; "self-esteem," Blm 264—Blm leaves *amour-propre* untranslated) as synonyms or near-synonyms.

102. See JA XIII 7–10.

103. JA XIII 135–36; Scholz 73–74; Gio 183–84; Gio 130–31.

pushiness," that "hardly a man still lives who is less pushy than I have been from childhood on,"[104] this childish protest for the purpose of completely silencing the letter to Mendelssohn just cited already proves by itself that the reproach, dismissed as it was by Jacobi, actually affected him. On the other hand, as far as Mendelssohn's cautious reaction is concerned, perhaps Jacobi himself again supplies a bit of proof concerning it, inasmuch as he remarks in passing against Mendelssohn: "Were I in his [sc., Mendelssohn's] place—yet I am far from putting on such airs. . . ."[105] Yet these suspicions can be properly left aside. One returns to more secure ground by leaving it at the assertion that Mendelssohn and Jacobi each raised a claim that was thoroughly incompatible with the other's claim: the claim to be the legitimate heir, the legitimate interpreter of Lessing. These conflicting claims led initially to a preliminary skirmish in the controversy over *Something that Lessing Said*. The result of this controversy may now be evaluated more adequately. Before it broke out, Jacobi was wavering as it were between two conceptions of Mendelssohn's cast of mind, between a complimentary one that had been suggested to him by Lessing himself, and another one.[106] Which conception he decided on depended on Mendelssohn's behavior toward him. Mendelssohn's critique of *Something that Lessing Said* proved to him fully that Mendelssohn had not comprehended Lessing's thoughts as deeply as he had; his "Objections to 'Thoughts of Various Men'" {xxix} was, on the whole, a superior critique of Mendelssohn's objections. But there was something in Mendelssohn's critique that irritated Jacobi. Jacobi had reported on a statement that Lessing had made to him. Mendelssohn had not heard Lessing's statement but, supported by his intimate acquaintance with Lessing's cast of mind and mode of expression, believed he was able to interpret Lessing's statement and thereby make it innocuous for his own standpoint: wasn't the self-centeredness that "has the audacity to administer truth to suit oneself"[107] showing up here? "How many there are," wrote Jacobi in an essay that appeared two months after the "Objections to 'Thoughts of Various Men,'"

---

104. RK IV.2 184. {LS}
105. RK IV.2 199. {LS}
106. Jacobi expressed himself in a complimentary sense in the aftermath of the quarrel over Lessing's Spinozism; thus in a statement from 1788 the discussion is about an "excellent" remark "of no less than Mendelssohn" (RK II 487); in the essay "Über den transzendentalen Idealismus" [On Transcendental Idealism] from 1787, the beautiful and perspicuous presentation of the Leibnizian doctrine in the *Phädon* is mentioned in passing (RK II 301n). {LS}
107. RK IV.2 410.

to whose soul what mattered was not cognition, insight; not knowing, but only outwitting and being a know-it-all; who did not want to obey the truth but to control it, to have it in their service.[108]

With his "Objections," Jacobi believed he had imparted a stinging[109] reprimand.[110] But Mendelssohn was amazingly thick-skinned: he had "been satisfied" with Jacobi's "Objections."[111] Probably he did not take Jacobi as seriously as Jacobi took himself. When he later said,

> Basically, I had never known Mr. Jacobi. I knew of his merits as an author; but I had never seen anything by him in the metaphysical department[112]

—he thereby also gave expression to his having regarded *Something that Lessing Said* only as "literature," not as a philosophical essay.

Jacobi was therefore irritated over Mendelssohn's reaction to *Something that Lessing Said* and the "Objections" for various reasons. He found himself tactically in a very favorable situation.[113] He was the younger one, {xxx} the more flexible one, who could survey and in fact did survey Mendelssohn's position and its resources: still, he believed that he was not spared the trouble of tracing Mendelssohn's standpoint back to its roots. Mendelssohn, older, by nature more cautious in his thinking, and now further weakened for more than ten years by his illness,[114] was groping completely in the dark at Jacobi's intentions: this attack spewing forth about atheism and Christianity, about Spinoza and Pascal, about Hobbes and Rousseau, against everything that was close to his heart, against everything middle-of-the-road,

---

108. RK II 417. — In the same essay, citing Lessing's "Second Anti-Goeze," he denies "that seeking in some manner to give cold, symbolic ideas something of the warmth and life of natural signs is utterly damaging [to the truth]"; RK II 423 [quoting LM XIII 149]. {LS}
(LS's quotation of RK II 423 omits the words I have interpolated in square brackets; for the fuller quotation, see IMH xxxvn145, below.)

109. Lit.: sensitive. In LS's next sentence, "thick-skinned" is, literally, "unsensitive."

110. When Mendelssohn later wrote in *To the Friends of Lessing*, "Basically, I had never known Mr. Jacobi," Jacobi replied, "Not so! He knew me only too well," namely, from the controversy over *Something that Lessing Said*; see RK IV.2, 199–200. {LS}

111. RK IV.2 201. {LS}

112. See IMH xxIIn62, above

113. The excellent description of this tactical situation in Lucien Lévy-Bruhl, *La philosophie de Jacobi* (Paris: Félix Alcan, 1894), 143–44, should be emphatically pointed out. {LS}

114. Mendelssohn's illness began in February of 1771. {LS's editorial annotation to *Morgenstunden* 3.4ff.}
For fuller details, see Altmann, MMBS 264–71.

this "rash," fanciful movement between opposites was really unintelligible to him, although he was familiar with it firsthand from Lessing. And now the quarrel hit bottom over just what the meaning of Lessing's legacy was and who—Mendelssohn or Jacobi—had the calling to administer it. Lessing had spoken to Jacobi with an openness such as he had never shown toward Mendelssohn. So the quarrel was already decided almost before it began. Jacobi, aroused to the quarrel by Mendelssohn without the latter's knowledge, began it. His cause stood so well that he needed only to come out with half of his arguments, fatal as they were for his opponent: what Lessing had said to him about his practiced reserve toward Mendelssohn, he meanwhile kept secret.

So much has had to be recalled for one to understand Jacobi's insincere first communication to Elise Reimarus concerning Lessing's Spinozism. To make Mendelssohn's answer understandable, four sentences suffice. Mendelssohn did not in fact know Jacobi's qualities. Being the harsh critic that he was of *Nouvelle Héloise*,[115] he would not especially have liked *Allwill* and *Woldemar* at all. He believed he recognized in *Something that Lessing Said* the crypto-papist tendentiousness of an obscurantist. Above all, however, the careless use of Lessing's oral statements may have embarrassed him as being an indiscretion, as "trafficking in anecdotes."[116]

In July of 1783, a few months after the controversy over *Something that Lessing Said*, {xxxi} the "hint" that Lessing had been a decided Spinozist had been tossed off to him by a man so insufficiently known to him as to awaken his distrust. One might guess his reaction: Once again an anecdote! No more

---

115. Mendelssohn's review of Rousseau's novel *Julie, ou la nouvelle Héloise* [Julie, or the New Heloise] (1761) in *Literaturbriefe* ##166–71 (JA V.1 366–89) reads, in part: "To be sure, you find here and there in this *compilation* excellent *letters* that are worthy of a *Rousseau*. But what sort of letters are they? Those in which *Rousseau* treats particular matters as a philosopher. As for the *reading of books*, the *duel*, *suicide*, *music*, *education*, the *satisfactions of a hardworking country life*, you know what one can expect from a *Rousseau* about these matters! When it comes to eloquence and reasons, this philosopher has already shown himself to be a master. But how seldom does a novelist have occasion to bring these talents to bear, and how little is an author who possesses these talents only, albeit in the highest degree, cut out for novel writing! A fruitful and inexhaustible poetic power; knowledge of the human heart that does not so much dwell on universal moral considerations as penetrate into the peculiarities of each character; the great gift of narrating, and the even greater one of making dialogue; the genuine language of the passions, which kindles a sympathetic fire in the reader's heart and, rather than wax enthusiastic, communicates enthusiasm up to the limits of the reader's imagination. These are the attributes that one admires in a [*Samuel*] *Richardson* but will seek in vain in the work of a *Rousseau*." (*Literaturbrief* #166, JA V.1 366–67) In the foregoing, "philosopher" is *Weltweise*; see IPM xviiin23. Also, "making dialogue" is *Dialogiren*; cf. IMH xiin11. Finally, "wax enthusiastic" and "communicates enthusiasm" are *schwärmen* and *mit zu schwärmen*, respectively; see IMH lxivn297.

116. "I considered him"—*sc.*, Jacobi—"a fine mind that also looks around for philosophical news," he wrote on November 18 to the Reimarus siblings [JA XIII 156]. {LS}

did he take the anecdote seriously than he did the anecdote-trafficker. Lessing a decided Spinozist—this claim seemed to him as absurd as the onetime supposition of the Berlin Academy, "Pope a metaphysician!"[117] The justification for this judgment that he gave in that same letter offers testimony to his thorough acquaintance with Lessing:

> If Lessing was in the position of understanding himself so simply, without any closer determination, in terms of the system of any man, then Lessing was no longer himself at the time, or in his peculiar humor for asserting something paradoxical....[118]

In fact, Lessing in his conversation with Jacobi, which Mendelssohn still did not know about at all when he made the judgment cited, had in no way professed himself unreservedly in favor of Spinozism. He had said, to be sure, "There is no philosophy other than the philosophy of Spinoza," but he had previously said, "*If* I am to name myself after anyone, I know of nobody else" but Spinoza;[119] and shortly afterward, when Jacobi had declared "my credo is not in Spinoza," he had replied, "I would hope that it is not in any book."[120] To that extent, Mendelssohn had fended off Jacobi's attack successfully once and for all. But in that it had been made clear that Lessing was unable to swear *in verba ullius magistri*,[121] it was not yet in any way proved that in his speculative endeavors he had not distanced himself from theism in a direction toward Spinozism. That this had been the case, that Lessing had adhered to a "purified" Spinozism, and that this had been familiar to him for a long time, Mendelssohn later asserted in *Morning Hours* and *To the Friends of Lessing*. It is important to keep in mind that not the faintest trace of this assertion is found in his first reaction to Jacobi's communication.[122] It has to be said: Jacobi surprised Mendelssohn. Not reckoning with

---

117. To Elise Reimarus, August 16, 1783 [JA XIII 124]. {LS}
118. *Ibid.* [JA XIII 123].
119. Scholz 77 [cf. Gio 187; cf. Val 85; cf. Nis 243; cf. Got 132]. {LS; the emphasis is LS's}
120. Scholz 80n [cf. Gio 189; cf. Val 88n; cf. Nis 245; cf. Got 133]. — Cf. also Mendelssohn's playful remark about Lessing and the Kabbalah in the same letter, with Jacobi's report that in his dialogue with Lessing he "could, when pressed, raise the suspicion of Kabbalistic opinions" against him. Scholz 92 [cf. Gio 195; cf. Val 97; cf. Nis 252]. {LS}
The German *Cabbalisterey*, rendered as "Kabbalistic opinions," resembles both *Schwärmerey* (IMH LXIV) and *Spinozisterey* (IMH LXXXIII, LXXXIX), as well as "*Anekdotenkrämerey*" ("trafficking in anecdotes"; IMH XXX).
121. Lat.: to the words of any master. Cf. Horace, *Epistles* I.1.14 (Fai 252), with Lessing, "Rettungen des Horaz" [Vindications of Horace], LM V 299. LS quotes the Lessing passage in his editorial annotation to *Pope!* 51.27–36; see appendix 2, supplement to IPM XVIIIn24.
122. In the letter of August 16, 1783, to E. Reimarus [JA XIII 123–25]. {LS}

the possibility that Jacobi could have had a more exact notion of {XXXII} Spinozism—and he would have reckoned with this possibility if Jacobi had laid out for him the report about his conversation with Lessing right away—Mendelssohn clung to what all the world understood by Spinozism: to the "atheistic system of Spinoza's, notorious as it is for being so."[123] He did not once take the trouble merely to recall also what he himself had written about Spinozism in his *Philosophical Dialogues*.[124] He therefore denied not merely Lessing's decided Spinozism *explicite*, but also his "purified" Spinozism *implicite*.[125] If he was showing that he was ready to grant that Lessing could have professed himself in favor of Spinozism, then it was only because for Lessing, "in his peculiar humor for asserting something paradoxical," "no opinion [was] so absurd that he was not capable of assuming it out of a love for acumen."[126] Furthermore, Mendelssohn in the same letter disclosed a sensitive weakness with his question about which system of Spinoza's had supposedly been adopted by Lessing: "the one expounded in his *Tractatus theologico-politicus* or in his *Principia philosophiae cartesianae*, or the one that Ludovicus Meyer published in his name after his death?"[127] About these questions, Jacobi later was to judge: "they are uniquely and solely apposite to my opponent's unfamiliarity with Spinoza's writings."[128] Above all, however, the tone of Mendelssohn's letter suggested distinctly what he later granted explicitly, that Jacobi's report was "highly disagreeable" to him.[129] And to be sure, it was also disagreeable to him initially with respect to Lessing's reputation: Lessing's orthodox enemies would triumph over this proof of Lessing's unbelief, exceeding as it did all their expectations. Despite this apprehension, he was ready for the public announcement of the facts in the framework of his planned writing about Lessing's character. The one condition whose prior fulfillment he insisted on was that Jacobi give more exact information about the specifics of Lessing's profession of Spinozism.

The content of Mendelssohn's letter was forwarded to Jacobi by Elise Reimarus on September 1, 1783, in an excerpt that was not quite complete.[130]

123. *Ibid*. [JA XIII 123].
124. See IMH xxiiin71, above.
125. Lat.: explicitly . . . implicitly.
126. JA XIII 123, 125.
127. JA XIII 123. Mendelssohn is referring to Spinoza's *Theologico-Political Treatise* (1670), his *Principles of Cartesian Philosophy* (1663), and his posthumously published *Ethics Demonstrated in a Geometrical Order* (1677), respectively.
128. RK IV.2 202 [cf. Gio 200; cf. Val 103]. {LS}
129. *Freunde* 189.7 [Scholz 296; cf. Val 130; cf. Got 155]. {LS}
130. Scholz 69–71 [Gio 182–83; Val 81–82]. {LS}

Elise Reimarus also felt a certain uneasiness with respect to Jacobi's communication. Jacobi, on the other hand, had

> not the least hesitation about meeting {xxxiii} this challenge [*sc.*, of Mendelssohn's, to give more exact information about Lessing's remark] and on the fourth of November sent off a follow-up letter to Mendelssohn, unsealed, in an envelope to my friend [*sc.*, E. Reimarus].[131]

In the accompanying letter to Elise Reimarus, likewise dated November 4, 1783, Jacobi identifies himself, in advance no less, as a martyr not so much for the truth as for the "appearance of [his] being":

> I hardly expect the best thanks from [Mendelssohn] for my trouble, since my perspective[132] is somewhat different from his. . . . But I am prepared once and for all to put up with come-what-may from the appearance of my being and just to keep showing this as it is. Some courage and renunciation will be required for this, but that is why one also has the inner repose that at other times can never be preserved.[133]

Jacobi's hefty letter to Mendelssohn—thirty-three pages long in Scholz's edition[134]—which was also available to Elise Reimarus as well as to her brother J. A. H. Reimarus, begins with a self-characterization of Jacobi, then lets follow with the report about the conversations with Lessing and ends with the mention "of a few specific questions" of Mendelssohn's. About his answers to these questions—he calls these answers "difficulties"—he himself says that he may "well" have "presented" them "somewhat harshly."[135] The rather irritated tone, in fact, of his answers would have to be explained in that, to him, Mendelssohn's questions seemed to presuppose an ignorance in Jacobi, an ignorance "in which perhaps I *could have* found myself— but nothing overt called for you to entertain the suspicion of that and to reveal it so blithely."[136] Mendelssohn was in essence satisfied with Jacobi's

---

131. Scholz 71 [cf. Val 82].
132. Lit.: mode of seeing. Cf. IMH xli–xlii and lvi–lvii, below.
133. Scholz 71n [cf. Val 82n]. {LS}
134. Scholz 72–105 [Gio 183–201; Val 83–104]. {LS}
135. Scholz 105 [cf. Gio 201; cf. Val 104]. {LS}
136. Scholz 103 [cf. Gio 200; cf. Val 103]. — Jacobi later (RK IV.2 203) gave another explanation: he would have seen himself as the one insulted and reproached, so as not to have to reproach Mendelssohn, "the deserving and in so many respects venerable man," with "ignorance, and, to be sure, of the severest kind, in a matter about which he was raising questions with so much complacency." {LS}

answer. He frankly confessed that Jacobi was entitled to be indignant toward him:

> and if the tone in which he let me feel my wrong is no compensation, then I am prepared to beg forgiveness formally. I had misjudged the knight whom I so {xxxiv} insolently challenged to a duel.[137]

Jacobi had therefore succeeded in luring Mendelssohn into a challenge.

Mendelssohn's letter to the Reimarus siblings of November 18, 1783, in which the aforecited confession is found, has a claim to special attention for the reason that it contains Mendelssohn's first statement concerning Jacobi's conversations with Lessing now that they were available to him. He received his incredulous proclamation, "Lessing a decided Spinozist!" in silence. Not the slightest doubt was voiced about the reliability of Jacobi's report. Nor is there found even the trace of an indication of Lessing's "purified" Spinozism and of Mendelssohn's familiarity with his late friend's efforts in that direction; and, moreover, not for the same reasons as before: "the so-called Spinozist system . . . always remains a skeleton."[138] Striking, then, is the judgment, favorable on the whole, about Goethe's poem "Prometheus,"[139] which Jacobi had given Lessing to read at the beginning of the decisive conversation—it is strikingly favorable in comparison with the judgment in *To the Friends of Lessing*: whereas in the latter publication[140] the Goethean poem is dismissed as a "wretchedness," the private letter of November 18, 1783, reads:

> The poem ["Prometheus"] pleased me. A good persiflage. The so-called Spinozist system cannot be shown more happily in its complete nakedness.[141]

Mendelssohn therefore did not feel as such the difficulty that has caused many interpreters of the Lessing-Jacobi conversations so much racking of brains—the unmediated transition from "Prometheus" to Spinoza—and, moreover, evidently for the same reasons for which Jacobi himself saw this

---

137. To Elise and J. A. H. Reimarus, November 18, 1783, JA XIII 157.
138. *Ibid.*, 158.
139. The poem (Goe I 261–62) is quoted in full in Scholz CI–CIII or 75–76 (trans. Val 7–9; Nis 242–43; Gio 185–86).
140. *Freunde* 192.1 [Scholz 299; cf. Val 133; cf. Got 158]. {LS}
141. JA XIII 158.

transition as quite natural: they both were still too closely bound to the theistic tradition for them not to have been forced to see in the atheism (and "Spinozism is atheism")[142] a result of anti-theism, of rebellion against God. Since Mendelssohn therefore knew nothing to oppose to Jacobi's report about Lessing's Spinozism, i.e., atheism, nothing else remained for him but to distance himself from Lessing: if even now in his writing about Lessing's character he still wants to speak of Lessing's final sentiments, he does so with the aim "of faithfully warning lovers of speculation and {xxxv} showing them through glaring examples what danger they expose themselves to if they give themselves over to it without any guide." Lessing's Spinozist aberration is therefore to be offered as an admonitory example. Under the first impression of Jacobi's conversations with Lessing, Mendelssohn sensed very vividly the kinship of Jacobi's style of thinking with Lessing's; in a letter to Elise Reimarus a few weeks later,[143] he says of "Lessing *or* Jacobi": "The confusion and jumbling of concepts are due to mere acumen; and such quick minds have this in overabundance." Mendelssohn had meanwhile noticed, therefore, that Jacobi's failing did not consist in his ineptness in the "metaphysical department." As has already been indicated, this conspicuous change of judgment about Jacobi shows up earlier in the letter to the Reimarus siblings of November 18, 1783; there one reads:

> ... Nevertheless so much philosophical acumen shines from the building Mr. Jacobi has erected for himself, all at his own expense, that I might very well grasp how a Lessing has been taken in by it and been able to bring an unlimited confidence to the builder himself.[144]

Indeed Mendelssohn even now complains—and these complaints are repeated—about the "wealth of images in [Jacobi's] notions."[145] The difficulty of Jacobi's presentation of the Spinozist axiom and, even before that, the unexpected broadening of the subject—now "Lessing and Spinoza" instead of "Lessing"—prompted Mendelssohn then and there to postpone further the working out of *Lessing's Character*:

---

142. Scholz 173; Gio 233; Val 123; Got 137.
143. On January 5, 1784 [JA XIII 168]. {LS; the emphasis that follows is LS's}
144. JA XIII 157, with IMH xxin62 and xixn112, above.
145. Here the Lessing citation that is found in an essay of Jacobi's published in April of 1783 has to be recalled once more [cf. IMH xxixn108, above]: it would not be true "that seeking in some manner to give cold, symbolic ideas something of the warmth and life of natural signs, is utterly damaging to the truth." {LS}

Before I write about Lessing's character, however, I will request Mr. Jacobi's clarification about one thing or another that is contained in his essay. For now, it is still quite impossible for me to think straight either about Lessing or about Spinoza. Better late than badly. It will depend, then, primarily on friendly advice from both sides by Mr. Jacobi and by you about what use is to be made of this discussion [*sc.*, Lessing's] with Jacobi.[146] {XXXVI}

Mendelssohn's stance toward Jacobi's detailed report, indeed his whole further behavior in the quarrel with Jacobi as well, is influenced by the opinions of the Reimarus siblings. The children of the "Fragmentist," who had concealed his unbelief even from her who "slept at his bosom,"[147] had inherited their father's circumspection. In the letter in which she acquainted Mendelssohn with Jacobi's first communication, Elise Reimarus already seemed to have given expression to her fear in the face of a public announcement of Lessing's final sentiments. Her brother, in his letter of November 11, 1783, which accompanied the transmission of Jacobi's detailed report to Mendelssohn, shared with him the advice "not to [set forth] the matter in too much detail, lest outsiders rejoice over it."[148] His judgment about Lessing's Spinozism agrees with Mendelssohn's. He too had been inclined initially to assume "that defending Spinozism could have been a whimsy or a paradox that Lessing posed." But now, after having read Jacobi's detailed report, he must confess: "Jacobi's account puts the matter [*sc.*, Lessing's Spinozism] almost beyond doubt."[149] Furthermore, Reimarus expresses the wish that Mendelssohn nevertheless might "still put those delusions that confused the great Spinoza and others after him into a brighter light some day." The first suggestion for Mendelssohn's Spinoza critique therefore goes back to J. A. H. Reimarus; and as *Morning Hours* was originally conceived as a refutation of Spinozism, so one has to glimpse (with Bruno Strauss)[150] in

---

146. JA XIII 157.
147. Ger.: "*so in seinen Armen schläft.*" The expression is Lessing's, "Von Duldung der Deisten," LM XII 258. The translation is LS's, WPP 189.
148. JA XIII 155.
149. Cf. also the statement of E. Reimarus in her letters to Jacobi of November 14, 1783, and April 2, 1784—RK IV.2 188–89 and 194–95. {LS}
150. LS does not cite a published souce for the words in quotation marks that follow. During the 1930s, Bruno Strauss was engaged in editing and annotating Mendelssohn's correspondence for JA XI-XIII. JA XI, containing Mendelssohn's correspondence of 1754–62, appeared in 1932. Despite delays and uncertainties about the future of JA following the collapse of the Weimar Republic and its replacement by the Nazi regime in 1933, JA XII was complete in manuscript in 1936 and awaiting publication in 1938, along with JA III.2 (containing Mendelssohn's *Morning Hours* and *To the Friends of Lessing*, edited by LS), JA VIII (originally containing Mendelssohn's

the aforecited statement of Reimarus's "a first encouragement for *Morning Hours*."

As a consequence of Jacobi's communication and Reimarus's wishes, the plan for *Lessing's Character* was therefore immediately pushed back considerably. To be sure, initially it still remained undecided "what use" was to be made of Jacobi's conversations with Lessing; but Mendelssohn saw immediately that he would not be able in his planned writing to take a critical view of Lessing's Spinozism.[151] {xxxvii} And he saw at once what the indispensable guide is for all speculation, by the spurning of which Lessing had been driven into the arms of Spinozism; this guide is—the details in *Morning Hours* and *To the Friends of Lessing* leave no doubt about it—sound commonsense. Having now become evident, Lessing's defection from the natural theology of the Leibniz-Wolffian Enlightenment must have further corroborated Mendelssohn in the thought whose growth might well have also been encouraged beforehand by Kant's defection,[152] already well-known to him for a long time: that the retreat from the science of natural theology to the natural religion of sound commonsense had become virtually inevitable. Mendelssohn did indeed keep himself from giving in to that

---

Psalms translation, *Jerusalem*, etc., edited by Simon Rawidowicz), and JA XIV (the first of six volumes of Mendelssohn's Hebrew writings, edited by Haim Borodianski/Bar-Dayan). Of these, JA XIV alone came into print that year. Here is the rest of the story as told by Alexander Altmann in 1971, in his foreword to the facsimile reprint of JA I, as editor-in-chief of the entire reprinted and resumed JA:

> Volume 14 ... was seized by the Gestapo and evidently destroyed. Only a few copies of it were preserved. Volumes 3.2, 8, and 12 never appeared. Fortunately, the completed parts of volumes 3.2 and 8 are still extant.... A deep tragedy shrouds volume 12 of the letters, which was seen to by Bruno Strauss and was completely ready to go. When he emigrated to Holland, he took the manuscript with him. It was lost, however, during his escape from Holland. Professor Bruno Strauss, who reached the United States of America and died of old age in 1969, never got over the loss of his manuscript. Regrettably, the commendable searches undertaken by Friedrich Frommann Verlag in 1965 with a view to finding the manuscript in Holland or Germany brought no results. As Professor [Bruno] Strauss wrote to me on October 16, 1965, the volume lost in manuscript went up to about the middle of the 1770s. A third volume of letters, to be worked on by him, had been planned. (JA I vii; cf. JA XI 520ff., JA XII.1 vii)

Had circumstances permitted, the words of Bruno Strauss that LS is quoting might have shown up in the then-anticipated third volume of Mendelssohn's letters—though as things turned out, Altmann himself ended up editing JA XII-XIII from scratch. Meanwhile the words in question found their way, unannotated, into IMH here as LS's (and Altmann's) understated homage to an esteemed colleague.

151. Indeed, in view of his bad health, he postpones for the time being Reimarus's challenge that he write a critique of Spinozism: in turn, he demands of Reimarus that he expand this critique, in which he will, within his powers, by all means "stand alongside" him "as a faithful henchman or shieldbearer." {LS}

152. Cf. IMH LXIX, below.

thought entirely, from letting the retreat turn into a flight. "Sound commonsense," he wrote to Elise Reimarus on April 19, 1784,[153] and certainly he thought so at the beginning of the quarrel with Jacobi,

> can be of little service here; for the Spinozist must protest against this right at the start. Therefore pure reason, exclusively and by itself, should and must have the say.

For when it comes to "conquering hair-splitting doubts," one must, as had already been set forth in the *Treatise on Evidence*, "take . . . one's refuge in the strictest proofs."[154]

It has been emphasized that in his first answers to Jacobi's communications, Mendelssohn, being thrown off guard by him, had made use not of the latter's more exact, if for that very reason not necessarily correct, concept of Spinozism, but of the vulgar one. In the next months, he found the occasion to remember his forgotten Spinoza studies. In his letter to Elise Reimarus of January 5, 1784, he says with respect to "the essay of Mr. Jacobi's":

> the refuter has a Sisyphean labor. Now he is going back to the first concepts and ruminating on them without nausea: on what substance, truth, cause and, primarily, on what objective existence is, which it appears to come down to mostly. . . .[155]

This statement is remarkable for several reasons. To begin {xxxviii} with, it shows that Mendelssohn, having now given in to the Reimarus siblings' pressure, has decided on the working out of a Spinoza critique. In it, then, is announced for the first time the thematic scope of the "Prior Cognition" of *Morning Hours* (First through Seventh Lectures). Above all, however, in it is betrayed, for the first time since the beginning of the controversy with Jacobi, Mendelssohn's peculiar concept of Spinozism. If the concept of "objective existence" is the decisive concept for the refutation of Spino-

---

153. Mendelssohn's letter is listed but not reproduced at JA XIII 192. As Alexander Altmann points out in his editorial annotation (JA XIII 398, on #642), the letter is now missing, though parts of it are quoted by Elise Reimarus in her letter to Jacobi of July 4, 1784. See RK IV.1 99–100; cf. Scholz 108n, which does not quote the passage in question, however. Cf. also IMH xxxixn162, xln167, and lxxiin339, below.

154. *Evidenz* 313 and 328–29 [Dah 293 only]. {LS}
Dah omits the latter passage to which LS refers. For an explanation, see ITE xlvi–xlvii and lii–liii, with liiin62.

155. JA XIII 168.

zism, then Spinozism is no longer to be understood as atheism, but as subjectivism, more exactly as a doctrine of divine solipsism ("Egoism"). Mendelssohn had presented it as such in the *Philosophical Dialogues*, in order to show "under which [configuration] Spinoza's system could be consistent with reason and religion":[156]

> Spinoza ... believed that there had never actually come to be a world outside God and that all visible things down to this hour were to be found merely in the divine understanding.[157]

And he will again present it as such in his *Morning Hours*, in the discussion of Lessing's "purified" Spinozism: the decisive question, which is directed to the opponents of the representative of "purified" Spinozism, reads,

> how do you convince him of this objective existence outside the divine understanding?[158]

and the same is said of just this "purified" Spinozism, that it would make God "tantamount to an infinite Egoist."[159] Admittedly, at the moment in question (the beginning of 1784) Mendelssohn is still far removed from the subsequently clear distinction between authentic Spinozism, to be understood as the atheistic God as the sum of all finite things, and Lessing's "purified" Spinozism, which would be not atheism but acosmism. All the same, the conception of Spinozism as the doctrine of divine solipsism had again entered into his purview even then.

By recalling this conception, Mendelssohn had arrived at an essential clarifying of his task. But with respect to carrying it out, he felt himself even now still quite incapable. That is why on January 5, 1784, he sent the Jacobi manuscript to J. A. H. Reimarus {xxxix} with the request for feedback: "There is still time for it, a few more months at least."[160] During the next months, it became clear to him that the refutation of Spinozism would probably fall outside the framework of *Lessing's Character* and would require the working out of a separate writing. He writes on April 19, 1784—immediately

---

156. *Gespräche* 17.8–10 [also *Schriften* 352.9–11; Dah 108]. {LS}
157. *Gespräche* 17.15–18 [also *Schriften* 352.16–20; cf. Dah 108]. {LS}
158. *Morgenstunden* 116.6–7 [Scholz 18; cf. DaDy 84; cf. Got 147]. {LS}
159. *Morgenstunden* 116.14–15 [Scholz 18; cf. DaDy 84]. — Cf. also the juxtaposition of Idealism, Egoism, and Spinozism in *Morgenstunden* 79.24–27 [DaDy 57]. {LS}
160. JA XIII 169.

after the Jacobi manuscript had been sent back to him again[161]—to Elise Reimarus: "If I have enough health and leisure this summer, then perhaps I will put *Lessing's Character* to one side and first venture a round with the Spinozists."[162] About three months later, one finds the suspicion hardened into a certainty; in his letter to Jacobi of August 1, 1784, Mendelssohn writes that he is "at the point of giving up the intent to write about Lessing's character, and of a mind . . . to draft something about Spinozism first."[163] The plan to abandon for now the working out of *Lessing's Character* and at once work out a refutation of Spinozism is identical with the conceiving of *Morning Hours*: *Morning Hours* was conceived in the spring, if not the summer, of 1784 as a refutation of Spinozism.[164] "Already a year and a half ago," reports Nicolai in his obituary for Mendelssohn dated January 7, 1786,[165]

> [Mendelssohn] disclosed to me . . . specifically his idea of the style in which he wanted to publish a detailed work about it [*sc.*, about the concept of God and His attributes]. The first part has meanwhile appeared under the title *Morning Hours*.

For, that the planned refutation of Spinozism had previously been intended to treat the principles of natural theology in general is almost self-evident: "Spinozism is atheism." That Mendelssohn's temporary abandonment of the working out of *Lessing's Character* also signifies that in his refutation he was initially planning to recall in so many words Lessing's Spinozism, or at least his putative profession of Spinozism, may not be asserted definitively, but may nevertheless be assumed with a certain probability. {XL}

When Mendelssohn in April of 1784 came for the first time to the thought of devoting a separate[166] book to the refutation of Spinozism, he did not quite know initially in what manner he should conduct the quarrel. He would have preferred, as he says in his letter to Elise Reimarus of April 19, 1784, to have taken on "a definite opponent, with whom we start

---

161. See Scholz 107n [Val 106n] and 108n. {LS}

162. Scholz 108n. See IMH XXXVIIn153, above.

163. Scholz 110 (cf. Val 107); JA XIII 217. I have corrected LS's quotation: where Scholz and JA XIII have *entwerfen* ("to draft"), LS repeats *schreiben* ("to write") from earlier in Mendelssohn's sentence.

164. That the essential purpose of *Morning Hours* is the refutation of Spinozism is further divulged in Mendelssohn's letter to E. Reimarus of April 29, 1785 [JA XIII 281], and *Freunde* 213.30–33 [Scholz 317–18; Val 145]. {LS}

165. See IMH XIIn14, above.

166. Lit.: self-standing. Likewise at IMH XXXIX, above. Cf. IMH LXXIVn361, below, with IPM XVn5.

out from a certain point, presuppose certain principles as given, and then investigate something further."[167] He may have had his eye on Jacobi as the "definite opponent" even then, as he wrote another nine months later.[168] For just that reason, it was indispensable for him to confront more closely at last Jacobi's report about his conversations with Lessing, and especially the Spinoza interpretation contained in that report. He did so in the "Objections of Mr. Jacobi," which he sent to Jacobi on August 1, 1784,[169] and which may have been written in July of the same year.

Even in these "Objections," not the slightest doubt is found about the reliability of Jacobi's report; even in them, no indication of Lessing's "purified" Spinozism is met up with at all. To be sure, Mendelssohn discounted—entirely in the sense of his earlier remarks about Lessing's paradoxes—as "peculiar whimsies" a number of statements that Lessing had made in Jacobi's presence;[170] but in no way did he characterize in this manner the statements of Lessing immediately relevant to Spinozism.[171] The critique of Spinoza or of Jacobi's conception of Spinoza—for the two can scarcely be separated—which is found in the "Objections" is characterized by a complete misapprehending of the questions raised by Jacobi—a misapprehending that is admittedly due to a certain extent to the all too summary and not always pellucid presentation that Jacobi had given in his dialogues with Lessing. Mendelssohn cannot for a moment disregard his own° presupposition that the ultimate cause of the world is an infinite understanding.[172] Just this presupposition had been denied by Spinoza in that, to be sure, he granted "thinking" (*cogitatio*) to the infinite substance, but denied understanding (*intellectio*).[173] And recognition of the necessity {XLI} by virtue of which Spinoza had been led to this dark thesis was nothing less than the center of Jacobi's Spinoza interpretation: he took the trouble to "retrace" this thesis back to its source—according to his assertion, the basic principle "*a nihilo nihil fit*"[174]—and, going forward from there, to grasp how Spinoza, though granting to the infinite substance the two attributes of thought

---

167. Scholz 108n. See IMH xxxviin153, above.
168. See the letter to E. Reimarus of January 28, 1785 [JA XIII 263–64]. {LS}
169. Scholz 109ff. (Val 107ff.); JA XIII 216–17, with *Freunde* 200–207.
170. *Freunde* 205.5–19 [found in Scholz 117–18; cf. Val 113]; cf. also 203 [found in Scholz 115; cf. Val 111]. {LS}
171. Cf. also the identification of Jacobi's view with that of Lessing at *Freunde* 204.14–15 [found in Scholz 116–17; Val 112]. {LS}
172. Cf. esp. *Freunde* 210.18–21 [Scholz 313; Val 142]. {LS}
173. See *Ethica*, pt. II, props. 1, 5, and 7 corr., with pt. I, prop. 31 schol. (Geb II 86, 88, 98. with 72; WhSt 46–47, 49, 50, with 29). Cf. Scholz 79 (Gio 188).
174. Lat.: "nothing comes to be from nothing."

and extension in an equal manner, nevertheless in fact claimed priority for extension over thought and so arrived at materialistic consequences. Mendelssohn, far from perceiving the connection among these reflections, enters into them with a concept of Spinozism that makes an understanding of them completely impossible for him: he has distanced himself from the vulgar conception of Spinoza in the direction exactly opposite to Jacobi's. According to what is now for him the authoritative conception, Spinozism's doctrine is that finite things do not exist outside the divine understanding. This conception, developed in the *Philosophical Dialogues*, has therefore now brought the vulgar conception, according to which Spinoza understands by God the sum of all finite things, almost to the vanishing point: precisely those statements of Jacobi's that seemed to be meant in the sense of the vulgar view, and that Jacobi for just that reason later rejected as inadequate, are now regarded by Mendelssohn as at best confusing,[175] and since he found in Jacobi's presentation enough statements that contradicted the vulgar conception, without further ado he then interpreted these statements erroneously in the sense of the conception developed in the *Philosophical Dialogues*.[176] The result is that he sees himself driven around by Jacobi in a circle that he cannot find his way out of.[177] In spite or because of this, even now he does not yet come to his later, clear distinction between two concepts of Spinozism—between authentic, atheistic Spinozism, and "purified," acosmic Spinozism: he applies to the critique of Spinoza an argument of Wolff's that is in keeping only with the vulgar conception[178] and that in *Morning Hours*[179] is used for the critique of authentic Spinozism, and on the other hand {XLII} he sketches an argument by which in *Morning Hours* he attempts to refute "purified" Spinozism in particular[180] yet that is entirely otiose in connection with the critique of Spinoza himself. He understands Jacobi's own position rather than Jacobi's conception of Spinoza. Needless to say, Jacobi's characterizing as "believing" the mode of knowledge that is distinguished from knowing qua speculation provokes his protest. Just as he had accused Jacobi's liberal critique of (enlightened) despotism of a

175. Cf. *Freunde* 203 §4, 205 §3 to 206.5, 206 §2 [found in Scholz 115–20; cf. Val 111–14]. {LS}
176. Cf. *Freunde* 200.14–19 [found in Scholz 111; Val 108] with *Morgenstunden* 121.16–122.2 [Scholz 25; DaDy 88]. {LS}
177. *Freunde* 206 §2 [found in Scholz 120; Val 114]. {LS}
178. *Freunde* 206.35–207.13 [found in Scholz 120; Val 114–15]. {LS}
179. See *Morgenstunden* 110.7ff. [Scholz 11; DaDy 79], which refers to the pertinent passage in Wolff's *Theologia naturalis*. LS quotes the passage, TN II §706, in his editorial annotation to *Morgenstunden* 110.9–111.3; see appendix 2, supplement to IMH XLIIn179.
180. Cf. *Freunde* 200.24–28 [found in Scholz 111; Val 108–9] with *Morgenstunden* 120.21ff. [Scholz 23ff.; DaDy 87ff.]. {LS}

crypto-papist tendentiousness, so he misinterprets Jacobi's liberal concept of belief (derived from Hume)[181] as the attempt at a restoration of the Christian belief in revelation, which he would have had to reject in deference to his rational Judaism:[182] his suspicion that in Jacobi he had before him an obscurantist had been considerably reinforced since the reading of Jacobi's conversations with Lessing.[183]

Jacobi had been informed about Mendelssohn's reaction to his communications, as well as about the changes resulting from them in Mendelssohn's literary plans, partly by Elise Reimarus,[184] partly by Mendelssohn himself.[185] In June and July of 1784, he had composed his "Letter to Hemsterhuis"[186] about Spinozism, which he sent off to Mendelssohn on September 5, 1784. The "Letter to Hemsterhuis," which therefore had been written before Jacobi knew of Mendelssohn's "Objections," should have served as a precursory answer "to the most important thing" in the "Objections," as Jacobi says in the writing accompanying the mailing of the "Letter." The tone of this accompanying writing is of an almost insulting severity, for which the tone of neither the "Objections" nor Mendelssohn's letter to Jacobi of August 1, 1784, gave the least right. Jacobi was no doubt miffed about Mendelssohn's actual lack of understanding of his Spinoza interpretation, but even more about the latter's putative misinterpretation of his real intention: he believed Mendelssohn regarded him as a Spinozist, whereas in actuality he had described him as a "Christian philosopher." Mendelssohn did not feel Jacobi's letter of September 5, 1784, to be hurtful, or at least he cleverly hid his feeling.[187] {XLIII}

The "Letter to Hemsterhuis" is of significance for the emergence of *Morning Hours* for various reasons. To begin with, on account of its form: it is penned in the form of a dialogue between Jacobi as an opponent of Spinoza and Spinoza himself. The liveliness of the discussion that is brought about by this form appealed to Mendelssohn so much that he meanwhile thought "of using Mr. Jacobi's lively lecture [in the presentation of Spinozism] and letting him [sc., Jacobi] speak in Spinoza's place."[188] He abandoned this aim

---

181. LS quotes the pertinent passage from Jacobi's *David Hume on Belief* in his editorial annotation to *Freunde* 205.23–30; see appendix 2, supplement to IMH XLIIIn181.
182. *Freunde* 205.19ff. [found in Scholz 118; Val 113]. {LS}
183. Cf. also in this context the letter to Zimmermann of September 1, 1784 [JA XIII 221–23]. {LS}
184. Cf. Scholz 105–6 [Gio 201–2; Val 105]. {LS}
185. Letter of August 1, 1784 [JA XIII 216–17]. {LS}
186. Scholz 123–36; Gio 202–15.
187. Cf. his letter to E. Reimarus of November 15, 1784 [JA XIII 232]. {LS}
188. To E. Reimarus, January 28, 1785 [JA XIII 263–64]. {LS}

a short time afterward. But—besides the conversations between Jacobi and Lessing—the model of the "Letter to Hemsterhuis" may have been determinative for Mendelssohn's having put forward his presentation and critique of "purified" Spinozism in the Fourteenth Lecture of *Morning Hours* in the form of a dialogue between himself as the opponent of this Spinozism and Lessing as its adherent. Presumably, then, by the full-blown distinction right at the beginning of it between Spinoza's "system" and his "geometric method," the "Letter to Hemsterhuis" again brought Mendelssohn close to the thought of distinguishing explicitly between authentic Spinozism and a more complete form of Spinozism freed from the fetters of the geometrical method (a "purified" Spinozism).[189] Finally, it must be mentioned that, in this second presentation of Spinozism, Jacobi emphasizes Spinoza's denial of divine intelligence no less emphatically than in the first.[190]

Mendelssohn would begin the working out of *Morning Hours* in the last third of 1784 at the earliest.[191] In his letter to Elise Reimarus of January 28, 1785,[192] he can already give a rough estimate of the number of pages in the manuscript. As it turns out from the same letter, at this point in time he is not yet occupied with Spinozism itself, but with "a sort of revision of the proofs of the existence of God in general." Even now, he can still {XLIV} "not say how soon his manuscript will be in shape to be submitted to Mr. Jacobi." He is already inquiring, however, whether Jacobi will perhaps give permission "to make public use of his philosophical letters some day." This use would not have to consist in the publication of Jacobi's letters as such, but in the utilizing of these for Mendelssohn's presentation of Spinozism: Mendelssohn evidently thought to draw Jacobi, as he had in a similar way drawn J. A. H. Reimarus,[193] into collaborating in *Morning Hours*, for whose fully independent working out he felt himself too weak. Since Mendelssohn, in an evident protest to the distribution of roles in Jacobi's conversations with Lessing, wanted to have not Lessing but Jacobi

---

189. Cf. *Morgenstunden* 114 ¶1 [Scholz 15–16; DaDy 83; Got 146–47] with Jacobi, RK IV.1 124–25 [Scholz 123–24; Gio 204–5] {LS}

190. Cf. IMH XXI-XXII, above.

191. From his letter to Zimmerman of September 1, 1784 [JA XIII 222–23], it would have to have turned out that at the very least he had begun the gathering of material at this point in time. {LS}

192. JA XIII 263–64.

193. See [Mendelssohn's introductory] annotation to [his] "Annotations and Additions" to *Morgenstunden* (JA III.2 159.2–5 [DaDy 117]). {LS; in the German text of JA III.2 XLIV, LS's parenthetical citation lacks the page and IMP numbers}

For Mendelssohn's annotation and LS's editorial annotation to it, see appendix 2, supplement to IMH XLIVn193.

enter as the champion of Spinozism, this aim implies that Mendelssohn in no way anticipated talking about Lessing's Spinozism in the work being planned. In his letter to Elise Reimarus of January 28, 1785, he goes on as follows: "I would like this"—that is to say, for Jacobi to let him make use of his philosophical letters in such a way that he might avail himself of Jacobi's "lively lecture" in his presentation of Spinozism—"but to hear soon if possible, since I must arrange my presentation accordingly."[194] In the same letter, Mendelssohn inquired after the whereabouts of Jacobi's answer to the "Objections." Jacobi was made acquainted with the content of this letter in February of 1785 by Elise Reimarus. The rest is best heard from Jacobi himself:

> I wrote Mendelssohn immediately at° that moment to permit him the free use of my letters and promised him the specific answer he was still waiting for [*sc.*, to the "Objections"] in the coming month without fail. Just then I succumbed to an illness, from which I began to recover at the end of March. I reported this delay to my friend [*sc.*, E. Reimarus], so that she might inform Mendelssohn about it and assure him at once that I am now actually on the job.[195]

Mendelssohn's answer to this communication is surprising in the greatest degree: on April 29, 1785, he has to ask Jacobi, through Elise Reimarus, "not to rush with the response to my 'Objections.'" "I have decided," he goes on to say, {XLV}

> to have the first part of my brochure printed after the Leipzig Fair.[196] In it I am concerned mainly, to be sure, with Pantheism, but there is still no mention of our correspondence. I am saving this for the second part, for which however there is still a lot of time. Mr. Jacobi must read this first part of my writing before he responds to my "Objections"; at least he will be able to respond to both at once and through my writing perhaps get an occasion to explain himself more distinctly. Anyway, my "Objections" contain mere precursory remarks, which do not go far enough. I

---

194. JA XIII 264.
195. Scholz 139 [cf. Gio 216; cf. Val 117]. {LS}
196. I.e., the Leipzig Bookfair. Likewise at IMH XLVI and L–LI, below. See Lucien Febvre, *The Coming of the Book: The Impact of Printing 1450–1800*, trans. David Gerard (London: NLB, 1976), 233; Henri-Jean Martin, *The History and Power of Writing*, trans. Lydia G. Cochrane (Chicago: University of Chicago Press, 1994), 247–48, 250, 386.

am now having the manuscript copied in order to send it to you; not for Mr. Jacobi, however, whom I am sparing from it until it is published, but your brother [*sc.*, J. A. H. Reimarus] must read everything in the manuscript beforehand; for without his assessment nothing can appear publicly in the matter.[197]

What had happened in the meantime? Why did Mendelssohn now no longer need Jacobi's answer to the "Objections" and also his earlier "philosophical letters" for his presentation of Spinozism? Why should Jacobi now learn of the book-in-progress only in published form, whereas it was still self-evident three months earlier that the manuscript was to be submitted to him? And why is the discussion about a later public mention of the Jacobi-Mendelssohn correspondence concerning Lessing's Spinozism now of such definiteness, whereas earlier a yet-to-be-determined use of Lessing's exchange with Jacobi, or rather of Jacobi's philosophical letters in general, had at most been contemplated?[198]

Considered in the light of the history of its emergence,[199] the expositions of Lessing's "purified" Spinozism contained in *Morning Hours* are its most striking characteristic. The discussion in Mendelssohn's answers to Jacobi's communications and letters had gone on with no word of this "purified" Spinozism. And Mendelssohn would have had in truth every reason to speak of it. Was there from his standpoint a better answer to Jacobi's aggressive communication that Lessing had been a {XLVI} decided Spinozist than the dry and considered reply that Jacobi, perhaps led astray by certain overstatements of Lessing's, must have misunderstood Lessing's "purified" Spinozism, of which Mendelssohn naturally had known for decades? A cleverer answer was, from his standpoint, not thinkable: he answered Jacobi in just this manner in *Morning Hours* and *To the Friends of Lessing*. In *Morning Hours*, he cited *in extenso*[200] a unique documented proof for his assertion that Lessing had adhered to a "purified" Spinozism: Lessing's "Christianity of Reason."[201] To be sure, as he explains repeatedly, Mendelssohn had already learned of

---

197. JA XIII 281.
198. The explanation that Mendelssohn gives in *To the Friends of Lessing* 213.24–26 [Val 124–25; Got 167] is already unacceptable for the reason that it does not make intelligible why he wanted Jacobi not to see the manuscript of *Morning Hours*. {LS}
199. Or: History of Its Emergence. See the translator's remark on *Entstehungsgeschichte* at IMH XIIn2, above.
200. Lat.: extensively.
201. "Das Christenthum der Vernunft," LM XIV 175–78 (Cha 99–101; Nis 25–29). See *Morgenstunden* 133.25–136–21 (Scholz 40–43; Val 74–76; DaDy 97–99), with IMH XLV–XLIX, LXXX, XCI–XCIII, below.

this early Lessingian writing soon after the beginning of his friendship with Lessing. But that it had completely vanished from his memory, that at least its possible connection with Spinozism—for the discussion in it is, after all, by no means about Spinoza—had never come to mind during the critical timespan, is proof of his deep silence about Lessing's "purified" Spinozism in the whole controversy with Jacobi preceding the publication of *Morning Hours*. Now, "Christianity of Reason" had been published for the first time for the Easter Fair of 1785 in the framework of Lessing's unpublished theological writings[202]—it is this edition, not the manuscript, that Mendelssohn cites in *Morning Hours*—, therefore shortly before Mendelssohn emancipated himself from Jacobi's presentation of Spinozism. I see no other explanation: only on the occasion of the reading of Lessing's unpublished theological writings in April 1785, does Mendelssohn again recall "Christianity of Reason." Pointed by Jacobi to Lessing's Spinozism, there occurred to him for the first time a connection between this writing and his late friend's Spinozist tendencies. Only at this moment did he conceive his real and final answer to Jacobi's communication, and therefore especially the presentation that he would have to give of Lessing's Spinozism in his book-in-progress. Only at this moment did he conceive Lessing's "purified" Spinozism. Now he was sitting in the saddle again. As far as the understanding of Spinoza is concerned, Jacobi could always {XLVII} confidently assert and prove his superiority. So what![203] Thanks to the disclosure of Lessing's "purified" Spinozism, which was, after all, distinguished from the credo of the moderate Enlightenment only by a subtlety, Lessing, the moderate Enlightenment, and Mendelssohn himself were from now on protected from Jacobi's underhanded attempt to drive a wedge between Lessing and the moderate Enlightenment. In order for him to be able to bring about unhindered the regrouping of the fighting forces that had been put into confusion by the enemy for some time, the enemy had to hear of it only after the accomplished fact, from the published book. Now there was also no longer the least objection to a later publication of Jacobi's letters about his conversations with Lessing: after the disclosure of Lessing's "purified" Spinozism, these conversations, publicized and properly introduced by Lessing's

---

202. See annotation to *Morgenstunden* 133.10–11 [Scholz 39; Val 73; DaDy 96]. {LS}
 For LS's editorial annotation to *Morgenstunden* 133.10–11; see appendix 2, supplement to IMH XLVIIn202.
203. How untroubled Mendelssohn was in this respect is shown especially in *Freunde* 211.11–15 [Scholz 314; Val 142; Got 165]; cf. the annotation. {LS}
 For LS's annotation to *Freunde* 211.14–15, see appendix 2, supplement to IMH XLVIIn203.

oldest friend, would no longer serve as warning signs of the dangers of unguided speculation, as Mendelssohn had originally contemplated,[204] but at most as warning signs of the dangers of uncircumspect conversation,[205] especially with rash young people; the complete, infinite harmlessness of Lessing's statements, apparently so dangerous, would—Mendelssohn was now confident of being able to show this—leap to the eye in view of Lessing's documentably proven "purified" Spinozism.

A seemingly weighty objection arises against this explanation: Mendelssohn already had Lessing's unpublished theological writings in his hands some two years before their publication. As is it turns out from the letters from Lessing's brother Karl Gotthelf to Mendelssohn of April 22 and May 8, 1783,[206] the unpublished theological writings reached Mendelssohn in the last week of April and the first week of May of 1783, for his evaluation of their worthiness and suitability for publication. But: there is no basis for assuming that Mendelssohn at that time devoted special attention to the "Christianity of Reason" fragment; he seems to have taken a (disapproving) interest above all in Lessing's writings that were critiques of revelation. And quite apart from this: nothing speaks in favor of, {XLVIII} everything speaks against, his having recognized "Christianity of Reason" as a Spinozist document, even if it had specifically occurred to him in April or May of 1783. He was disposed to such a recognition only after Jacobi's detailed report about his conversations with Lessing had forced him to take seriously the possibility that Lessing had been a Spinozist; i.e., he was not disposed to such a recognition before November of 1783. And only in April of 1785 did Lessing's unpublished theological writings fall into his hands again.

A few days after Mendelssohn had tasked Elise Reimarus with letting Jacobi know that there was no rush for the answer to the "Objections," he came into possession of this answer, which had been sent off on April 26, 1785.[207] This answer is of importance for the emergence of *Morning Hours* for the reason that an exposition contained in it made the demarcation of authentic and "purified" Spinozism easier for Mendelssohn. Mendelssohn in his "Objections" had described as "the greatest difficulty... in Spinoza's system" the fact "that he wants to let the limited emerge out of the aggre-

---

204. To the Reimarus siblings, November 18, 1783 [JA XIII 157]. {LS}
205. Ger.: *Konversation*. In the next paragraph, however, "conversations" is, as usual, *Gespräche*. See IMH XIIIn11, above.
206. JA XIII 104, 106–7.
207. JA XIII 280.

INTRODUCTION TO *MORNING HOURS* AND *TO THE FRIENDS OF LESSING* 99

gate of the unlimited."[208] Jacobi in his answer protested against this conception of Spinozism, by explaining in the seventh paragraph:

> This sum [of all finite things] is no absurd composite of finite things that make up an infinite; but, in accord with the strictest meaning, it is a whole whose parts can only be in it and in accord with it, and be thought in it and in accord with it.[209]

Mendelssohn in *Morning Hours*[210] makes this explanation his own, by determining the distinction between authentic and "purified" Spinozism by means of it: "purified" is distinguished from authentic Spinozism just in that it does "not" let "the necessary being consist in the sum of infinitely many contingent beings, as Spinoza himself asserted," but teaches rather "that the one necessary being must be infinite in its unity and in accord with its power."[211] A correction of what Mendelssohn had remarked about Jacobi's {XLIX} "retreat under the banner of belief" forms the conclusion of Jacobi's answer to the "Objections,"[212] which is "completely in the spirit of [Jacobi's] religion."[213] He distinguishes emphatically between natural belief, which is the ground of all certainty about nature, and Christian belief. But in an immediate follow-up to this illuminating distinction, he plunges into a hymn-like profession of the Christian belief in God's becoming man, so that he would have to have completely intimidated Mendelssohn, who had "already experienced very often the same well-meaning attempts by [his] contemporaries" to "lead him into the womb of [Christian] belief,"[214] if he had not already freed himself entirely from Jacobi in the meantime.

In no way did Mendelssohn in the working out of *Morning Hours* let himself be disturbed by Jacobi's answer to the "Objections."[215] On June 28, 1785, he is already able to send the manuscript of the "entire first part" of *Morning*

---

208. *Freunde* 206.35–37 [found in Scholz 120; cf. Val 114]; cf. *Morgenstunden* 110.7ff. [DaDy 79ff.] {LS}
209. Scholz 146 [cf. Gio 218]. {LS}
210. Cf. *Freunde* 214.9–13 [Scholz 318; Val 145; Got 167] and annotation. {LS}
LS's editorial annotation to *Freunde* 214.9–13 (JA III.2 333) merely quotes the passage in Jacobi's answer to Mendelssohn's "Objections" which has just been quoted in the text of IMH XLVIII.
211. *Morgenstunden* 115.11–21 [cf. DaDy 84] {LS; JA III.2 XLVIII reads, erroneously, 215.11–21}
212. Scholz 168ff. (Val 120ff.).
213. *Freunde* 205.19ff. [found in Scholz 118; cf. Val 113] {LS}
214. *Freunde* 196.14ff. [Scholz 305; cf. Val 137; Got 162]. {LS}
215. Cf. also the letter to E. Reimarus of May 24, 1785 [JA XIII 282–83]. {LS}

Hours to the Reimarus siblings with the request for an evaluation.[216] The book appeared in the first days of October the same year.

Morning Hours had originally been conceived as, so to speak, the first, preparatory part of *Lessing's Character*: its original purpose is the critique of Spinozism that was to prepare for the presentation of Lessing's Spinozism in the second part. The finished work does not suggest in the least the actual history of its emergence,[217] whether by its title (*Morning Hours, or Lectures on the Existence of God*) or by its structure (the chapters devoted to Spinoza and Lessing are added to the presentation of the proofs of God and do not form a part by themselves) or, for that matter, by the remarks of the "Preface" about the history of the emergence of the book. That this is no accident, but the result of a tactic, scarcely needs to be said. With the help of Mendelssohn's correspondence with Elise Reimarus, one may follow out how there was formed in his mind the image of the purpose and emergence of *Morning Hours* which, in view of the finished book, is imposed on the reader ignorant of the history of its emergence. Mendelssohn had written to Elise Reimarus on April 29, 1785, that in the first part of his brochure he had "to deal *mainly*, to be sure, with Pantheism, {L} only there is still no mention of our correspondence [*sc.*, the correspondence with Jacobi]."[218] In the letter written to Elise Reimarus four weeks later, on the other hand, one already reads:

> I am therefore publishing the first part of my *Morning Hours*, am still saying nothing in it about our correspondence, but am also *touching on* Pantheism and trying to refute it.[219]

Mendelssohn not only wants to make Jacobi's communication about Lessing's Spinozism innocuous by paving the way for its public announcement with a critique of Spinozism and an account of Lessing's "purified" Spinozism; he wants at the same time to disguise these reassuring expositions—for, as such, every identifiable reassurance is at the same time unsettling—by introducing them as a mere excursus in a presentation of the proofs of God. The remarks about the history of its emergence that are offered in the "Preface" also serve this disguise specifically. According to them, *Morning Hours*

---

216. See JA XIII 289.
217. Ger.: *Entstehungsgeschichte*. See IMH xiin2, above. Likewise later in this paragraph and the next.
218. JA XIII 281; the emphasis is LS's. Cf. IMH xlv, above.
219. JA XIII 282–83; the emphasis is LS's.

emerged essentially on the basis of the home instruction that Mendelssohn had given to his eldest son and two other young people, whereas the quarrel with Jacobi about Lessing's Spinozism was only "a special occasion for the present announcement of this writing."[220] That the significance that is thereby granted to the home instruction is exaggerated, to say the least, needs no further proof after what has been said. Indeed, what has been detailed above warrants expressing the following suspicion, which is further reinforced by the probability of the fact that the home instruction did not begin before the end of 1784: only when Mendelssohn, prompted by the quarrel with Jacobi, had begun to concern himself again with natural theology did he come to the thought of presenting the later content of *Morning Hours* to his circle of pupils for the purpose of clarifying his reflections.

Mendelssohn believed that by the disclosure of Lessing's "purified" Spinozism, by the concealment of the disclosure from Jacobi beforehand, and by the mode of his treatment of both the Lessing-Spinoza question and the history of the emergence of *Morning Hours*, he had preempted his opponent in a manner decisive for the quarrel. Only on July 21, 1785, did he inform Jacobi that at the next fair a writing concerning their quarrel {LI} would appear from his pen; in this writing he hopes "to establish . . . the *status controversiae*[221] and thereby introduce the quarrel properly."[222] He did not once take the trouble of notifying Jacobi unambiguously about whether his writing would deal only with Spinozism in general or also with Lessing's Spinozism or, for that matter, also with Jacobi's communication as such. The explicit request in the same letter for a copy of the "Objections" contained at most an inkling, scarcely intelligible to Jacobi, about the division of his work that Mendelssohn was mulling over, according to which "everything that concerns Jacobi and Lessing in particular"[223] was to be discussed in the second part of *Morning Hours*:

> for I am of a mind to get closer to our quarrel now, and to this end . . . to go through both your essays once more. Here, however, is where the "Objections," to which your answer is directed, necessarily belong.

On October 4, 1785, Mendelssohn sent off the printed copy of the first part of *Morning Hours* to Jacobi with a very friendly cover letter, which con-

---

220. *Morgenstunden* 5.16–17 [cf. DaDy xx].
221. Lat.: state of the controversy.
222. JA XIII 292. Ditto for the block citation in the sentence after the next.
223. Letter to Elise Reimarus, May 24, 1785, JA XIII 283.

cludes with the request for Jacobi's "heartfelt affection and friendship."[224] Four days afterward at the latest,[225] he was in possession of Jacobi's *On Spinoza's Doctrine, in Letters to Mr. Moses Mendelssohn*.

Jacobi had been informed since May 26, 1785, about a part of the content of Mendelssohn's letter to Elise Reimarus of April 29, 1785, i.e., about Mendelssohn's publishing aim—not about Mendelssohn's explicit explanation, of course, given that he could not let Jacobi see the manuscript—by Elise Reimarus.[226] Despite the advice of Hamann[227] and Herder, Jacobi had forgone the separate publication of his conversations with Lessing. "About your wish that I publish my discussion with Lessing in particular independently of Mendelssohn," he had written to Herder on June 30, 1784,

> I have thought it over and found at each reconsideration that I have to advise myself not to. The guise that this matter has by now taken on through events [*sc.*, which had been brought about by Jacobi] must keep them intact°; I will let them continue their historical course quietly, without worrying about the further development {LII} and the end. [228]

Now that he could no longer be certain that the historical course of events would correspond to his wish and plan as a result of Mendelssohn's surprising publication decision, whose background causes were unknown to him and always remained unknown, he was compelled to influence the development and the end actively. When on May 26, 1785, he heard of Mendelssohn's publication decision, a month had passed since he had sent Mendelssohn the answer to the "Objections." He

> still hoped for a response from Mendelssohn. After [he] had waited three months in vain, [he] was gradually moved to reach a decision for [himself] alone, and felt more and more inclined to bring to light, by means

---

224. JA XIII 308–9.
225. See the letter to Nicolai of October 8, 1785 [JA XIII 309]. {LS}
226. Scholz 172 [Gio 232; Val 122]. {LS}
227. In his letter to Jacobi of November 14, 1784; see RK I 389. {LS}
228. RK III 491–92. Jacobi's German word that I have translated as "matter" is *Sache*—more or less literally, "cause" (in the sense of, say, Mendelssohn's *Sache Gottes* or Leibniz's *Causa Dei*; on these, see IGC). It shows up in a statement in Lessing's letter to Mendelssohn of May 1, 1774, concerning Leibniz's philosophizing, which I have quoted as the epigraph to my interpretive essay: "it is incontestably better to defend an unphilosophical cause [or matter: *Sache*] very philosophically than to want to reject and reform it unphilosophically" (JA XII.2, 47). Cf. also IMH LVIInn258–61, below.

of the letters inserted here [*sc.*, to Mendelssohn and Hemsterhuis], a presentation of Spinozism such as [he] found useful at the present time.[229]

In June of 1785, he had heard through Hamann something more exact about the title and publication of *Morning Hours*.[230] At the end of July, he came into possession of Mendelssohn's formal announcement of the imminent appearance of *Morning Hours*. "Now there was no further need for any long reflection about what I had to do":[231] Jacobi set himself to putting before the public the record of the quarrel that he had carried on with Mendelssohn about Lessing's Spinozism,[232] with the addition of a conclusion devoted to the critique of the Enlightenment. He could not know what Mendelssohn in *Morning Hours* would say about Spinozism, about Lessing, and perhaps even about Jacobi himself; for Mendelssohn's explicit assurance in his letter to Elise Reimarus of May 24, 1785, that he would do without "the setting forth" of "everything that applies to Jacobi and Lessing in particular"[233] remained unknown to him. He was especially afraid that Mendelssohn would present him as a defender of Spinozism.[234] {LIII} In view of Mendelssohn's silence, he believed he had to be prepared for anything. Since he was no longer holding back the part of his argument that was for Mendelssohn the most dangerous, being literally fatal for the latter, he made known in his *Spinoza Letters* what Lessing had said to him about his practiced reserve toward Mendelssohn and about his reasons for it.[235] Thus he had far outstripped his opponent, who believed he had gained a decisive advantage by his disclosure of Lessing's "purified" Spinozism: without knowing of this disclosure, Jacobi had completely devalued it through the communication, adequate as it was for escaping all traps, that Lessing had kept silent about his explicit explanation in accord with his credo vis-à-vis Mendelssohn.

How much this communication affected Mendelssohn, how deeply it

---

229. Scholz 173 [cf. Gio 233; cf. Val 122–23]. {LS}
230. RK IV.3 53–54 and 63. {LS}
231. Scholz 182 [cf. Gio 235; cf. Val 125]. {LS}
232. With the exception, above all, of the "Objections," whose publication he did not consider warranted and which he regarded as "a sort of hostage" — Scholz 142n. {LS}
233. JA XIII 283.
234. Scholz 183 [Gio 236; Val 125]; cf. already Jacobi's letter to Mendelssohn of September 5, 1784 [JA XIII 223–24]; supplying a certain justification for this fear is Mendelssohn's explicit aim in the letter to Elise Reimarus of January 28, 1785 [JA XIII 263], of "letting" Jacobi "speak in Spinoza's stead," an aim to which Jacobi had raised no objection at all, in any case. {LS}
235. See IMH XXVI, above.

pained him, his letter to Kant of October 16, 1785,[236] and the corresponding passage in *To the Friends of Lessing*[237] show especially. The pure expressions of the pain of the friend are more perceptible to our ear than the strained outbreaks of the annoyances of the outsmarted whose carefully devised tactic has come to naught. The pain over the barrier that separated him from Lessing, of which he had only now become aware, was so deep that words failed him for properly describing the brutality with which Jacobi had brought this barrier to his awareness.[238] Not merely had there fallen on his friendship with Lessing, which was the greatest happiness of his life, a shadow that, in a truly forgivable manner, crushed his self-esteem. Together with this, his trust toward the non-Jewish world had been shaken: after all, unreserved friendship with Lessing was at the same time also the oldest and most trustworthy bridge that connected him with that world at all, the testimony most precious to him of the possibility of complete understanding between men of opposite background. One can appreciate again by now how great the hurdles must have been, despite which Mendelssohn kept working on his trust in non-Jewish friends—he who was as free of pathological sensitivities as a mere human can be, who bore no greater distrust {LIV} than what is justified sufficiently by the experiences of the Jews at all times. Without assuming such a justified distrust toward the non-Jewish world, one cannot, as things stand, understand his behavior in the quarrel with Jacobi, nor, for that matter, his behavior toward Bonnet in the quarrel with Lavater.[239] To be sure, the same natural hatred against the Jews did not then yet have the principle of nationalism at its disposal; but even so, the anti-Jewish theory and practice of the Christian Churches supplied it with weapons scarcely less effective. So it is self-evident that Mendelssohn could toy with the (absurd) thought that Jacobi was looking to convert him to Christianity.[240] For the proper understanding of his reaction to Jacobi's public communication, however, one has to keep in mind Mendelssohn's

236. JA XIII 312–13. Altmann's translation of the relevant paragraphs may be found in MMBS 705–6.
237. *Freunde* 190.37ff. [Scholz 298ff.; Val 132ff.; Got 157]. {LS}
238. Cf. the letter to Garve of November 7, 1785 [JA XIII 324–25]. {LS}
239. Cf. JA VII LXXXVIII–LXXXIX. {LS}
LS's reference is to Simon Rawidowicz's editorial introduction to Mendelssohn's *Gegenbetrachtungen*, JA VII LXXXI–CV. For further details of Mendelssohn's controversies with Johann Caspar Lavater (1741–1801) and Charles Bonnet (1720–93), see Rawidowicz, JA VII XI–LXXX, and Altmann, MMBS 201–42, 247, 257–63, 270, 280, 730–35, 744–45, 749, 792n24 (on Lavater) and 216, 221–22, 223, 227, 228, 239–41, 246–49, 256 (on Bonnet).
240. Cf. also on this the report of J. F. Reichardt about the conversation he had with Mendelssohn on December 13, 1785, in the *Vossischen Zeitung*, 1786, No. 18, February 11, 1st supplement [trans. Altmann, MMBS 732ff., *passim*]. {LS}

experience of the distrust of the non-Jewish world toward the Jews, no less than his own distrust as a Jew toward the non-Jewish world. Had even Lessing, therefore, not bestowed his full trust on him? This suspicion was incomparably more tormenting than the already sufficiently hurtful certainty that he believed he had to infer from Jacobi's publication, that the latter had trusted him to break his given word.[241]

Mendelssohn had decided "not [to put] the pen [to the reply to Jacobi's book] until [he] was completely free of all sensitivity."[242] He waited with the working out of his response to Jacobi's presentation in fact some two months. On December 31, 1785—four days before his death—he brought the manuscript of *To the Friends of Lessing* to the publisher.

This writing fulfills, in the main, the purpose for which Mendelssohn had intended the second part of *Morning Hours*. The plan for this second part had been "torn" from him by Jacobi's publication,[243] since the correspondence with Jacobi {LV} about Lessing's Spinozism had already been published by Jacobi. There remained nothing further for him but to oppose his own presentation of the course and subject of the quarrel to the one that Jacobi had given and, in turn, to bring into print the few documents that had not been published by Jacobi (the "Objections," the beginning of Jacobi's answer to the "Objections," and Mendelssohn's letter to Elise Reimarus of May 24, 1785).[244] *To the Friends of Lessing* is, contrary to Mendelssohn's intention, written throughout "in the irritated mood that Jacobi's writing had aroused in him."[245] This is not to deny, but perhaps in part to explain, that it shows Mendelssohn's power as author to an unusual degree, above all in contrast to Jacobi's diffuse style of writing. The image of the facts that is offered in *To the Friends of Lessing* is even more convoluted than the one that *Morning Hours* offers. Right on the first page, it says that *Morning Hours* was "drafted a few years ago," an assertion that has already been proven to be an exaggeration by his friend Nicolai's report, cited above.[246] With the help of our remarks, the reader will have no difficulty in being able to discover the otherwise small inaccuracies that in part bring the chronology completely into confusion. It must be emphasized that Mendelssohn now

---

241. *Freunde* 217 [Scholz 322–23; Val 148; Got 170]. Cf. Mendelssohn's statement to Reichardt, *loc. cit.* {LS}
242. To E. Reimarus, October 21, 1785 [JA XIII 320]; cf. also the letter to Garve of November 7, 1785 [JA XIII 324–25]. {LS}
243. *Freunde* 181 [Scholz 287]. {LS}
244. *Freunde* 200–207, 208–9, 215–16; cf. Got 168–69 (letter to Elise Reimarus only).
245. MMGS V 634n. {LS}
246. IMH xxxix. {LS}

contests, if only in an ambiguous form, the authenticity or at least the seriousness of all the important statements Lessing had addressed to Jacobi and that he categorizes Jacobi's book as a complaint raised against Lessing, and Jacobi himself as an obscurantist enemy of the free-spirited Lessing. To be sure, Jacobi had made such an interpretation of his aims plausible, at least in Mendelssohn's eyes, chiefly by the appeal to Lavater, with which he had let himself get carried away at the conclusion of his book;[247] but Mendelssohn himself knew that this interpretation does not correspond with the facts: in his letter to Kant of October 16, 1785, he describes Jacobi as a "*Schwärmer*,"[248] i.e., as a fanatic,[249] of philosophy, in emphatic contradistinction to the "*Schwärmern*" of positive religion. While his invectives against Jacobi's cast of mind therefore convolute the actual issue, {LVI} his statements about Jacobi's character, about his dishonesty and crudeness, do not go beyond what he had to assert on the basis of his experiences. Although in his reply to Mendelssohn's writing, *Against Mendelssohn's Accusations in His "To the Friends of Lessing,"* which appeared shortly after Mendelssohn's death, Jacobi was therefore easily able to show those invectives to be unfounded, on the other hand he could at best provide these statements with snide comments, but not invalidate them. This finding, however, should not obscure the fact that Jacobi's refutation of *To the Friends of Lessing*, no less than his *Spinoza Letters*, is of inestimable worth for the correction of the not inconsiderable inaccuracies that are found in *Morning Hours* and *To the Friends of Lessing*.

On the whole, it will have to be said that Jacobi's presentation of the quarrel is more trustworthy than Mendelssohn's—as far as the particulars go. Jacobi's dishonesty shows up only in general, that is, when it becomes clear why he communicated the content of his discussions with Lessing to Mendelssohn *privatim*[250] instead of unambiguously taking the responsibility from the start for announcing it to the public, and when one considers the mode in which he put the communication to work on Mendelssohn. He had devised his game so minutely, he had from the start maneuvered the guileless and self-certain Mendelssohn into such an unfavorable stance, that after the latter had committed the imprudence of involving himself in

---

247. Cf. also Reichardt, *loc. cit.* [IMH LIVn240, above], *ad loc.* {LS}

248. JA XIII 313; trans. MMBS 706. See the translator's note on *Schwärmerey* at IMH LXIVn297, below. "*Schwärmern*" later in the sentence is the dative plural of "*Schwärmer*" in LS's original German.

249. Cf. Mendelsohn, "Enthusiast, Visionair, Fanatiker" [Enthusiast, Visionary, Fanatic], JA III.1 315–16. {LS}

250. Lat.: privately.

the private communication at all instead of hauling Jacobi into the public forum right away, hardly any other choice remained for him except to resort to tactics and dishonesty in turn. This is to say nothing at all about his having been pressured into such a resort by the Reimarus siblings, indeed by Jacobi himself,[251] even before he himself could have reached any decisions to that effect. From the start and during the whole course of the quarrel, he was facing Jacobi's style of thinking and type of temperament without understanding them. It has been remarked[252] that Jacobi's intellectual freedom was missing in him and that, as a result, Jacobi's shifting between atheism and Christianity remained incomprehensible to him: he actually did not know all along whether in Jacobi he had before him an atheist or a Christian; {LVII} only for a moment was he able to rise to the insight that Jacobi was a philosopher. The intellectual daring in Jacobi, however, was bound up with a no less remarkable moral cowardice: he who later boasted that no one before him would have risked his name to speak of Spinoza with such high respect, with such admiration and love as he did,[253] had on the other hand an anxiety, shocking for a man of his rank, over possibly being represented to the (incompetent) public as a Spinozist. His moral cowardice becomes more identifiable when it is defined more closely as a mixture of self-pity with a brutal disregard for others. Its root is an unrestrained self-esteem that takes on the appearance of love of freedom. For the indulging of self-esteem one may blame Rousseau, who throughout his whole oeuvre had supplied a justification for this emotion that charmed the century, although or because he was combating it as the detestable source of detestable institutions—the brutality has darker origins than Rousseau's sermon and the general revolutionary movement of that time. For what characterizes Jacobi's being is the complete absence of the *"générosité"*[254] that, however questionable, formed the revolutionary spirit's patent of nobility. Mendelssohn did not shy away from stating, in regard to his behavior in the quarrel with Jacobi, that he may well have "received no proper con-

251. See IMH XV–XVI, above. {LS}
252. See IMH XL–XLII, above.
253. See annotation to *Freunde* 188.11–34. {LS}
For LS's editorial annotation to *Freunde* 188.11–34; see appendix 2, supplement to IMH LVIIn253.
254. Fr.: "generosity." Cf. Mei 146 or Mas 131–32, with René Descartes, *Les passions de l'âme*, pt. II, §145, pt. III, §§153–64, 187, 202–3 (AT XI 437–38, 446–56, 469–70, 479–80; Vos 98, 104–10, 120–21, 128–29); Spinoza, *Ethica*, pt. III, prop. 59 schol.; pt. III, Definitions of the Emotions no. 48 ("Explanation"); pt. IV, props. 46, 73, and appendix ch. 11; pt. V, props. 10 schol., and 41; *Tractatus politicus* VII, §11 (Geb. II 188–89, 203, 245, 265, 269, 287–88, 306, III 312; WhSt 145, 157 ["nobility of soul"], 197–98, 216, 219, 236, 254; Wer 343 ["nobility of soul"]).

cept of honor and *point d'honneur*[255] in [his] early education"[256]—compared with Jacobi, however, he proves to be a gentleman.[257] Jacobi's brutality stands in a not unintelligible connection with his deep dishonesty: His conscience did not raise an objection when he directed the following sentence to Mendelssohn:[258]

> I want to move out against you from the perfectly *quiet*[259] line of defense in which I have been standing and venture a sally on your circle with but one perfect[260] thrust.[261]

Facing a Jacobi who as a tactician was superior to him by far, Mendelssohn developed a tactic whose ineptitude proves {LVIII} he was at bottom without guile and that calls forth our compassion rather than our protest. Yet to judge it is a matter for the reader; the editor's obligation is to uncover it. {LIX}

II. ANALYSIS OF THE CONTENT

Morning Hours is a compendium of what Mendelssohn has "previously gathered and [him]self thought" about natural theology.[262] To a considerable extent, it merely contains either abbreviated reiterations or fuller expansions of reflections he had already presented in the *Thoughts on Probability*,[263] the *Phädon*, and especially the *Treatise on Evidence*. If one adds that in *Morning Hours* is also found the definitive formulation of the results at which his aes-

---

255. Fr.: point of honor.
256. Reichardt, *loc. cit.* [MMBS, 737]. {LS}
257. Here LS uses the English word.
258. In his answer to the "Objections"—Scholz 141. {LS}
  LS quotes the third sentence of the letter in question, whose first thirteen sentences are omitted by Gio (as is indicated by the bracketed ellipsis, Gio 216), following the first rather than the second edition of Jacobi's *Spinoza-Briefe*: Jacobi himself calls attention to his having withheld those sentences from the first edition and inserting them only in the second edition (after Mendelssohn's death), inasmuch as they "resonate somewhat harshly, and I did not believe that I would have to deal in my book with Mendelssohn's 'Objections,' which would have explained and justified" them (Scholz 142n).
259. The emphasis is LS's.
260. Lit.: precise. Likewise earlier in Jacobi's sentence.
261. Cf. the interpretation of the turn of phrase, "I will let events take their historical course *quietly*," in Jacobi's letter to Herder cited above, IMH LI–LII. {LS; the emphasis is LS's}
262. *Morgenstunden* 3.1–3 [cf. DaDy xix]. {LS}
263. "Gedanken über die Wahrscheinlichkeit" (1756), JA I 147–64; renamed "über die Wahrscheinlichkeit" [On Probability] in *Schriften*, JA I 497–515 (Dah 233–50).

thetic investigations aimed[264] and that in *To the Friends of Lessing*, which is of course not to be separated from *Morning Hours*, is found a recapitulation of his view of the essence of Judaism,[265] one may say that these two writings contain the definitive presentation of most of Mendelssohn's reflections.[266] Newly added are the reflections on truth, appearance, and error in the "Prior Cognition," the critique of Spinozism and the attempt at a new proof of God that accompanies that critique, the critique of Jacobi's philosophy of belief, and, finally and above all, the interpretation of Lessing's philosophical efforts. The evaluation of *Morning Hours* and *To the Friends of Lessing* has to be limited to these themes, peculiar as they are to the two writings.[267]

The inner connection of the themes mentioned has occasionally been indicated in the "History of Their Emergence."[268] To make it completely visible requires just one remark about the significance of the "Prior Cognition." This introduction[269] is of significance not because it attempts (in imitation of Lambert)[270] a corrective to Leibniz-Wolffian Rationalism in the sense of English Empiricism,[271] but because it lays the basis for the discussions of the relationship of speculation {LX} and sound commonsense that run through the two writings like a scarlet thread.[272] If the significance of the

---

264. *Morgenstunden* 61–62. [DaDy 42–43] {LS}
On Mendelssohn's distinction here between the "faculty of approval" and the faculties of cognition and of desire, see LS's editorial annotation to *Morgenstunden* 61.26–62.21 (JA III.2 284–85), in appendix 2, supplement to IMH LIXn264.

265. *Freunde* 196ff. [Scholz 305ff.; Val 137ff.]. {LS}

266. In this connection, let it be recalled that the application of natural theology to natural right and ethics was perhaps also to be brought about in the second part of *Morning Hours*, and therefore the theme of the first part of *Jerusalem* was in a certain manner to be taken up again. {LS}

267. See below, IMH LX–LXIX, LXX–LXXV, LXXV–LXXVII, and LXXVII–XCV, respectively.

268. I.e., part I of IMH. See IMH XIIn2, above.

269. I.e., to the remainder of *Morning Hours*. Cf. IMH XXXVIII, above.

270. On Johann Heinrich Lambert (1728–77), see LS's annotation to *Morgenstunden* 141.20–21 (JA III.2 306–8), in appendix 2, supplement to IMH XIIn9.

271. Cf. *Morgenstunden* 10.6ff., 11.4ff., 20.30–21.9, 39.6–40.28, 61.12–15 [DaDy 3–4, 11, 26–27, 42] and annotations. {LS; LS's German text reads 10.8ff. instead of 10.6ff.}
For LS's editorial annotations to *Morgenstunden* 10.6ff., 11.4ff., 20.30–21.9, 39.6–40.28, and 61.12–15 (JA III.2 278–79, 279, 280, 282, 284), see appendix 2, supplement to IMH LIXn271.

272. Incidentally, the speculation/sound-commonsense opposition is the, on the one hand, radicalized and, on the other hand, coarsened form of the Rationalism/Empiricism opposition. The kinship of the two pairs of opposites is asserted by Tetens in the following words (*Philosophische Versuche* [see IMH LIXn257, above], I, 570–71): "Formerly, sensible cognition was opposed to rational cognition . . . and philosophers investigated how these two sorts of representations comport with each other. If more recent philosophers have investigated how sound commonsense and its cognitions relate to higher discursive reason and its scientific insights, it

introduction to *Morning Hours* is grasped in the manner indicated, then the multiplicity of themes peculiar to *Morning Hours* and *To the Friends of Lessing* can be understood from one and the same point of view. The two writings are documents of the final crisis of modern metaphysics of the Cartesian-Leibnizian stamp; their particular subject is the solutions to this crisis that were being taken up within Mendelssohn's purview. He saw before him, as such solutions: (1) the philosophy of sound commonsense, (2) Spinozism, (3) Jacobi's philosophy of belief, and (4) the philosophizing of Lessing.[273]

To understand the position he took toward the crisis of modern metaphysics, one must first recall what, in his view, the characteristic distinction between modern and premodern metaphysics consists in. He knew premodern philosophy chiefly from the Jewish philosophy of the Middle Ages, especially Maimonides' *Guide of the Perplexed*,[274] on the one hand, and the Platonic dialogues as well as later Platonism as it had been transmitted to him specifically through Cudworth,[275] on the other. Since the Jewish philosophy of the Middle Ages is determined considerably by Platonism, or rather by Neo-Platonism, it has to be said that Mendelssohn knew premodern metaphysics chiefly in its (Neo-)Platonic form. Now this metaphysics is, in {LXI} his view, utterly inferior to modern metaphysics.[276] Characteristic of the distinction between the two is, e.g., that modern metaphysics is equipped with better concepts of the value of the human body than Platonic metaphysics°;[277] it has—against the otherworldly tendencies of the older view—rehabilitated the this-worldly, the body, sensuality, the "delights of the senses"; it has shown that this world is no prison, no vale of sorrows, but a potential paradise.[278] And it has been able to do so only because it has known the senses, the body, and this world as a "divine creation," whereas the earlier metaphysics was not in a position to contradict thoroughly the "obviously absurd" view of the eternity of matter, advocated by "Plato and

---

is almost the same questions and the same considerations, except that they come up in another form." {LS}

273. See IMH LIXn267, above.

274. LS uses the traditional Hebrew title, *Moreh Nevuchim*. Mendelssohn, like most of his European fellow-Jews, read the *Guide* in Hebrew translation (i.e., not in the original Judeo-Arabic).

275. On Mendelssohn's use of Cudworth, see LS's editorial annotations to *Phädon 3* 152.30 and 153.18ff. (JA III.1 417–18), in appendix 2, supplement to IP XXVIIn85.

276. Cf. *Phädon 3* 150.38–151.6 [Nob 153], as well as *Evidenz* 269–70 [Dah 253–54]. {LS}

277. *Phädon* 8.26–27 [Nob 42]. {LS}

278. *Schriften* 393.18–27 [Dah 140] and *Sendschreiben* 102.9–19. {LS}
LS quotes the latter passage in part at IEL XXIII; cf. also IGC CVII.

his sect and also many sons of our people."²⁷⁹ Modern metaphysics is therefore closer to the Bible than premodern metaphysics, and, to be sure, not merely in the doctrine of creation but also in the doctrine of providence. Whereas the earlier philosophers recognized only general providence and denied special providence, modern metaphysics, especially the Leibnizian, has learned to appreciate that God's providence reaches "down to the smallest changes and unique events" in the sublunary world.²⁸⁰ But not merely does modern metaphysics free this world—earth, body, and senses—from the blemish that the earlier metaphysics had imputed to it, by proving that each human soul must ultimately arrive at eternal happiness; it also takes all terror from death and the beyond: "in our time" one can no longer say with Epicurus and Lucretius "that the concept of a future life makes death terrifying for us"; "in our time" "the most reasonable part make for themselves... instead the most consoling representations of the future, which make death even worth wishing for."²⁸¹ This thoroughly consoling and calming conception of this life as well as of the next one has its foundation in the conviction that God has created man for man's happiness without placing all too high demands²⁸² on him; and {LXII} this conviction is cogently justified through the proofs for the existence of God as "a supremely benevolent being."²⁸³ Metaphysics as Mendelssohn understands and appropriates it culminates in taking away from man the fear of divine anger and of death, in vindicating "an, as it were, just claim to a further progress to higher perfections [*sc.*, after death],"²⁸⁴ without forcing him to make considerable cutbacks in his demands for happiness in this life.

The inherent questionableness of this "rather Epicurean"²⁸⁵ theism was not felt by Mendelssohn. To him, only doubts about the adequacy of demonstrations securing this theism posed difficulties. Now admittedly, modern philosophy's demonstrations were its pride: "... il est étrange," Leibniz had said,²⁸⁶ "qu'on ne voit point d'ombre de démonstration dans Platon

---

279. See Mendelssohn's *Commentary on Maimonides' "Millot HaHiggayon"* ["Logical Terms"], ch. 9, annotation 11 [JA XIV 80–81; cf. JA XX.1 106]. {LS}
280. *Morgenstunden* 127–28 [Scholz 32–33; cf. Val 68–69; cf. DaDy 93–94]. {LS}
281. *Literaturbrief* #99, April 24, 1760 [JA V.1 191]. {LS}
282. The noun *Anspruch*, which shows up frequently in IMH, has previously been translated as "claim." In what follows, it is translated as either "claim" or "demand," depending on the immediate context.
283. Cf. *Morgenstunden* 70.19–37 [cf. DaDy 50–51]. {LS}
284. *Sache Gottes* §79. {LS}
285. To Sophie Becker, December 27, 1785 [JA XIII 333]. {LS}
286. *Nouveaux Essais* IV, ch. 2, §9 [Ger V 352; cf. ReBe 371]. {LS}

et dans Aristote (excepté ses analytiques premiers), et dans les autres philosophes anciens."[287] In this methodological superiority of the modern philosophers over the earlier ones was seen the reason for all the advances of modern times in the knowledge of things. As has already been mentioned, Mendelssohn in *Morning Hours* considers the adequate justification of the doctrine of special providence, which had been accomplished only by Leibniz (and Shaftesbury),[288] to be such a progress of the highest significance: in antiquity, that important doctrine was promulgated not by the philosophers, but by the "popular system of the poets and priests."[289] Let no one be puzzled why Mendelssohn in this context silently bypasses revelation. He was not forced to speak of it, since in *Jerusalem* he had shown in detail that there could not be a revelation of eternal truths.[290] The same thing that is said clearly enough of the "popular system of the poets and priests," therefore, is valid of revealed religion (as belief in the revealed character of eternal truths): that its legitimate claim has been fulfilled by modern metaphysics, only by this and by this all the more, and that as a result it has even become superfluous. One could not rest content with the "popular {LXIII} system"[291] for the reason that, as much as it is to be preferred to unbelief, it does not offer adequate security against the other defective extreme, superstition.[292] For securing human happiness against superstition on the one hand and unbelief on the other, there is but a single, though fully adequate, means: demonstration.

Our peace of mind, threatened as it is by the terrors of superstition and the despair of unbelief, is in danger until "by a simple series of incontrovertible reasons," by "a chain of distinct inferences," we have assured ourselves of the blissful truth in such a mode that "we can recall it . . . at all

287. Fr.: ". . . it is strange . . . that not a shadow of demonstration is seen in Plato and Aristotle (his *Prior Analytics* excepted) and the other ancient philosophers."
288. Cf. . . . Leibniz's judgment on Shaftesbury's work [sc., *Characteristicks*] which Mendelssohn cites in the *Litteratur-Briefe* (of September 11, 1760, Letter #126): "*J'y trouve d'abord presque toute ma Théodicée (mais plus agréablement tournée) avant qu'elle eût vu le jour. . . . Il ne manque presque que mon harmonie préétablie, mon bannisement de la mort, et ma réduction de la matière, ou de la multitude aux unités, ou aux substances simples.* [I find in it, to begin with, almost all my *Theodicy* (but conveyed more agreeably) before it had seen the light of day. . . . It lacks, more or less, only my preestablished harmony, my banishment of death, and my reduction of matter or multiplicity to unities or simple substances.]" {LS's editorial annotation on *Pope!* 76.22–23 (JA II 387)}
Cf. also Altmann, MMFM 104n56.
289. *Morgenstunden* 127–28 [Scholz 32–33; cf. Val 68–69; cf. DaDy 93–94]. {LS}
290. *Jerusalem* 160ff.; Ark 93ff.; Got 83ff.
291. Cf. also *Sache Gottes* §§55–57. {LS}
292. Cf. *Morgenstunden* 127.33–128.26 [Scholz 32–33; DaDy 93] and 71.34–72.25, and *Evidenz* 314–15 [Dah 293–94]. {LS}

times."[293] To strike superstition and unbelief at the root, however, one must undertake the total transformation of our confused representations into clear and distinct concepts, one must "at least once in one's life"[294] have called into question, from the ground up, the world within which alone "prejudices" can flourish: the world of confused concepts, of experience. It was Descartes who, by his radical doubt, had gotten the fundamental reform of philosophy on the road: "before his time, one had been used to making principles of experience the foundation even in philosophy."[295] The transformation of philosophy into a purely demonstrative knowing, free of all empiricism, had to remain incomplete, however, so long as philosophers were given over to language; thus there resulted the desideratum of a purely scientific language, fundamentally distinguished from the usual language of men, the "*mathesis universalis*."[296] In this desideratum, the most important consequence of the Cartesian-Leibnizian transformation of philosophy in the present context comes to the clearest expression; this philosophy was, even and especially in its "language," incomparably further removed from the language of sound commonsense than the earlier philosophy; it tended toward extreme unpopularity. In that way, however, it became wholly incapable {LXIV} of displacing the "popular system" and therefore of fulfilling one of its most important functions, that of "Enlightenment." No wonder, then, that "*Schwärmerey*"[297] raised its head anew. No wonder either, however, that when it became clear to sound commonsense, which had let itself

---

293. *Phädon* 81.16–19 [cf. Cul 98; cf. Nob 105]; cf. on this point Epicurus, *Letter to Herodotus, in princ.* [Bai 18–20] and *passim.* {LS}

294. *Morgenstunden* 18.5–6 [DaDy 9] — *semel in vita* is found in Descartes. {LS}
The Latin expression means "once in one's° life"; see the first sentence of Descartes's *Meditations* I (Hef 86–87).

295. *Evidenz* 294.29–31 [cf. Dah 276]. {LS}
Mendelssohn's word for "philosophy" here is *Weltweisheit*. In LS's surrounding discussion, "philosophy" is *Philosophie*, and "philosophers" is *Philosophen*. See IPM XVIIIn23.

296. *Evidenz* 290.19ff. [Dah 272ff.] {LS}
The Latin expression means "universal mathematical symbols"; cf. the last sentence of Descartes's *Meditation* V (Hef 182–83).

297. See J. C. Adelung, *Grammatisch-kritischen Wörterbuch* (1811), s.v.: "1. As an abstract noun . . . , the tendency to make confused representations, or imaginings, and indistinct representations, or feelings, the basis for determining one's judgments and actions, while overriding clearer and more distinct representations. *Schwärmerey* in religion is the tendency to accept images and feelings as divine effects and truths, which includes [religious] enthusiasm and fanaticism, the former appealing to images, the latter appealing to feelings. In the broadest though not the most usual understanding, *Schwärmerey* is sometimes the tendency to accept other sources of cognition as Holy Scripture, since it agrees with superstition here. 2. As a concrete noun, opinions and actions insofar as they are based on confused and indistinct representations, while overriding clearer and more distinct ones."

become enlightened by modern metaphysics as much as it could, that it had to expect a new obfuscation of its insights from the "subtleties" of this metaphysics, it abruptly dismissed its governess and declared itself to be grown-up. No one described the illusion it was succumbing to more aptly than Mendelssohn:

> This is the property of all moral truths. As soon as they are brought to light, they are so closely united with the language of society and combined with men's everyday concepts that they become illuminating to commonsense, and now we wonder how one could have stumbled before on such a smooth road. But we do not consider the price it cost to smooth this climb through the wilderness.[298]

The confrontation with the difficulties that resulted from the demonstrative character of modern philosophy shows up throughout Mendelssohn's entire literary output. Very telling is the form in which it is treated by him at first, in the letters *On the Sentiments*.[299] The clear and distinct knowledge of modern metaphysics had rehabilitated the this-worldly, the body, the senses, the delights of the senses; now the noblest of these delights, the enjoyment of beauty, i.e., of sensory perfection, became a rival authority over° against the longing for clear and distinct concepts: isn't the "sense"[300] or "feeling" of beauty, an essentially indistinct representation, destroyed if it is severed from reason? and doesn't the earthly happiness of man, which the supremely benevolent Creator according to the doctrine of that metaphysics did not want to deny him, depend precisely on this feeling? The letters *On the Sentiments* rebut this objection by accepting the peculiarity of the "feeling" of beauty, its proper[301] right over° against clear and distinct repre-

---

298. *Jerusalem* 106 [cf. Ark 36]. {LS}
299. Mendelssohn's *Über die Empfindungen* contains fifteen chapters, each in the literary form of a letter. Originally published anonymously as a separate treatise (1755), it was subsequently included in Mendelssohn's *Philosophische Schriften* (1st ed. 1761, JA I 41–123; 2nd ed. 1771, JA I 233–334, Dah 7–95). In his preface to it and elsewhere, Mendelssohn refers to it as "*die Briefe 'Über die Empfindungen'* [the letters *On the Sentiments*]."
   The word *Empfindung* occurs frequently in IMH. Except where noted otherwise, it is always either "sensation" or "feeling"—though "feeling" in LS's next few sentences is *Gefühl*. (Apart from Mendelssohn's book title, "sentiment" is always *Gesinnung*.) *Empfindlichkeit* is either "sensitivity" or "sensuality," and *empfindlich* is usually "sensitive," though at IPM xix and IMH xxv (in the quotation from Mendelssohn), above, and in the next sentence, below, it is "sensuous"; at IMH xxix, above, it is "stinging," etc.; and at IGC cii it is "sensory."
300. Ger.: *Empfindung*. See the previous note. Cf. IPM xviiin25.
301. Or: peculiar. The German here is *eigentümliches*. "Peculiarity" earlier in the sentence is *Eigentümlichkeit*.

sentation. Implicit in this acceptance was that, whereas reason is the authoritative faculty in the realm of the theoretical and the moral, {LXV} reason is subject to another authority in the realm of the beautiful; this other authority is "taste."[302] It is in "taste," therefore—and self-evidently not in "belief," but also not really in "feeling" and also not yet in "sound commonsense"—that Mendelssohn initially sees reason's needed complement; in this original choice of his, the essence of the "civilized,"[303] pre-Rousseauian eighteenth century comes to sight. The difficulties that stood in the way of demonstrative philosophy in the realm of beauty, however, were not the most pressing by far. Mendelssohn was at once forced to note corresponding difficulties with respect to ethics. Ethics too had been transformed into a demonstrative discipline. Precisely its demonstrative character distinguished modern from ancient ethics, whose greatest merit consisted in ethical sayings and graphic description of character.[304] As for demonstrative ethics, Mendelssohn in the *Treatise on Evidence* now had to admit that "the proofs in this science can be far less illuminating, less perspicuous, than even those in the first principles of metaphysics or natural theology."[305] That is why, in the application of the principles, "conscience and a good sense for the truth (*bon sens*)"[306]—i.e., skills in correctly distinguishing good from evil or rather true from false through indistinct consequences[307]—"take the place of reason in most situations." Concerning these skills, one reads further—and here Mendelssohn's orientation by "taste" betrays itself again—that it is "in its area what taste is in the domain of the beautiful and the ugly."[308] In the *Treatise on Evidence*, however, doubt is directed {LXVI} not merely against the adequacy of demonstrative ethics, but even against the ade-

302. "Verwandtschaft des Schönens und Gutes" [Kinship of the Beautiful and Good], JA II 183.4–8. Cf. [Mendelssohn to Lessing, first half of December 1756,] JA XI 84.24–37. {LS}
303. For this term, see Mendelssohn's remark concerning Rousseau that LS quotes at IEL XXI. Cf. also PPH 126–27, HCR 111.
304. Variant Readings to JA I 419.21–420.6; *Evidenz* 315.34–36 [Dah 295] and *passim*. Pride in this progress, together with the incapacity inseparable from it to understand the character of the Aristotelian ethics that Maimonides had adopted, shows up clearly in [Mendelssohn's letter to (Rabbi) Jacob Emden of October 26, 1773,] JA XVI 178–79 [Got 32ff.; for a German translation of Mendelssohn's original Hebrew, see JA XX.2 262ff.] {LS}
305. *Evidenz* 322.12–15 [cf. Dah 301]. {LS}
306. Fr.: sound commonsense. Cf. IP xxvn75, IMH LXVIII.
307. Cf. ITE LI–LII.
308. *Evidenz* 325.6–15 [Dah 303]. In the *Philosophische Schriften*—JA I 417–24 [Dah 162–68]—doubt about the evidentness of demonstrative ethics had been expressed, to say the least, much less decisively. Cf. also [Mendelssohn's letter to Friedrich Gabriel Resewitz of May 15, 1756,] JA XI 45.37ff., as well as the annotation to JA XI 181.20. {LS}
There is no editorial annotation to JA XI 181.20. Conceivably, this should read JA II 181.29ff. For this Mendelssohnian passage, and Fritz Bamberger's editorial annotation *ad. loc.* (JA II 404), see appendix 2, supplement to IMH LXVn308.

quacy of the central demonstrative discipline, metaphysics itself, as well. The attempt of Wolff and his school to give metaphysics the evidentness of mathematical proofs had failed: would he[309] have "been able to find such a welter of contradiction" otherwise?[310] The transitoriness of all systems—for demonstrative philosophy necessarily took on the form of a system, the system of an I that, like Leibniz, could speak of *"mon système"*[311]—seemed to suggest "that the sense[312] of beauty and order, or taste, is far more steadfast and trustworthy than reason or conviction about philosophical truths."[313] Mendelssohn coped with the predicament by granting to demonstrative philosophy the certainty, of course, but not the perspicuity of mathematics. He went beyond this in assigning to metaphysics the task of defending against "hairsplitting doubts" the knowledge available to and trustworthy for man independently of metaphysics.[314] In just that way, he took the first step in the direction toward the philosophy of sound commonsense, from which he was admittedly far removed in the *Treatise on Evidence*; in this writing, he speaks of the (relative) priority of sound commonsense over reason only in the discussion of the evidentness of ethics. The quarrel over his Judaism, from which there ensued initially the writings against Lavater and Bonnet,[315] and then and above all *Jerusalem*,[316] became of decisive significance for his coming closer to the philosophy of sound commonsense. Forced to defend his Judaism and his Rationalism at the same time, he had to present Judaism as a merely rational religion. But the Bible's doctrine, at any rate, is not demonstrative. He could not, in keeping with his modern presuppositions, follow the course of Maimonides, who had attributed to the Prophets an intellectual insight superior to demonstration.[317] The vindi-

---

309. I.e., Mendelssohn. For the fuller excerpt from which the following quotation has been taken (and adapted), see ITE XLVIII.

310. *Evidenz* 271.3–12 [cf. Dah 255]. {LS}

311. Fr.: "my system." See Leibniz, *Théodicée*, preface, toward the end (Ger VI 40–45 *passim*; Hug 64–69 *passim*).

312. See IMH LXIVn299, above.

313. *Evidenz* 269.2–21 [cf. Dah 253]. {LS}

314. Cf. ITE LII–LIII. {LS}

315. See IMH LIVn239, above.

316. Cf. Altmann, MMBS 421–552.

317. Cf. his elaboration of the sixth and seventh of Maimonides' Articles of Faith; see Kayserling, *Moses Mendelssohn* (Leipzig, 1862), 567–68 {LS}

Mendelssohn's elaborations read (*loc. cit.*): "6. I know as true and certain that God confers the gift of prophecy on a few human beings who are pleasing to him, i.e., at times makes known to them through divine bestowal things that are unknown to other human beings, and makes known and transmits his divine will and his commandments through them. 7. I know as true and certain that Moses our teacher has been the greatest of all prophets that have ever been and will be, and that no mortal is to be supposed equal to him in the gift of prophesying."

cation of Judaism was possible for him only in such a manner as to limit considerably the legitimacy and significance of demonstration. That is why it says in *Jerusalem* about the {LXVII} scientific[318] knowledge of God that it

> [is] not necessary or useful . . . all the time. Very often, as the Psalmist says, the babbling of children and infants is enough to confound the enemy.[319]

The connection between his increased inclination toward the philosophy of sound commonsense and his defense of Judaism becomes fully distinct in the following statement in *To the Friends of Lessing*: Judaism

> consists uniquely and only in revealed laws of divine worship, and presupposes natural and rational conviction about the truths of religion, without which no divine lawgiving can take place. When I talk of rational conviction, however, and I want to presuppose this as undoubted in Judaism, the talk is not about metaphysical argumentation as we are used to carrying it on in books, not about pedantic demonstrations that all meet the test of the subtlest skepticism, but about the claims and judgments of a simple, sound commonsense, which looks things right in the eye and reflects calmly.[320]

During the course of his life, Mendelssohn therefore yielded more and more to the critique of the adequacy of demonstrative philosophy.[321] The final stage of this development, which was no doubt further accelerated by Jacobi's communication about Lessing's falling away from Leibniz-Wolffian metaphysics, is the doctrine of *Morning Hours* and *To the Friends of Lessing* on the relationship of speculation and sound commonsense.[322]

Even now, Mendelssohn still does not join the philosophy of sound

---

For the Maimonidean original—*Commentary on the Mishnah, Tractate Sanhedrin*, Ch. 10, introduction—see *Mishnah im perush Rabbenu Moshe ben Maimon, makor v'targum: Seder Nezikin*, ed. and trans. Yosef Kafih (Jerusalem: Mossad HaRav Kook, 5725/1964), 212–13; Isadore Twersky, ed., *A Maimonides Reader* (New York: Behrman House, 1972), 418ff. Cf. also LSGS II 106–7; PL 117–18.

318. Ger.: *wissenschaftlichen*. I.e., rational or demonstrative.
319. *Jerusalem* 161 [cf. Ark 95; cf. Got 85]. — Cf. also the critique of civilization intimately connected with the critique of demonstration that characterizes the whole second part of *Jerusalem*, i.e., the defense of Judaism. {LS}
320. *Freunde* 197.10–21 [Scholz 306–7; cf. Val 137–37; cf. Got 162]. {LS}
321. He says in his letter to Hennings of November 5, 1785 [JA XIII 323]: "I too am now no longer in favor of it"—*sc.*, of "scholastic brooding"—"though formerly I was even extraordinarily fond of it." {LS}
322. Cf. also IMH XXXVII, above. {LS}

commonsense unreservedly. In his controversy with Basedow,[323] he points emphatically to the necessity of speculation, of demonstration. Even now, he still attempts to mediate between the claims of speculation and those of sound commonsense. In this, {LXVIII} and even so in the mode in which he attempts to determine the relationship of speculation and sound commonsense more exactly by reducing both to a common origin, he follows Tetens, who in the Eighth Essay of the First Part of his *Philosophical Essays*[324] had dealt with "the relationship of the higher cognitions of discursive reason to the cognitions of ordinary commonsense." But precisely the comparison with Tetens shows how close Mendelssohn now is to the philosophy of sound commonsense. Originally he had judged the relationship of speculation and sound commonsense as follows:

> I know how easily[325] consequences can be drawn from any philosophical system that declares the thing that is called sound commonsense, or *bon sens*, to be absurd. How far would one get in the demonstrative sciences if one had wanted to be left merely to the guidance of *bon sens*, which distinguishes objects by a very blinding light?[326]

Tetens's opinion is:

> One must investigate them both, the judgments of commonsense and the judgments of reason. Of these, the one type is in general no more and no less suspect than the other, even if in special cases the one can have more presumption in its favor than the other.[327]

---

323. *Morgenstunden* 69.14–72.37 [DaDy 50–52]. {LS}
Johann Bernhard Basedow (1723–90), "well known as a liberal-minded author in the field of theology and a tireless laborer for the improvement of the quality of German education and instruction" (*Allgemeine Deutsche Biographie*). For the personal relations of Mendelssohn and Basedow, refer to their correspondence (from 1768–69) and the annotations to it in our edition. {From LS's editorial annotation to *Morgenstunden* 69.14–23 (JA III.2 286)}

For the pertinent correspondence, see JA XII.1 157–58 and 159–60, with 307 and 308. By "our edition," LS is referring instead to the original manuscript of JA XII, edited by Bruno Strauss, which had been ready for publication in 1936. As has been related above (see IMH XXXVIIIn150), Bruno Strauss's manuscript never came into print and was subsequently lost during his escape from Nazi-occupied Europe. What became JA XII.1 and 2 was later edited from scratch by Alexander Altmann.

For the remainder of LS's editorial annotation to *Morgenstunden* 69.14–25, see IMH LXXVIIn373, below.

324. Cf. IMH LXn272, above.

325. Ger.: *leicht*. This word is missing from the text of JA III.2 LXVIII, but present in that of JA V.1 77, which LS cites in the following note.

326. *Literaturbrief* #54, September 13, 1759 [JA V.1 77]. Cf. also "Verwandtschaft des Schönens und Gutes," JA II 185.24–25. {LS}

327. *Loc. cit.*, I, 585. {LS}

In *Morning Hours*, on the other hand, one reads:

> Whenever reason lags far behind sound commonsense, or even deviates from it and is in danger of getting on the wrong track, the philosopher[328] himself will not trust his reason and contradict sound commonsense, but will prefer to impose a silence on it when the effort to lead it back to the beaten path and reach sound commonsense does not succeed for him. Let us attempt, therefore, to help reason out as far as we ... can.[329]

The relationship of reason and sound commonsense is here seen to be determined in exactly the same way as the relationship of reason and belief had been determined earlier: reason, being insufficient, has to be subjugated to sound commonsense, without whose guidance it necessarily errs; the sound commonsense of the simple-minded is the authority for {LXIX} reason. Admittedly, all the shortcomings that had brought belief into discredit among many are missing from sound commonsense: whereas belief is exclusionary, otherworldly, and humbling, sound commonsense is a bond of union among all men, is partial to this world and its joys, and is—sufficient: "The man whose reason has not yet been corrupted by sophistry need only follow his plain sense, and his happiness stands firm."[330] The blissful truth is neither an undeserved, paradoxical gift from above, nor the result of strenuous investigation, but a matter of sheer self-evidence. How self-evident it is for Mendelssohn is shown by his remark: "I cannot believe that any one of these absurdities [*sc.*, Idealism, Egoism, Skepticism, and Spinozism] has ever been asserted in earnest."[331] The schools of thought that deviate from sound commonsense, that rest on "over-refined speculation," are therefore completely harmless:

> On the long road that one has to take from this over-refined speculation to practical matters of religion and ethics, there are so many resting places where one can turn again from the side-road onto the open highway.[332]

---

328. Ger.: *Weltweise*. See IPM xviiin23.
329. *Morgenstunden* 79.38–80.9 [DaDy 57]. Cf. also *Morgenstunden* 82.15–22 [cf. DaDy 59–60; cf. Got 143], as well as the letter to Winkopp of March 24, 1780 [JA XII.2 184–85]. {LS}
330. *Freunde* 199.4–6 [Scholz 309; cf. Val 139; cf. Got 164]. {LS}
331. *Morgenstunden* 79.29–30 [cf. DaDy 57]. {LS}
332. *Morgenstunden* 136.27–31 [Scholz 43–44; cf. Val 77; cf. DaDy 99]. {LS}

That is why Mendelssohn is very inclined "to explain all the quarrels of the philosophical schools as mere quarrels about words, or at least to derive them originally from quarrels about words."[333] Just this "maxim," this "artifice" that "the subtle man, now almost reduced to half, [makes use of] in his *Morning Hours*, where he does not want to go on to the solution to the difficulties," Kant[334] thought worthy of a critique that begins with the contention "that in matters that have been quarreled over for quite some time, especially in philosophy, at bottom it has never been a quarrel about words, but always a genuine quarrel about things."[335] {LXX}

The moment the theistic metaphysics of Leibnizian provenance had to seek refuge in the neutral island of sound commonsense, the metaphysics of Spinoza, whether acosmic or atheistic, made its incursion into the realm of speculation. By satisfying important concerns of the revelation-believing tradition, Leibnizian metaphysics had contributed considerably to the shaking of this tradition: the presuppositions that justified the proof for the creation of the world and special providence, on the one hand, were the same as those that justified Determinism and Optimism, on the other. It had thus made minds receptive to a view that was yet much further removed from revealed religion, indeed that even contradicted it openly, Spinoza's view.[336] That is why the reception of Spinozism in the last decades of the eighteenth century signifies, to begin with, a considerable progress of unbelief. Toward the start of the century, Leibniz with the support of his metaphysics, which was putatively in harmony with revealed religion throughout, had attacked Bayle's thesis that there was no equivalence between belief in revelation and a theistic philosophy that contradicted revelation on every important point;[337] toward the end of the century, Mendelssohn had to defend Leibniz's metaphysics against Jacobi's thesis that there was no equivalence between belief, which was naturally theistic, and demonstration, which necessarily led to atheism. Whereas back then the belief in revelation, which was still as good as unshaken in the general awareness, had to confront natural theology, which was asserting its suf-

---

333. *Morgenstunden* 104.30–33 [cf. DaDy 75; cf. Got 144]. {LS}
334. "Einige Bemerken zu Ludwig Heinrich Jakobs Prüfung der Mendelssohn'schen Morgenstunden" [A Few Remarks on Ludwig Heinrich Jakob's Examination of the Mendelssohnian *Morning Hours*; IKW IV 481–85; the remark quoted is on 482]. {LS}
335. About the application of the maxim cited in Mendelssohn's *Über Freiheit und Notwendigkeit* [On Freedom and Necessity]—JA III.1 343–50—Kant, *loc. cit.*, judges that it would be "as if he wanted to stop a tidal wave with a wisp of straw." {LS}
336. Concerning Spinoza's Optimism, cf. Pope! 47.5–7 [Gal 46]. {LS}
337. Cf. SCR 8, with 271n12, or LAM 232, with 257n12.

ficiency, now the discussion is in general no longer about revelation (in the strict sense of the word). Whereas back then, judged from the standpoint of the tradition, Rationalist theism was the most serious enemy, now a far more dangerous enemy appeared on the battlefield in Spinozism. Whereas back then the possibility of rational knowledge of the existence of God from creation, from nature, was recognized by both sides,[338] now this possibility is contested. At the same time, the reception of Spinozism signifies the reawakening of speculative seriousness after decades of the dominance of materialistic positivism, {LXXI} psychology, popularizing, and the philosophy of feeling. Even Mendelssohn saw that although Spinozism could not be reconciled with sound commonsense, pure reason would have to make the effort.[339] But the speculative arguments against Spinozism had not yet been united "with men's everyday concepts."[340] For this reason, it was already a far more dangerous opponent for Mendelssohn's position than, for instance, French materialism. So it is not surprising that the confrontation with Spinoza forced him into a more radical meditation on his own presuppositions than any other confrontation carried out by him. Admittedly, the confrontation with Spinozism as such did not exert this pressure: the arguments he brings forward in the thirteenth chapter of *Morning Hours* against authentic Spinozism are more or less commonplaces of the Spinoza critique handed down to him, especially Wolff's.[341] The critique of Spinozism that is peculiar to him, he presented chiefly in the form of a critique of Lessing's "purified" Spinozism. This circumstance again corroborates what the History of Its Emergence[342] shows step by step, that the real motive for Mendelssohn's conception and working out of *Morning Hours* was his interest in Lessing: only on the basis of his interest in Lessing did he let himself move to the critique of Spinozism. It is in the critique of Lessing's "purified" Spinozism, whose essential argument is admittedly applicable also to authentic Spinozism, and not in the explicit critique of authentic Spinozism that Mendelssohn comes closer to the knowledge of his own presupposition[343] than in any other of his reflections.

338. Cf. Leibniz, *Théodicée* §146 [Ger VI 196–97; Hug 214–15]. {LS}
339. To [J. A. H. and] Elise Reimarus, April 19, 1784. {LS}
This letter is now missing. See JA XIII 192, 398. Cf. IMH XXXVIIn150, above.
340. See IMH LXIVn292, above.
341. See LS's editorial annotations to *Morgenstunden* 104.5–14, 104.20–21, 104.23–26, 105.31–34, 106.28–107.28, 110.9–111.3, and 111.25–38 (JA III.2 294ff. *passim*).
342. I.e., part I of IMH. See IMH XIIn2, above.
343. Ger.: *Voraussetzung* (singular). Perhaps, however, it should read *Voraussetzungen* (plural), in agreement with "presuppositions" earlier in this paragraph. Cf., on the other hand, IMH LXXIII–LXXV, below.

The thesis of "purified" Spinozism amounts to saying "that we ourselves and the world that surrounds us are [nothing] more than mere thoughts of God."³⁴⁴ The justification of this thesis runs that no criterion can be given that lets one decide between God's thought of a thing and the thing itself in question. Mendelssohn asserts on the contrary that there "[are] undeceptive signs that distinguish me as an object from me as a representation in God; distinguish° in the most undeceptive way me as an archetype from me as an image in the divine understanding." This {LXXII} undeceptive criterion Mendelssohn finds in the "awareness of myself, combined with complete ignorance of everything that does not accordingly fall within the circle of my thought." The awareness of myself as a limited, finite being "is the most telling proof of my substantiality outside God, my archetypal existence."³⁴⁵ For since God is the most perfect being of all, for that reason "the thought in God . . . which has a limited being for its object cannot, in [God], arrive at any individual, as it were torn-off awareness,"³⁴⁶ and such an "individual," "discrete"³⁴⁷ awareness of myself is the most evident phenomenon. The motive of this critique appears at first glance to be the interest in insisting on God's transcendence, the infinite distance that separates the utterly perfect Creator from finite creatures, against the "mystics," who "are not satisfied with God's transcendence."³⁴⁸ But were Mendelssohn in fact guided by a genuinely theological interest, it could not occur to him to describe finite creatures repeatedly³⁴⁹ as "archetypes" and God's thoughts of them as "images," and thereby assert that God in his knowing is independent of the finite creatures that he knows. Let it not be said that this manner of expression is a mere *lapsus calami*.³⁵⁰ For even assuming that this were the case, then by the very same token it would be proved that Mendelssohn is not guided by any genuinely theological interest: just because he can commit this *lapsus calami*, because he can unreflectively make the transition from

---

344. *Morgenstunden* 116.7ff. [Scholz 18; cf. DaDy 84; cf. Got 147]. {LS}
345. *Morgenstunden* 117.36–118.16 [Scholz 20–21; cf. DaDy 85–86; cf. Got 149]. {LS}
346. *Morgenstunden* 120.21–34 [Scholz 23–24; cf. DaDy 87]. {LS}
347. *Morgenstunden* 123.2–3. [Scholz 27; cf. DaDy 89]. {LS}
348. Hermann Cohen ["Spinoza über Staat und Religion, Judentum und Christentum," in Cohen, *Jüdische Schriften*, ed. Bruno Strauss, intro. Franz Rosenzweig (3 vols.; Berlin: C. A. Schwetzschke & Sohn, 1924), III, 371; reprinted in Cohen, *Werke*, ed. Helmut Holzhey (Hildesheim and New York: Georg Olms, 1997–), vol. 16: *Kleinere Schriften*, ed. Hartwig Wiedebach (6 vols.), V, 425]. Cf. LSGS I 264; SCR 208.] {LS}
349. *Morgenstunden* 117.8ff. and 20ff.; 117.27ff. and 38ff.; 118.4 [Scholz 19–20 *passim*; cf. DaDy 85 *passim* ("prototype"); Got 148]. {LS}
350. Lat.: slip of the pen.

the human knowing whose representations are the "images" of things qua "archetypes" to the divine knowing whose representations are the "archetypes" of all created things qua "images." That is why one cannot rest content with the interpretation that Mendelssohn's paradoxical "switching" of the "concepts of archetype and image" proves how "deeply ... he [probes] into the actuality of things outside of God."[351] Against this interpretation, it must first be recalled that, to Mendelssohn, his critique of "purified" Spinozism comes down not so much to the actuality of things outside God, as to the actuality of man qua I outside God.[352] {LXXIII} And second and above all, Mendelssohn asserts not merely the I's being outside God, its substantiality, but also the I's being archetypal. What he therefore wants to secure over against Spinozism, "purified" as well as authentic,[353] more exactly, what for him is the decisive objection against Spinozism because for him it is a self-evident presupposition, is not so much God's transcendence as it is the archetypal substantiality of the I as a "closed-off" awareness, in the sense that even God's thoughts of the finite I are simply images of this archetype.[354] That is why the least that must be said is that a certain equality of God and man, self-evident as it is for Mendelssohn, is for him the authoritative presupposition.

The equality presupposed by him may be determined more exactly. It is a certain equal entitlement,[355] a certain equality of rights, on the part of God's rational demands on the one hand and man's on the other. Were he not to presuppose such an equality, he could not say in *Jerusalem* that God's "rights can never come into quarrel and confusion with ours."[356] He presupposes that each man possesses a definite natural sphere of right, in which no other man, nor likewise God, may or can interfere. He understands God's lordship over men on the analogy of a constitutional monarchy. Man is,

---

351. Gottfried Fittbogen, *Die Religion Lessings* (Leipzig: Mayer & Müller, 1923), 261n. {LS}

352. Cf. *Morgenstunden* 117.36–118.4, 119.14–18, 119.25–33, 123.6 to the end of the Fourteenth Chapter [Scholz 20, 22 *passim*, 27–29; Val 65 (for LS's last citation only); DaDy 85, 86, 87, 89–90; Got 149 (for LS's first citation only)]. {LS}

353. Cf. *Morgenstunden* 121.7ff. [Scholz 24–25; DaDy 88ff.]. {LS}

354. Cf. also the original determination of the difference between Spinozism and theism in *Morgenstunden* 105 and 106–7 [Scholz 4–7; DaDy 76–77]; the two doctrines differ originally not with respect to the being and attributes of God, but with respect to the substantiality of the finite thing, of the I. {LS}

355. More or less lit.: a certain equality under the law. LS's German expression is *eine gewisse Rechtsgleichheit*. The nearly identical German expression immediately following, which I have translated "a certain equality of rights," is *eine gewisse Gleichheit der Rechte*.

356. *Jerusalem* 127 [cf. Ark 59]. {LS}

as he likes to say in imitation of Leibniz,[357] a "citizen in God's State."[358] He means by this just what Leibniz does: far from its being the case that only a small part of the human race, a "remnant," belongs to the City of God, all men on the contrary have the unalienable quality, the unalienable rights of citizens in God's State, and they have these rights fundamentally, even over against the Chief of this State. Nothing in this {LXXIV} fundamental view is altered by the limitation that, in consideration of the wise benevolence of God, there is not and cannot be any assertion of these rights over against God.[359]

When Mendelssohn in *Morning Hours* ascribes to the finite I an archetypal substantiality, therefore, it is hardly a matter of an insignificant faux pas, nor in any case a well-thought-out statement, but an involuntary disguising of his hidden presupposition. Understandably, this presupposition does not come out in, say, his controversy with Christianity. For, for him, this controversy mainly comes down to securing natural religion against Christian dogma, or rather securing the sufficiency of reason against belief in the revelation of eternal truths. As for what concerns the content of natural religion itself, however, Mendelssohn recognizes God's transcendence (and His creation of the world as well as His providence) on the one hand and a future life on the other, just as his opponent does. Thus one gains

---

357. *Ep. ad Wagnerum de re activa* §5 [Ger VII 531], *Système nouveau* §8 [Ger IV 479–80; Wie 110 or ArGa 145 or FrWo 147]. {LS}

358. *Phädon* 112–13 [cf. Cul 176; cf. Nob 134], *Sache Gottes* §60 line 20, MMGS V 309 and 397 [= JA VI.1 22.5–6 and 55.26]. {LS}

359. Cf. also IGC, as well as the Variant Reading to *Morgenstunden* 122.3–13 [JA III.2 271]. {LS}

Morgenstunden 122.3–13 [Scholz 26; cf. DaDy 88–89] reads:

... if all God's thoughts have what is required of existence merely because they are God's thoughts, then none of them can actually exist in fact. Yet in the end so much is undeniable about existence: that the existence of a certain determination excludes the opposite determination; that the present changes of things cannot be equally as actual as the past and future changes of them; that I who am now sitting and speaking, am no longer lying down and sleeping. It may always be that, according to Spinoza (as, at bottom, according to the truth), the sequence of various states-of-affairs takes place only in me as a limited being....

The variant reading (JA III.2 271 *ad loc.*) consists of a handwritten notation crossed out in the right-hand margin of a manuscript containing a rough draft of the last third of the Fourteenth Lecture of *Morning Hours*. Had Mendelssohn adopted the variant reading, the foregoing sentences would instead read:

... if all God's thoughts have what is required of existence merely because they had an equal right to be actual, then none of them could ever become actual. It may always be that, according to Spinoza (just as according to the truth), the sequence of various states-of-affairs takes place only in me as a limited being....

See also JA III.2 263 (LS's editorial remark concerning Manuscript No. 2).

the impression that Mendelssohn's essential difference from Christianity, and in a certain manner also from the Jewish tradition, consists not in the content of the natural religion recognized by him, but simply in his attitude toward revelation (eternal truths). To be satisfied with this impression, however, is to misunderstand the revolution that had been accomplished within natural religion itself in the age of the Enlightenment. To be sure, the theological expression of this upheaval is the assertion of the absolute priority of God's undemanding benevolence over His glory and retributive justice, which is everywhere so distinctly visible that it could not escape any historian; but precisely whether that theological expression renders appropriately the real sense of the fundamental upheaval is questionable. What shows up in Mendelssohn's confrontation with Spinozism is that what motivates him definitively[360] is no routine theological interest, but interest in the substantiality, the discreteness, the autonomy, the individual right of the I: that is why the undemanding benevolence of God is privileged, since only it is compatible with the demands of the autonomous[361] I, {LXXV} since only it can "never come into quarrel and confusion"[362] with this demand. That it was precisely Spinozism that provoked the disclosure of this presupposition, however, is ultimately explained in that Spinozism—being akin here to the "emanation system of the ancients" as well as to "kabbalistic *Schwärmerey*"[363]—called the substantiality of the individual decidedly into question.

What we have been saying about Mendelssohn's critique of Spinozism is corroborated within certain limits by the comparison of this critique with the new proof of God (in the Sixteenth Lecture) that accompanies it. The proof is introduced as the "Attempt at a New Proof for God's Existence from the Incompleteness of Self-Cognition." The same evident phenomenon, therefore, the incompleteness of self-knowledge with respect to which Mendelssohn first proved man's substantiality as an I outside God,[364] is now to serve as the foundation for a new proof of God. Nevertheless, as one considers this proof more closely, one notes that for Mendelssohn it comes down to the peculiarity of self-knowledge for external, methodological reasons exclusively: the self is privileged in general simply as the

---

360. Lit.: what determines him authoritatively.
361. Lit.: self-standing. LS's German here is *selbständigen*. Cf. also IMH XLn166. For Mendelssohn's use of this term, see, e.g., IGC CIX. Earlier in LS's sentence, "autonomy" is *Eigenständigkeit* (more or less literally, "standing on one's own").
362. See IMH LXXIIIn356, above.
363. See note on *Schwärmerey* at IMH LXIV, above.
364. Cf. esp. *Morgenstunden* 118.6–10 and 123.7–8 [Scholz 20 and 27; DaDy 85–86]. {LS}

most indubitable case of an actual thing. Thus is explained Mendelssohn's passing instinctively from the incompleteness of our knowledge of our soul to the incompleteness of our knowledge of our body[365] or, for that matter, "of a single mote in a sunbeam,"[366] and, above all, in the summary of the "chain of argument" at the end of the proof, his speaking only about "everything actual" and not about the I.[367] And in the proof itself, the discussion is, on the whole, more about actual things in general than about the I in particular—in marked contradistinction to the critique and reinterpretation of "purified" Spinozism, in which "I, man" is the persistently recurring password.[368] The new proof of God's existence does not come down decisively to the I as such. The I, on the other hand, is the decisive objection against Spinozism.

Spinozism stood further from Mendelssohn than did the view of the man who had pressed the confrontation with Spinozism onto him. The conviction that Jacobi was asserting in opposition to Spinozism, the belief in "an intelligent personal cause {LXXVI} of the world" and in "final causes,"[369] was also Mendelssohn's belief. And just as Mendelssohn "turns back from the side road [of over-refined speculation] onto the open highway [of sound commonsense]" to vindicate this belief,[370] Jacobi goes back from "the wilderness of speculation . . . to the smooth and secure path of belief."[371] Mendelssohn thoroughly recognized this kinship: he identified the "*salto mortale*" out of speculation with the orienting of speculation to sound commonsense.[372] In fact, both Jacobi's "*salto mortale*" and Mendelssohn's retreat to sound commonsense are, in an equal manner, the expression of (1) the knowledge that modern metaphysics' attempts at justifying belief's concept of God by means of unbelieving speculation have collapsed, and (2) the identification of metaphysics in general with modern metaphysics. In the controversy between Mendelssohn and Jacobi, the tone is naturally set more by the difference than by the agreement of "belief" and "sound commonsense." The difference consists in that reason and sound commonsense are "at bottom the same," that their opposition is accidental, whereas reason and belief, as Jacobi at this time understands "reason," are essen-

---

365. *Morgenstunden* 141.37–142.10 [DaDy 103]. {LS}
366. *Morgenstunden* 142.34–143.3 [cf. DaDy 104]. {LS}
367. *Morgenstunden* 147.6ff. [DaDy 107] {LS}
368. See *Morgenstunden* 123–24 [Scholz 27–28; cf. Val 65; cf. DaDy 89; cf. Got 149–50].
369. Scholz 80–81 [cf. Gio 189; cf. Val 88; cf. Nis 245–46; cf. Got 133–34]. {LS}
370. *Morgenstunden* 136.26–30 [Scholz 44; cf. Val 77; cf. DaDy 99]. {LS}
371. *Freunde* 194.8–9 [Scholz 302; cf. Val 135; cf. Got 159]. {LS}
372. *Freunde* 202.35ff. [found in Scholz 114–15; cf. Val 111] Cf. above, IMH XXII–XXIII. {LS}

tially opposed to each other: reason is proud and belief is humble. Mendelssohn's real objection against Jacobi's philosophy of belief—in *Morning Hours*, where he did not want to mention his correspondence with Jacobi, he presents this objection in the form of a critique of Basedow's principle of the "obligation to believe"[373]—amounts to saying that it would make "cognition without investigation" into a foundation and, in that way, promote "prejudice and blind belief," "superstition and *Schwärmerey*."[374] In actuality, belief as Jacobi understands it is much less of a danger to speculation than sound commonsense is. For sound commonsense lets the blissful conviction appear as sheer self-evidence, whereas the assumption that this conviction is believed implies, or at least can imply, knowledge of ignorance and, with that, an impulse to speculation. Admittedly, Jacobi's discussion of {LXXVII} "belief," especially vis-à-vis Mendelssohn, was easily exposed to misunderstandings. The misleading manner of expression had its ultimate ground in Jacobi's unclarity in principle about the implications of his critique of Spinoza. He objects to Spinoza: "If there are simply efficient causes and no final causes, then in the whole of nature the thinking faculty is merely the looking on,"[375] then I only think "what I do" while yet in truth "I do what I think."[376] The view of Spinoza's that he is combating, he formulates elsewhere as follows: "If we look on closely, we find that in all things action precedes reflection, *which is only the action in its° continuation*."[377] Just this insight, however, is the presupposition of Jacobi's critique of the Enlightenment. He objects to the Enlightenment: "Can living philosophy ever be anything other than history?"[378] And he determines this objection more closely by repeating, probably unreflectively, a turn of phrase of his Spinoza interpretation:

> just as every age has its own truth, the content of which is as the content of the experiences, just so it has its own living philosophy also, which presents the age's dominant way of acting *in its continuation*.[379]

---

373. *Morgenstunden* 69.14–72.25 [cf. DaDy 50–52]. {LS}
 On Basedow, see the first part of LS's editorial annotation to *Morgenstunden* 69.14–25 (JA III.2 286), in IMH LXVIIIn323, above. For the remainder of LS's editorial annotation (*ibid.*, 286–87), see appendix 2, supplement to IMH LXXVIIn373.
374. See note on *Schwärmerey* at IMH LXIV.
375. Ger.: *Zusehen*. Likewise as a verb in Jacobi's next full sentence. For this expression, cf. LS's remarks on Hobbes and Hegel in PPH 105–6 (LSGS III 124–25 in the German original).
376. Scholz 81 and 89 [cf. Gio 189, 193; cf. Val 89, 94; cf. Nis 246, 250; cf. Got 134, 135]. {LS}
377. Scholz 134 [cf. Gio 213]; the emphasis is Jacobi's. {LS}
378. Scholz 187 [cf. Gio 239]. {LS}
379. Scholz 188–89 [Gio 239]; emphasis Jacobi's. {LS}

Had he held fast to his Spinoza critique to the end, he would have not been able to appeal against the Enlightenment from[380] history, nor from belief as understood within the horizon of the concept of history, and so he would also have made Mendelssohn's misunderstanding impossible.

But what did Jacobi matter to Mendelssohn? What did Spinozism itself matter to him? The important thing for him was what Lessing had thought. The answer he could have given to this question thanks to his longstanding intimate acquaintance with Lessing is not able° to be gathered from *Morning Hours* without further ado. Even the answer that is explicitly given in *Morning Hours* is not as straightforward as is usually assumed. The dialogical form in which this book is at least partly composed allowed him to give two answers in it. Initially (in the Fourteenth Lecture) he himself asserts, by putting the exposition and defense of "purified" Spinozism into Lessing's mouth, that Lessing was an adherent of "purified" Spinozism. Speaking against Mendelssohn, {LXXVIII} "Friend D." asserts (in the Fifteenth Lecture) that Lessing was a decided adherent of radical-Rationalist theism and consequently in no way a Spinozist. The two assertions are brought into harmony by the reflection that Lessing's "purified" Spinozism is distinguished from the "religion of reason" of the Enlightenment only by a subtlety "which has not the least influence on human actions and happiness," "which can never become practical,"[381] that "purified Spinozism . . . is quite compatible with everything that religion and ethics have of practical relevance°."[382] As for the response to the question about Lessing's opinions, however, it admittedly came down, as Mendelssohn very well knew, not at all to the practical dangerousness or innocuousness of these opinions in the first place, but entirely to the ever subtle difference between Lessing's opinions and "our system,"[383] i.e., the opinions of the theistic Enlightenment. The reconciliation of the two mutually contradictory assertions is therefore only apparent; it serves to let Lessing's heresy, already reduced to "purified" Spinozism, appear completely innocuous. The result of this is that M.'s assertion—let Mendelssohn as the speaker in the Fourteenth and Fifteenth Lectures be designated as M., to distinguish him from the author of *Morning Hours*—and D.'s assertion are distinguished fundamentally, even if the two assertions were not to contradict each other directly in every particu-

---

380. Lit.: to. Likewise in the next phrase.
381. *Morgenstunden* 133.2–6, 124.1–5 [Scholz 39, 28; cf. Val 73, 65; cf. DaDy 96, 90; cf. Got 152 (only)]; compare *Morgenstunden* 136.21–31 [Scholz 43–44; Val 76–77; DaDy 99]. {LS}
382. *Freunde* 188.19–21 [Scholz 295; cf. Val 130; cf. Got 155]. {LS}
383. *Morgenstunden* 123.37 [Scholz 28; Val 65; DaDy 90; Got 149]. {LS}

lar. That is why one will ask oneself initially which of these two opinions corresponds with Mendelssohn's own view. Or rather, one will consider this question entirely superfluous since M.'s assertion is self-evidently Mendelssohn's assertion. That this question must be asked, however, and, at the same time, that the answer to the general question apropos Mendelssohn's view about Lessing's beliefs cannot be gathered from *Morning Hours* without further ado, are recognized as soon as one has become clear about the structure and purpose of the discussion carried on in the Fourteenth and Fifteenth Lectures of *Morning Hours*. To this end, however, one must first answer the question: why does Mendelssohn in these Lectures make such conspicuous use of the dialogical form?[384] {LXXIX}

It is already a striking use of the dialogical form that "Friend D." enters exclusively in the Fifteenth Lecture and therefore is specifically introduced for the purpose of the discussion about Lessing's opinions. The young students of Mendelssohn with whom M. is conversing in the remaining Lectures were obviously unsuited for this purpose: Mendelssohn needed a mature man, an experienced, well-informed expert on all of Lessing's writings, an expert also on the background of the quarrel over the "Wolfenbüttel Fragments," and of course a personal friend of Lessing's,[385] as the antagonist for his dialogue about Lessing's opinions. A dialogue is a type of drama; a drama, as a poetic production, is an idealized portrayal of nature, in special cases an idealized portrayal of actual events; and art is cheerful, whereas life is serious. The dialogue between M. and D. is an idealized, "cheerful" portrayal of the actual, serious dialogue between Jacobi and Mendelssohn. Or, to describe the content somewhat differently, the dialogue between M. and D. is a simulated fight that represents the actual fight between Jacobi and Mendelssohn: the simulated fight that is being represented, which recapitulates from Mendelssohn's standpoint the actual fight in the most perfect form, is to prepare the public for the report about the actual fight that has preceded it, which is still unknown.

The structure of the fictional discussion in the Fourteenth and Fifteenth Lectures of *Morning Hours* follows by and large the course of the actual discussion between Jacobi and Mendelssohn. The fictional controversy begins with M.'s putting forth the assertion that Lessing was a "purified" Spino-

---

384. The distinction between D.'s and M.'s opinions is made noticeable yet again in *To the Friends of Lessing*, inasmuch as Lessing is characterized initially—187.8–10 [Scholz 293; Val 129]—as an adherent of the religion of reason, and afterward—188–89 [Scholz 294–96; cf. Val 130–31]—as an adherent of "purified" Spinozism. {LS}

385. *Morgenstunden* 130.24–25 and 132.7–10 [Scholz 36, 38; Val 71, 72; DaDy 95]. {LS}

zist, just as the actual controversy had begun with Jacobi's putting forth the assertion that Lessing was a "decided" Spinozist. From M.'s fictional disclosure—it is doubly fictional, since it rests on the explicit fiction that Lessing was {LXXX} present at the last Lecture—there follows the fictional protest of D., Lessing's friend, that Lessing could not possibly have been the "defender of such an erroneous, notorious system" as Spinozism, that indeed he must never be depicted as a defender of this system, just as from Jacobi's actual disclosure there had followed the actual protest of Mendelssohn, Lessing's friend, that the assertion that Lessing was a decided Spinozist is as absurd as the Berlin Academy's assuming that Pope was a metaphysician. In the fiction, M. answers D.'s incredulous protest with the documentary proof for Lessing's "purified" Spinozism by citing "Christianity of Reason," just as in actuality Jacobi had answered Mendelssohn's incredulous protest with the documentary proof for Lessing's decided Spinozism by submitting the record of his conversations with Lessing. And as in actuality Mendelssohn had ultimately rested content with Lessing's "purified" Spinozism, so in the fiction D. rests content with the "purified" Spinozism that is doubly purified, namely, further criticized and circumscribed by M.

What is the purpose of this fiction? Jacobi's report about Lessing's Spinozism was to have been communicated in the second part of *Morning Hours* in some form or other. The portrayal in the first part is to prepare for this communication, to make it inoffensive in advance. The preparation for the communication is accomplished in two ways. First, the substantive critique of Spinozism takes out of the hands of the enemies of radical-Rationalist theism the argument that they might have believed they could find in Lessing's defection from that theism: if Lessing had actually fallen into Spinozism, so much the worse for him, for he had chosen error instead of the proven truth. Second and above all, the portrayal of Lessing's Spinozism in the first part of *Morning Hours* serves to prepare for and blunt the communication of Jacobi's report by furnishing the evidence that Lessing's Spinozism was an altogether innocuous, "purified" Spinozism; in that way, Jacobi's report was brushed off in advance as an exaggeration, and Lessing's oral statements in Jacobi's presence as paradoxes. After all these preparations, it would be an easy thing {LXXXI} to communicate Jacobi's disclosure to the public. The public was to remain, and had to remain, spared the painful surprise that Jacobi had inflicted on Mendelssohn and the Reimarus siblings. But a certain painful surprise was unavoidable: the public, which was used to seeing in Lessing "the great, admired defender of theism and the religion of reason,"[386] now had to be made acquainted with the thought that Lessing's forte was not, as Friend D. opined,

> the same calm conviction that was so emblematic [of the Fragmentist], the same impartial distance from any skepticism, the same straightforwardness of sound commonsense in regard to the truths of the religion of reason,[387]

i.e., with the thought that Lessing somehow had something to do with Spinozism. Mendelssohn's task was to inflict this weakened shock on the public. That is, Mendelssohn had to adopt the role of discloser before the public that Jacobi had played in the narrow circle of friends; he played it as M. Now to be altogether sure that the public would react appropriately, however, it was best if one demonstrated to it *ad oculos*[388] how it had to react. One needed for this purpose a typical, an ideal representative of the public, i.e., of the community that revered Lessing as a theist, a friend of Lessing's if possible, to whom the disclosure would be made in the fiction: the reaction of the ideal representative of the public was the reaction being recommended as ideal for the public. The representative of the Lessing community—Friend D.—therefore had to play before the public the role that had fallen to Mendelssohn and the Reimarus siblings in the narrow circle of friends: he had to experience and withstand the weakened shock, just as Mendelssohn and the Reimarus siblings had experienced and withstood the original shock.

Mendelssohn's task was yet a considerably more delicate one than the previous remarks suggest. *Morning Hours* appeared only seven years after the quarrel that Lessing had had to carry on with the Lutheran Church on account of the so-called "Wolfenbüttel Fragments," published by him as the work of an Unnamed.[389] The author of the Fragments, {LXXXII} Hermann Samuel Reimarus, in his work had contested all revealed religion, and especially Christianity, from the standpoint of Rationalist theism with a decisiveness and detail which had been unheard of previously, at least in the German language. Lessing had carried on the quarrel over the Fragments explicitly as a Christian, if also no longer as an orthodox Lutheran. Men-

---

386. *Freunde* 187.9–10 [Scholz 293; cf. Val 129; cf. Got 153–54]. {LS}
387. *Morgenstunden* 126.4–11 [Scholz 30; cf. Val 67; DaDy 92]. {LS}
388. Lat.: visually.
389. See IMH xivn26, above.

delssohn now had to acquaint the public with the fact that Lessing was not merely no Christian, but not even a radical theist who denied revelation, a Reimarian. It was now, as is self-evident, impossible to maintain the fiction of Lessing's Christianity any longer. One recognizes Mendelssohn's circumspection in that he himself in *Morning Hours* does not give away this fiction unreservedly. He says: "With the defense of the Fragmentist, Lessing also *seems* to have adopted his entire sentiment."[390] The fiction would be given away completely only when Jacobi had published his conversations with Lessing; only in *To the Friends of Lessing* does Mendelssohn give it to be understood that perhaps Lessing in his early writings was never "a strict adherent of Athanasius" and that he had later become, or at least could have become, "an adherent of the Jew Baruch Spinoza."[391] If Lessing was therefore not to appear tainted with a double blemish—the denial of revelation and the denial of theism—then to begin with, in any case, Reimarianism now had to be portrayed in full public as the most unthreatening, most respectable thing in the world. That is why it must have mattered all the more to Mendelssohn that, as the children of the "Fragmentist," the Reimarus siblings be significantly[392] involved in the quarrel that had broken out between Jacobi and Mendelssohn over Lessing's beliefs. Obeying the urgent wish of the Reimarus siblings, Lessing had never given away the name of the author of the Fragments. He had simply "warned the Unnamed not to behave so mischievously and schoolboyishly that one would not have to be all too ashamed if it were ultimately discovered who he was."[393] Mendelssohn in *Morning Hours* therefore now makes a circumspect use of the weapon recommended by Lessing himself as the most highly effective one for the defense of Reimarianism, the disclosure of the identity {LXXXIII} of the author of the Fragments: he gives it to be understood that the Fragmentist had composed not merely the able critique of revelation, but also masterful portrayals of the religion of reason.[394] In that way Reimarianism, along with Lessing's defense of it, was legitimized as well as possible. The praise of the sublime religion and morals of *Nathan the Wise*[395] immediately alongside

---

390. *Morgenstunden* 125.35–126.2 [Scholz 30; cf. Val 66; xd. DaDy 91; cf. Got 151]. {LS; the emphasis is LS's}
391. *Freunde* 188.27–32 [Scholz 295; cf. Val 130; Got 155]. {LS}
392. Lit.: authoritatively.
393. "Ninth Anti-Goeze," toward the end [LM XIII 199]. {LS}
394. *Morgenstunden* 125.27–33 [Scholz 30; Val 66; DaDy 91; cf. Got 150–51]. — That Mendelssohn with this statement gives away the secret of the "Fragments" is recognized by Fittbogen, *Die Religion Lessings*, 241n1. {LS}
395. LM III 1–177 (trans. R. Dillon-Boylan, in LDW I 227–382).

the reference to Lessing's defense of the Fragments did something further: the most favorable light was reflected onto the publication and defense of the Fragments from *Nathan*. The glorification of the Fragments quarrel together with *Nathan*, the introduction of Reimarianism as a sentiment of unimpeachable propriety, had to be undertaken by the representative of the Lessing community, Friend D. In that way, Mendelssohn had the game under control: M. did not have to defend Lessing's *Spinozisterei*[396] over against orthodoxy, but over against Reimarianism—a task he could fulfill without difficulty with the help of an equivocation, by the proof that Lessing's "purified" Spinozism was distinguished from the Reimarian religion of reason only by a subtlety.

In light of the tactical considerations he had to take into account in *Morning Hours*, Mendelssohn's actual view of Lessing's opinions cannot be gotten from his portrayal of Lessing in this work. On the contrary, his actual view, the view he had formed on the basis of longstanding, intimate acquaintance with Lessing, is to be gotten rather from occasional, if always sparse, statements of his and then applied as a standard for the critique of the portrayal in *Morning Hours*. In his letter written to Lessing in May of 1763, he calls him a "brother in Leibniz."[397] He therefore knew until May of 1763, in any case, that he was at one with Lessing in professing Leibnizian philosophy. But since Lessing's writings composed after 1763, those published by him himself as well as those edited from his unpublished writings, betray a decided sympathy for Leibniz, to say the least, it will {LXXXIV} have to be assumed that in the presence of Mendelssohn the Leibnizian even after 1763 Lessing expressed himself about Leibniz no differently than before. Until autumn of 1783, he had no reason to see anything else in Lessing but a "brother in Leibniz." If one adds his expression for this characterization in the letter to Elise Reimarus of August 16, 1783, that Lessing was never in the position of seriously "understanding" himself "simply, without any closer determination, in terms of the system of any man,"[398] then one can summarize his original judgment about Lessing, unshaken as it was until autumn of 1783, as his having taken him to be an independent[399] Leibniz-

---

396. More or less lit.: Spinozist opinions. The term is understood by analogy with "*Schwärmerey*" (see IMH LXIVn297, above). LS here uses the twentieth-century spelling, in contrast to that of Mendelssohn's contemporaries, which he retains at IMH LXXXIX.
397. JA XII.1 9.
398. JA XIII 123.
399. Ger.: *selbständigen*. See IMH LXXVn361, above. Likewise in the first sentence of LS's next paragraph. At IMH XCI, below, "independence" is *Selbständigkeit*. Normally, "independence," etc., is *Unabhängigkeit*, etc.

ian who was going his own way. For just that reason, he cannot possibly have taken him to be an adherent of "our system," i.e., of the opinions of the radical-Rationalist theism of the Reimarian or Mendelssohnian type. For since he had read "Leibniz on Eternal Punishments" and "The Education of the Human Race,"[400] he must therefore have known, he therefore knew, that contrary to the German Enlightenment of the eighteenth century, Lessing went back to Leibniz's genuine[401] doctrine, whereas the cautious Mendelssohn was connected more narrowly with the Wolffian school and, moreover, aimed at the unification of Leibniz's doctrine with Locke's, whom the later Leibniz took to be a rather insipid philosopher.[402]

So much for the conception of Lessing's opinions that must have suggested itself to Mendelssohn if not on the basis of conversations with Lessing, in any case on the basis of both aforenamed writings, and which, reduced to the formula that Lessing was an independent Leibnizian, is supported by Mendelssohn's own statements. Against this conception, the conception that Friend D. presents in the Fifteenth Lecture of *Morning Hours* must be brought up. D. understands Lessing to be a decided adherent of the "religion of reason" of the Mendelssohnian or rather the Reimarian persuasion. As proof for this assertion, he appeals first to all the essays Lessing had written in defense of the Fragmentist,[403] and second and above all to *Nathan the Wise*. As for the first point, he asserts in particular that Lessing was, to be sure, already acquainted with the religion of reason in his earliest writings, but that only after his acquaintance with the Fragmentist's critique of revelation {LXXXV} did he express himself with complete clarity "in regard to the truths of the religion of reason."

> With the defense of the Fragmentist, Lessing also seems to have adopted his entire sentiment [*sc.*, the denial of all revealed religion in the interest of the religion of reason].[404]

This is as much as to say that Lessing was originally an adherent of "revelation-believing Rationalism" and only through Reimarus became convinced of the "Impossibility of a Revelation That All Men Could Be-

---

400. LM X1 461–87, XIII 413–36; Cha 82–98; Nis 37–60, 217–40.
401. Here LS uses the English word.
402. Cf. Leibniz, *Nouveaux Essais*, preface, 2nd par. (Ger V 42; ReBe 48).
403. See IMH XXIIIn76, above.
404. See IMH LXXXIIn390, above.

lieve in a Well-Founded Mode"—as the "Second Fragment" is titled.[405] The sentence with which the discussion of Lessing's defense of the Fragmentist concludes must be quoted literally:

> only after his acquaintance with the Fragmentist does one notice in his writings, in all the essays that he wrote in defense [of the Fragmatist], the same calm conviction that was so emblematic of him, the same impartial distance from any skepticism, the same straightforwardness of sound commonsense in regard to the truths of the religion of reason.[406]

No proof is needed that Mendelssohn was not so naïve as to believe what Friend D. believes: that certain writings of Lessing's, and now even the writings of the '70s and finally the writings of the Fragments quarrel, are marked by "impartial distance from any skepticism" and by the "straightforwardness of sound commonsense." That he did not believe it, his statements about Lessing in his letters to Elise Reimarus of November 18, 1783, and January 5, 1784,[407] indeed even his remark in *Morning Hours* about Lessing's "investigative spirit"[408] prove sufficiently. "The new and the striking were worth more to [Lessing] than truth and simplicity," to cite only the most pointed of these statements.[409] Mendelssohn's stance toward Lessing is therefore very different from D.'s. As far as D.'s assertion is concerned, were Lessing's adherence to the religion of reason corroborated by the Fragmentist, he would have been able to cite, out of a need for it to be sure, an ambiguous statement of Lessing's in the "Seventh Anti-Goeze," which reads:

> I have not only not said explicitly that I am partial to the opinion of my Unnamed; I have also, down to the point in time when I concerned myself with the publication of the "Fragments," never written or publicly asserted the least thing {LXXXVI} that could put me in suspicion of being a secret enemy of the Christian religion. Indeed, I have written more

---

405. "Unmöglichkeit einer Offenbarung, die alle Menschen auf eine gegründete Art glauben könnten," LM XII 316–58.
406. *Morgenstunden* 125.27–126.11 [Scholz 30; cf. Val 67–68; cf. DaDy 91–92; cf. Got 151]. {LS}
407. JA XIII 158, 168 (reading *Januar* for *Juni* in LS's German).
408. [Ger.: *Geist der Untersuchung.*] *Morgenstunden* 132.6ff. [Scholz 30; cf. Val 73 ("spirit of inquiry"); cf. DaDy 96 ("spirit of investigation"); cf. Got 152 ("spirit of inquiry")]. {LS}
409. JA XIII 158. LS quotes the pertinent statement from JA XIII 168 at IMH xxxv, above.

than one trifle in which I have not only shown the Christian religion generally in the best light in keeping with its doctrines and teachers, but also defended the orthodox Lutheran-Christian religion, especially against Catholics, Socinians, and tyros.[410]

But Mendelssohn had perhaps read, e.g., the "Vindication of Cardanus"[411] or the first two pieces of the *Hamburg Dramaturgy*[412] sufficiently closely to know what to make of Lessing's aforecited assurance. Above all, however—who knew better than Mendelssohn, to whom Lessing had written it on January 9, 1771, that, since his acquaintance with the Fragmentist, the question of whether by throwing out certain prejudices he might not have thrown out a little too much of what he would have to recover had become, if possible, even more pointed for Lessing?[413] More likely, Friend D.'s assertion about Reimarus's influence on Lessing betrays such an influence on Mendelssohn himself, who had all along been taken to be the author of the Fragments. In fact his *Jerusalem*, composed after the acquaintance with the Fragmentist, expresses a much more decisive critique of revealed religion than his earlier writings.[414] Mendelssohn was therefore not so naïve as to believe what Friend D. says about Lessing; he was also not naïve enough to pass it off as his own° insight: he puts it into Friend D.'s mouth. When Jacobi therefore comments mockingly on the sentence in which the discussion is about Lessing's "impartial distance from any skepticism"[415] and the like,

Oh, the clever housekeepers! Oh, the wise ones without fraud and hypocrisy![416]

his mocking is not sufficiently fine-tuned to catch Mendelssohn completely: he himself is forced to ascribe the sentence cited to "D. or Mendelssohn." If it was impossible for such important components of D.'s assertion to have

---

410. LM XIII 182–83.
411. LM V 310–33.
412. LM IX 184–92; trans. H. Zimmern, LPW 227–39.
413. JA XII.2 1.
414. Julius Guttmann, "Mendelssohns Jerusalem und Spinozas Theologisch-politischer Traktat," *Bericht der Hochschule für die Wissenschaft des Judentums in Berlin* 48 (1931), 65–66 ["Mendelssohn's *Jerusalem* and Spinoza's *Theologico-Political Treatise*," trans. Alfred Jospe, in *Studies in Jewish Thought: An Anthology of German Jewish Scholarship*, ed. A. Jospe (Detroit: Wayne State University Press, 1981), 385n36] has indicated that "particular turns of phrase from *Jerusalem*" "resonate clearly" in the second "Wolfenbüttel Fragment." Special attention should be paid to the conclusion of this "Fragment." {LS}
415. See IMH lxxxvn406, above.
416. Scholz 336 [cf. Val 153]. {LS}

been accepted by Mendelssohn, however, the suspicion is reinforced that not everything D. says corresponds with Mendelssohn's view, or at least not without {LXXXVII} further ado. For his assertion that Lessing was an adherent of theism, D. appeals first to Lessing's writings in the Fragments quarrel. As for what this argument concerns, "M." refrains from any statement in regard to it. If, therefore, Jacobi remarks, again mockingly, about D.'s assertion that the Fragmentist's "adherence to natural religion went so far that out of zeal for it he would suffer no revealed religion alongside it" and "with the defense of the Fragmentist, Lessing seems also to have adopted his entire sentiment,"

> Should one want Lessing's adherence to natural religion to follow from his zeal against all revealed religion? ... Then a similar adherence could also be ascribed to Spinoza,[417]

even here his mockery somehow misses its target: not without reason had Mendelssohn taken precautions to allow "M." to agree with D.'s assertion. Friend D. appeals afterward and above all to *Nathan the Wise*. "M." validates this argument insofar as he appropriates the conception of *Nathan* as a vindication of providence.[418] But it was clear to him that even if this conception is correct, one cannot possibly infer from *Nathan* Lessing's "system." Together with Lessing, he had expatiated on the reason for this impossibility in *Pope a Metaphysician!* Friend D. might take *Nathan* to be a "dramatic didactic poem" as much as he liked,[419] the poem as such was not a "system brought ... into a meter," it was as such the work not of a philosopher but of a "philosophical poet," who seeks "a lively impression rather than a deep conviction" and who for that reason "[has] no other means but to express one truth according to one system and another according to another."[420] Like Horace in his philosophical poems, Lessing too, in his, leaves "everywhere ... untouched those hairsplittings that have no influence on morals."[421] Thus, for Mendelssohn, *Nathan* proved in fact that Lessing agrees by and large with what theism's doctrine of providence "has of practical relevance°";[422] more it did not prove to him. Only for this practical

---

417. Scholz 335 (cf. Val 152), with IMH LXXXVn404, above.
418. *Morgenstunden* 129.35–130.5 [Scholz 35; cf. Val 70–71; DaDy 94]. {LS}
419. *Morgenstunden* 129.24 [Scholz 35; cf. Val 70; cf. DaDy 94]. {LS}
420. *Pope!* 50–51; cf. also 72 [cf. Gal 48, also 56–57]. {LS}
421. "Rettungen des Horaz" [Vindications of Horace], LM V 299. {LS}
422. See IMH LXXVIIIn382, above.

consequence {LXXXVIII} of the theistic doctrine of providence, for the "devotion to God,"[423] can Lessing have been interested in *Nathan*, as in a poem; but this practical consequence resulted not only from the theistic doctrine of providence, but also from Spinozism as *amor fati*,[424] to apply Nietzsche's expression. Possibly this knowledge motivates the one substantive contribution that "M." offers to D.'s argument apropos *Nathan*; with an earlier literary plan of Lessing's in mind, he calls *Nathan* "a sort of anti-*Candide*."[425] With that, he recalls the basic sentiment common to himself and Lessing that could not be called into question by any "summersaults" and that is expressed in the opposition to Voltaire. *Nathan* is "a sort of anti-*Candide*" in any case; but would not Lessing also, and especially if he had been a decided Spinozist, have had to reject the moral preached in *Candide* of "*travailler sans raisonner*,"[426] together with its foundation, the Manicheanism of the Bayleist persuasion? Had Mendelssohn actually taken *Nathan* to be an adequate proof of Lessing's theism, he would have said a word about it in the statements in his letters addressed to the Reimarus siblings and Jacobi. Here too, Jacobi again catches D. rather than Mendelssohn himself, when, again mocking, he counters:

> Mr. Mendelssohn does not know how to call on this *Nathan* often enough.... Yes indeed, even Voltaire could be praised to the skies as a zealot and a witness for the Christian religion on account of his *Alzire* and *Zaïre*.[427]

To recapitulate: Friend D.'s opinion about Lessing is not Mendelssohn's own opinion. If one does not exactly want to assert an opposition between the two opinions, one must at least say that D.'s opinion is the popular, exoteric version of the opinion that Mendelssohn had of Lessing's beliefs originally, i.e., until Jacobi's communication. Friend D.'s Lessing corresponds

---

423. See Jacobi, *Wider Mendelssohns Beschuldigungen in dessen Schreiben An die Freunde Lessings* [Against Mendelssohn's Accusations in his *To the Friends of Lessing*], in Scholz 337; cf. Val 153.
424. Lat.: love of fate. Friedrich Nietzsche, *Die fröhliche Wissenschaft* §276 (KSA III 521; *The Gay Science*, Kau 223); *Ecce Homo*, "*Warum ich so klug bin*" §10 (KSA VI 297; "Why I Am So Clever," GaKa 714). Cf. also LSGS I 258, 269 (SCR 202, 211), SCR 17–18 or LAM 242–43.
425. *Morgenstunden* 129.35ff. [Scholz 35–36; cf. Val 70–71; cf. DaDy 94]. {LS}
426. Fr.: "working without trying-to-reason." See Hav 111; cf. Woo 79.
427. Scholz 337 [cf. Val 153]. {LS}
Cf. Mendelssohn's reference to Voltaire's *Zaïre* (and Lessing's *Miss Sara Sampson*) in *Schriften* 275 [Dah 42–43], with Dah's note: "In Voltaire's *Zaïre*, first staged in Paris in 1732, the Sultan Orosman mistakenly kills Zaïre out of jealous rage, only to kill himself after he learns that she in fact loved him and that his jealousy was completely unfounded" (Dah 42n3).

with Mendelssohn's fantasy-image of Lessing—he would have preferred to adopt the Fragmentist's entire sentiment than, e.g., "[to] let himself imagine [the idea of 'The Education of the Human Race'] under the influence of I-don't-know-what historian of mankind"[428]—rather than with his actual notion of him: he is the Lessing for the school- and home-use of the Enlightenment, {LXXXIX} the Lessing *in usum Delphini*.[429]

Admittedly, D.'s opinion agrees with Mendelssohn's original opinion on one point, namely, that Lessing was in no way a Spinozist. Mendelssohn's "bewildered outcry" in the letter to Elise Reimarus of August 16, 1783,[430] followed by not one reservation in connection with a "purified" Spinozism, already proves by itself that before setting eyes on Jacobi's descriptions of his conversations with Lessing, he simply did not take into account the possibility of Lessingian "*Spinozisterey*."[431] Jacobi's detailed report immediately convinced Mendelssohn to the contrary, just as it did the Reimarus siblings: for Mendelssohn as for the Reimarus siblings, Lessing's Spinozism is a proven fact from then on. The statements of both Mendelssohn and the Reimarus siblings that were discussed in the History of Their Emergence[432] make it completely implausible that Mendelssohn actually believed what he lets "M." say in *Morning Hours* and repeats in *To the Friends of Lessing*: that it was already known to him since the beginning of their friendship that Lessing had adhered to "purified" Spinozism.

Mendelssohn must have ascribed "purified" Spinozism to Lessing just because he could not possibly represent before the public that his late friend had distanced himself even further from the dominant view. "Purified" Spinozism was the most he allowed himself to represent, to apologize for. A proof of this is that Mendelssohn in *Morning Hours* allows the doctrine under consideration to be represented by the fictional Lessing and that he attributes it to the actual Lessing only after he has completely diffused D.'s objections.

And a further proof of this is that in both writings he ascribes "purified" Spinozism to Lessing only with a certain hedging: he does not ascribe to

---

428. *Jerusalem* 162; cf. Ark 95; cf. Got 86.
429. Lat.: the Delphin Classics Lessing. "The Delphin Classics, *in usum Delphini*, were prepared about 1670–80 under the direction of Pierre Daniel Huet for the education of the Grand Dauphin, son of Louis XIV. They included some sixty volumes by thirty-nine editors." (*The Oxford Companion to Classical Literature*, ed. Sir Paul Harvey [rev. ed.: Oxford: Clarendon Press, 1940], s.v. "Editions of Collections of the Classics," 153.)
430. JA XIII 124.
431. See IMH LXXXIIIn396, above.
432. See IMH XII–LVIII *passim*, with XIIn2, above.

him purified Spinozism so much as purified Pantheism. To be sure, the word "Pantheism" already comes up in the title of the Thirteenth Lecture, which deals with authentic Spinozism; within this chapter itself, however, the discussion is nowhere about "Pantheism," but exclusively about "Spinozism." Whereas in the title of the Thirteenth Lecture "Spinozism" as {xc} well as "Pantheism" is spoken of, in the title of the Fourteenth Lecture, in which the fictional Lessing defends purified Spinozism, the discussion is only about "Pantheism." In the Fourteenth Lecture, "Lessing" now explicitly replaces "Spinozism" with "Pantheism,"[433] and generally in this Lecture "Pantheism" is spoken of more frequently than "Spinozism." But the Fourteenth Lecture deals explicitly with a fictional profession of Lessing's as regards Spinozism. In the Fifteenth Lecture, which deals explicitly with the opinions of the actual Lessing, the discussion is almost exclusively about "Pantheism"; only a single time[434] is "Pantheism or Spinozism" spoken of. In *Morning Hours*, Lessing is described as the "defender of purified Spinozism" only within the fiction of the Fourteenth Lecture:[435] to the actual Lessing is ascribed only a "refined" Pantheism quite compatible with Christian orthodoxy. And in *To the Friends of Lessing*, Mendelssohn with unambiguous words attributes only "Pantheism" to Lessing.[436] Jacobi understood the purpose of this distinction very well. He says in his letter to Elise Reimarus of November 7, 1785: "Mendelssohn just at the present time was in need of a tolerable Spinozism that could be purified into an even more tolerable Pantheism and ascribed to Lessing in case of trouble."[437] Meanwhile, as the repeated equatings of "Spinozism" and "Pantheism" prove, the distinction is simply verbal.[438] In fact, Mendelssohn ascribes to Lessing a "purified" Spinozism in both writings.

It is with this assertion that Mendelssohn answers Jacobi's thesis that Lessing was a "decided" Spinozist. The reply can be broken down into two arguments. First, it expresses the certainty, prior to any investigation of documents, that Lessing could not be understood absolutely and without qualification in terms of the system of any man. This first argument does not turn up in either writing; it is met up with in no other statement that Men-

---

433. "Spinozism or Pantheism, if you will" — *Morgenstunden* 114.20–21 [Scholz 16; cf. DaDy 83] {LS}
434. *Morgenstunden* 132.8. [Scholz 38; Val 72; DaDy 96]. {LS}
435. *Morgenstunden* 124.1 [Scholz 28; cf. Val 65; cf. DaDy 90]. {LS}
436. Cf. *Freunde* 188 [Scholz 295; Val 130; Got 155]. {LS}
437. Scholz LXXXIX. {LS}
438. Here LS uses the English word.

delssohn made after reading Jacobi's detailed report; it {XCI} is found only in the letter to Elise Reimarus of August 16, 1783.[439] It was Mendelssohn's original argument and at the same time his strongest: it was fully reinforced by the oral statements of Lessing that were reported by Jacobi himself. *Morning Hours* now attempts to give a closer determination of Lessing's independence vis-à-vis Spinoza, which had been asserted in general from the outset; and this closer determination is Mendelssohn's second argument against Jacobi: Lessing's independence vis-à-vis Spinoza consists in the fact° that he has "purified" Spinozism.

Scarcely separable from this substantive argument, which is peculiar to *Morning Hours* (and *To the Friends of Lessing*), is an *argumentum ad hominem* that Mendelssohn combined with it: Mendelssohn further asserts that he has known of Lessing's "purified" Spinozism for a long time. He cites a single document as proof for both the substantive argument and the one concerning himself: Lessing's "Christianity of Reason," which Lessing "read aloud" to him "right at the beginning of our acquaintance."[440] This Lessingian fragment is by and large defined by Leibnizian views. The assertion set forth in §3 that "to envisage, to will, and to create" are "one thing in God" recalls Spinoza.[441] From this presupposition, rejected in principle by Leibniz,[442] two significant conclusions follow: the conclusion that the world therefore does not subsist outside the divine understanding is admittedly not drawn explicitly, but it glimmers in the assertion that the creation of the world consists in God's having been thinking of "his perfections severally" (§§13–14). The second conclusion by which Lessing distances himself from Leibniz is the thesis that the distinction of possibility and actuality in reference to God, and with it the conception of the actual world as the best of all possible worlds, loses its sense; he says in §15: "therefore, there *could possibly* be infinitely many worlds, if God were not always thinking the most perfect one"; therefore, they are in fact not possible.[443] {XCII} Lessing's profession of the doctrine of the unfreedom of the will, which he tossed off in

---

439. JA XIII 123. For the full statement, see IMH XXXI, above.
440. *Morgenstunden* 133.12–14 [Scholz 39; cf. Val 73; DaDy 96]; cf. *Freunde* 188.35ff. [Scholz 295–96; cf. Val 130; Got 155]. {LS}
441. *Ethica*, pt. I, prop. 17 schol. [Geb II 61–63; WhSt 56–58]: identity of God's understanding, willing, and power. {LS}
442. *Monadologie* §§48 and 55 [Ger VI 615–16; Wie 542, 544, or Sch 155, 156, or FrWo 274, 275]; *Théodicée* §§149–50 [Ger VI 198–99; Hug 217–18]. {LS}
443. Cf., on the other hand, *Théodicée* §§171ff. [Ger VI 215ff.; Hug 233ff.]; §173 is explicitly directed against Spinoza. For Spinoza, cf. especially *Ethica*, pt. I, prop. 33, schol. 2 [Geb II 74–76; WhSt 69–71]. {LS; the emphasis in the preceding Lessing quotation is LS's}

Jacobi's presence some thirty years later, has its basis in this deviation from Leibniz.[444]

The examination of "Christianity of Reason" therefore leads to the result that the young Lessing already distanced himself from Leibniz's doctrine by the adoption of Spinozistic thoughts. To that extent, it is understandable that a decided Leibnizian, so to speak, like Mendelssohn describes the standpoint from which the Lessingian fragment is written as a "purified" Spinozism, namely, a Spinozism improved by Leibnizian thoughts. But did he already conceive the fragment in this manner at the time Lessing was making it available to him? Did he ever conceive it in that way at all before the possibility of a Lessingian Spinoza was suggested to him by Jacobi? About the stance he originally took toward the fragment, it is known with certainty only that he expressed considerable objections to it, by which Lessing "[had been] put off at once from thinking seriously about it again for [him]self."[445] The objections might have been related to the construal of the Trinity that Lessing attempts in §§5–12. It is highly probable that Mendelssohn rejected the (Leibnizian) doctrine developed in §§16–17 and 24 about the hierarchical ordering of beings.[446] The correspondence between Lessing and Mendelssohn in 1774 discusses the fragment very briefly. Mendelssohn recalls on this occasion the kindred doctrine of "our Kabbalists"[447] but says no word of a relation to Spinoza.[448] {XCIII} Nevertheless, it seems to have been none other than Mendelssohn himself who posited an explicit connection between Spinozism and the conclusion implicit in the fragment, that the world does not subsist outside the divine understanding.

Under which configuration "Spinoza's system could be consistent with reason and religion" is set forth in the second of his *Philosophical Dialogues*, which appeared in 1755 and was probably composed in 1754. What is being attempted is therefore a "purifying" of Spinozism. According to it, Spino-

---

444. In a revision from 1755, Lessing proclaimed "the thoughtful manner" in which "Prémontval presented his doubt about freedom" and which "could seem suspect to a few Christian bleeding-hearts" (LM VII 12). Even at that time, therefore, Lessing was "not in the least frightened" by the consequences that result from the doctrine of the unfreedom of the will; cf. Scholz 82 [cf. Gio 189–90; cf. Val 89; cf. Nis 246]. {LS}

445. Lessing to Mendelssohn, May 1, 1774 [JA XII.2 47]. {LS}

446. Cf. IPM xx. {LS}

447. To Lessing, February 1, 1774 [JA XII.2 40]. {LS}

448. In *Morgenstunden*—104.20–22 [Scholz 3–4; DaDy 75; Got 144]—he assumes a connection between Spinozism and Kabbalah; but perhaps only because for tactical reasons it is convenient for him to validate a connection between Spinozism and Judaism as a positive religion. Cf. also *Morgenstunden* 136 [Scholz 43; Val 77; DaDy 99]. {LS}

zism is precisely the doctrine that the world, that all visible things are "down to this hour found merely in the divine understanding."[449] Is anyone else besides Mendelssohn the originator of "purified" Spinozism? Still, whether the Spinoza interpretation sketched in the second of the *Philosophical Dialogues* does not go back to a brainstorm of Lessing's cannot be said absolutely. That the *Philosophical Dialogues* is influenced in style by Lessing is evident. The first two *Dialogues* contain a "vindication" of Spinoza, and Lessing loved to "vindicate" heretical men.[450] The two persons who talk with each other in the first three *Dialogues*, Philopon and Neophil, behave toward each other like Mendelssohn and Lessing: Philopon is a decided Leibnizian, and Neophil behaves toward Leibniz as a doubting admirer and an admiring doubter.[451] Philopon, who knows him, knows from the outset that Neophil's praise of Leibniz will be followed by a "But...."[452] On the other hand, Neophil defends an apparently trivial answer of Leibniz's by saying that it is directed against "Bayle the critic" and not against "Bayle the philosopher"—"against Bayle the critic, I say, who has not seldom made crimes out of minor historical inaccuracies."[453] Neophil's mode of speaking and type of thinking are qualified by "small[454] indiscretions" from which something can be learned.[455] A subject with which Neophil seems to be especially occupied is Leibniz's cast of mind, and the mode in which {xciv} he determines it points ahead to "Leibniz on Eternal Punishments" and "Wissowatius":

Leibniz presented his opinion only under various configurations, just as his purpose required each time;[456]

Leibniz, he who was not only the greatest philosopher, but also the most cautious.[457]

---

449. *Gespräche* 17 [retained in 2nd ed., *Schriften* 352; cf. Dah 108]. {LS}
450. Cf. JA I xviii–xxiii. {LS}
451. Lit: doubting with admiration and admiring with doubt.
452. *Gespräche* 25.22–23 [not retained in 2nd ed.] {LS}
453. *Gespräche* 4.28 to 32 [retained in 2nd ed., *Schriften* 338; cf. Dah 97]. {LS}
454. The German words for "trivial" (*kleinliche*) and "minor" (*kleinern*) in LS's previous sentence are, literally, "smallish" and "smaller." In the passage LS quotes from Lessing's "Seventh Anti-Goeze" at IMH lxxxv–lxxxvi, above, "trifle" is *Kleinigkeit*. Cf. also IPM xixn36.
455. *Gespräche* 3.17–24. [retained in 2nd ed., *Schriften* 337; cf. Dah 86]. Cf. Lessing's letters to Mendelssohn of December 18, 1756, at the beginning, and September 14, 1757, in JA XI 159.5–6. This last passage is cited by Mendelssohn in his "Hauptzügen" [Characteristics]. {LS}
456. *Gespräche* 6.7–8 [retained in 2nd ed., *Schriften* 340; cf. Dah 98]. — Cf. Lessing to Mendelssohn, November 1756, JA XI 64.35–38. {LS}
457. *Gespräche* 12.1–3 [retained in 2nd ed., *Schriften* 346; cf. Dah 104]. {LS}

It is this Neophil who is described entirely in Lessing's image, therefore, who puts forth the assertion that Leibniz adopted the doctrine of preestablished harmony from Spinoza and who anticipates the "purifying" of Spinozism. It has to be said: Mendelssohn already puts "purified" Spinozism into Lessing's mouth in the *Philosophical Dialogues*. And it has to be suspected that "purified" Spinozism, if not a brainstorm of Lessing's, was nevertheless a result of the discussion between Mendelssohn and Lessing about "Christianity of Reason." That Lessing in the review of *Philosophical Dialogues* describes the full-blown reinterpretation of Spinozism in this writing as one of "very bold but, as it seems to us, also very felicitous thoughts"[458] may at least be mentioned. Did Mendelssohn therefore take Lessing to be an adherent of "purified" Spinozism in 1754 and 1755? Since Lessing "had been put off at once" from "Christianity of Reason" by Mendelssohn,[459] it can at most be assumed that Mendelssohn found him on the road to becoming a "purified" Spinozist then but held him back from this road just in time. Nevertheless, here one is not simply pointed to suspicions. Lessing returns to the first *Philosophical Dialogue* in his letter to Mendelssohn of April 17, 1763.[460] He is now "no longer so very satisfied" with Mendelssohn's attempt to trace the doctrine of preestablished harmony back to Spinoza. About the reinterpretation of Spinoza he says no word at all. And not only this; he wonders "that no Leibnizian has taken up against you yet." Lessing therefore stands on Leibniz's side, not on Spinoza's. Then too, in his letter to Lessing of May of the same year, Mendelssohn calls him "a brother in Leibniz."[461]

With this correspondence from 1763, the question is also answered whether a third document of Lessingian {xcv} speculation did not prove to Mendelssohn that Lessing was an adherent of "purified" Spinozism: the essay "On the Actuality of Things Outside God." The essay was addressed to Mendelssohn. The thoughts developed in it were perhaps also available to Mendelssohn through letters now lost,[462] assuming that the essay had not accompanied any one of these letters. In any case, there is reason for the supposition that the presentation of "purified" Spinozism in the Fourteenth Lecture of *Morning Hours* was written with the aid of the Lessingian essay.[463] But had Mendelssohn through this essay come to the thought that "puri-

---

458. LM VII 14. {LS}
459. JA XII.2 47. See also IMH xcii, and IPM xx.
460. JA XII.1 5ff. For the two quotations from Lessing's letter that follow, see 6–7.
461. JA XII.1 9. See IMH lxxxiii, above.
462. LM XIV 292n. {LS}
463. Cf. *Morgenstunden* 116.6–118.18 [Scholz 18–21; DaDy 84–85; Got 147–49] and the annotations. {LS}

fied" Spinozism was Lessing's belief in 1763, he would not have described him as a "brother in Leibniz." And had he come to this thought later, some trace of it would have shown up in his answer to Jacobi's communications.

But even granted that the view that is developed in the essay on the actuality of things outside God can be brought into connection with Spinoza, this view should not be described from Lessing's viewpoint as "purified" Spinozism. For if Lessing undertook a restructuring of Spinozism, his aim was definitely not to "purify" or "refine" it or, to apply an expression Lessing himself uses in a kindred context, to satisfy himself "with a lovely quintessence" by means of which one can avoid "every suspicion of freethinking."[464] If Jacobi was touched by Lessing's spirit nowhere else, he surely is in his critique of the conception of a "purified" Spinozism. Of the sentences that he devotes to this conception in his *Against Mendelssohn's Accusations in His "To the Friends of Lessing,"* perhaps Lessing himself would not have been ashamed.

For LS's editorial annotations to *Morgenstunden* 116.6–118.18 (JA III.2 302–303), see appendix 2, supplement to IMH xcvn463.

464. *Literaturbrief* #49, August 2, 1759; LM VIII 127. {LS}

10

[1936/1962/ 1974]

Introduction to Mendelssohn's *God's Cause, or Providence Vindicated*[1]

What is known about this writing through direct report—by the date on the title page of the first printing in the *Gesammelte Schriften*,[2] which probably goes back to a corresponding date in the manuscript, now missing—is merely this: Mendelssohn wrote it in the year 1784. That is why, even for knowledge of the circumstances of its emergence, one is entirely given over to the investigation of the content.

God's Cause is a recasting of Leibniz's *Causa Dei asserta per justitiam ejus cum caeteris ejus perfectionibus cunctisque actionibus conciliatam*.[3] It stands to its model as does the *Phädon* to the Platonic *Phaedo*. Here too, Mendelssohn adopts the framework—and that means, in the present case, almost the whole arrangement[4]—and the part of the content that appears acceptable to him, while he replaces those passages in the model that he believes he must reject with the doctrines that he holds to be correct. But if he was able in the *Phädon* to replace merely tacitly the Platonic passages that he viewed as false or inadequate with the doctrines that were in his opinion correct, the less obliging form of the Leibnizian writing allowed him an explicit polemic against his model as well. Some two-fifths of *God's Cause* sets forth a—more or less literal—translation of the Leibnizian writing: §§1–55 (beginning) correspond to §§1–55 of *Causa Dei*, §§61–69 to §§60–68. Already Mendelssohn's remarkable deviations from Leibniz show up in this part.

---

1. First published in *Einsichten: Gerhard Krüger zum 60. Geburtstag* (Frankfurt am Main: Vittorio Klostermann, 1962), 361–75; JA III.2 xcvi–cx; LSGS II 514–27. LS cites *Sache Gottes oder die gerettete Vorsehung*, in JA III.2 219–60; henceforth *Sache Gottes*, followed by the pertinent Mendelssohnian section number(s). Interpolations inside square brackets in quotations in LS's text are LS's; those in LS's annotations are the translator's. Unless otherwise noted, emphases in LS's quotations are LS's.

2. MMGS II 411.

3. *God's Cause Upheld through His Justice having been Reconciled with His Remaining Perfections and the Entirety of Actions* (Ger VI 437–71; translated as *A Vindication of God's Justice Reconciled with His Other Perfections and All His Actions*, Sch 114–47). LS cites the Latin original according to Leibniz's section numbers.

4. Cf. the sole deviation from Leibniz's remarks concerning the arrangement: annotation to *Sache Gottes* §62. {LS}

For LS's editorial annotation to *Sache Gottes* §62 (JA III.2 340), see appendix 2, supplement to IGC xcviii4.

§§55–60 contain the explicit polemic against Leibniz. From §70 on, a simple one-to-one correspondence of single paragraphs to paragraphs of *Causa Dei* is no longer possible. This most striking deviation is based on the fact° that the (disproportionately long) concluding part of the Leibnizian writing[5] is devoted to the justification of the Christian doctrine of sin and grace. Once having decided not to follow his model any further, not even by way of contesting it, Mendelssohn distanced himself from it even where in substance he thoroughly agreed with it: in §83 of *God's Cause*, he renders the discussion offered {xcvii} in §§102–108 of *Causa Dei*, of the relationship between human freedom and divine providence, in an appropriately freer form, specifically one that is quite independent of Leibniz's paragraph divisions. Generally speaking, the entire concluding part of *God's Cause*, insofar as it is not devoted to the polemic against Christianity and, in that way, against Leibniz too, mostly reproduces Leibnizian doctrines. But since Mendelssohn presents these doctrines at a place where in the model quite different themes are being dealt with, namely, peculiarly Christian ones, even by this apparently merely literary difference he gives expression to a substantive critique of Leibniz. That is why it has to be said on the whole that *God's Cause*, which is to be characterized from a literary point of view as a recasting of a Leibnizian writing, sets forth in its content a controversy with Leibniz.

Mendelssohn's relationship to Leibniz is, first of all, the relationship of Jew to Christian. That Mendelssohn qua Jew has recast a writing by Leibniz qua Christian shows up initially in a particular feature: he drops Leibniz's references to Christian sources and gives references to Jewish sources.[6] He is not satisfied with this mode of recasting, however, which would be tantamount to an implicit critique in any case. In §60, he polemicizes explicitly against Leibniz as a "Christian philosopher,"[7] who as such must have been compelled to assert the eternal damnation of the wicked; in §77, he continues the polemic against the "system of a religion familiar to us," plainly Christianity; in the concluding paragraphs,[8] he gives a survey of the Christian doctrine of sin and grace in order to indicate "the great confusion that has had to emerge from the combination of [the] popular concepts with philosophy" and to suggest the repudiation of the combination "of this hodge-

---

5. *Causa Dei* §§74–144 [Ger VI 450–60; Sch 130–45]. {LS}
6. See *Sache Gottes* §§2, 3, 22, 24, 30, 34, 36, 39, 49, and the annotations. {LS}
For LS's editorial annotations on *Sache Gottes* §§2, 3, 22, 24, 30, 34, 36, 39, and 49 (JA III.2 335–38 *passim*), see appendix 2, supplement to IGC xcviin6.
7. Ger.: *Weltweise*. See IPM xviiin23.
8. I.e., *Sache Gottes* §§78–84. The passages quoted subsequently in this part of LS's sentence are from §84.

podge of picturesque religious concepts with philosophical hairsplittings," i.e., of Christian dogmatics; whereas he says about the "popular system" in general, i.e., about the doctrine of otherworldly reward common to all the revealed religions, that it contains "much that is true,"[9] he describes the representations of "the people's religion's" that are peculiar to Christianity as simply "false."[10] And he accomplishes this critique on {xcviii} the basis of "our religion [and] our reason."[11] The expression "our religion" occurs synonymously with "my religion," "religion of my fathers," "Judaism," "the Jewish religion," etc., in the writings prompted by the quarrel with Lavater;[12] the expression "my religion and my philosophy,"[13] which corresponds fully to the expression "our religion [and] our reason," also comes up in the *Letter to Lavater*. Undoubtedly, therefore, by "our religion" is to be understood Judaism: in *God's Cause*, Mendelssohn pits himself qua Jew against Christianity in general and, for that reason, against the Christian Leibniz in particular.

This finding is of significance for knowledge of the circumstances surrounding the emergence of the writing under discussion. The expression "our religion" has reminded us of the writings that resulted from the quarrel with Lavater. The circumstance that Mendelssohn's clearest and most coherent critique of Christianity is found in one of them, the "Counterreflections on Bonnet's '*Palingénésie*',"[14] already points back to those writings; Mendelssohn himself described this writing simply as a "manuscript against the religion of the Christians."[15] Now, the "Counterreflections" was to be published only if and when Mendelssohn *had* to do so for the sake of the defense of Judaism,[16] and indeed it was never to be published by him in its present form. Mendelssohn had the "firm intention" of never letting the manuscript out of his hand.[17] This behavior corresponded to his explicit principle "of avoiding all religious controversies and of speaking in published writings only about those truths that must be equally important to all religions."[18] Only the necessity of defending his Judaism when it had

---

9. *Sache Gottes* §57. {LS}
10. *Sache Gottes* §84. {LS}
11. *Sache Gottes* §60. {LS}
12. Cf. especially *Gegenbetrachtungen* 101.34 [Got 26]. {LS}
13. *Loc. cit.*; cf. also *Lavater* 10.26 [Sam 55]. {LS}
14. *Gegenbetrachtungen* 65ff. {LS}
15. [Letter to Elkan Herz, November 15, 1771] JA XVI 153. {LS}
16. *Lavater* 12.17ff. [Sam 57ff.; Got 10ff.] {LS; JA III.2 xcviii reads, erroneously, 12.37ff.}
17. [Letter to Elkan Herz, November 15, 1771] JA XVI 153; cf. also [to the Hereditary Duke of Brunswick-Wölfenbüttel] JA VII 305. {LS}
18. *Lavater* 10.28–30 [cf. Sam 55; cf. Got 9]. {LS; the German text at JA III.2 xcviii reads, erroneously, 10.36–38}

come under attack could wring from him the publicly taken stance against Christianity in the *Letter to Lavater*. Under these circumstances, the fact that Mendelssohn in *God's Cause* unambiguously contests Christianity, and therefore attacks it, without having been compelled to—and moreover attacks it explicitly qua Jew—is proof that publication of this writing was not left in abeyance accidentally: {xcix} in keeping with Mendelssohn's basic principles, *God's Cause* was not intended for publication.

Admittedly, *God's Cause* was not written for the sake of the critique of Christianity contained in it. Rather, this critique was merely the consequence of the aim of recasting Leibniz's *Causa Dei*. Once having resolved on the latter, Mendelssohn had to take a stance on Leibniz's Christian assertions, and if he forwent publication from the outset, he could take the stance on Christianity explicitly and openly. But what occasion did he have in general, and especially just in the year 1784, to recast Leibniz's writing?

The opinion has been advocated that *God's Cause*, as a "fragment drafted in paragraphs," must have been "intended as the second part of *Morning Hours*."[19] The writing would hardly have been described as a fragment if it had been noticed that it is a recasting of Leibniz's *Causa Dei*: the model is already "drafted in paragraphs." *God's Cause* is unfinished, it lacks the final revision;[20] but one needs only to read the final paragraphs to see that it is no fragment. If therefore it can in no way be regarded as a draft for the second part of *Morning Hours* either, it could be a kind of study for this book, which was being planned by Mendelssohn. But then, how does one know that the subject of *God's Cause*—the problem of theodicy—was to be the subject of the second part of *Morning Hours*? Not on the basis of direct reports, in any case, which hardly say anything other than that Mendelssohn in the second part of *Morning Hours* wanted to treat in detail what in *To the Friends of Lessing* he detailed only in brief.

In terms of its content, therefore, *God's Cause* does not belong with *Morning Hours*. {c} To ascertain its true place among Mendelssohn's writings, one must recall the context in which he had treated the problem of theodicy—

---

19. M. Kayserling, *Moses Mendelssohn: Sein Leben und seine Werke* (Leipzig 1862), 440; judging similarly: Ch. A. Brandis in his "Einleitung zu Mendelssohns philosophischen Schriften," MMGS I 90n2; Hettner, *Geschichte der deutschen Literatur im 18. Jahrhundert*3, II, 234; M. Brasch, *Mendelssohns Schriften zur Philosophie, Aesthetik und Apologetik* I (Leipzig 1880), 501n; Jakob Auerbach, "Moses Mendelssohn und das Judenthum," *Zeitschrift für Geschichte der Juden in Deutschland* I (Braunschweig, 1887), 8. {LS}

20. See *Sache Gottes* §46 and annotations. {LS}

For LS's editorial annotations to *Sache Gottes* §46 (JA III.2 337–38), see appendix 2, supplement to IGC xcixn20.

more generally, of providence—in the most depth. This context is the problem of immortality,[21] which is the theme of the Third Dialogue of the *Phädon*.[22] This Dialogue had emerged as a consequence of Mendelssohn's attempt to dispose of the objections that Thomas Abbt had raised against the Leibniz-Wolffian doctrine of providence.[23] It was Herder's critique of the *Phädon*,[24] more than anything else, that seems to have convinced Mendelssohn of the inadequacy of his answer to Abbt's objections. In any case, for a while he had in mind to revise the Third Dialogue of the *Phädon*. Only around 1780 did he finally give up this aim. But even at this time he still considered it necessary to take a fresh stance on the questions treated in that Dialogue.[25] A few years earlier presumably, he had continued the discussions of the Third Dialogue of the *Phädon* in his Hebrew treatise on the immortality of the soul;[26] in this treatise he explicitly promulgates a theodicy.[27] Besides, it happens that the Third Dialogue of the *Phädon* is referred to twice in *God's Cause*,[28] whereas no reference at all is found in this writing[29] to a treatise, whether written or to be written, on the existence and attributes of God. *God's Cause* does not belong with *Morning Hours*, therefore, but with the Third Dialogue of the *Phädon*: it sets forth Mendelssohn's final attempt to invalidate Abbt's considerations against the German Enlightenment's doctrine of providence.[30] Nevertheless, the attempt to bring *God's Cause* into connection with *Morning Hours* was not entirely misguided. The connection consists less in the content of the two writings, however, than in the circumstances of their emergence. Jakob Auerbach[31] has remarked that *God's Cause* "was intended for [Mendelssohn's] coreligionists." As proof of this, it is enough to point to the Hebrew citations in §§2 and 49, if one considers that Mendelssohn does not cite in Hebrew in any philosophical writing in which he also addresses non-Jews. {CI} Besides, the description of Christianity as "a religion familiar to us"[32] was inserted in a writing probably

---

21. See IP XV. {LS}
22. *Phädon* 102–28; Cul 151–212; Nob 125–46.
23. See IP XVI–XVII.
24. See IP XXX–XXXII.
25. In the "annotations to Abbt's Friendly Correspondence"; see IP XXXIII. {LS}
26. I.e., *HaNefesh*. See the following note.
27. IS XL, and *Seele* 208.32–33 [at www.press.uchicago.edu/sites/strauss/*ad loc.*]. {LS}
28. In *Sache Gottes* §§57 and 79. {LS}
29. I.e., in *Sache Gottes*.
30. Cf. the annotations to *Sache Gottes* §§56–60 and 76. {LS}
  For LS's editorial annotations *Sache Gottes* §§56–60 and 76 (JA III.2 339–40, 341), see appendix 2, supplement to IGC cn30.
31. *Op. cit.* [IGC XCIXn19, above]. {LS}
32. *Sache Gottes* §77. {LS}

intended only for Jews. Auerbach's finding allows for a closer determination: *God's Cause* was intended only for Jews and, as has been shown, was not intended for publication; it was therefore intended only for Mendelssohn's Jewish acquaintances. The emergence of the writing has been declared to be in 1784, i.e., at about the time when Mendelssohn was giving philosophical instruction to his son Joseph.[33] Out of this instruction came *Morning Hours*, as Mendelssohn narrates in the "Preface";[34] at any rate, he presented the main content of this writing to his domestic circle of students, to which two other young Jews besides Joseph belonged; and *Morning Hours* insofar as it arose in the context of the home instruction was also not intended for publication.[35] Therefore, one has to take into account the possibility that *God's Cause* came about, just as in a certain way *Morning Hours* did, out of Mendelssohn's aim "to guide" his son Joseph "at an early age to the knowledge of God."

God's Cause has a claim to special attention for the reason that it is the only writing in which Mendelssohn has controverted Leibniz. Leibniz was for him the highest philosophical authority. That is why, in his explicit controversy with Leibniz, the views peculiar to him are brought out most pointedly. These views, be it noted in advance, are not peculiar to him as an individual; nor are they to be traced altogether to his Judaism; they are instead the common coin of the later German Enlightenment: the progress that the Enlightenment has made in Germany since Leibniz comes to thoughtful expression in the difference between *God's Cause* and *Causa Dei*.[36]

Admittedly, the first impression that one gains in comparing Mendelssohn's writing with its model is that the difference between Mendelssohn's and Leibniz's views coincides with the difference between Judaism and Christianity. Yet closer inspection shows that this impression does not correspond with the facts of the case. Mendelssohn deviates from Leibniz not merely {CII} because qua Jew he cannot go along with a Christian, but also and above all because qua philosopher[37] in the style of the eighteenth century he has to distance himself considerably further from all posi-

---

33. Cf. IMH XIIf.
34. *Morgenstunden* 3–4.
35. See variant readings to *Morgenstunden* 4.26. {LS}
   The pertinent variant reading entry to *Morgenstunden* 4.26 ("I know that my philosophy is no longer the philosophy of the times") reads (JA III.2 266): "*Previously crossed out before* 'I': 'They were originally not intended for this use.'" ("They" refers to the seventeen Lectures—or "essays," as Mendelssohn calls them at 4.24—of *Morgenstunden*; "this use" refers to their publication.)
36. Cf. IMH LXX–LXXI.
37. Ger.: *Weltweise*. See IPM XVIIIn23.

tive religion than did the very much freer Leibniz. It has been emphasized that Mendelssohn drops Leibniz's references to Christian sources or else replaces them with references to Jewish sources.[38] What is more remarkable is that he cites many fewer Jewish sources than Leibniz does Christian ones and that, in one passage in particular where Leibniz adduces a Jewish (biblical) example, he leaves it unmentioned.[39] In that same context he uses the religious vocabulary far less uninhibitedly than Leibniz: he speaks of "actions and concerns" and of "meditation on divine perfections," rather than of "prayers";[40] he avoids talking of "pious men" and "piety";[41] he emphasizes the anthropomorphic character of certain expressions about God.[42] It is not quite as certain to him as it is to Leibniz that there is a sensory reward and punishment after death.[43] To be sure, he does decide to deal with the question of miracles; but it concerns him so little that he literally forgets his purpose.[44] This same tendency shows up fully in his explicit critique of Leibniz: what forces him into the critique at first is by no means a peculiarly Christian doctrine, but the "*universal*[45] popular ethical doctrine," allegedly accepted by Leibniz, ". . . in which every virtue would result in a reward."[46] One cannot characterize the difference in question any better than Mendelssohn himself does *implicite*[47] in that in §2 he renders "*vere Orthodoxi*"[48]

38. See IGC xcviiif., above.
39. *Sache Gottes* §30 and annotation. {LS}
For LS's editorial annotation to *Sache Gottes* §30 (JA III.2 336), see appendix 2, supplement to IGC xcviiin6.
40. See *Sache Gottes* §§44 and 48, and the annotations. {LS}
For LS's editorial annotations to *Sache Gottes* §§44 and 48 (JA III.2 337, 338), see appendix 2, supplement to IGC ciiin40.
41. See *Sache Gottes* §§1, 61 and 69, and the annotations. {LS}
For LS's editorial annotations to *Sache Gottes* §§1, 61 and 69 (JA III.2 335), see appendix 2, supplement to IGC ciiin41.
42. See *Sache Gottes* §44 and annotations, as well as §49 {LS}
For LS's editorial annotations to §44 (JA III.2 337), see appendix 2, supplement to IGC ciiin40.
43. See *Sache Gottes* §52 and annotations. {LS}
For LS's editorial annotations to §52 (JA III.2 338), see appendix 2, supplement to IGC ciiin43.
44. See *Sache Gottes* §46 and annotation; cf. §11 and annotation. {LS}
For LS's editorial annotation to *Sache Gottes* §11 (JA III.2 335), see appendix 2, supplement to IGC ciiin44.
For LS's editorial annotations to *Sache Gottes* §46 (JA III.2 337–38), see appendix 2, supplement to IGC xcixn20.
45. The emphasis is LS's.
46. *Sache Gottes* §55. {LS}
47. Lat.: implicitly.
48. Lat.: "the truly Orthodox." The corresponding paragraph in *Causa Dei* to which LS is referring (§2 [Ger VI 439; cf. Sch 114]) is quoted in full in LS's editorial annotation to *Sache Gottes* §2, translated in appendix 2, supplement to IGC xcviiin6.

by "the true religion of reason": Mendelssohn distinguishes himself qua man of reason from Leibniz qua orthodox (according to his own explicit view, at any rate).

The critique of orthodoxy in the name of reason makes its appearance initially as a critique of the "popular ethical doctrine" in the name of a "higher," "stricter" morality: against the "popular ethical doctrine, . . . in which every virtue would result in a reward," Mendelssohn appeals to the "higher ethical doctrine of the wise," according to which the reward for virtue is simply virtue.[49] {CIII} Let it remain unsettled with what right Mendelssohn finds the meaning of the "popular ethical doctrine" spelled out in the words cited from Leibniz in §54 of *Causa Dei*.[50] What is decisive is that in the passages where Leibniz expresses himself thematically about the principle of morality, he leaves no doubt about the priority in principle of *amor verus* over *amor mercenarius*[51] according to the Christian tradition, which does not distinguish itself from the Jewish tradition in this regard. And as for occasional accommodations to the context of the vulgar imagination, Mendelssohn is scarcely entitled, or even quite seriously willing, to reject them out of hand[52]—he who shortly before had said, in *Jerusalem*,[53]

> Without God, providence, and a future life, charity is but an inborn weakness, and goodwill is little more than a folly into which we seek to lure one another so that the simpleton will toil while the clever one can enjoy himself and have a good laugh at the other's expense.[54]

Mendelssohn thinks differently than Leibniz not about the relationship of virtue and reward, but about the relationship of vice and punishment: the struggle against mercenary morality is a struggle that is not so much for the purity of virtue, as it is against the harshness of punishments.

The struggle is directed chiefly against the harshest of all punishments, against eternal damnation. Leibniz had deemed it good to defend the Chris-

---

49. *Sache Gottes* §§55 to 59. Cf. the deviations from Leibniz in *Sache Gottes* §§28 and 32. {LS}
 In this connection, see LS's editorial annotations to §§28 and 32 (JA III.2 336), in appendix 2, supplement to IGC CIIIn49.
50. See annotation to *Sache Gottes* §55. {LS}
 For LS's editorial annotation to *Sache Gottes* §55 (JA III.2 338), see appendix 2, supplement to IGC CIIIn50.
51. Lat.: true love . . . mercenary love.
52. Cf. *Sache Gottes* §57. {LS}
53. *Jerusalem* 131; cf. Ark 63.
54. Cf. in this connection E. Zeller, *Geschichte der deutschen Philosophie seit Leibniz* (Munich: R. Oldenburg, 1873), 345. {LS}

tian "dogma" of the "eternal damnation of the wicked." Mendelssohn rejects it as wholly incompatible with God's justice.[55] In doing so, he adopts Leibniz's conception of justice as benevolence governed by wisdom.[56] Despite this agreement in regard to the principle, there turns out to be a diametrical contrast in regard to the application of the principle to the question of eternal punishments, since Leibniz puts the emphasis on the moment of wisdom, whereas Mendelssohn on the contrary puts it on the moment of benevolence.[57] This means that the purpose of creation for Leibniz is chiefly the beauty and order of the cosmos; for Mendelssohn, {CIV} on the contrary, it is chiefly the happiness of man, of each man.[58] The result of this is that for Leibniz all suffering is in principle justified in the upward glance at the universe—indeed, all suffering is grounded, and thereby justified, in the universal order—whereas for Mendelssohn the suffering of any one human being remains a decisive objection against the perfection of the universe insofar as this suffering does not redound to the benefit of that same individual.[59] It is for just that reason that Mendelssohn, in contrast to Leibniz, is sentimental.[60] And as Leibniz can justify all suffering in the upward glance at the universe, so he can justify in particular even the most extreme

---

55. *Sache Gottes* §60. {LS}
56. *Sache Gottes* §§40–41 {LS}
57. See *Sache Gottes* §§12, 36, 52 and annotations; on this deviation from Leibniz, typical as it is of later Leibnizians, cf. the remarks of Zeller, *op. cit.*, 307. {LS}

For LS's editorial annotation to *Sache Gottes* §12 (JA III.2 335), see appendix 2, supplement to IGC CIIIn57.

For LS's editorial annotations to *Sache Gottes* §36 (JA III.2 337), see appendix 2, supplement to IGC XCVIIn6.

For LS's editorial annotations to *Sache Gottes* §52 (JA III.2 338), see appendix 2, supplement to IGC CIIn43.s

58. Cf. Leibniz, *Théodicée* §§118ff. [Ger VI 168 ff.; Hug 188ff.], with *Evidenz* 319.1–7 [Dah 298] and annotations; cf. meanwhile, e.g., Leibniz, *Système nouveau de la nature* §5 [Ger IV 479–80; Wie 108–9 or ArGa 140 or FrWo 146]. {LS}

For LS's editorial annotations to *Evidenz* 319.1–7 (JA II 425), see appendix 2, supplement to IGC CIVn58.

59. See *Sache Gottes* §§1, 12, 40, 47, 50, and annotations; but cf. also the similar expression of Leibniz in "Principes de la nature . . ." §18 [Ger VI 606; Wie 532–33 or ArGa 212–13 or FrWo 265–66]. {LS}

For LS's editorial annotations to *Sache Gottes* §1 (JA III.2 335), appendix 2, supplement to IGC CIIIn41.

For LS's editorial annotations to *Sache Gottes* §12 (JA III.2 335), see appendix 2, supplement to IGC CIIIn57.

For LS's editorial annotations to *Sache Gottes* §40, 47, and 50 (JA III.2 337, 338), see appendix 2, supplement to IGC CIVn59.

60. [LS uses the French (or English) word.] See *Sache Gottes* §§41 and 48, and annotations; cf. IP XIXff. {LS}

For LS's editorial annotations to *Sache Gottes* §§41 and 48 (JA III.2 337, 338), see appendix 2, supplement to IGC CIVn60.

suffering, eternal damnation, which admittedly becomes impossible if, as Mendelssohn assumes, creation's purpose, which is not to be shaken by any human lapse, is the happiness of each human individual.[61] Mendelssohn's concept of God's benevolence results especially in the denial of a merely mercenary punitiveness: God always punishes each individual whom He punishes for his own betterment as well, therefore He punishes no sinner eternally.[62] Leibniz on the contrary, thanks to his conviction concerning the priority of the universe and thus of contemplation, can accept, besides *"justice corrective,"* a

> justice punitive, qui est proprement vindicative, . . . qui contente non seulement l'offensé, mais encore les sages qui la voient: comme une belle musique ou bien une bonne architecture contente les esprits bien faits. . . . C'est ainsi que les peines des damnés continuent, lors même qu'elles ne servent plus à détourner le mal.[63]

Admittedly, Leibniz did not believe in eternal damnation as it was understood by the Christian tradition.[64] The fact that he could nevertheless defend the Church doctrine has its ultimate ground in just that conviction that makes up the content of his defense: in the conviction concerning the unconditional priority of the beauty and order of the whole over the happiness of the part, of human beings therefore as well {cv}, and in the conviction inseparable from it that happiness consists in the observation of the universal order. For with the ideal of contemplation comes the splitting up of the human race into the "wise" and the "multitude," and with this the acceptance of a twofold manner of communicating truths, an esoteric and an exoteric one. Such a distinction Mendelssohn could not accept unreservedly; his presuppositions forced him into popular philosophy.[65] The acceptance or denial of the fundamental natural order of rank has a

---

61. *Sache Gottes* §§60, 77, and 82. Cf. *Phädon* 102 [Cul 153–54; Nob 125]. {LS}
62. Cf. also *Seele* 231–32 and annotations. {LS}
  For LS's editorial annotations to *Seele* 231–32, see www.press.uchicago.edu/sites/strauss/, ad loc.
63. *Théodicée* §§73–74 [Ger VI 141ff.; cf. Hug 161–62]. {LS}
  Fr.: "corrective justice . . . punitive justice that is appropriately retributive, . . . that satisfies not only the injured, but also the wise who see it: as a beautiful piece of music, or indeed a good piece of architecture, satisfies cultivated minds. . . . Thus it is that the sufferings of the damned continue, even when they no longer serve to ward off the evil."
64. See esp. *Théodicée* §272 [Ger VI 280–81; Hug 293–94]. {LS}
65. Cf. his critique of "Ernst and Falk" in the letter to Lessing of November 11, 1777 [JA XII.2 98–99]. {LS}

certain connection with the acceptance or denial of hierarchies legitimized through custom. Leibniz expressed the thought of the unconditional priority of the beauty and order of the whole over the happiness of the part in a parable that is very instructive in this regard. Against that thought, Bayle had objected that a prince of true magnanimity would prefer comfortable architecture to grand architecture: for that reason, he would take care that the inhabitants of a city to be built for him found all sorts of comforts. Leibniz remarks, on the contrary, that in the case of a conflict over the beauty of the structure of the palace, "the comfort of a few domestics" should be sacrificed.[66] That Mendelssohn does not share Leibniz's courtly taste, but Bayle's bourgeois one, needs no proof. But if it needed a proof, then it could perhaps be found precisely in his recasting of *Causa Dei*. In any case, it deserves to be remarked that he considers it necessary to add an example of a "store clerk" to Leibniz's passing example of dueling soldiers.[67]

So long as one remains within Mendelssohn's own purview, belief in the priority of benevolence as a love that is not demanding, but "softly dispensed" and "tender,"[68] over any other divine attribute shows up as the radical presupposition by whose acceptance Mendelssohn turns out to be in contrast with Leibniz. Between the recourse to God's benevolence understood in that way and the distancing from positive religion that the discussion has been about up till now, there exists a connection that cannot be adequately understood from Mendelssohn's {CVI} own statements. The isolating of divine benevolence was a reaction against the isolating of divine ruling power and glory, particularly as it had been brought about by supralapsarian Calvinism. Since the spokesmen for this "despotic"[69] representation of God appealed, not without the appearance of some justification, to the tradition founded in the Bible and especially to Jewish tradition, there seemed no other way open for the extreme opponents than that of countering the positive theology of sovereignty and glory with a natural theology of pure benevolence, independent of all positive theology. It was Bayle who

---

66. *Théodicée* §215 [Ger VI 247; Hug 262]. {LS}
67. See *Sache Gottes* §67 and annotations. {LS}
For LS's editorial annotations to *Sache Gottes* §67 (JA III.2 340), see appendix 2, supplement to IGC cvn67.
68. For these items, see IP xixn46, xixn48.
69. Cf. Leibniz, *Théodicée* §§6, 167, with §82 [Ger VI 106, 209–10, with 146–47; Hug 127, 228, with 166]; *Causa Dei* §§2, 76, 131 [Sch 114, 130, 142]; for Leibniz's understanding of theological "Despotism," see *Causa Dei* §2—quoted in LS's editorial annotation to *Sache Gottes* §2; see appendix 2, supplement to IGC xcviin6.

had brought about this countering. From the concept of God as the most perfect being of all, he deduced that God could have created the world out of benevolence alone and therefore only for the sake of the happiness, the absence of suffering, of human beings and that for that reason, taking into consideration divine omnipotence and omniscience, the whole of creation must in fact serve the purpose of the happiness of human beings. From this concept of *"bonté idéale,"*[70] there resulted for him the elimination of divine punitiveness specifically:

> comme tout doit être heureux dans l'empire d'un souverain être infiniment bon et infiniment puissant, les peines n'y doivent point avoir lieu.[71]

What is valid for benevolent fathers is valid *a potiori*[72] for the all-benevolent God; now, benevolent fathers would not chastise their children with rods if they were convinced that *"une complaisance sans bornes"*[73] were the effective means of education:[74]

> Ils se serviroient du sucre, et de tout ce qui seroit le plus [au goût de l'enfant], s'ils espoirent de trouver là un meilleur remède.[75]

Now admittedly, Bayle himself had meant the aforementioned deduction in his tentative and tempting manner: he made it clear that the a priori deduction would come to naught over the experience of human suffering, that by making that deduction he was meanwhile putting into doubt not merely positive (Christian) theology but also natural theology; yet he confessed that experience as distinguished from {cvii} the a priori deduction does not speak in favor of the theology of pure benevolence, but of dualism in the sense of Marcion or the Manicheans.[76] In other words: the

---

70. Fr.: "ideal goodness"; "ideal benevolence."
71. Fr.: "as all ought to be happy in the empire of an infinitely good and infinitely powerful sovereign being, sufferings ought to have no place in it."
72. Lat.: even more.
73. Fr.: "an unlimited kindness."
74. DHC, s.v. *"Origène," remarque* E. — As Mendelssohn distances himself from Leibniz in the direction of Bayle in general, so too in his statements about divine punitiveness in particular; cf. the repeated *"allenfalls"* ["perhaps"] in *Sache Gottes* §57, as well as the explicit mention of reward with a simultaneous veiling of punishment in *Phädon* 123 at the bottom [Cul 201; Nob 143 top]. {LS}
75. Fr.: "They would make use of sugar and of all that would be most [to the child's taste], if they hoped to find a better remedy there."
76. DHC, s.v. *"Marcionites," remarque* F, and *"Manichéens," remarque* D [Pop 144–52]. {LS}

theology of pure benevolence that excludes punitiveness was feasible only if the "otherworldly" tendencies of the Christian tradition were raised to the Gnostic extreme. It was in answer to Bayle's skepticism that Leibniz devised his *Théodicée*. He managed to restore natural theology by restricting Bayle's principle of pure benevolence, not, to be sure, by means of the principle of sovereignty and glory, nor by means of the principle of justice, but by means of the principle of wisdom, i.e., of regard for the beauty and order of the universe.[77] Unlike the natural theology of pure benevolence, the natural theology of benevolence governed by wisdom was not demonstrated by experience, but simply confirmed by experience: by the latest results of natural science.[78] And by drawing from his natural theology of benevolence delimited by wisdom the inference that the world, i.e., "this" world, must be the best of all possible worlds, Leibniz managed not only to hold in check the "otherworldly" tendencies connected with the theology of pure benevolence, but to uproot them: the world ceases to be that "vale of sorrows" of which "a multitude of gloomy enthusiasts" had known how to talk so much.[79] In the present context, everything comes down to Leibniz's having brought about the restoration of natural theology by having benevolence delimited by wisdom and not by justice. For, by doing just that, he accepted as a matter of course the elimination of divine justice and punitiveness that had been, if not the original aim, in any case the result, of Bayle's deduction. Indeed, he gave that elimination a secure foundation precisely by rejecting the classical concept of justice as a steadfast will to grant each his due: by his concept of justice as benevolence governed by wisdom, the peculiar essence of justice dissolved into the two moments of wisdom and benevolence, {cviii} and thereby evaporated. This modification of the concept of justice might always be passed off—and particularly by Mendelssohn—as a formal improvement of the classical definition, supposedly inadequate formally;[80] in truth, it had a revolutionary character,

---

77. See esp. *Théodicée* §151 [Ger VI 199–200; Hug 217–18]; cf. on the contrary Kant, *Kritik der praktischen Vernunft*, ed. Vorländer, 166–67 [*Critique of Practical Reason*, trans. Lewis White Beck (Indianapolis: Library of Liberal Arts/Bobbs-Merrill, 1956), 150–51]. {LS}

Cf. also Strauss, CM 39.

78. Cf. *Causa Dei* §143 [Ger VI 460; Sch 144–45]. {LS}

79. Cf. *Sendschreibung* 102, as well as *Jerusalem* 108–9 [Ark 39–40]. {LS}

The two phrases of Mendelssohn's which LS is quoting here are also found in the Mendelssohnian passage LS quotes at IEL xxiii. Cf. also IMH lxi.

80. See *Evidenz* 291.29ff. [Dah 273–74] and annotations. {LS}

For LS's editorial annotations to *Evidenz* 291.29ff., see appendix 2, supplement to IGC cviiin80.

as came to be clearly recognized by the opponents[81] and at least occasionally pointed out by the adherents.[82] As for God's punitiveness in particular, Leibniz did make the attempt to preserve it by appealing to retributive justice; in fact, however, following the adoption of his opponents' presuppositions, it was impossible for him to assert the meaning peculiar to punishment: punishment, insofar as it is more than mere disciplining, became for him an utterly beautiful spectacle. That is why it has to be said on the whole that, by restricting Bayle's principle considerably, Leibniz guaranteed the viability of that principle. It is for just that reason that the contrast between Leibniz and Mendelssohn is not as radical as it presents itself initially.

Natural theology as it had been restored by Leibniz was initially adopted root and branch by Mendelssohn: Voltaire's *Candide*, which is a veiled defense of Bayle's "Manicheanism" over against Leibniz's "Optimism"—Martin, the most rational character in the novel, is a Manichean,[83] and he is "un pauvre savant qui avait travaillé dix ans pour les libraires à Amsterdam"[84]—found him wholly on Leibniz's side.[85] And when Abbt again attacked the Leibniz-Wolffian Enlightenment's doctrine of providence in the name of Bayle, he explicitly implored the "spirit of the great Leibniz."[86] But since Leibniz's success was for him a self-evident possession, and since he could thereby believe that by this very success° both superstition and unbelief would be overcome once and for all, for this reason he could again emancipate to a certain degree the principle of pure {CIX} benevolence taken up by Bayle that had been "disposed of"[87] in the *Théodicée* and thereby bring about that contrast with Leibniz. The form in which this emancipation came about, however, was now decisively determined once again by Leibniz. A sign of this is that Mendelssohn validates the central reservation that he has to

---

81. See Wolff's polemic against it in TN I §1067 note. {LS}
82. Cf. *Gegenbetrachtung* 73.6–7 and moreover the following statement by Mendelssohn's friend Eberhard in his *Neue Apologie des Sokrates*, I (Berlin and Stettin, 1776), 123: "An enlightened philosophy recognizes *no* justice in God *except* his essential benevolence insofar as it is governed by wisdom." {LS}
83. Cf. *Candide*, ch. 19 and 20 [Hav 60–68; Woo 42–48]. {LS}
84. Fr.: "a poor savant who had worked ten years for publishers in Amsterdam" (Hav 64; cf. Woo 46).
85. *Philosophische Gespräche* 356ff. [Dah 112ff.]; cf. the Fifteenth Lecture of *Morgenstunden* [*idem* 125–37; Scholz 29–44; Val 66–77; cf. Got 150–52 (for *Morgenstunden* 125–26 and 132–33 only)]. {LS}
86. *Orakel* 21.27.
87. Ger.: "*aufgehoben*." Cf. *Théodicée* §241 (Ger VI 261; cf. Hug 276), where Leibniz speaks of our now being "débarrassés enfin de la cause morale du mal moral" [finally disencumbered of the moral cause of moral evil].

raise against Leibniz's justification of all suffering, even of the most extreme suffering—he does not present it as emphatically and as precisely in any other writing as he does just in *God's Cause*—chiefly in expressions whose Leibnizian provenance is unmistakable.[88] If, to the "excuse that the evil in the parts is due to the perfection of the whole," he objects that "every perceiving and thinking being is a system unto itself, has its own interest in existence, therefore cannot without injustice suffer for the sake of another's well-being," that the I is as it were an atom that "transforms the course of its own destinies,"[89] then he owes the possibility of doing so to Leibniz,[90] who had discovered the one "spontanéité peu connue jusqu'ici"[91] of the monads, "qui sont les seuls et vrais atomes de la nature,"[92] and had understood monads as self-sufficient beings, beings° independent of all external causes. And even if Mendelssohn says of the "only self-standing beings" that they "have a long progress to higher perfections, resembling a legal claim,"[93] if he therefore almost awards creatures an absolute claim, a claim even over against God, not even with that does he go beyond Leibniz. For Leibniz too had said,[94] "dans les idées de Dieu une monade demande avec raison que Dieu en réglant les autres dès le commencement des choses ait regard à elle."[95] {cx} Besides, Leibniz had specifically awarded to all rational minds the unalienable quality of citizens in God's State.[96] Above all, however, by

88. *Sache Gottes* §§60, 76, 78, 79, 82. {LS}
89. Or: determinations.
90. *Théodicée* §§59 and 89 [Ger VI 135 and 152; Hug 155 and 172]. {LS}
91. Fr.: "spontaneity little known previously." The translation is LS's; see JPCM 102.
92. Fr.: "which are the sole and true atoms of Nature."
93. *Sache Gottes* §79. {LS}
94. *Monadologie* §51 [Ger VI 615; cf. Wie 543 or Sch 156 or FrWo 274–75]. Cf. also *Monadologie* §54 [Ger VI 616; Wie 544 or Sch 156 or FrWo 275]. — Mendelssohn was pointed to the significance of this thought for the understanding of Leibnizian philosophy by Boscovich, toward whose critique, developed in the appendix to his *Philosophia naturalis*, he takes the following stance in *Literaturbrief* #56 (September 20, 1759) [JA V.1 86]: "On the system of the best world, Mr. Boscovich has very strange thoughts. He believes that if this were the best world, we would have no need to thank God for our existence; for surely He would have had to call us into existence on account of our merit, since the other creatures, which He might have left in their nothingness, do not suit the best world as well as we do. Even if one wanted to exempt Him from the *having to*, that would nevertheless require yet another weighty limitation here; what odd concepts Mr. Boscovich has concerning gratitude!" — Cf. also Kant's exposition of Genesis 3:22 in "Mutmasslicher Anfang der Weltgeschichte" ["Conjectural Beginning of Human History," trans. Emil L. Fackenheim, in *Kant: On History*, ed. Lewis White Beck (Indianapolis: Library of Liberal Arts/Bobbs-Merrill, 1963), 59]. {LS}

On Father Roger Joseph Boscovich, S.J. (1711–87), cf. LS's editorial annotations to *Phädon 3* 148.36 and *Phädon* 62.15–66.14 (JA III.1 414, 403), in appendix 2, supplement to IGC cixn94 and n32 *ad loc.*

95. Fr.: "in God's ideas, it is reasonable for a monad to demand that God in ruling the others since the beginning of things have regard for it."
96. Cf. IMH LXXIII.

the dissolution of the classical concept of justice, in which the original sense of justice as obedience to law had been preserved, he had considerably advanced the process that aimed at the suppression of law as obligation in favor of right as claim.[97] What distinguishes Mendelssohn from Leibniz on this point is, rather, merely that he, the author of *Jerusalem*, was incomparably more strongly interested in the practical consequences that had to result from the change of the basic concepts, i.e., in reclaiming the rights of man, than was his teacher.

97. Cf. IMH XVII–XIX, XXII, LXI–LXII, LXXIV–LXXV.

APPENDIX 1

[1937]   Strauss Preliminary Remark to
A Reminder of Lessing[1]

The present explanation of Lessing's intentions is the attempt of an amateur, not a scholar; it is the fruit of hours of leisure, not years of labor. It is uncertain whether only years of scholarly labor earn one° the right to an amateurish exposition. But certain it is that no one becomes a proper scholar without having been an amateur at first and becoming an amateur over and over again. Scholars in the making have the obligatory privilege that only their leisure justifies their labor.

The foregoing justification is needed, and apt, simply for addressing the fact that its Jewish author, instead of tidying up his own doorstep, attempts to make a Christian-born philosopher's confrontation with Christianity more familiar to Jewish readers. Let it therefore be noted from the outset that, to be sure, much is altered in detail, but little in principle, if wherever Christianity is spoken of in the present writing, one thinks of Judaism. This manner of reading is requested of the gentle reader, in the interest of the issues and therefore in his own interest. The author had the weakness of preferring to give his attention to a Jew. But despite searching in earnest among the apostate or suspect Jews of modern times, he found not one man with Lessing's intellectual freedom. Besides, the author was not unmindful of the obligation of thanks that is owed by his nation[2] to that great son of the German nation,[3] especially at this moment of farewell.

Cambridge, England, on . . .

---

1. LSGS II 607–8. "Unpublished. A manuscript, written in ink with pencil corrections. Leo Strauss papers, Box 11, Folder 7, Department of Special Collections, University of Chicago Library." (Heinrich Meier's editorial annotation, LSGS II 626)
2. I.e., by the Jewish nation.
3. I.e., to Lessing.

APPENDIX 2
Supplements to Translator's Notes

SUPPLEMENT TO IPM XVIn12

Bruno Strauss's editorial annotation on Prémontval (JA XI 391)

In 1752 André Pierre le Guay, known by the name of Prémontval (1716–64), after living as an itinerant adventurer came to Berlin, where he was accepted into the Academy in the very same year. His numerous philosophical works, mostly only sketches, in their critical parts combat the adherents of the Leibniz-Wolffian school (cf. Christian Bartholmèss, *Histoire philosophique de l'Académie de Prusse* [2 vols.; Paris: M. Ducloux, 1850–51], II, 207ff.). The fourth of Mendelssohn's *Philosophical Dialogues* (1755) defends Leibnizian views against the attacks that Prémontval in his *Pensées sur la liberté* (1754), as well as in his *Du Hazard sous l'Empire de la Providence* (1755), had directed against the Leibnizians (cf. the stinging but respectful words that Prémontval devoted to this Mendelssohnian polemic in his *Vues philosophiques* of 1756; available to me only in the 2nd ed. of 1761, pp. 276–77). A further polemical passage in Mendelssohn's letters *On the Sentiments*, which Prémontval in agreement with Michaelis and others took as applying to himself (see JA XI 17), led then to Mendelssohn's entering first into a literary correspondence with Prémontval and, subsequent to Prémontval's warm response, into a personally friendly one. Cf. also Mendelssohn's judgment about Prémontval in JA XI 110, 117, the restrained discussion in the 94th *Litteratur-Brief* (JA V.1 174ff.), and the interesting circumstance that Mendelssohn, in the acknowledgment of Prémontval as "a scholar who, it is certain, is not lacking in the acumen deserving of the name of a true philosopher," which the first edition of his *Dialogues* contains, replaced the word "acumen" by "talent" in 1761 (JA I 32 and 370 [cf. Dah 123]).

Attestations to Mendelssohn's (missing) letter to Prémontval in October 1755, are: Mendelssohn to Lessing, no. 10 [JA XI 17–18] and Prémontval to J. D. Michaelis, January 6, 1756 (Buhle I, 114): "J'ai su de Mr. Moses ce, que j'ai l'honneur de Vous écrire. C'est ce philosophe juste, auteur de Traité des Sensations et des Entretiens philosophiques. Je le trouve home d'esprit et de mérite, et je Vous dois cette conoissance. Il m'écrivit il y a quelque tems pour se justifier de m'avoir en vue dans certaines qualifications fort dures, ou Vous n'étiez cependant pas le seul, Monsieur, qui crussiez qu'il m'en voulait. Sur la cordialité de ma réponse il me vint voir, et nous liâmes amitié...." [I have known of Mr. Moses what I have the honor of writing you. He is that equitable philosopher, author of *Treatise on the Sentiments* and *Philosophical Writings*. I find him a man of intellect and merit, and I owe you this knowledge. He wrote me some time ago to justify himself for having me in mind in certain very harsh characterizations, where meanwhile you were not the only one, Monsieur, who believed that he meant me by them. Following the cordiality of my reply he came to see me, and we established a friendship....][1]

SUPPLEMENT TO IPM XVIIn15

LS's editorial annotation to Pope! 46.8 (JA II 379)

Leibniz's doctrine was first described as "Optimism" by his opponent Crousaz (cf. annotation to *Pope!* 62.4–6), as Gottsched remarks in his pamphlet against the Berlin Academy's prize competition for the year 1755 (*De optimismi macula diserte nuper Alexandro Popio Anglo, tacite autem G. G. Leibnitio, perperam licet, inusta*, Leipzig, 1753, IV).

LS's editorial annotation to Pope! 47.7–10 (JA II 379)

On Pope's behalf and against the opponents of "Optimism," Warburton (see annotation to 62.4–6)[2] and Gottsched (*loc. cit. passim*) had argued that "Optimism" is the common coin of the whole philosophical and theological tradition. In doing so, Warburton had called attention to Plato and Shaftesbury, and Gottsched to Thales, Chrysippus, Plato, Augustine et al. For Spinoza, cf. Mendelssohn's *Philosophical Dialogues* (JA I 17–18 [or JA I 352–53; Dah 108–9]).

SUPPLEMENT TO IPM XVIIn16

LS's editorial annotation to Pope! 46.3ff. (JA II 379)

The competition announcement° read, literally: "On demande l'examen du Système de Pope, contenu dans la proposition: Tout est bien. Il s'agit: 1. De

---

1. Mendelssohn's word for "philosopher" here is *Weltweise*; see IPM XVIIIn23, below. On Mendelssohn's "letters *On the Sentiments*" (called by Prémontval the "*Traité des Sensations*"), see IMH LXIVn299. On Bruno Strauss, see IMH XXXVIn150. On the anti-Leibnizianism of the Berlin Academy, see also supplement to IPM XIXn34, below.
2. For LS's editorial annotation to *Pope!* 62.4–6, see IPM XVIIIn11.

determiner le vrai sens de cette proposition, conformément à l'hypothèse de son auteur. 2. De la comparer avec le Système de l'Optimisme, ou du choix du meilleur, pour en marquer exactement les rapports et les différences. 3. Enfin d'alléguer les raisons qu'on croira les plus propres à établir ou à détruire ce Système." [What is being asked for is the examination of Pope's system as contained in the proposition "All is good." It is a matter of (1) determining the true meaning of this proposition in conformity with the hypothesis of its author, (2) comparing it with the System of Optimism, or of the choice of the best, in order to note exactly the similarities and the differences, and (3) finally, adducing the reasons most proper for establishing or destroying this System.] (According to GAW II 306.)

SUPPLEMENT TO IPM XVIIn17

From Bruno Strauss's editorial annotation on Maupertuis (at JA XI 392)

Pierre Louis Moreau de Maupertuis (1698–1759), natural scientist, mathematician, and philosopher, was president of the Berlin Academy since 1746. . . . Maupertuis [in 1756] joked about Mendelssohn that there was nothing of being a great man that was lacking in him except a little foreskin.

SUPPLEMENT TO IPM XVIIn18

LS's editorial annotation to Pope! 64.10–38 (JA II 384–85)

E.g., *Théodicée* §§9, 21, 22, 74, 84 [Ger VI 107–8, 115–16, 142, 147–48; Hug 79, 87–88, 115–16, 120–21]; *Monadologie* §§87–89 [Ger VI 618; Wie 551–52, or Sch 162–63, or FrWo 280–81]; "Principes de la nature et de la grâce" §§11, 15 [Ger VI 608–9; Wie 529–31 or ArGa 210–12 or FrWo 263–65]. — Maupertuis spells out the relationship of Malebranche's, Leibniz's, and Pope's theodicies in the following way: "Les uns, pour conserver sa sagesse (*sc.*, la sagesse de Dieu), semblent avoir diminué sa puissance; disant qu'il a fait tout ce qu'il pouvoit faire de mieux (Leibniz, *Théodicée* §§224–25 [Ger VI 251–52]): qu'entre tous les Mondes possibles, celui-ci, *malgré ses défautes*, étoit encore le meilleur. Les autres, pour conserver sa puissance, semblent faire tort à sa sagesse. Dieu, selon eux, pouvoit bien faire un Monde plus parfait que celui que nous habitons; mais il auroit fallu qu'il y employât des moyens trop compliqués; et il a eu plus en vue la manière dont it opéroit, que la perfection de l'ouvrage (Malebranche, *Méditations chrétiennes et métaphysiques* VII [see *Oeuvres complètes*, 22 vols. (Paris: Vrin, 1958–84), X, 69–81]) . . . . Je ne parle point d'une autre espèce de Philosophie, qui soutient *qu'il n'y a point de mal* dans la nature: Que tout ce qui est, est bien (Pope)." [Some, to preserve his wisdom (*sc.*, God's wisdom), seem to have diminished his power, saying that he has made everything he could have made the best (Leibniz, *Theodicy* §§224–25 [Ger VI 252; Hug 267–68]): that among all possible worlds, this one *despite its defects* is still the best. The others, to preserve his power, seem to do damage to his wisdom. God, according to them, could well have made a world more perfect than the one that we inhabit; but he would have had to employ means that were too complicated; and he had in mind the manner in which it would operate more than the perfection of the work (Malebranche, *Christian and Metaphysical Meditations*, VII). . . . I am not speaking of another species of philosophy, which maintains *that there is no evil* in nature: that everything that is, is good (Pope).] (*Oeuvres* [Berlin, 1753], I, 16–18). — I have emphasized the passages [*sc.*, here in Maupertuis's *Essai de cosmologie*] proving that Maupertuis held that Pope's doctrine was not identical with Leibniz's doctrine—cf. IPM xvii.

SUPPLEMENT TO IPM XVIIIn24

LS's editorial annotation to Pope! 51.4–11 (JA II 381)

In the foreword ("The Design") to the *Essay on Man*, Pope says: "If I could flatter myself that this *Essay* has any merit, it is . . . in forming a temperate, yet not inconsistent; and a short, yet not imperfect system of Ethics. This I might have done in prose; but I chose verse, and even rhyme, for two reasons: The one will appear obvious; that principles, maxims, or precepts so written, both strike the reader more strongly at first, and are more easily retained by him afterwards." Pope explicitly required limiting himself to the "large, open, and perceptible parts," knowledge of which would be more useful than subtler investigations and would not, like the latter, give occasion for quarrels and arouse the understanding more than the heart. Pope therefore claims to be a philosophical[3] poet only in the sense in which Lessing and Mendelssohn ascribe that title to him.

LS's editorial annotation to Pope! 51.6–7 (JA II 381)

Essay on Man I.16: ". . . vindicate the ways of God to Man."

---

3. In the editorial annotations included in the present supplement, Mendelssohn and Lessing's German words for "philosopher" and "philosophy" are *Weltweise* and *Weltweisheit*, respectively; "philosophical," however, is *philosophischen*; and "philosophy" in LS's parenthetical interpolation in his editorial annotation to *Pope!* 51.27–36 is *Philosophie*. See IPM xviiin23.

LS's editorial annotation to Pope! 51.7–8 (JA II 381–82)

The following further judgments of Mendelssohn's about Pope are to be compared here: In his review in the *Bibliothek der schönen Wissenschaften und der freyen Künste* of 1759 (JA V.1 266), he says of Pope that he is "a poet whose characteristic strengths consist in fine figures of speech, in melodiousness, in the choice of epithets, and in general in a pithy but nevertheless extremely pleasant poetic delivery, who poetizes informatively more than inspirationally, with understanding more than with imagination." And a *Literaturbrief* (Letter 126, of September 11, 1760) reads: "Our didactic poets are excellent when they present the systems of the philosophers, when they soar to the heights of the immeasurable, when they sing of the Creator and his works; on the other hand, they sink below the mediocre once they stoop to the morals of nations and of individual men. . . . You know that my taste is especially weighted in favor of philosophical poems that venture something higher." Mendelssohn counts the *Essay on Man* in the latter genre.

LS's editorial annotation to Pope! 51.27–36 (JA II 382)

In "Vindications of Horace," Lessing says: "It is even harder, or rather quite impossible, to infer his (*sc.*, Horace's) opinions from his poems, as they may well have to do with religion or philosophy; it must be, then, that he had explicitly wanted to expound various ones in authentic didactic poems. The subjects with which he is occupied force him to borrow the most beautiful thoughts for developing them in all respects, without investigating much which system they belong to. He will not be able to say much that is sublime about virtue without seeming to be a Stoic; nor much that is stirring about pleasure without taking on the look of an Epicurean" (LM V 298). Cf. also, on the remark at *Pope!* 48.15–17 [cf. Gal 47] that the poet "'in the ripe autumn of his years' can 'quite easily veil himself in the philosophical cloak,'" the following passage from the "Vindications": ". . . what, then, is ultimately known about it (*sc.*, about Horace's philosophy)? This, that *in his old age*, when he began to make a serious business of it, he swore to the words of no philosopher but took the best where he found it; everywhere, however, he left undisturbed those hairsplittings that have no influence on morals" (LM V 299). On the concept of the "philosophical poet," cf. the following characterization of Horace: "He, the philosophical poet who brought wit and reason into a more than sisterly bond and, with the refinement of a courtier, knew how to give the most serious doctrines of wisdom the well-wrought essence of friendly reminiscences and bestowed on them delightful harmonies, the more unerringly to give them entry into the heart" (LM V 273–74).

LS's editorial annotation to Pope! 51.32 (JA II 382–83)

Lessing in 1754 was occupied in depth with "the verses of Seneca"; see his *Von den lateinische Trauerspielen, welche unter dem Namen des Seneca bekannt sind* [On the Latin tragedies that are known as Seneca's] (LM VI 167–242).

SUPPLEMENT TO IPM XIXN34

Fritz Bamberger on the Berlin Academy's Anti-Leibnizianism (JA I xix–xx)

The *Philosophical Dialogues*, "this small work consisting of four dialogues on metaphysical truths" (Lessing, in his notice in [the *Berlinische Priviliegierte Zeitung* of March 1, 1755]), treats themes of Leibnizian philosophy. This was important, for at that time, around the middle of the eighteenth century, Leibniz's doctrine was *again* at the focal point of philosophical discussion. The interest . . . was neither purely theoretical, nor did it have only historical grounds. At the universities of Germany and inside its Academies, the adherents and the opponents of Christian Wolff had until recently been in the most vehement quarrel. The Wolffian system had been considered from each point of view, refuted from each and defended from each. That one had to go back to its origin and compare it with the doctrines of Leibniz was thus self-evident as well. Thus the opponents of Wolff, depending on their position, either had to show that Wolff had misconstrued or denied the truths of Leibniz, or else had to demonstrate that his views were false *along with* those of Leibniz. Precisely in Berlin, this interest in Leibniz . . . was especially intense. In this commotion, however, the Berlin Academy, as author and fomenter of the quarrel, stood with the philosophers in the first echelon—against Leibniz and against Wolff. In 1747, it had advertised a prize for an exposition and critique of the doctrine of monads in which the correctness or falsity of the Leibnizian concept of monads was to be demonstrated, and the prize was awarded to the writing of an ignoramus, one Herr von Justi. Justi *attacked* the doctrine of monads and, with that, provoked countless articles and rejoinders, all of which were on a very low level, with the exception of the arguments against monads of Crusius [i.e., Crousaz; cf. supplements to IPM xvIIn11 and xvIIn15, above]. In 1751, the Academy asked for the critique of Leibnizian Determinism—this too, like the foregoing, being a theme that Mendelssohn took up in his first writing [*sc.*, the *Philosophical Dialogues*]. And this theme of the Academy's, led as it was by French philosophers—Maupertuis was its president, and Prémontval, whom Mendelssohn attacked in his *Dialogues*, was a prominent member of it and a heated opponent of German scholastic philosophy[4]—goes against the Leibniz-Wolffian position until the time of Mendelssohn's beginnings as a writer. Maupertuis, who did not let up in his struggle against Leibniz and Wolff, proposed for the competition in 1753 the investigation "of the Popeian system that is contained in the principle 'All is right.'" The contempt for Leibniz in the theme went so far as to prompt Mendelssohn, together with Lessing, to write his *Pope a Metaphysician!* In this pamphlet, a front is made against the Academy openly, but in the *Philosophical Dialogues* too the spearhead against the anti-Leibnizianism of prominent Academicians is unmistakable.

SUPPLEMENT TO IPM XIXN41

LS's editorial annotation to Pope! 45.18 (JA II 379)

Cf. on this point Lessing's letter to Mendelssohn of February 18, 1755 [JA XI 14]: "Supposing, now, that we had won first prize in this learnèd lottery...."

SUPPLEMENT TO IPM XXN42

LS's editorial annotation to Pope! 67.11–28 (JA II 385)[5]

The following passages from Lessing's fragment "The Christianity of Reason" are to be compared with this critique: "§15 God could think of His perfections divided in an infinite number of ways.... §16 The most perfect way of thinking of His perfections discretely is that of thinking of them as divided by infinite degrees of more and less that follow one another in such

---

4. On Maupertuis and Prémontval, see supplements to IPM xviiin12, xviiin17, and xviiin18, above, and ITE xlvii.

5. *Pope!* 67.11–28 reads as follows [cf. Gal 12]: "On what grounds can *Pope* prove that the chain of things in the best world must be ordered in terms of a gradual downgrading of perfection? Let anyone cast eyes on the visible world before us! If *Pope's* principle is well-grounded, then it is impossible for our world to be the best. Things in it are alongside one another according to the order of effects and causes, but in no way according to a gradual downgrading. Sages and fools, animals and trees, insects and stones are all wonderfully mingled with one another in the world, and one would need to gather together limbs from the most distant animals in the world if one wanted to form such a chain as reaches gradually from nothingness to divinity. What *Pope* calls coherence, therefore, has no place in our world, and nevertheless it is the best and nevertheless no gap can be discovered in it. Why is this? Is not one led here to the Leibnizian system, namely, that by virtue of divine wisdom all beings in the best world must be grounded in one another, that is, ordered alongside one another according to the series of effects and causes?"

a way that there is nowhere a leap or a gap between them. §17 The beings in this world must therefore be ordered by such degrees. . . . §27 Since there cannot possibly be a leap in the series of beings, beings must also exist that are not aware of their perfections with sufficient clarity . . ." (LM XIV 177–78 [cf. Cha 100, 101; cf. Nis 27, 29]). Cf. the annotation to 62.19–63.21 [immediately below].

LS's editorial annotation to Pope! 62.19–63.21 (JA II 384)

Leibniz's and Pope's views on this point in no way differ as the text asserts. Leibniz and Pope both understand by the coherence of the world the interaction of all cosmic elements as well as the hierarchical ordering of forms (interaction—Leibniz, *Théodicée* §§7–9 [Ger VI 106–8; Hug 77–79], *Monadologie* §§ 56, 61, 63 [Ger VI 616–18; Wie 220–21 or Sch 156–58 or FrWo 275–77], "Principes de la nature et de la grâce" §§3, 13 [Ger VI 598, 604; Wie 523–24, 529–30, or ArGa 207–8, 211, or FrWo 259–60, 264], Pope, *Essay* I 23ff., 165–72, 247ff., III 7ff.; hierarchical ordering—Leibniz, *Théodicée* §§14, 31, 120 [Ger VI 110, 121, 172–74; Hug 128, 141–42, 191–93], *Sur le principe de vie* (Erd 431 [Wie 190–91]). Only this much is correct, that the discussion of the hierarchical ordering is comparatively more frequent in Pope than in Leibniz. — Cf. the editor's introduction [to *Pope a Metaphysician!*]. Mendelssohn speaks about the hierarchical ordering, etc., in the Third Dialogue of the *Phädon* [105.4ff.; Cul 158ff.; Nob 127ff.] and at the conclusion of the "Investigation into the Synthesis of the Soul with the Body" [i.e., *Seele* 233].

SUPPLEMENT TO ITE XLVIn**12**

Bruno Strauss's editorial annotation on Mendelssohn's letter to Lessing at the end of October 1755 (JA XI 393)

. . . the words "Oh the young scholar lies, etc." [in that letter] point to the attack that Mendelssohn in the fourth of his *Philosophical Dialogues* had directed against the Berlin Academician Johann Bernhard Merian's (1723–1807) treatise on *Le Principe des indiscernables* [The Principle of Indiscernibles]. He had spoken of him as the "young scholar" and added: "This half-witted author has scarcely deserved that a refutation be made to his objections." The remark, manifestly perceived as deprecating by the "young scholar" (more exactly, philosopher),[6] Mendelssohn now wants to soften by pointing, in contrast, to his own youth. In the second edition [of the *Philo-*

---

6. The word for "philosopher" here is *Weltweise*; see IPM xviiin23.

sophical Dialogues], Mendelssohn removed the adjective "young," as well as, in general, the entire harshness of the passage (JA I 370 [cf. Dah 123]). Later on, Merian's writings found a congenial critic in Mendelssohn (cf. JA V.1 174).

SUPPLEMENT TO ITE XLVII_N26

LS's editorial annotation to Evidenz 271.15–19 (JA II 416–17)

Hume, for one, has this view; cf. his *An Enquiry Concerning Human Understanding*, §XII, pt. III [here LS cites the German translation, *Versuche über die menschliche Erkenntniß* (Hamburg and Leipzig, 1755), 387–88]: "It seems to me, that the only objects of the abstract sciences or of demonstration are quantity and number, and that all attempts to extend this more perfect species of knowledge beyond these bounds are mere sophistry and illusion." — Here, however, one will have to think above all of Maupertuis, in whose "Examen philosophique de la preuve de l'existence de Dieu employée dans l'*Essai de Cosmologie*" (in *Histoire de l'Académie Royal des Sciences et Belles-Lettres, Année 1756* [Berlin, 1758]) . . . one reads: ". . . Cet accord à la verité et cette evidence ne se trouvent que dans les sciences mathématiques: tandis que toutes les autres parties de nos connaissances sont sujettes à des disputes éternelles, dans la Géometrie tout le monde est d'accord; cette science fixe le Sceptique le plus incertain, convainc l'esprit le plus obstiné." [. . . This agreement as regards truth and this evidence are found only in the mathematical sciences: whereas all the other parts of our knowledge are subject to eternal disputes, in Geometry everyone is in agreement; this science settles the most uncertain Skeptic, convinces the most stubborn mind.] (392) On the significance of Maupertuis's treatise for the history of the emergence of the *Treatise on Evidence*, see ITE.

SUPPLEMENT TO ITE XLVIII_N29

LS's editorial annotation to Evidenz 286.27–28 (JA II 419)

This definition of philosophy goes back to Baumgarten, who defines philosophy as *"scientia qualitatum in rebus sine fide cognoscendarum"* [the science of the qualities that are to be known in things without recourse to faith] (see *Acroasis logica* [Halle, 1761], §1). Kant ("[*Untersuchung*] über die Deutlichkeit des Grundsätze der natürlichen Theologie und der Moral," I, Betrachtung §4 [IKW II 182–83; Wal 255]) and Abbt (*Vermischte Werke*, IV [Berlin and Settin, 1780], 108) appeal to this concept of philosophy in their answers to the Berlin Academy's prize question.

LS's editorial annotation to Evidenz 286.29 *(JA II 419)*

"Science" according to Wolff is *"habitus asserta demonstrandi, hoc est, ex principiis certis et immotis per legitimam consequentiam inferendi"* [the steady habit of demonstrating, that is, of inferring a legitimate consequence on the basis of certain and unchanging principles] (*Logica, Disc. praelim.* §30).

SUPPLEMENT TO ITE XLVIIIn33

LS's editorial annotation to Evidenz 269.3–6 *(JA II 416)*

This objection to metaphysics was being made above all by Voltaire. Cf., e.g., *L'esprit de Monsieur Voltaire* (London, 1759), 211: "Plus je vais en avant, et plus je suis confirmé dans l'idée, que les systèmes de Métaphysique sont pour les philosophes, ce que les romans sont pour les femmes. Ils ont tous la vogue les uns après les autres, et finissent tous pour être oubliés. Une vérité Mathématique reste pour l'éternité, et les fantômes Métaphysiques passent comme des rêves de malades." [The more I go on, the more I am confirmed in the idea that systems of metaphysics are for philosophers what novels are for women. They all come into fashion one after the other and all end up by being forgotten. A mathematical truth remains for eternity, and metaphysical phantoms pass like madmen's dreams.] (*Oeuvres de Voltaire, éd.* Beuchot [54 vols.; Paris: Garnier, 1877–85], XXXVIII, 526). Further statements of a similar sense in the article *"Philosophie"* . . . , *loc. cit.*

SUPPLEMENT TO ITE XLVIIIn34

LS's editorial annotation to Unkörperlichkeit 176.9 *(JA III.1 425)*

Jean Lerond d'Alembert (1717–83), famous as a physicist and as editor of the *Encyclopedia*.

LS's editorial annotation to Unkörperlichkeit 176.13–20 *(JA III.1 425–26)*

D'Alembert, after he has brought up the arguments translated by Mendelssohn in [*Unkörperlichkeit* 176.26–177.10] against the spirituality of the soul, continues: "Telles sont les raisons de certains Philosophes pour douter de la spiritualité de l'âme. Mais ôtent-elles quelque force aux preuves que nous avons données plus haut de cette spiritualité? . . . d'après le peu de connoissance que nous avons de l'essence de la matière, et d'après l'obscurité même de l'idée sous laquelle nous nous la représentons, il seroit téméraire (la religion même étant mise à part) d'affirmer que la pensée et le sentiment pussent l'appartenir." [Such are the reasons of certain philosophers for doubting the spirituality of the soul. But do they display any force as regards the proofs of this spirituality that we have given above? . . . given the little knowledge that we have of the essence of matter and given the very obscurity of the idea by which we represent it, it would be rash (setting religion itself aside) to affirm that thought and sensation could belong to it.] (*Mélanges de Littérature, d'Histoire et de Philosophie*, vol. 5, p. 128) A few sentences later: ". . . la spiritualité de l'âme est une vérité qui est du ressort de la raison . . . , puisque la raison en fournit les preuves; mais la foi est nécessaire pour faire le complément de ces preuves, auxquelles même elle n'ajoute rien, qu'en nous assurant que la force des preuves est réelle, et que celle des objections n'est qu'apparente, et en nous donnant ainsi le moyen de nous décider entre les unes et les autres. En vain, dirait-on, que suivant l'opinion de quelques savans homes, très-attachés d'ailleurs à la Religion, la spiritualité de l'âme n'est énoncée clairement en aucun endroit de l'Écriture, et par conséquent ne nous est point confirmée par la révélation. Mettons cette discussion à part, l'objection dont il s'agit est bonne tout au plus pour ceux qui bornent la révélation à l'Écriture, mais non pour ceux qui y joignent l'autorité de l'Église, destinée à suppléer à l'Écriture quand elle ne s'explique point ou ne s'explique assez: or cette dernière autorité ne nous laisse aucun doute sur la spiritualité de notre ame." [. . . the spirituality of the soul is a truth that is within the competence of reason . . . , since reason furnishes the proofs of it; but faith is necessary to make up the complement of these proofs, to which it itself adds nothing except in assuring us that the force of the proofs is real and that that of the objections is only apparent, and in thus giving us the means for deciding between the one and the other of these. In vain would it be said that according to the opinion of a few wise men, who are moreover very attached to Religion, the spirituality of the soul is not enunciated clearly in any passage in Scripture and that consequently it is not confirmed by revelation. If we put aside this discussion, the objection that it has to do with is all the more valid for those who limit revelation to Scripture, but not for those who join to it the authority of the Church, which is intended to supplement Scripture when it is not self-explanatory or not self-explanatory enough: the latter authority does not leave us any doubt about the spirituality of our soul.] (pp. 134–35)

SUPPLEMENT TO ITE XLIXn39

LS's editorial annotation to Evidenz *295.11ff. (JA II 421–22)*

Formey expresses himself similarly in his *Mélanges philosophiques*: ". . . il ne découle des vérités Mathématiques aucune consequence, qui intéresse notre Coeur et nos passions; au lieu qu'il n'en est pas de même des notions Métaphysiques, qui influent nécessairement sur la Théologie Naturelle, et sur la Morale. Ce qui fait qu'on envisage différemment ces Principes, et les vérités qui en naissent, c'est que l'intérêt qu'on prend dans les unes, ne se trouve pas dans les autres." [. . . there does not flow from Mathematical truths any consequence that interests our Heart and our passions—instead of their being like Metaphysical notions, which have of necessity an influence on Natural Theology and Morals. What makes these Principles and the truths arising from them be considered differently is that the interest taken in the one is not found in the other.] (I, 8) Further: ". . . s'il étoit possible que la connaisance de Dieu ne nous obligeât à rien, et n'influât point sur notre conduit, elle n'aurait jaimais été un sujet de contestation parmi les hommes." [. . . if it were possible that knowledge of God did not oblige us in any way and had no influence on our conduct, it would never have been a subject of contention among human beings.] (I, 12.)

SUPPLEMENT TO IP XVIn29

Bruno Strauss's editorial annotation on Thomas Abbt (JA XI 456)

Thomas Abbt (1738–66), by birth a Schwabian from Ulm, had attended the gymnasium in his home town and in 1756 moved to the University of Halle as a theology student. He was educated there in the theology college of Siegmund Jakob Baumgarten's, but very soon turned to philosophy and mathematics. Active early on as an author, familiar also with modern English and French as well as German literature, steeped in a thorough study of philosophy and history, he habilitated at Halle in May 1759 in order to go to Viadrina University at Frankfurt-on-the-Oder just a year later. Here the intense experiences of the war filled him once again with passionate admiration for the Philosopher King [as Friedrich II was called], and from this personal life-experience came, in 1760, his first great writing, *Vom Tode fürs Vaterland* [*On Death for the Fatherland*], which appeared in Nicolai's press in 1761. With this, his latest publication, he then became acquainted through Nicolai with Mendelssohn, who recognized in the twenty-three-year-old professor of mathematics a proper collaborator for the *Literaturbriefe*, which had fallen on hard times with Lessing's move to Breslau. At his advice, Nicolai wrote to Abbt on January 29, 1761, to offer him the coeditorship at the *Literaturbriefe*. On the very next day, Abbt accepted this offer with delight. Thus begins the correspondence between the young Frankfurt professor and the two Berlin friends, which, as far as it involves Mendelssohn, occurs initially through Nicolai, but soon is addressed directly to Mendelssohn....

SUPPLEMENT TO IP XVIn**32**

LS's editorial annotation to Phädon 7.8−9 (JA III.1 391)

Johann Joachim Spalding (1714–1804), Lutheran clergyman, prior, and member of the higher consistorial court in Berlin from 1764 on. His *Betrachtung über die Bestimmung des Menschen* [Meditation on the Destiny of Man], considerably expanded and titled *Die Bestimmung des Menschen* [The Destiny of Man], first appeared in 1748; Abbt's review was based on the seventh edition, which appeared in 1763.

SUPPLEMENT TO IP XXIn**58**

LS's editorial annotation to Phädon 39.14−17 (JA III.1 399−400)[7]

On the alteration of the text in the later editions, cf. Riedel's review of the first edition (*Klotzens Deutsche Bibliothek* [1767], 135): "Almost throughout, the author translates too freely and, instead of the eloquent but, notwithstanding this, the° stern and grave Plato, gives us a sweet, fashionable philosopher, instead of Greek simplicity a Frenchifying tone, occasional antitheses where none exists in the text, and almost always a certain courtliness that contrasts with the gravity of the material in a wonderful manner." — See further the review in the *Göttingische Anzeigen* (1767), 987−88: "'... seldom come now to Athens' is not οὐδεὶς πάνυ τι ἐπιχωριάζει τὰ νῦν Ἀθήναζε, and how stilted is 'What did the man speak before his death?' as against τί οὖν δή ἐστιν ἄττα εἶπεν ὁ ἀνὴρ πρὸ τοῦ θανάτου." In addition, the announcement of the second edition in *Klotzens Deutsche Bibliothek* (1769), 260−61, which was combined with a review of the *Phaedo* translation

---

7. *Phädon* 39.14−17 reads: "ECHECRATES: What did the man speak before his death? How did he die? If only someone would tell me everything point for point! Phliasian citizens seldom come to Athens now, and also no guest has come to us from there for a long time now who could bring such reports over to us."

by J. Bernhard Köhler. Köhler's translation—"'Now what did the man then speak before his death?'"—one reads there, "is obviously more suitable to the original, has more naïveté, shows more curiosity: 'What did the man speak,' etc., sounds cold and frosty. (Köhler translates, 'I'd be glad if. . . .') Mr. M.'s 'If only someone would tell me everything point for point!'—What made him do that?—The former sentence°, *ibid.*, is acceptable in Mr. K., for there is no one actually coming now—to Athens. On the other hand, Mr. M.'s 'The Phliasians seldom come now' is against Plato's meaning . . . —there is absolutely no one coming—and 'they seldom come' is hardly the same. . . . Mr. M. translates ξένος as 'guest,' which will not do. . . . (Köhler: 'and also no one has come to us from there for a long time now.')"

LS's editorial annotation to Phädon *40.2 (JA III.1 400)*[8]

On the alteration of the text in the later editions, cf. Riedel's review (*loc. cit.*, 136): "'The dismal ship" (!) makes the artistry that conveys the dialogue from one mouth to another, by virtue of which the first person begins a conversation and the other continues it, into something° altogether natural, makes it into something° naïve! Certainly Plato was never acquainted with it. It is a refined turn of phrase of a fashionable man, but far from the Greek simplicity." Further, the announcement of the second edition in *Klotzens Bibliothek* (1769), 261: "Mr. K.'s 'And what ship is this?' Right. . . . Mr. M. weakens the question and there is, '[ECHECRATES:] And this ship—')."

SUPPLEMENT TO IP XXVIIN84

LS's editorial annotation to Phädon *3 152.9–18 (JA III.1 415–17)*

Mendelssohn does not characterize this proof in Descartes's sense. One who wants to prove "that matter cannot think" presupposes the existence of matter as secured, in order to prove on the basis of this presupposition the existence of the soul as an immaterial being, which still remains in question; he steps onto the soil of materialism in order to refute it. Characteristic of Descartes's argumentation, however, is precisely that he disposes of the materialist presupposition in advance by doubt of the existence of the corporeal world: the existence of the corporeal world is more uncertain than the existence of the mind, the corporeal world is less "well-known" than the mind. His proof for the real difference of soul and matter has two presuppositions: 1) nothing of the concept of body is contained in the con-

---

8. *Phädon* 40.2 reads: "[ECHECRATES:] And this ship—"

cept of soul, and nothing of the concept of soul is contained in the concept of body; our clear and distinct ideas of soul and body are wholly different; 2) everything we cognize clearly and distinctly is in actuality, in the exact manner as we cognize it. From these two presuppositions he concludes: "ea omnia, quae clare et distincte concipiuntur, ut substantiae diversae, sicuti concipiuntur mens et corpus, esse revera substantias realiter a se mutuo distinctas" [all the things that are clearly and distinctly conceived as diverse substances, as mind and body are conceived, are in truth substances that are really mutually distinct from each other] (*Meditationes, Synopsis*, AT VII 13 [cf. Hef 81]). The first presupposition—so Mendelssohn gives it to be understood—is secured against any objection; what is controversial is the second presupposition and, with it, the conclusion: that the *real* difference of soul and body follows from the disparateness of our clear and distinct *ideas* of soul and body (that "an attribute that may not be distinctly conceived through the *idea* of a thing" can "not belong to this *thing*"). Mendelssohn's formulation for Descartes's "well-known first principle," therefore, revises Descartes's principle of clear and distinct knowledge—cf. the parallels with *de Luc* 197.14–23—which in fact "found a welter of contradiction" from the outset: the objections by Caterus (*Objectiones in Meditationes, Primae*, in AT VII 100), Arnauld (*Objectiones, Quartae*, AT VII 200–201), Ludovicus Wolzogen (*Opera* [Irenopoli, 1656], II, 79ff.), Huëtius (*Censura Philosophiae Cartesianae* [Paris, 1689], c. II §9 and c. III §5) et al. against Descartes's proof for the real difference of soul and body are directed above all against that "well-known first principle" presupposed in the proof. As comparison with the parallel passages in the *Treatise on Incorporeality* documents, however, Mendelssohn seems to be thinking here of Locke's critique; Locke asserts that the immateriality of thinking cannot be concluded securely from the disparateness of our ideas of matter and thinking (which is granted by him), since we have no clear and distinct cognition of substances at our command (cf. the annotation to *Unkörperlichkeit* 167.25–27 [immediately below]).

LS's editorial annotation to Unkörperlichkeit *167.25–27 (JA III.1 422)*

The objection[9] results immediately from Locke's central assertion: cognition of substances is not possible; Locke certainly considered it to be just as "insurmountable" as his critique of substance-cognition. Mendelssohn is

9. *Unkörperlichkeit* 167.25–27 reads: "But I believe that the Englishman [Locke] himself did not consider his notion [*sc.*, that the immateriality of thinking cannot be concluded securely from the disparateness of our ideas of matter and thinking] so insurmountable."

right, however, insofar as Locke, despite his skepticism about the rational demonstrability of the doctrine of immortality, held to this doctrine quite energetically (cf., *inter alia*, bk. IV, ch. III, §6 of the *Essay*, cited in the annotation [to *Unkörperlichkeit* 167.22; translated immediately below]). Mendelssohn's remark recalls the difference between Locke himself and the French Enlightenment, insofar as the latter propagated Locke's ideas in the service of radical unbelief.

LS's editorial annotation to Unkörperlichkeit *167.22 (JA III.1 421)*

Locke, *An Essay concerning Human Understanding*, bk. IV, ch. III, §6 [Nid 541]: "... I see no contradiction in it, that the first eternal thinking Being, should, if he pleased, give to certain Systems created of senseless matter, put together as he thinks fit, some degrees of sense, perception, and thought: Though, as I think, I have proved, *Lib.* 4. *c.* 10th, it is no less than a contradiction to suppose matter (which is evidently in its own nature void of sense and thought) should be that Eternal first thinking Being."

SUPPLEMENT TO IP XXVIIN85

LS's editorial annotation to Phädon *3 152.30 (JA III.1 417)*

From the letter to Nicolai of February 1768, it would have to follow that Mendelssohn first learned in general of the Plotinian proof only incidentally through the English Platonist Ralph Cudworth, whose work *The True Intellectual System of the Universe* (London, 1678) he made use of in Mosheim's Latin translation (*Systema intellectuale huius universi* [Jena, 1733]). Cudworth "further amplified" the Plotinian proof in the sense demanded by Mendelssohn; see the annotation to 153.18ff.

LS's editorial annotation to Phädon *3 152.33–153.6 (JA III.1 417)*

Ennead 4, bk. VII, *c*. 2. Mendelssohn's translation, faithful by the way, reproduces the text with an omission in the middle.

LS's editorial annotation to Phädon *3 153.8–17 (JA III.1 417)*

Ennead 4, bk. VII, *c*. 5. Here too Mendelssohn leaves a passage in the text untranslated.

LS's editorial annotation to Phädon *3 153.18ff. (JA III.1 417–18)*

Cudworth (*loc. cit.*, 1110–11 [cf. Roy II 823–24]) first cites the two Plotinus passages cited also by Mendelssohn, and then continues:

Physicos quidem si consulamus, qui atomos totam rerum universitatem contineri arbitrantur, corporae qualitates et formae ex varia corpusculorum et particularum compositione et textura nascuntur, nec ullum corpusculum per se formae aliquid et qualitates possidet:

> ... ne ... ex albis alba rearis
> Aut ea, quae nigrant, nigro de semine nata.

Sed haec ratio tota dissimilis est hujus sententiae. Namque formae ac qualitates non sunt naturae reapse a magnitudine, figura, situ ac motu particularum diversae, sed coagmentationes tantum particularum sensus nostros vere afficientes. Vita vero et ratio, mens et animus res sunt ipsa natura sua seiunctae a magnitudine, figura, situ et motu partium, neque animi tantum notiones et commenta, aut rerum syllabae, verum res simplices, nec compositae.

[If we were to consult the physicists who judge that the whole universe of things is contained in the atoms, corporeal qualities and forms are born from the varied composition and texture of both corpuscles and particles, and no corpuscle per se possesses any forms and qualities:

> ... lest you reason that white things are born of white ones
> Or those that are black from black seed. (Lucretius, *De natura rerum* II 731, 733)

But that whole reasoning is unlike this tenet. For forms and qualities are not really of a different nature from the magnitude, figure, position, and motion of the particles, but are only combinations of the particles truly affecting our senses. In truth, life and reason, mind and spirit are things that by their very nature are joined together by magnitude, figure, position, and motion, and not just notions or contrivances of the spirit, but simple things, and not composite ones.]

SUPPLEMENT TO IP XXVIIIn90

LS's editorial annotation on Christian Garve's review (JA III.1 409: Assessments of the 1st edition, item 3)

Neue Bibliothek der schönen Wissenschaften und der freyen Künste VI, 80–107 and 313–32. (The author, according to Friedländer's report in his preface to the 5th edition of the *Phädon*, is Garve.)

From Alexander Altmann's editorial annotation to Garve's letter to Mendelssohn of May or October 1769 (JA XII.1 313)

... Christian Garve (1742–98), a native of Breslau, ... held an associate professorship of philosophy at the University of Leipzig from 1769 until 1772. But he resigned this position as early as 1772 for reasons of health and retired to Breslau, where he lived on his own means. An edition of his *Collected Works* appeared in Breslau in 1801–3.

SUPPLEMENT TO IP XXIXn91

LS's editorial annotation to Unkörperlichkeit 165.27–167.2 (JA III.1 421)

Mendelssohn here presents the proof for the immateriality of the soul as it is usually presented in the contemporary literature, without therefore making it as precise as he had in the *Phädon* (see our intro. to the *Phädon* [i.e., IP]). Cf. Cudworth, *Systema intellectuale*, ed. Mosheim (Jena, 1733), 1112; Henry Moore, *Scripta philosophica* (London, 1679), II 332ff.; Samuel Clarke, *A Letter to Mr. Dodwell* (London, 1706; cf. *Acta Eruditorum* 1707, 214–15); Condillac, *Essai sur l'origine des connaissances humaines* (Amsterdam, 1746), vol. I, sec. 1, ch. 1, §6; Bayle, *Historisches und critisches Wörterbuch* (Leipzig, 1742), Gottsched's annotation on remark C of the article "Dicäarchus"; Spalding, *Bestimmung des Menschen*, ed. Stephan, 56.

SUPPLEMENT TO IP XXXn96

LS's editorial annotation to Phädon 3 143.17–20 (JA III.1 410–11)

Here are a few examples [of contemporaries' applause for Mendelssohn's literary art]. Iselin had a few "small points" to offer on the art of writing; he did not know what to do with the "metaphysical subtleties of the First Dialogue"; but "the rest of the work touched and captivated me extraordinarily—and during the third reading even more than during the first and during the other one." He praises the "excellent prose" of the work. A few years later he declares the *Phädon*, along with Arrian's *Epictetus* and Spalding's *Destiny of Man*, to be his "handbook"—which in the context amounts to saying: book of consolation (to Zimmermann, June 7, 1770). — Nicolai to Gerstenberg (March 21, 1767): "The simplicity of the art of writing merits much applause, I believe." And Gerstenberg to Nicolai (January 31, 1767): "Mr. Moses is a man whom I esteem quite highly. I await his *Phädon* with longing. I have often wished that someone might make our public ...

more familiar with the works of Plato, Xenophon, and Shaftesbury, in order to divert it from our academic philosophy, as is greatly needed. Who can do this better than he?" Gerstenberg to Nicolai (December 5, 1767): "This much I can set down with truth, that for me *Phädon* is one of the most beautiful philosophical books I have ever read: but the system, very ingenious as it is in itself, has not convinced me...." — H. P. Sturz to Lessing (September 23, 1767): "... Moses is one of the few who succeeds in teaching deep wisdom with the language of sentiment and in strewing the gulches of metaphysics with flowers...." — Riedel (*Deutsche Bibliothek* [1767], 144–45), who has many considerations against the style and argumentation of the *Phädon*, nevertheless, following a report about the content of the work, says with reference to its concluding sentence: "And this is the end of a book that, of all the German philosophical books of our century that I have read, is the most refined, the most distinct, and, I might almost say at the same time, the most profound. To all our academic philosophers, as important as they may keep thinking themselves to be, from professor to adjunct and from the latter to schoolmaster, I recommend the reading of this writing with due reverence. They ought to learn from it how one can think thoroughly and yet beautifully, deeply and yet humanely, and express the most ingenious thoughts so purely, so distinctly, so illuminatingly that they are understandable even to the exoteric friend of wisdom, the layman." — The reviewer in the *Jenaische Zeitungen von Gelehrten Sachen* (1767), who basically forgoes criticism of the proofs, declares the *Phädon* to be "a classic book, which will still be read in future generations, when all our *compendia*, large and small, Latin and German, are long outmoded and forgotten with their authors"; he praises the author: "He thinks acutely and writes purely, elegantly, and classically, without any neologisms." — In an "Epistle to a Friend..." (*Unterhaltungen* [1767]), one reads in reference to the *Phädon*: "I wish that we had been able to read the beautiful dialogue together.... So much noble simplicity and sublimity, so much true beauty of expression with all the thoroughness of the philosopher, so much sentiment and religion predominate in it, that I believe it might become our favorite book" (906).

SUPPLEMENT TO IP XXXIIn103

From LS's editorial annotation on Phädon 143.7 (JA III.1 409: Assessments of the 1st Edition, item 2)

... (*Klotzens*) *Deutsche Bibliothek der schönen Wissenschaften* (1767), 124–61. (The author is Friedrich Justus Riedel [1742–85], as it turns out from his correspondence with Klotz—cf. Fr. J. Riedel's collected *Werke* [Vienna, 1787], IV, 333–38.)

SUPPLEMENT TO IMH XII<small>N</small>9

From LS's editorial annotation to Morgenstunden 111.25–113.6 (JA III.2 301)

As is suggested in *Morgenstunden* 111.38–112.2, the argument focuses on the proof for the immateriality of the soul in the Second Dialogue of the *Phädon*. The thought of "transforming" this proof "into a proof for the immateriality and unity of God" had been a "brainstorm" of Iselin's. Mendelssohn at once had the second thought that "it must also be shown that God is no world-soul..." (to Iselin, September 10, 1767 [JA XII.1 145]). Cf. further von Platen's objection to the Second Dialogue of the *Phädon* (to Mendelssohn, August 10, 1769 [JA XII.1 188–95]); in Mendelssohn's reply to this objection (to von Platen, December 29, 1769 [JA XII.1 203]), the discussion is already about the error of his "brother Spinoza," who makes "our thinking into a mere determination of the divine Being." Both Iselin's brainstorm and Spinoza's error were then noted in principle in the attachment to Mendelssohn's letter to Camper of January 6, 1781 (""Beweis, daß weder die sinnliche Welt das göttliche Wesen, noch Zeit und Raum Eigenschaften Gottes seyn können" [Proof not only that the Sensible World cannot be the Divine Being, but also that Space and Time cannot be Attributes of God] [JA XIII 2–4]); this polemic is not explicitly directed against Spinoza, however, but against Newton and Hemsterhuis.

LS's editorial annotation to Morgenstunden 141.20–21 (JA III.2 306–8)

As for the proof that begins here, the following is to be noted. Mendelssohn was led to his "new proof" by his critique of the received proof that concludes the existence of God from the presence of eternal truths. I cite this proof in Leibniz's formulation: "... on demandera..., où seraient ces idées si aucun esprit n'existait, et que deviendroit alors le fondement réel de cette certitude des vérités éternelles. Cela nous mène enfin au dernier fondement des vérités, savoir, à cet esprit suprême et universel qui ne peut manquer d'exister, dont l'entendement, à dire vrai, est la région des vérités éternelles, comme saint Augustin l'a reconnu...." [... it will be asked ... where these ideas would be if no mind existed, and what would then become the real foundation of this certainty of eternal truths. This leads us at last to the ultimate foundation of truths, to wit, to that supreme and universal mind that cannot fail to exist, whose understanding is, to speak truly, the region of eternal truths, as St. Augustine has recognized. . . .] (*Nouveaux Essais*, pt. IV, ch. 11, §13 [cf. Ger VI 447; ReBe *ad loc.*]; cf. also *Monadologie* §§43–44 [Ger VI 614; Wie 541 or Sch 154–55 or FrWo 273–74], *Théodicée* §189 [Ger VI 229; Hug 246], and *Causa Dei* §8 [Ger VI 440; Sch 115]; cf. further Cudworth, *Systema intellectuale*, 905–9 [Roy II 728–36]). This proof was not satisfying to Mendelssohn, as comes out in his review (published in 1766) of the first volume of Lambert's *Neues Organon*; in this review, one reads: "Mr. Lambert seeks . . . the ground of all truths, as usual, in the divine understanding; and he holds the truths to be the *principium cognoscendi* of the existence of God to the extent that an eternal *Suppositum intelligens* can be concluded from eternal truths. We would have liked this proof to have been carried out somewhat more clearly, because the conclusion from the possibility of representations to the existence of a representing Being seems to make for a few more difficulties. To be sure, that the divine understanding would also have to be held to be the source of all truths is easily grasped once one is convinced of its existence on other grounds. From this it seems to flow naturally that the existence of the divine understanding could also be concluded in reverse from the truths; all the same, this path is not as easy as it came to be represented" (JA V.2 45). What Mendelssohn had to object to in the received argument may be recognized more distinctly from the changes that he makes in that argument. First, instead of the presence of eternal truths, he starts from the presence of self-knowledge as incomplete knowledge (see the title of the Sixteenth Lecture). To judge this departure correctly, it must be observed that Mendelssohn starts from self-knowledge because, and only because, he wants to secure the proof against the Idealist doubt of the existence of the corporeal world (cf. *Morgenstunden* 141.25–142.7 with 83.38–39 [DaDy 103 with 61]); in the proof itself, he does not speak about self-knowledge so much as about knowledge of every actual thing (cf. the whole discussion beginning in *Morgenstunden* 142.8 [DaDy 104], especially the "chain of inferences" at the end of the Lecture): the I takes precedence in the proof only because it is that actual thing that "is above and beyond all doubt." Knowledge of the actual is now privileged by Mendelssohn over knowledge of eternal truths because it is essentially infinite (cf. *Morgenstunden* 142.38–143.3 [DaDy 104] with 105.15–16 [Scholz 4–5; DaDy 76]), and therefore, on the presupposition that everything thinkable—everything actual must be thinkable (*Morgenstunden* 143.15–16 [DaDy 104])—must also be actually thought, it can only be ascribed to an infinite understanding. Mendelssohn's second departure from the received argument consists in his attempting to prove the necessity presupposed in his argument, that everything thinkable must also be actually thought. This proof is the nerve of his argument (cf. *Morgenstunden* 143.13–22) [DaDy 104]. He concludes as follows: Everything actual is thinkable, i.e., it is possible for it to be thought; now "everything possible, insofar as it is merely possible," is "not an objective predicate of things" (*Morgenstunden* 144.23–24 [DaDy 105]), however, but has its "ideal existence in the thinking subject"; i.e., each possibility always presupposes an actual thinking subject beforehand that "(ascribes)" the possibility "qua thinkable to the object" (145.13–16 [cf. DaDy 106]); therefore, everything thinkable is also actually thought (and therefore, on account of its infinity, everything actual is thought only by an infinite understanding). — For the genesis of this proof, one may refer to *Morgenstunden* 111.4–113.14 [Scholz 13–15; DaDy 79–81] and the annotations [immediately below].

LS's editorial annotation to Morgenstunden *111.6–112.13 (JA III.2 300)*

Cf. on this point A. W. Rehberg, *Abhandlung über das Wesen und die Einschränkungen der Kräfte* (Leipzig, 1779), 83–84: "Spinoza assumed that extension was something real. He could therefore be answered that that very same basic concept, one Being in various spatial combinations, is no longer one. . . . But Leibniz and his followers have shown that the existence of extended Being is impossible. This makes the answer to the difficulty that I have just drawn from Spinoza more difficult. . . . We must therefore look around for another refutation. We must prove that the soul is an actual substance that exists on its own."

LS's editorial annotation to Morgenstunden *111.9–24 (JA III.2 300–301)*

Cf. on this point de Jariges, "Über das System des Spinoza," *Hißmanns Magazin für die Philosophie und ihre Geschichte* V (Göttingen und Lemgo, 1782), 17: "But if, as Spinoza asserts, the reality of this substance consists uniquely and solely in extension, or in a completely homogeneous matter, then the question is, When and how did it lose its absolute unity and homogeneity? . . . If the matter persistently stays the same, as it does in Spinoza's system, then how does it happen that the matter of which the pen I am now writing with consists cannot be transformed into gold, and why hasn't the matter that is in the sun shifted to the moon? . . ." — Cf. further Jacquelot, *Dissertations sur l'existence de Dieu* (den Haag, 1697), 453: "Spinoza dit, qu'il n'y a qu'une seule substance. Cela est obscure, qu'entend-t-il par une seule substance?

Est-ce une substance semblable? Ou est-ce une substance singulière unique en nombre, comme on parle dans l'École? Posons un corps A qui se meut vers l'Orient, et un corps B qui se meut vers l'Occident, dira-t-on que c'est le même corps? Non sans doute. On peut dire tout au plus, que ce sont des corps de même nature, s'ils sont semblables. Puis donc que ce sont deux corps, ils ont chacun leur existence proper, et différent l'une de l'autre. Ce que Spinoza peut répondre, sera, que ces deux corps font partie d'une même matière: alors la dispute ne sera plus que sur le nom. Ce que nous appelons deux corps, il le nomme deux parties d'une même matière. De même aussi, posons un sujet C qui pense aux propriétez d'un triangle, et un sujet D, qui pense au flux et reflux de la mer, dira-t-on, que c'est un même sujet qui pense à ces choses? Non, il faudra raisonner de ces deux sujets comme on a fait ci-dessus des deux corps. Ainsi cette unité de substance ne signifie autre chose que la conformité de son essence et de sa nature dans plusieurs sujets distinquez." [Spinoza says that there is one substance only. What he understands by "one substance only" is obscure. Is it an apparent[10] substance? Or is it a single substance, one in number, as they say in the School? Let us posit a body A that moves toward the East and a body B that moves toward the West: will it be said that it is the same body? No, undoubtedly. All one can say is that they are bodies of the same nature, if they are alike.[11] It therefore follows that they are two bodies, each having its own existence and differing from the other. What Spinoza can reply will be that these two bodies make up part of one and the same matter: then the quarrel will only be about the name. What we call two bodies, he calls two parts of one and the same matter. So too, let us posit a subject C that thinks about the properties of a triangle, and a subject D that thinks about the ebb and flow of the sea—will it be said that it is the same subject that thinks about these things? No, it will be necessary to reason from these two subjects as has been done above from the two bodies. Thus this unity of substance does not mean anything other than the conformity of its essence and its nature in several distinct subjects.]

LS's editorial annotation to Morgenstunden 111.25–28 (JA III.2 301)

Wolff also makes use of these thoughts in his Spinoza critique, in concluding from the ideality of spatial unities that extension cannot be an attribute of God. Cf. TN II §691.

---

10. Fr.: *semblable*.
11. Fr.: *semblables*. Cf. the preceding note.

SUPPLEMENT TO IMH XIIIn19

LS's editorial annotation to Morgenstunden 4.10–25 (JA III.2 277–78)

The reports of Nicolai's and Joseph Mendelssohn's are detailed in the "Introduction [i.e., IMH]." Cf. further D. Jenisch's introduction to *Moses Mendelssohns kleine philosophische Schriften* (Berlin, 1789), 49 and 59, as well as (von Schütz,) *Leben und Meinungen Moses Mendelssohns* (Hamburg, 1787), 86. — The oldest and most reliable reports know nothing of any participation by Humboldt in the philosophical home instruction. (Cf. also Albert Leitzmann in Wilhelm von Humboldt's *Gesammelte Schriften Akademie Ausgabe* [17 vols.; Berlin: B. Behr, 1903–36; reprint, Berlin: de Gruyter, 1968], I, 430.)

The dating of the instruction is uncertain. The earliest possible date would have to be 1783 (Joseph Mendelssohn was born in 1770); but it is not to be ruled out, indeed it seems to me more plausible, that the instruction did not begin before the end of 1784. On September 1, 1784 [JA XIII 222–23], Mendelssohn writes to Zimmermann: "I feel that I am much too weak to complete this sublime work (*sc.*, a contesting of atheism which would be adequate in every respect). Meanwhile, for as long as providence keeps my° life going, I want to supply the materials for it. Perhaps a lucky mortal will find them serviceable some day. And perhaps—this wish is consolatory for my weakness—perhaps the lucky one is my son!" Mendelssohn therefore seems at that time to have some reason for assuming that his son understands—or will understand?—his defense of natural religion currently in preparation. Has he therefore already presented this defense to him at that time? On November 20, 1784 [JA XIII 233–34], he writes to Herz Homberg, the former home instructor of his son, and instructs him on this occasion about the latter's scholarly education: the discussion in this letter contains no word of any philosophical instruction. Only in the letter to Homberg of September 6, 1785 [JA XIII 300], does Mendelssohn speak of his son's philosophical studies.

Karl Gotthelf Lessing's letter to Mendelssohn of May 8, 1783 [JA XIII 108], reads: "How very happy I am that you want to devote your morning hours to my brother's memory. For what has been written about him so far has not altogether pleased me, properly speaking." Here, as is self-evident, "morning hours" does not signify the title of Mendelssohn's planned Lessing book, but, literally, the hours of the morning, i.e., "the few hours of the day in which (Mendelssohn) was" usually "still cheerful" (*Morgenstunden* 4.10–11 [cf. DaDy xix]). (Cf. moreover the following passages from the letter to G. E. Lessing at the beginning of May 1756 [JA XI 39]: "The morning hours are devoted to you because they do not stop reminding me of you." Cf. further the following passage from Mendelssohn's letter to Hennings of July 29, 1779 [JA XII.2 160]: "... I had devoted these invigorating morning hours to you. ...") The title of the book recalls the title of a book putatively authored by Friedrich the Great, *Les matinées* (Berlin, 1766) (cf. Barbier, *Dictionnaire des ouvrages anonyms et pseudonyms* [Paris, 1923], II, 335).

SUPPLEMENT TO IMH XVIn31

LS's editorial annotation to Freunde 189.7–8 (JA III.2 319)

In this connection, Jacobi remarks (RK IV.2, 199): "That the offer (as he calls it)[12] on my behalf was most disagreeable to Mr. Mendelssohn, however—this he understood—and this I grasp perfectly. But why, then, did he not reject it out of hand? If I were in his place—though I have not been used to acting nobly for a long time—I would have answered on my behalf, 'Anecdotes!' and with that it would have been well and good."

SUPPLEMENT TO IMH XLIn179

LS's editorial annotation to Morgenstunden 110.9–111.3 (JA III.2 299–300)

"Realitas omnis infinita ac in specie cogitatio infinita non componitur ex realitatibus finitis, quae numero infinitae sunt ... quotiesqucumque sumas intellectum qui non omnia discernibilia distinguere valet, non tamen inde prodibit intellectus, qui omnia in quocumque objecto discernibilia actu distinguit, sed saltem multitudo intellectuum quorum unusquisque omnia discernibilia in objecto distinguere minime valet, consequenter intellectus finites infinito prorsus heterogeneous est" [Any infinite reality, and infinite thought specifically, is not composed of finite realities that are infinite in number. ... Regardless of how many times you assume an understanding that does not avail for distinguishing all discernibles, even an understanding that actually distinguishes all discernibles in any object will not go that far, but it will take a multitude of understandings at least, each of which hardly avails for distinguishing all discernibles in the object. Consequently, a finite understanding is utterly different in kind from an infinite one] (TN II §706). Mendelssohn already refers to this critique of Wolff's in the *Philosophical*

---

12. This parenthetical insertion is LS's.

Dialogues (JA I 16.25–28 [also JA I 351.25–30; Dah 108]). Cf. also *Phädon 3* 154.34–155.27 [Nob 156–57]. — Spinoza in loose discussion (cf., e.g., *Tractatus theologico-politicus*, ch. XVI, §4 [Bruder]) occasionally expresses himself in the sense that the critique presented here presupposes; his thematic statements on the problem of infinity (in *Ethica* I, props. 12, 13 and 15 Schol. [Geb II 55–56, 57ff.; WhSt 12–13, 14ff.] as well as in the Letters to Ludovicus Meyer [#12; Geb IV 52–62; Sh 101–107], to Oldenburg of November 20, 1665 [#32; Geb IV 169–76; Sh 192–97], and to Tschirnhaus of May 5, 1676 [#81; Geb IV 304; Sh 352]), Mendelssohn leaves out of consideration.

SUPPLEMENT TO IMH XLIIn181

LS's editorial annotation to Freunde *205.23–30 (JA III.2 330–31)*

Cf. with this Mendelssohn's remarks on Hume's *Dialogues on Natural Religion* in annotation *g* to his correspondence with Abbt (see JA XI 486 [or JA VI.1 33]). He may also have been thinking of Pascal, perhaps also of Bayle. — Jacobi remarks on the foregoing passage in *David Hume on Belief* (RK II 144–45 [Gio 265]): "Mendelssohn had saddled me, without the least cause, with Christian motives that were in fact neither Christian nor mine, and against them he set his own, which he presented as Jewish, when he said: 'My religion [knows of no obligation to remove doubts of this sort otherwise than through reason; it commands no belief in eternal truths. I have one more ground, therefore,] for seeking conviction.' — It was easy to detect in this sarcastic sally the accusation that I was trying to save myself by the back door. But since I did not want to counter it with a refutation that would have involved me in questions in which I did not want to get involved, I just gave the following answer: 'If every assent to truth not derived from rational grounds is belief (since this opposition between rational cognition and belief had been adduced by Mendelssohn himself), then conviction based on rational grounds must itself derive from belief and receive its force from belief alone.'" — Shortly afterward (RK II 147 and note [cf. Gio 266]), one reads: "Once again, language has no other word (*sc.*, than 'belief'). Even Mendelssohn uses it. See *Morning Hours*, 1st ed., 106 [*sc.*, *Morgenstunden* 54.33; DaDy 38]."

SUPPLEMENT TO IMH XLIVn193

Mendelssohn's introductory annotation to his "Annotations and Additions" to Morgenstunden (JA III.2 159.2–5 [DaDy 117])

One of the most thorough philosophers[13] of this age, who out of his friendship for me has perused these essays, has communicated to me a few annotations on them, which I do not want to withhold from my readers.

LS's editorial annotation (JA III.2 310–11) to the foregoing

The "philosopher" who communicated the annotations to Mendelssohn is J. A. H. Reimarus. Reimarus sent Mendelssohn one part of his annotations—not made use of in the following—on June 18, 1785 [see JA XIII 284–88]. That the annotations used in the following that are not directly attested to in the Reimarus-Mendelssohn correspondence also stemmed from Reimarus, comes out also in Reimarus's preface to his *Über die Gründe der menschlichen Erkenntniß und der natürlichen Religion* [On the Bases of Human Cognition and of Natural Religion] (Hamburg, 1787), in which one reads: ". . . Now the blessèd Mendelssohn wanted me to communicate to him my opinion concerning his soon-to-be-published work, of which he sent me a copy of the first part. I had to read through it fleetingly and, without going into his system in general, only sketched out one thing or another, which he also quoted in the 'Additions.' I had also drafted a couple of annotations on the other part that he sent me, and also touched on a few other things that were recalled afterwards from the reviews. They were delivered too late, however, when the book was already in press, and were not put in."

SUPPLEMENT TO IMH XLVIn202

LS's editorial annotation to Morgenstunden 133.10–11 (JA III.2 306)

Gotthold Ephraim Lessings theologischer Nachlaß (Berlin, 1784) "in actuality did not appear until the Easter Fair of 1785, edited by Karl Gotthelf Lessing" (LM XXII 477). "Christianity of Reason" emerged in 1753 (LM XIV 175n).

---

13. Ger.: *Weltweiser*. Likewise in the following annotation. See IPM xviiin23.

SUPPLEMENT TO IMH XLVIIn203

LS's annotation to Freunde 211.14–15 (JA III.2 332)

Mendelssohn's doubt is understandable only on the presupposition that the doctrine of the *Ethics* (pt. I, appendix [Geb II 77–83; WhSt 35–41]) has completely vanished from memory.[14]

SUPPLEMENT TO IMH LVIIn253

LS's editorial annotation to Freunde 188.11–34 (JA III.2 316–17)

On this point, Jacobi remarks (RK IV.2 225ff.), after citing the passage, "Lessing is a follower [of Spinoza? So what? What do speculative axioms have in common with the man? Who would not rejoice to have Spinoza himself as a friend, as much as he was also a Spinozist? Who would refuse] to give [Spinoza's genius and excellent character] their due?" (*Freunde* 188.11–16 [Scholz 294–95; cf. Val 130; cf. Got 154–55]): "Exactly what I myself think and have also expressed everywhere. Who before me has, at the risk of his name, spoken of Spinoza with the respect, with the admiration and love with which I have spoken of him? Let anyone look at the passage where Lessing interrupts me with the words, 'And you are not a Spinozist, Jacobi?' — Let anyone look at the beginning of the letter to Hemsterhuis and throughout the whole work. I spoke out with similar uninhibitedness in earlier writings, especially *Something that Lessing Said*; and not only about Spinoza, but also about other, no less suspect authors, like Machiavelli and Hobbes. — And yet Mendelssohn would say to me, in connection with the words just cited, *The name Jew and Spinozist could hardly be either as shocking or as troublesome to me as it may well be to Mr. Jacobi!* [*Freunde* 188.32–34; Scholz 295; cf. Val 130] — What is unsayable (language has no milder word) — what is manifestly *unsayable*, if not this? — Mr. Mendelssohn is therefore of the opinion that 'speculative axioms . . . made no difference' (*Freunde* 188.11, 19 [Scholz 294–95; cf. Val 130; cf. Got 154–55]). That is the very man's very opinion and straightforward story. — Otherwise why these words immediately afterwards . . . (*sc*. ['As long as no one was accusing my friend of having been

---

14. The "doubt" to which LS is referring is Mendelssohn's uncertainty about whether Jacobi is serious in saying (in the "Letter to Hemsterhuis") that Spinoza considers the doctrine of final causes to be "the greatest derangement of the human intellect" and "true nonsense" (*Freunde* 211.12, 14). See Scholz 124, 131 [cf. Gio 205, 211], cited as LS's editorial annotations to 211.11–13 and 13–14, respectively.

a secret blasphemer, and therefore also a hypocrite, the report that Lessing was a Spinozist made no difference to me. I knew that there was also a purified Spinozism that is quite highly compatible with everything religion and morality stand for, practically speaking, as I myself showed extensively in *Morning Hours*; I knew that, in general, this purified Spinozism might be united very well with Judaism and that Spinoza, his speculative doctrine aside, could have remained an orthodox Jew if he had not contested authentic Judaism in other writings and thereby withdrew himself from the Law'], *Freunde* 188.19–27 [Scholz 295; cf. Val 130; cf. Got 155])? Therefore, if there were no purified Spinozism as in *Morning Hours*, if Spinoza could remain in his own speculative doctrine no orthodox Jew, *would the speculative axioms then still have something in common with the man? Would one then not enjoy having Spinoza himself, with such an unpurified Spinozism, as a friend? Would one then refuse to give Spinoza's genius and excellent character their due?* — Would Mr. Mendelssohn then also be very *astonished*[15] about the report that Lessing had been a Spinozist? Would it have had an influence on his friendship for Lessing? Would his concepts of Lessing's genius and character have suffered by that? *Or not*? Let the choice be made! My mind and soul are not up to knowing how to find one's way out of such difficulties."

SUPPLEMENT TO IMH LIXN264

LS's editorial annotation to Morgenstunden 61.26–62.21 (JA III.2 284–85)

The full-blown distinction here of the "faculty of approval" from the faculty of cognition and the faculty of desire is in effect the most precise formulation that Mendelssohn found for the peculiarity of behavior toward the beautiful. The expressions used by him recall Kant's discussion of "disinterested satisfaction." The connection between "approval" and the "sentiment of pleasure and displeasure" explains why, in a handwritten note from 1776 [JA I 125–31], Mendelssohn could distinguish the faculty that he now calls the "faculty of approval" from the faculty of cognition and the faculty of desire (*Schriften* 276–77 [Dah 44–45]). Originally—in the second edition of the *Philosophische Schriften* (1771)—he had distinguished between understanding, will, and feeling (*Schriften* 393.21–23 [Dah 140]). Cf. also the distinction of taste, reason, and moral sentiment that shows up in JA II

---

15. Concerning Jacobi's reference to Mendelssohn's being *astonished*, see *Freunde* 187.34ff. (Scholz 294; Val 129; Got 154), with Scholz 69 (cf. Gio 182).

183.4–8, the distinction of enjoying and wanting in JA I 225.13ff., and the distinction of pleasure and pleasing sentiment in JA I 131.28ff. — In order not to overestimate the significance of the foregoing expression [*sc.*, "faculty of approval"], one has to consider two facts. 1. The threefold division of the faculties of the soul was in any case already quite current in the '70s of the eighteenth century. Tetens writes in his *Philosophische Versuche* [*über die menschliche Natur und ihre Entwicklung* (Leipzig, 1776–77)], I, 619–20: "Most name, as the catechism, two (basic faculties of the soul), understanding and will. . . . To others, yet a third principle seems to be required by the name of sentimentality, a faculty of having sentiments." (Cf. also A. Palme, *J. G. Sulzers Psychologie und die Anfänge der Dreivermögenlehre* [Berlin, 1905], 57). 2. Mendelssohn himself in the following makes no use of the threefold division introduced by him, but employs only the usual twofold division (see esp. *Morgenstunden* 63.36–37 [DaDy 44], 69.29–30 [DaDy 50], and 115.29 [DaDy 84; Got 147]: "faculty of approval *or* of desire"). Cf. also the twofold division into faculties of cognition and approval in *Jerusalem* 137.32–35 [Ark 70; Got 72]. The threefold division is a casual remark that remains without consequences. Besides, the entire discussion that begins here is not transparent. Mendelssohn speaks initially (*Morgenstunden* 63.16 [DaDy 44]) of the relationship of the faculty of approval with the faculty of desire; one should expect that in the following the relationship of the faculty of approval and the faculty of cognition is discussed; instead of this, the distinction of the faculty of cognition and the faculty of approval or desire is discussed.

SUPPLEMENT TO IMH LIXn271

LS's editorial annotation to Morgenstunden 10.6ff. (JA III.2 278–79)

The discussion leads from the nominal definition of truth as *consensus judicii nostri cum objecto, seu re repraesentata* [the agreement of our judgment with the object, or the thing being represented] (Wolff, *Logica* §505) to the real definition of truth. (Cf. also Kant, *Critique of Pure Reason*, A58: "The nominal explanation of 'truth,' namely, that it is the agreement of knowledge with its object, is here granted and presumed; one demands to know, however, what the universal and certain criterion of the truth of each and every knowledge is.") Mendelssohn does not make the Wolffian real definition of truth as *determinabilitas praedicati per notionem subjecti* [the ability to determine the predicate by the notion of the subject] (*loc. cit.*, §513) his own, however, and, to be sure, because he has a definition that is applicable in an equal manner to both rational and sensible knowledge. Cf. *Morgenstunden* 12.29–13.2 with 22.21–25, 39.14–20, and 45.17–22.

LS's editorial annotation to Morgenstunden 11.4ff. (JA III.2 279)

Mendelssohn here, following Leibniz (see, e.g., *Monadologie* §§36ff. [Ger VI 612ff.; Wie 540ff. or Sch 153ff. or FrWo 272ff.]), deals first (*Morgenstunden* 13.33, below [DaDy 5]) with the truths of reason, which rest on the principle of contradiction, and then with the truths of fact, which rest on "another principle." As the latter principle, however, he does not designate the principle of sufficient reason, as does Leibniz, but—"the evidence of sensory cognition," that is to say, induction.

LS's editorial annotation to Morgenstunden 20.30–21.9 (JA III.2 280)

Cf. the essentially "more Rationalistic" assertion in the *Treatise on Evidence* (JA II 302.19–25 [Dah 284]).

LS's editorial annotation to Morgenstunden 39.6–40.28 (JA III.2 282)

Cf. Locke, *Essay*, IV, ch. 2, §§1–6.

LS's editorial annotation to Morgenstunden 61.12–15 (JA III.2 284)

Cf., on the other hand, JA II 290.25ff. [Dah 272–73].

SUPPLEMENT TO IMH LXVn308

From Mendelssohn's Verwandtschaft des Schönen und Guten [Kinship of the Beautiful and Good], JA II 181.29ff.

Socrates wanted to investigate what *universal justice* is. Since this is not so easy to discover in an individual man, he considered universal justice in view of a whole state, so as to take it up in the case of an individual man too by downsizing[16] afterwards. He found that the universal justice of a state is a condition in which all members accord with the perfection of the society. In a similar manner, he concluded, the universal justice or righteousness of an individual man consists in a condition in which all his powers and capabilities are in accord with the perfection of the whole. He considers, that is to say, the different capabilities of men as citizens of a republic. The city

---

16. Ger.: *durch die Reduktion*.

must take care that each citizen find means for being as happy as can be consistent with the happiness of the whole. The man must train each of his capabilities as befits the perfection of the whole man. The happiness of a state consists in a complex relationship to the happiness of the individual citizens and their accord with the whole. The perfection of the man consists in the perfection of his individual powers and capabilities and in their relation to the whole. All duties toward ourselves he reduced to the law: *be just toward yourself.*

Fritz Bamberger's editorial annotation to JA II 181.29ff. (JA II 404)

The account more or less follows Plato's *Republic,* mainly the second and fourth books. In particular, one may point to II 368d–369a (turn from the individual to the state), IV 423c and 433a (the "universal justice" of the state as an organic arrangement), and° IV 4434c and 444d (the perfection of man in accord with his powers).

SUPPLEMENT TO IMH LXXVIn373

LS's editorial annotation to Morgenstunden 69.14–25 (JA III.2 286–87)

... Mendelssohn renders Basedow's opinion in an overstated form: according to Basedow, the obligation to believe, by itself, is no sufficient motive for the acceptance of the truths of natural religion, but "universal experience *and* the obligation to believe" (*Theoretische System der gesunden Vernunft* [Altona, 1765], bk. 3, p. 87). (What he understands by "universal experience" comes out in the following sentences: "The analogical mode of thinking ... infers with perfect confidence from very many similar examples. . . . That such analogical inferences are credible, true, and certain, that they have ordinary practical certainty, is one of the first main principles. . . . It has the name of the first main principle of universal experience." [*Philalethie* (Altona, 1764), II, 298–99]) The "rational obligation to believe" finds "a role ... when certain important principles ... remain at least apparent, when no theoretical certainty is to be arrived at, and when a doubt of whether this being-apparent is true interferes with and greatly endangers the important purposes of man, certain important principles ... remain at least apparent" (*Theoretische System, Vorbericht,* p. 5). "There are practical principles that in theory are and remain only apparent to us, but must be valid in practice if we do not want to act contrary to important principles and put ourselves in danger. . . . The principle of the immortality of souls and of future reward

... is an example of such principles as I am talking about. If the case were as I am positing, then immortality and reward would, theoretically speaking, be only apparent. But the obligation to believe makes them certain in one who thinks it over" (ibid., bk. 3, pp. 76ff.). "Once one sees that a doubt of God's existence and attributes puts our soul's welfare in danger, robs us of the purest satisfactions and consolations, then by virtue of the obligation to believe, the principle of God's existence must remain a certain moral and practical truth, even if the proof for it should not be fully forthcoming or should have been forgotten" (bk. 4, p. 144). In *Philalethie*, Basedow calls the principle of the obligation to believe "the rule of purposive knowledge"; this rule reads: "A cognition that is apparent and indispensable" (that is, one whose truth is very important for us and the world, and whose rejection is believed to be something of a danger to happiness, and doubt of which could have the most harmful consequences in the vicissitudes of life) "is to be utilized as true, and through this usage must ultimately be received with a well-established approval. At the appropriate time, I will prove that even if we had no higher light, nevertheless for a well-practiced reason the indispensable principles of the oneness of God, the immortality of the soul, and divine reward ... are also apparent principles, and this rule must therefore be applied to them.... But it is ... to be noted that this rule cannot be applied at all to the corroboration of such things as are never apparent but are altogether false" (II, 311–12).

SUPPLEMENT TO IMH XCVn463

LS's editorial annotation to Morgenstunden 116.6–15 (JA III.2 302)

Lessing, "On the Actuality of Things Outside God" (LM XIV 292–93; cf. Cha 102–3; cf. Nis 30–31]): "However I may explain to myself the actuality of things outside God, I must confess that I can form no concept of it. Let it be called the complement of possibility; I then ask, Is there a concept of this complement of possibility in God, or not? Who will assert this last? But if there is a concept of it in Him, then the thing itself is in Him, and all things in Him are themselves actual." (The essay's continuation and conclusion are in the annotation to *Morgenstunden* 117.8–118.18.)

LS's editorial annotation to Morgenstunden 116.12–15 (JA III.2 302)

The thesis that Spinozism is acosmism is found implicitly in the following alterations of Wolff's: "Spinoza potentiam naturae facit potentiam Dei et naturam omnem proprie sic dictam a corporibus, ex quibus mundus constat, removet, seu naturam proprie sic dictam non ens facit" [Spinoza makes the power of nature the power of God and removes all nature properly so called from the bodies of which the world consists, or makes nature properly so called into° nonbeing] (TN II §696). Cf. further Edelmann, *Moses mit aufgedecktem Angesicht*, 148: "alle Creaturen sind nichts; Er aber ist's gar . . ." [all creatures are nothing; He, however, exists emphatically . . .]. E. Platner, *Philosophische Aphorismen* (Leipzig 1776), 353: "Spinoza leugnet eigentlich nicht die Existenz der Gottheit, sondern die Existenz der Welt. Es ist also in seinem System nichts wirklich als Gott, d.h. das ewige unendliche Wesen." [Spinoza is really not denying the existence of the Divinity, but the existence of the world. There is therefore in his system actually nothing but God, i.e. the eternal infinite being.]" Cf. also A. W. Rehberg, *Abhandlung über das Wesen und die Einschränkung der Kräfte* (Leipzig, 1779), 50ff.

LS's editorial annotation to Morgenstunden 116.18–21 (JA III.2 302)

Cf. *An die Freunde Lessings* 205.38–206.3.

LS's editorial annotation to Morgenstunden 116.24–25 (JA III.2 302)

[Spinoza,] *Ethica* II, prop. 7, school., where "*quidam Hebraeorum* [some of the Hebrews]" is referred to (namely, Maimonides, *Guide of the Perplexed* I 68). Cf. the letter to Lessing of February 1, 1774 [JA XII.2 40].

LS's editorial annotation to Morgenstunden 117.8–118.18 (JA III.2 302–3)

Lessing, "On the Actuality of Things Outside God" (see annotation to *Morgenstunden* 116.6–15): "But, it will be said, the concept that God has of the actuality of a thing does not do away with[17] the actuality of a thing outside Him. No? Then the actuality outside Him must have something that distinguishes it from the actuality in His concept. That is, there must be something in the actuality outside Him of which God has no concept. An absurdity! But if there is nothing of the sort, if in the concept that God has of the actuality of the thing outside Him everything is to be found that is to be met up with in its actuality outside Him, then both actualities are one, and everything that ought to exist outside God exists in God. Or it might be said: The actuality of a thing is the sum of all possible determinations that

---

17. Ger.: *hebt . . . auf*. LS uses the past participle of this verb in quotation marks ("*aufgehoben*") at IGC CIX, where it has been translated "disposed of."

can apply to it. Must not this sum also be in the idea of God? What determination does the actuality outside Him have, if the archetype were not also to be found in God? Consequently, this archetype is the thing itself, and to say that the thing also exists outside this archetype means that its archetype is duplicated in a manner that is as unnecessary as it is absurd. To be sure, I believe that the philosophers say, To affirm the actuality of a thing outside God means nothing more than merely to distinguish this thing from God and to declare that its actuality is of another sort than the necessary actuality of God. But if they mean merely this, why shouldn't the concepts that God has of the actual things be these actual things themselves? They are still sufficiently distinguished from God, and accordingly their actuality becomes no less necessary because they are actual in Him. For in His idea, must there not also correspond an image of the contingency that they ought to have had outside Him? And this image is only their contingency itself. What is contingent outside God will be contingent in God, or God must have had no concept of the contingent outside Him. — I use this expression *outside Him* as it is commonly used, to show from its application that it ought not to be used. But, one will cry, to assume contingencies in the unchangeable being of God! So? Am I alone in doing that? You yourselves, who must attribute concepts of contingent things to God, has it never occurred to you that concepts of contingent things are contingent concepts?"

SUPPLEMENT TO IGC XCVIn4

LS's editorial annotation to Sache Gottes *§62 (JA III.2 340)*

The corresponding paragraph in Leibniz (§61 [Ger VI 448; cf. Sch 127]) reads: "Objicitur nempe Deum nimis concurre ad peccatum, hominem non satis" [It is objected that God concurs too much in sin, and man not enough]." The second part of the objection ("hominem non satis" [... man not enough]), or rather the refutation of it—*Causa Dei* §§74 to the end [Ger VI 450–60; Sch 130–45]—relates above all to the Christian doctrine of the Fall and Redemption.

SUPPLEMENT TO IGC XCVIIn6

LS's annotation to Sache Gottes *§2 (JA III.2 335)*

The paragraph in Leibniz reads: "Magnitudinis Divinae potius quam Bonitatis rationem habuere Theologi rigidiores; at laxiores contra: utraque perfectio aeque curae est vere Orthodoxis. Error Magnitudinem Dei infringentium Anthropomorphismus, Bonitatem tollentium Despotismus appellari posset." [The stricter Theologians have taken into account Divine Greatness rather than Divine° Goodness; the more lenient ones have done the opposite: both perfections are equally of concern to the truly Orthodox. The error of those who compromise God's Greatness could be called Anthropomorphism, that of those who deny His° Goodness could be called Despotism.] [cf. Ger VI 439; cf. Sch 114]

LS's annotation to Sache Gottes §3 (JA III.2 335)

The paragraph in Leibniz reads: "Magnitudo Dei studiose tuenda est contra Socianos imprimis, et quosdam Semisocianos, in quibus Conradus Vorstius hic maxime peccavit. Revocari autem illa potest ad duo Capita Summa, Omnipotentiam et Omniscientiam." [God's greatness is to be studiously protected, primarily against the Socinians and some half-Socinians, among whom Conrad Vorst has sinned here the most. It can be referred to two Main Headings, Omnipotence and Omniscience.] [cf. Ger VI 439; cf. Sch 114]

LS's annotation to Sache Gottes §22, line 3 (JA III.2 336)

[". . . as some philosophers[18] have believed."] Leibniz refers to the Stoic Diodorus and to Abelard, Wyclif, and Hobbes "among the Christians."

LS's annotation to Sache Gottes §24 (JA III.2 336)

In rendering this paragraph, Mendelssohn leaves out Leibniz's discussion of an alternative explanation of the division in question and thereby also its incidental pointers to peculiarly Christian themes.

LS's annotation to Sache Gottes §30 (JA III.2 336)

The paragraph in Leibniz reads: "Metaphysicum (sc. bonum et malum) generatim consistit in rerum etiam non intelligentium perfectione et imperfectione. Lilorum campi et passerum curam a Patre coelesti geri Christus dixit, et brutorum animalium rationem Deus habet apud Jonam." [Metaphysical (*sc.*, good and evil) consists, in general, in the perfection and imperfection of things, including those lacking in intelligence. Christ has said that the heavenly Father takes care of the lilies of the field and the sparrows; and according to Jonah, God takes the brute animals into account.] [cf. Ger VI 443; cf. Sch 120]

---

18. Ger.: *Weltweiser*. See IPM xviiin23.

LS's annotation to Sache Gottes §34 lines 7–17 (JA III.2 336)

"God can [allow some evil, i.e., although being contemplated as an evil it is an object of his hatred, nevertheless in His all-wise decrees He can° will not to prevent it so that a greater good be not lacking or even be prevented thereby. In cases of collision, the lesser good must give way to the better one, the smaller evil is preferred to the greater one. No collision takes place in the antecedent will, for in it we contemplate each good and each evil in and for itself, out of context. On the other hand, in the executing will or in the decree, collisions must emerge, and therefore exceptions must°] have a place." In Leibniz, it says: "Unde Thomas de Aquino post Augustinium non incommodo dixit, Deum permittere quadam mala fieri, ne multa bona impediantur." [Hence Thomas Aquinas, following Augustine, has said, not unfittingly, that God permits some evils to happen lest many goods be prevented.] [Ger VI 444; cf. Sch 121]

LS's annotation to Sache Gottes §36 line 2 (JA III.2 337)

"No one should do [evil for the purpose of serving the good]." — Leibniz: "neque enim (Apostolo monente) facienda sunt mala" [for (as the Apostle admonishes) evils are not to be done] [Ger VI 444; cf. Sch 121].

LS's annotation to Sache Gottes §36 line 9 (JA III.2 337)

"[according to the principle] of the highest wisdom and benevolence" — Leibniz: "*convenientiae* [of convenience]" [cf. Ger VI 444; cf. Sch 121].

LS's annotation to Sache Gottes §39 (JA III.2 337)

Mendelssohn leaves out Leibniz's concluding words, which read: "eo sensu quo Christus dixit oportere ut scandala existant" [in the sense in which Christ has said that it is necessary that there be offenses] [Ger VI 444; cf. Sch 122].

LS's annotation to Sache Gottes §49 (JA III.2 338)

The paragraph in Leibniz reads: "Optimae autem seriei rerum (nempe huius ipsius) eligendae maxima ratio fuit Christus Theanthropos, sed qui, quatenus Creatura est ad summam provecta, in ea Serie nobilissima contineri debebat, tanquam Universi creati pars, imo caput; cui omnis tandem potestas data est in caelo et in terra, in quo benedici debuerunt omnes gentes, per quem omnis creatura liberabitur a servitute corruptionis, in libertatem gloriae filiorum Dei." [The greatest reason for the choosing of the best series of events (namely, this very one) was Christ, God-become-Man, but who, insofar as He is a Creature raised to the highest, had to be the noblest one contained in that Series—as a part, indeed the head, of the created Universe: to whom ultimately all power has been given in heaven and on earth, in whom all peoples were to be blessed, and through whom every creature will be freed from the servitude of corruption, into the freedom of the glory of God's children.] [Ger VI 446; cf. Sch 124] — On Mendelssohn's explanation of Genesis 1:31, cf. the entirely different conception of the passage in Maimonides (*Guide of the Perplexed* III.10 and 13).

SUPPLEMENT TO IGC XCIXN20

LS's editorial annotation to Sache Gottes §46 lines 10–15 (JA III.2 338)

"Everything [acts commensurately with the wisest possible purpose; nothing ensues to which there does not correspond, on the one hand, an active secondary cause and, on the other hand, a purpose befitting God's perfection. The exception that miracles constitute in the systems of some philosophers][19] will be [dealt with in what follows]." — Mendelssohn's addition.

LS's editorial annotation to Sache Gottes §46, lines 13–15 (JA III.2 338)

["The exception that miracles constitute in the systems of some philosophers will be dealt with in what follows."] Mendelssohn has not followed out the view expressed here; cf. on the question of miracles, e.g., *Evidenz* 307.28ff. [Dah 288], JA III.1 278 and 279, JA VII 43.16ff. and 77.18ff., and *Morgenstunden* 128.3–4.

SUPPLEMENT TO IGC CN30

LS's editorial annotation to Sache Gottes §§56–59 (JA III.2 339)

To be compared with these paragraphs is the controversy between Mendelssohn and Abbt: Abbt's *Zweifel* and Mendelssohn's *Orakel* (JA VI.1 7–18, 19–25).

LS's editorial annotation to Sache Gottes §56 lines 3–4 (JA III.2 339)

["'He who does the good,' says the strict moralist, 'for the sake of the reward that he expects from it is at bottom profiteering and not a lover of

---

19. Ger.: *Weltweiser*. See IPM XVIIIn23.

the good.'"] Cf., e.g., Seneca, *De vita beata* 9.4; Spinoza, *Tractatus theologico-politicus* IV (§§14–16 Bruder) and *Ethica* V 42 [WhSt 255–56]; Leibniz, *Opera Philosophica* (ed. Erdmann), pp. 118, 246–47, 446 and 643; PPU I, §§345ff. Cf. also *Orakel*, annotation *r* [JA VI.1 43ff.].

LS's editorial annotation to Sache Gottes §56 lines 32–34 (JA III.2 339)

["'The gods themselves,' says *Seneca*, 'know no more pleasant spectacle than the virtuous, who struggle with fate and are not defeated.'"] The passage from Seneca (*De providentia*, 2) is also cited by Mendelssohn in his treatise *Über das Erhabene und Naive in den schönen Wissenschaften* (JA I 462.17–22).

LS's editorial annotation to Sache Gottes §57 lines 3–18 (JA III.2 339)

Cf. on this *Phädon* 16.5–8 [Cul viii–ix; Nob 47] and 18.36ff. [Cul xvff.; Nob 50–51] and annotation.[20]

LS's editorial annotation to Sache Gottes §57 lines 20–21 (JA III.2 339)

["We have seen on another occasion that without expectation of an infinite future no system of ethical doctrine can be established."] In the Third Dialogue of the *Phädon*; see especially the comprehensive remark in *Phädon* 123.16–19 [Cul 200; Nob 142].

---

20. There is no editorial annotation to *Phädon* 16.5–8.
LS's editorial annotation to *Phädon* 18.36–19.21 reads: "This supposed maxim of Socrates' was Mendelssohn's maxim; cf. especially his 'Letter to Deacon Lavater at Zurich' (*Lavater* 13–14 [Sam 59–60; Got 11–12]). — [John Gilbert] Cooper [*Life of Socrates* (London, 1750),] (27), unlike Mendelssohn, does not make the precise distinction between doctrines that are only theoretically false and those that are practically dangerous."
Mendelssohn's account of Socrates' "maxim" in *Phädon* 18.36–19.21 reads: "With regard to religion, he seems to have had in mind the following maxim. Each false doctrine or opinion that would manifestly lead to immorality, and is therefore opposed to the happiness of the human race, would be in no way spared by him but in public, in the presence of the hypocrites, the sophists, and the common people, would be contested, made laughable, and shown in its absurd and despicable consequences. Of this type were the doctrines of the writers of fables about the weaknesses, injustices, scandalous desires, and passions that they ascribed to their gods. Concerning such principles, as well as concerning incorrect concepts of God's providence and governance, also concerning the rewarding of good and the punishing of evil, he was never one to hold back, never doubtful even in appearance, but always resolute in advocating the cause of truth with the greatest intrepidity and, as the outcome showed, in sealing his confession with his death. A doctrine that was merely theoretically false and could not bring such great harm to morals as was to be feared from an innovation, he left unchallenged, instead professing the predominant opinion in public, observing the ceremonies and religious customs based on it, avoiding on the other hand all occasion for a distinctive explanation; and when it was not to be evaded, he then had a ready recourse that could never fail him: he pleaded *his ignorance*."
On Cooper's *Life of Socrates*, see LS's editorial annotation to *Phädon* 9.35 (JA III.1 392–93).

LS's editorial annotation to Sache Gottes §57 *lines 32–34 (JA III.2 339)*

["To be sure, we expect punishment in that life, but not to avenge ourselves on the tyrant who has oppressed us here; this would be thirst for vengeance."] "We therefore do not expect retribution for injustice in that life as the satisfying of a sort of desire for vengeance, as Mr. Abbt calls it." *Anmerkungen zu Abbts freundschaftlicher Correspondenz,* annotation *r* (JA VI.1 46).

LS's editorial annotation to Sache Gottes §57 *lines 34–36 (JA III.2 339)*

["'A reasonable man,' says Plato, 'does and wishes nothing evil for the evil to happen; if he punishes or is glad to see punishment happening, it is so that he might not see further evil.'"] *Protagoras* 324b. Cf. also *Laws* XI, 934a–b.

LS's editorial annotation to Sache Gottes §57 *lines 37–46 (JA III.2 339)*

". . . the most corrupt inclinations of all must have a natural foundation that is good and has been implanted in the soul by the Creator. . . . In this case, the basest rabble's desire for revenge has at bottom the inclination to see moral turpitude made known by means of physical evil." *Orakel,* etc. (JA VI.1 23, etc.)

LS's editorial annotation to Sache Gottes §60 *(JA III.2 339)*

Cf. *Gegenbetrachtungen* 72 and *Phädon* 102.

LS's editorial annotation to Sache Gottes §60 *lines 1–12 (JA III.2 339–40)*

Causa Dei §56: "Circa futuram vitam gravior adhuc est difficultas; nam objicitur ibi quoque bona longe vinci a malis, quia pauci sunt electi. Origenes quidem aeternam damnationem omnino sustulit; quidam veterum paucos saltem aeternum damnandos credidere, quorum in numero fuit Prudentius; quibusdam placuit omnem Christianum tandem salvatum iri, quorum aliquando inclinasse visus est Hieronymus." [Concerning the future life there is a still more serious difficulty; for here, too, it is objected that good things are far overcome by evils. Origen, of course, has done away with the eternity of damnation altogether; some of the ancients, among whose number was Prudentius, have believed that but few would be damned for eternity; some, to whom Jerome has sometimes seemed to have inclined, have been satisfied that every Christian was ultimately going be saved.] — §57: "Sed non est cur ad haec paradoxa et rejicienda confugiamus: Vera responsio est, totam amplitudinem regni coelestis non esse ex nostra cognitione aestimandam; nam tanta esse potest beatorum per Divinam Visionem Gloria, ut mala damnatorum omnium comparari huic bono non possint, et Angelos beatos incredibili multitudine agnoscit Scriptura, et magnam Creaturarum varietatem ipsa nobis aperit natura, novis inventis illustrata; quod facit ut commodius quam Augustinus et alii veteres praevalentiam boni prae malo tueri possimus." [But there is no reason to resort to these things, paradoxical and to be rejected as they are: The true answer is that the whole fullness of the heavenly kingdom is not to be estimated on the basis of our knowledge; for such can be the Glory of the blessèd through the Vision of God, that the evils of all the damned could not be compared to this good, and Scripture acknowledges blessèd Angels in an unbelievable multitude, and nature itself opens up to us the great variety of Creatures that is illuminated by new discoveries; this makes it more convenient for us than it was for Augustine and other ancients to defend the prevalence of good over evil.] — §58: "Nempe tellus nostra non est nisi satelles unius Solis, ete tot sunt Soles quot stellae fixae; et credibile et maximum esse spatium trans omnes fixas. Itaque nihil prohibet, vel Soles, vel maxime regionem trans Soles habitari felicibus creaturis. Quanquam et planetae esse possint aut fieri ad instar Paradisi felices. In domo Patris nostri multas esse mansiones, de coelo beatorum proprie Christus dixit, quod Empyrium vocant Theologi quidam, et trans sidera seu soles collocant, etsi nihil certi de loco beatorum affirmari posit: interim et in spectabili mundo multas Creaturarum rationalium habitationes esse verisimile judicari potest, alias aliis feliciores." [Namely, our earth is only a satellite of one Sun, and there are as many Suns as there are fixed stars; and it is believable that there is also a very great space beyond the fixed stars. Accordingly, nothing prevents either the Suns, or especially the region beyond the Suns, from being inhabited by happy creatures. Even so, the planets too could be or become as happy as Paradise. "In our Father's house are many mansions," Christ himself has properly said of the heaven of the blessèd, which some theologians call the Empyrium and locate beyond the stars or suns, even if nothing certain can be affirmed concerning the place of the blessèd: meanwhile it can be judged plausible that even in the visible world there are many habitations of rational Creatures, some being happier than others.] — §59: "Itaque argumentum a multitudine damnatorum non est fundatum nisi in ignorantia nostra, unique responsione dissolvitur, quam supra innuimus, si omnia nobis perspecta forent, appariturum ne optari quidem posse meliora quam quae fecit Deus. Poenae etiam damnatorum ob perseverantem eorum malitiam perseverant: unde insignis Theologus Joh. Fechtius in eleganto libro de Statu damnatorum eos bene refutat, qui in futura vita peccata peonam demereri negant, quasi justitia Deo essentialis cessare unquam posset." [Accordingly, the argument drawn from the multitude of the damned is founded only on our ignorance and is dissolved by a single answer, as we have intimated above: if all things were to become thoroughly visible to us, it would appear that better things than those God has made could not even be wished for. Also, the punishments of the damned persevere on account of the perseverance of their malice: hence a distinguished Theologian, Johann Fechtius, in a fine book on the State of the damned has well refuted those who deny that sins committed in the hereafter deserve punishment, as if the justice essential to God could ever cease.] [cf. Ger VI 447–48; cf. Sch 125ff.]

LS's editorial annotation to Sache Gottes §60 lines 25–29 (JA III.2 340)

Likewise in *Anmerkungen zu Abbts freundschaftlicher Correspondenz* (JA VI.1 46–47).

LS's annotation to Sache Gottes §76 (JA III.2 341)

Cf. *Anmerkungen zu Abbts freundschaftlicher Correspondenz* (JA VI.1 45–46), as well as *Phädon* 120 [Cul 192ff.; Nob 139–40].

LS's editorial annotation to Sache Gottes §76 line 1 (JA III.2 341)

["We have seen in the foregoing that in fact reason does not know how to find any solution here, if death could be the transition either to annihilation or to eternal torment."] In §§57–60.

LS's editorial annotation to Sache Gottes §76 lines 11–12 (JA III.2 341)

["The accusation that the evil in the parts belongs to the perfection of the whole will not be answered here."] This is Voltaire's objection to the theodicy of Shaftesbury et al.; see *Dictionnaire philosophique portative*, art. 'Bien (Tout est)' [(London, 1764), 466–69; Gay 116–22]. Cf. also *Gegenbetrachtungen* 71.19ff.

SUPPLEMENT TO IGC CIIN40

LS's editorial annotation to Sache Gottes §44 lines 2–3 (JA III.2 337)

"actions and concerns" — Leibniz: "*preces laboresque* [prayers and works]" [Ger VI 445; Sch 123]. Cf. JA XI 55.37–56.1, as well as JA II 4.5–12.

LS's editorial annotation to Sache Gottes §44 line 5 (JA III.2 337)

"to speak in a human way" — Mendelssohn's addition.

LS's editorial annotation to Sache Gottes §44 lines 6–7 (JA III.2 337)

"concerns and actions" — Leibniz: "*preces . . . et aliae causae* [prayers . . . and other causes]" [Ger VI 445; Sch 123].

LS's editorial annotation to Sache Gottes §44 lines 17–22 (JA III.2 337)

"If therefore [my improvement right now, e.g., or my change of heart can move divine mercy to turn away a misfortune imposed on me, then this change of heart belonged to the best series of things all along and brought about in God's decree the very same thing all along which] is [now] being contemplated [as its consequence]." — Mendelssohn's addition.

LS's editorial annotation to Sache Gottes §48 line 1 (JA III.2 338)

"nothing to be more wished for" — Mendelssohn's addition.

LS's editorial annotation to Sache Gottes §48 lines 2–4 (JA III.2 338)

"and to [cling to his wishes and purposes in everything, as much as is in us, to] submit completely to his commands" — Mendelssohn's addition.

LS's editorial annotation to Sache Gottes §48, lines 5–6 (JA III.2 338)

"and find [our highest happiness] in [the contemplation of his perfections]" — Mendelssohn's addition.

SUPPLEMENT TO IGC CIIN41

LS's editorial annotation to Sache Gottes §1 line 2 (JA III.2 335)

"and nobly, to be sure" — Mendelssohn's addition.

LS's editorial annotation to Sache Gottes §1 lines 8–10 (JA III.2 335)

"the first [part will contain mere preliminary knowledge, or those truths that must be presupposed for God's justification. The second part contains the justification] itself." — Leibniz: "prior praeparatoria magis, altera principalis censeri potest" [the first (part) may be considered as rather preparatory and the second as the principal one] [Ger VI 439; cf. Sch 114].

LS's editorial annotation to Sache Gottes §1 lines 13–14 (JA III.2 335)

"[the rule of God which] extends [over all intelligent beings]" — Leibniz describes it more closely: "Regimen circa intelligentes, praesertim in negotio pietatis et salutis" [the rule that He exercises over intelligent beings, especially in the business of piety and salvation] [cf. Ger VI 439; cf. Sch 114].

LS's editorial annotation to idem (JA III.2 335)

"and capable of happiness" — Mendelssohn's addition.

LS's editorial annotation to Sache Gottes §61 lines 7–8 (JA III.2 340)

Mendelssohn leaves out the concluding sentence of the corresponding paragraph of *Causa Dei* (§60), which runs: "Sed quicquid hoc est difficultatis, Divini Luminis auxiliio etiam in hac vita ita superatur, ut pii et Dei amantes sibi, quantum opus est, satisfacere possint" [But whatever difficulty there is here, it can be overcome with the help of the divine light, even in this life, so that the pious and those who love God can satisfy themselves as much is needed] [Ger VI 448; cf. Sch 127].

LS's editorial annotation to Sache Gottes §69 line 9 (JA III.2 340)

Mendelssohn here leaves a sentence of Leibniz's untranslated, which runs: "Sed hic quoque Deus mentem illustrans sui est vindex in anima pia et veritatis studiosa" [But here too God, enlightening the mind, vindicates himself in a soul that is pious and studious of truth] (*Causa Dei* §68 [Ger VI 449; cf. Sch 128]).

LS's editorial annotation to Sache Gottes §69 lines 9–14 (JA III.2 341)

"We [therefore have to explain that, insofar as we can ascribe to God a concurrence in moral evil, we will see that only the material of sin, i.e., that which is yet good in the sin itself, and not the formality, or that which is really evil in the sin,] can [be ascribed to God's concurrence]." — Leibniz: "Explicabimus igitur quid sit Deum concurrere ad peccati materiale, seu quod in malo bonum est, non ad formale" [We will therefore explain what it is for God to concur vis-à-vis the material of sin, or in what is good in the evil, and not vis-à-vis the formality of sin°] (*ibid.*).

SUPPLEMENT TO IGC CIIN43

LS's editorial annotation to Sache Gottes §52 line 2 (JA III.2 338)

"probably"[21] — Mendelssohn's addition. Compare on this IP xxxi.

LS's editorial annotation to Sache Gottes §52 line 8 (JA III.2 338)

"unceasingly"[22] — Mendelssohn's addition.

LS's editorial annotation to Sache Gottes §52 lines 9–13 (JA III.2 338)

The complaints [themselves indicate for the most part the rarity of evil and very often carry their consolations with them. Whoever complains wishes in that way to ease his pain or to move the other to compassion. Let whoever complains disconsolately look at his present life in its] entire duration." — Mendelssohn's addition.

SUPPLEMENT TO IGC CIIN44

LS's editorial annotation to Sache Gottes §11 line 1 (JA III.2 335)

"God's influence [on the actions of] creatures" — Leibniz: "Concursus autem Dei (etiam ordinaries seu non miraculosus) . . ." [God's concurrence (even ordinary or non-miraculous concurrence°) . . .] [Ger VI 440; cf. Sch 115]. Cf. *Sache Gottes* §46, lines 13–15, and annotation.[23]

SUPPLEMENT TO IGC CIIN49

LS's editorial annotation to Sache Gottes §28 lines 5–6 (JA III.2 336)

["Certain things that ought not to be done can be allowed anyway"] ". . . well, sometimes one is duty-bound not to prevent them." — Mendelssohn's addition.

LS's editorial annotation to Sache Gottes §28 line 8 (JA III.2 336)

["The object of the permissive will in this case is not the action itself . . ."] "which remains disallowed at any time" — Mendelssohn's addition.

---

21. *Sache Gottes* §52 lines 1–2 read: "Physical good and physical evil meet us in this life and will probably never emerge for us also in that future."

22. *Sache Gottes* §52 lines 8–9 read: "the good that happens to us unceasingly."

23. For LS's editorial annotation to *Sache Gottes* §46 lines 13–15, see appendix 2, supplement to IGC xcixn20, above.

LS's editorial annotation to Sache Gottes §28 lines 8–9 (JA III.2 336)

["but the *permission*"] "which can sometimes be allowed, sometimes even be an obligation." — Mendelssohn's addition.

LS's editorial annotation to Sache Gottes §32 (JA III.2 336)

This paragraph in Leibniz reads: "Morale [*sc.*, bonum et malum] de earum [*sc.*, substantium intelligentium] actionibus virtuosis et vitiosis, quo pertinet Malum Culpae: et malum physicum hoc sensu a morale oriri solet, etsi non semper in iisdem subjectis [*sc.*, qui istam culpam incurrunt]; sed haec [*sc.*, malum] tamen quae videri possit aberratio cum fructu corrigitur, ut innocentes nollent passi non esse. Add. infra §55." [Moral good and evil have to do with the virtuous and vicious acts of intelligent substances, to which belongs the Evil of Guilt; and physical evil usually arises from moral evil in this sense, even if not always in the same subjects who incur that guilt; but this evil, which could seem to be an aberration, is nevertheless corrected with a reward, so that the innocent do not wish not to have suffered. See also *Causa Dei* §55, below.]"[24] [Ger VI 443; cf. Sch 120]

SUPPLEMENT TO IGC CIIIn50

LS's editorial annotation to Sache Gottes §55 (JA III.2 338)

The paragraph in Leibniz reads: "Itaque non tantum large compensabuntur afflictiones, sed inservient ad felicitatis augmentum; nec tantum prosunt haec mala, sed et requiruntur. Add. §32." [Accordingly, not only will afflictions be largely compensated, but they will serve the increase of happiness; not only are these evils useful, but they are even required. See also *Causa Dei* §32.][25] [Ger VI 447; cf. Sch 125.]

SUPPLEMENT TO IGC CIIIn57

LS's editorial annotation to Sache Gottes §12 lines 5–6 (JA III.2 335)

"and of happiness" and "tender" — Mendelssohn's additions.[26]

---

24. *Causa Dei* §55 is translated in appendix 2, supplement to IGC CIIIn50.
25. *Causa Dei* §32 is translated in supplement to IGC CIIIn49.
26. *Sache Gottes* §12 lines 5–6 read: "God, the father of light and of happiness, the tender giver of everything good."

SUPPLEMENT TO IGC CIVn58

LS's editorial annotation to Evidenz *319.1–7 (JA II 425)*

Wolff also argues from the createdness of man and the world to God's unlimited right to rule and men's obligation to obey (TN I §§963ff.). The "supplement" to this syllogism that Mendelssohn brings forward in the next paragraph rests entirely on presuppositions that are also accepted by Wolff (see the following annotation [*sc*., to *Evidenz* 319.25–28).[27] The difference is therefore not primary. Even so, it is interesting as proof of the progress of theological Rationalism on the way from Wolff to Mendelssohn. Incidentally, from this point of view, cf. also Mendelssohn's sentence (*Evidenz* 318.32–34 [cf. Dah 298]): "Can the wisest of all and most benevolent Being have any other aim than the perfection of creatures?" with Wolff's sentence "Patefactio summae Dei perfectionis seu manifestatio gloriae divinae est finis ultimus, quem per existentiam huius universi intendit" [The disclosure of God's highest perfection, or the manifestation of divine glory, is the ultimate end that God has intended by the existence of this universe].

SUPPLEMENT TO IGC CIVn59

LS's editorial annotation to Sache Gottes *§40 lines 13–14 (JA III.2 337)*

"and capable of happiness" — Mendelssohn's addition.

LS's editorial annotation to Sache Gottes *§47 lines 5–7 (JA III.2 338)*

"[whether with respect to the whole or with respect to each individual being capable of happiness] nothing better could even be wished for" — Leibniz: "[sapientem qui intellegeret, judicturum] ne optari quidem posse meliora" [the wise one who would understand will judge that nothing better could even be wished for] (Ger VI 446; cf. Sch 124).

---

27. LS's editorial annotation to Evidenz 319.25–28 (JA II 426) reads: "Wolff: 'Voluntas Dei tendit ad id, quod in se optimum' [God's will aims at what is best as such]. (TN I §383 — 'Facultas agendi moralis Jus dici solet' [The capacity to act morally is usually called Right]. (*loc. cit*., §954) — 'Differentia actionum liberarum quoad rectitudinem est id, quod moralitatis nomine venit' [What differentiates free actions as far as their rectitude is concerned is what goes by the name of morality]. (*loc. cit*., §951) — 'Bonitas divina est motivum servandi legem naturae, eamque minime transgrediendi' [Divine goodness is the motive for keeping the law of nature and transgressing it least]. (PPU II §409)."

LS's editorial annotation to Sache Gottes §50 lines 3–5 (JA III.2 338)

"by virtue of [which each intelligent being is allotted as much happiness as] can [be allotted to him]" — Mendelssohn's addition.

LS's editorial annotation to Sache Gottes §50 line 7 (JA III.2 338)

"or [the so-called] right to force" — Mendelssohn's addition.[28]

LS's editorial annotation to Sache Gottes §50 lines 9–13 (JA III.2 338)

"Thus to each intelligent creature, without regard to his merit or to a right that belongs to him, is allotted as much and as great a happiness as can be allotted to him without infringing on the highest wisdom." — Mendelssohn's addition.

SUPPLEMENT TO IGC CIVn60

LS's editorial annotation to Sache Gottes §41 line 2 (JA III.2 337)

"highest" and "unalterable" — Mendelssohn's additions.[29]

LS's editorial annotation to Sache Gottes §41 line 5 (JA III.2 337)

"one . . . can say with the highest certainty" — Leibniz: *dicendum* [it is to be said]. Cf., on this alteration, the corresponding deviation from Plato in *Phädon* (see IP xxiii–xxix).

LS's editorial annotation to Sache Gottes §48 line 1 (JA III.2 338)

"nothing more desirable" — Mendelssohn's addition.[30]

LS's editorial annotation to Sache Gottes §48 lines 2–4 (JA III.2 338)

"and to cling to his wishes and aims in everything, as much as is in us, to submit to his commandments fully" — Mendelssohn's addition.

LS's editorial annotation to Sache Gottes §48 lines 5–6 (JA III.2)

"and to find our highest happiness in the contemplation of his perfections" — Mendelssohn's addition.

---

28. *Sache Gottes* §50 line 7 reads: "right in the strictest sense or the so-called right to force."
29. *Sache Gottes* §41 lines 1–3 read: "Since the benevolence of God, which is revealed in creation, or his providence, which serves the highest wisdom as the unalterable guideline...."
30. *Sache Gottes* §48 lines 1–3 read: "... nothing is more desirable, nothing happier than to serve such an all-benevolent Lord."

SUPPLEMENT TO IGC CVn67

LS's editorial annotation to Sache Gottes §67, lines 2–7 (JA III.2 340)

["it has already been remarked in the preceding that there are times when (moral evil) cannot be blamed on free will,[31] there being times when it is allowed, i.e., morally possible, or rather there are times when it is even an obligation, i.e., morally necessary; indeed, we have added that permission for moral evil is never merely allowed, but it is always either forbidden or an obligation."] In *Sache Gottes* §§28, 36 and 38.

LS's editorial annotation to Sache Gottes §67, lines 14–16 (JA III.2 340)

"nor could a store clerk know that his boss has perpetrated an injustice without betraying him" — Mendelssohn's addition.

SUPPLEMENT TO IGC CVIIIn80

LS's editorial annotation to Evidenz 291.29–30 (JA II 420)

["If one were to say to a beginner, for example, 'justice is a wisely administered benevolence'"] This is how Leibniz defines justice; see, e.g., *Principes de la nature et de la grâce* §9 [Ger VI 602; Wie 528 or ArGa 210 or FrWo 262–63]: ". . . la justice, prise généralement, n'est autre chose que la bonté conforme à la sagesse. . . ." [justice, taken generally, is nothing but goodness/benevolence in conformity with wisdom. . . .] Cf. also Wolff, *Theologia naturalis*, I, §1067.

LS's editorial annotation to Evidenz 291.33ff. (JA II 420)

On this critique of the traditional concept of justice, cf. Wolff, *De definitione justitiae Ulpiani*, bk. 10, *De justitia et jure* . . . (in *Horae subsecivae Marburgensis Anni 1729*, 230–31): "Ulpianus . . . justitiam definit, quod sit constans et perpetua voluntas jus suum cuique tribuendi; quae definitio ut intelligatur, doceri debet, tum quaenam voluntas constans dicatur, quaenam perpetua, tum quodnam alteri jus sit et quomodo ipsum tribuatur." [Ulpian . . . defines justice as the constant and perpetual will to grant each his own; for this definition to be understood, it has to be shown first what "constant will" means and what "perpetual" means°, then what the other's right is and how he might be granted it.] Likewise Bilfinger, *Dilucidationes* §445.

---

31. Ger.: *die freie Ursache*. More or less lit.: the free cause.

SUPPLEMENT TO IGC CIXN94

LS's editorial annotation to Phädon 3 148.36 (JA III.1 414)

Father Roger Joseph Boscovich, S.J. (1711–87, professor of philosophy and mathematics in Rome): *De continuitatis lege, et eius consectariis* (dissertation, Rome 1754); *Philosophiae naturalis Theoria* (Vienna 1759). Cf. Mendelssohn's review of the latter work in the *Literaturbriefen* (especially #42 of June 7, 1959). See annotation to *Phädon* 62.15–66.14.[32]

32. From LS's editorial annotation to *Phädon* 62.15–66.14 (JA III.1): "... cf. the following passage from Mendelssohn's review of Boscovich's *Philosophiae naturalis Theoria* (*Literaturbrief* #42, June 7, 1759 [JA V.1 58–60 *passim*]): 'Mr. Boscovich's whole system rests on the law of stability. The Father explains this general law of nature as follows: "if a quantity passes from one magnitude to another, then it must traverse all intermediate magnitudes that are to be met up with between the two magnitudes." In the intervening changes, therefore, each moment of time arrives at a determinate state that is distinct from both the preceding moment° and the following moment°. But just as the duration continues as one, and each moment is as it were only the transition from the preceding moment° into the following moment°, so therefore Mr. Boscovich considers the state that each moment arrives at as only the common boundary between the previous and the following magnitudes.... That such a law is really found in nature, Mr. Boscovich proves on one occasion by induction.... But Mr. Boscovich also proves his general law in a demonstrative manner. He presupposes that duration is stable in its sequence; any one moment is, as we touch on above, to be considered the common boundary of the preceding one and the following one. There are therefore no two moments that would be next to each other, i.e., between which an actual duration, an actual sequence would not have to be met up with; ... so it must be granted that changes are just as stable as time.'"

APPENDIX 3

From Mendelssohn's "Epistle to Mr. Lessing in Leipzig" (Passage cited in Strauss, *Natural Right and History*, p. 275, n. 41)[1]

... The state of nature [for Rousseau] is as it were the childish age of our race. The powers are weak, the capabilities limited, and man's entire nature is only a small step removed from the nature of beasts. Hence our duties are thereby enclosed within very narrow limits. But how so? Is the age of manhood supposed to prescribe no other obligations, no other duties to the human race than those with which it has been laden in its childhood years? How could this philosopher[2] have forgotten his own conclusions so easily?

If scholars have recognized at all times that it is necessary to consider man in his natural state in order to be able to build a right of nature on secure grounds, then they must have taken it quite otherwise [than Rousseau has], or else° asserted a manifest absurdity. I suppose the former. They will have taken man as he is now, with all the powers with which he is equipped and at the level of perfection to which he has raised himself after long labor. Had they robbed him of his capabilities, then they would have placed him down with the cattle, and the right of nature that would have been built on such grounds would be suitable for animals rather than for their masters. But they have torn man from society, that is, they have abstracted from all obligations that men willingly undergo for what is best for society. They have wanted to consider only what is legitimate in and for itself and without the consent of all peoples. Here is where they have grounded the right of nature, which can therefore be nothing else but *the laws of justice that flow from our essential condition and cannot be changed even if all the nations of the earth were united against them.*[3]

1. JA II 92. Interpolations in square brackets are my own. M.D.Y.
2. Ger.: *Weltweiser*. See IPM xviiin23.
3. The emphasis is Mendelssohn's.

APPENDIX 4

From Lessing's "The Education of the Human Race" (§§70–73)[1]

§70. You have seen in the childhood of the human race,[2] concerning the teaching of the oneness of God, that God also reveals mere truths of reason directly, or permits and encourages mere truths of reason to be taught for a long time as truths directly revealed, in order to spread them quickly and establish them more firmly.

§71. In the adolescence of the human race,[3] you experience the very same concerning the teaching of the immortality of the soul. In the second, better primer, it is *preached* as revelation, not *taught* as the result of human inferences.

§72. As we can now dispense with the Old Testament's teaching of the oneness of God, and as we can gradually begin to dispense with the New Testament's teaching of the immortality of the soul, could there not be mirrored in the latter still more of the same sort of truths that we are to be astonished at as revelations for as long as it takes, until reason learns to derive them from its other truths that it has made out and to combine them with them?

§73. E.g., the teaching of the Trinity. — How would it be if this teaching were to bring human reason at last, after infinite wanderings right and left, on the way to recognizing that it is impossible for God to be able to be *one* in the sense that finite things are *one*; that even his oneness would have to be a transcendental oneness that does not exclude a kind of plurality? — Must not God at least have the most perfect representation of himself, i.e., a representation in which is found everything that is in himself? Would everything be found in it that is in himself, however, if even of his *necessary actuality* there were found merely a representation, merely a possibility, just as of his remaining attributes? This possibility exhausts the being of his remaining attributes: but of his necessary actuality as well? Myself, I think not. — Consequently, either God cannot have any complete representation

---

1. LM XIII 430–31 (Cha 94–95; Nis 234–35). Includes passage cited in IPM xxn46 and IMH xxivn87.
2. I.e., in the Old Testament.
3. I.e., in the New Testament.

of himself at all, or this complete representation is just as necessarily actual as he himself is, etc. — Indeed, the image of me in the mirror is nothing but an empty representation of me, since it only has of me that of which light rays fall onto its surface. But then if this image were to have *everything*, everything without exception that I myself have, would it then also still be an empty representation, or not rather a true duplication of myself? — If I believe I recognize a similar duplication in God, then perhaps I do not err, but rather speech undermines my concepts; and perhaps so much remains forever indisputable that those who want to popularize the idea of it could hardly have expressed themselves more comprehensibly and fittingly than by the naming of a *son* that God begets from eternity.

PART II

An Interpretive Essay

Strauss on Mendelssohn: An Interpretive Essay

MARTIN D. YAFFE

> ... it is incontestably better to defend an unphilosophical cause very philosophically than to want to reject and reform it unphilosophically.
> —Lessing on Leibniz[1]

The story of Leo Strauss's philosophical introductions to ten writings by Moses Mendelssohn, as found in the Jubilee Edition of the latter's collected works,[2] is several stories in one.

I

First, there is the story of Mendelssohn as the leading Jewish figure of the German Enlightenment. Of the ten Mendelssohnian writings to which Strauss provides introductions, eight are in Mendelssohn's lively, erudite, widely read, and highly esteemed German prose. The other two are in Mendelssohn's Hebrew, for his fellow Jews. These writings indicate, among other things, the impressive scope of his literary and intellectual activity.

In *Pope a Metaphysician!*, he collaborates with his dearest friend and fellow defender of the philosophy of G. W. Leibniz, Gotthold Ephraim Lessing—the outstanding literary and intellectual figure of the German Enlightenment in his own right and Mendelssohn's early literary patron—to contest the Berlin Academy's misleading association, in an essay competition sponsored by the Academy, of Leibniz's metaphysical doctrines with Alexander Pope's didactic poem *Essay on Man*.[3]

In "Epistle to Mr. Lessing in Leipzig," he appends to his German translation of Jean Jacques Rousseau's *Discourse on the Origin and Foundations of*

---

1. Lessing to Mendelssohn, May 1, 1774 (JA XII.2 47, with IMH LIIn228—for these abbreviations, see notes 2 and 11, below). Cf. also note 111, below.
2. *Moses Mendelssohn Gesammelte Schriften Jubiläumsausgabe* (16 vols. planned, interrupted after 7 vols.; Berlin: Akademie der Wissenschaft des Judentums, 1929–37; facsimile reprint and continuation, 24 vols. in 36; Stuttgart–Bad Cannstatt: Friedrich Frommann Verlag Günther Holzboog, 1971–)—henceforth JA, followed by volume, part, and page numbers as appropriate.
3. *Pope ein Metaphysiker!* (JA II 47–80—henceforth *Pope!*), with JA II xv–xx, translated in the present volume as "Introduction to *Pope a Metaphysician!*" (henceforth IPM).

Inequality among Men a philosophical critique of Rousseau. The critique takes the form of a public letter addressed to Lessing in the wake of oral conversations the two friends were having about Rousseau before Lessing's relocation from Berlin.[4]

In *Commentary on Moses Maimonides' "Logical Terms,"* he explicates in Hebrew Maimonides' introduction to logic.[5]

In *Treatise on Evidence in Metaphysical Sciences*—his prizewinning entry in a Berlin Academy–sponsored essay competition—he examines whether or not metaphysical truths have the same "evidence" (that is to say, "certainty" and "perspicuity") as mathematical truths.[6]

In *Phädon, or On the Immortality of the Soul in Three Dialogues*, he adapts Plato's *Phaedo* to the literary taste of his German readers and updates its Socratic arguments for the immortality of the soul.[7]

In *Treatise on the Incorporeality of the Human Soul*—consisting of four separate essays on the imperishability of the soul, plus a fragment perhaps meant as an introduction to these, combined and published posthumously by a Viennese admirer—Mendelssohn responds to the scholarly controversy accompanying the popular success of his *Phädon*.[8]

In "On a Handwritten Essay of Mr. de Luc's," he complies with a request by the Swiss physicist Jean André de Luc for feedback on de Luc's sketch for a planned treatise on materialism. Mendelssohn's feedback was not published, except that de Luc translated the latter half of it into French for an annotation in his *Lettres physiques et morales sur l'histoire de la terre et de l'homme*.[9]

In *The Soul*—consisting of two separate treatises in Hebrew, posthu-

---

4. "Sendschreiben an den Herrn Magister Lessing in Leipzig" (JA II 81–109—henceforth *Sendschreiben*), with JA II xx–xxiii, translated in the present volume as "Introduction to 'Epistle to Mr. Lessing in Leipzig'" (henceforth IEL).

5. *Kommentar an den Termini der Logik des Mose ben Maimon* (JA XIV 23–119, Hebrew original; JA II 197–230, selection in Strauss's German translation—henceforth *Logik*)—translated online as *Commentary on Moses Maimonides' "Logical Terms,"* with JA II xli, translated as "Introduction to *Commentary on Moses Maimonides' 'Logical Terms'*" (henceforth ILT).

6. *Abhandlung über die Evidenz in metaphysischen Wissenschaften* (JA II 267–330—henceforth *Evidenz*), with JA II xlv–liii, translated as "Introduction to *Treatise on Evidence*" (henceforth ITE).

7. *Phädon oder über die Unsterblichkeit der Seele in drei Gespräche* (JA III.1 5–159—henceforth *Phädon*), with JA III.1 xiii–xxxiii, translated as "Introduction to *Phädon*" (henceforth IP).

8. *Abhandlung von der Unkörperlichkeit der menschlichen Seele* (JA III.1 161–88—henceforth *Unkörperlichkeit*), with JA III.1 xxxiv–xxxviii, translated as "Introduction to *Treatise on the Incorporeality of the Human Soul*" (henceforth IIS).

9. "Über einen schriftlichen Aufsatz des Herrn de Luc" (JA III.1 195–99—henceforth *de Luc*), with JA III.1 xxxviii–xxxix, translated as "Introduction to 'On a Handwritten Essay of Mr. de Luc's'" (henceforth IdL).

mously combined and published as one—he summarizes his argument for the spirituality and imperishability of the human soul.[10]

In *Morning Hours* and *To the Friends of Lessing*, Mendelssohn defends his late friend Lessing's moral and theological respectability in what came to be called the Pantheism Controversy—the publicly shocking and privately mortifying allegation by Friedrich Heinrich Jacobi (1743–1819) that Lessing had, unbeknownst to Mendelssohn, been a covert Spinozist (that is to say, atheist), and Mendelssohn's reply that he had known all along of Lessing's Spinozism but that, *pace* Jacobi, it was a "purified" Spinozism consisting of a morally salutary Pantheism rather than atheism.[11]

Finally, in *God's Cause, or Providence Vindicated*, he confronts the views of his chief philosophical authority, Leibniz, on divine providence.[12]

II

Second, there is the story of the unexpectedly long and intermittently uncertain coming into being of the Moses Mendelssohn Jubilee Edition (*Jubiläumsausgabe*; henceforth JA, followed by volume, part, and page numbers as appropriate)—its hopeful beginnings in Weimar Germany in the 1920s, its brutal suppression in Nazi Germany in the 1930s, and its eventual resumption in post–World War II Germany in the 1960s.

JA was to be the first comprehensive edition of Mendelssohn's works. The originally planned sixteen volumes—eventually expanded to twenty-four volumes in thirty-six parts—were to contain everything Mendelssohn had written in German (including his writings on philosophy and aesthetics and on Judaism; his extensive literary reviews; his translations of Plato, Rousseau, and the Bible; and his poems and personal correspondence) and in Hebrew (including his commentaries on biblical books and his aforementioned writings on Maimonides and on the soul). Publication began in Berlin in 1929, the 200th anniversary of Mendelssohn's birth, under the joint auspices of the Academy for the Science of Judaism, the Society for the Advancement of the Science of Judaism, and an honorary board of thirty-

---

10. *Die Seele* (JA XIV 121–44, Hebrew original—henceforth *HaNefesh*; JA III.1 201–33, Strauss's German translation—henceforth *Seele*—translated online as *The Soul* at www.press.uchicago.edu/sites/strauss/), with JA III.1 xxxix–xli, translated as "Introduction to *The Soul*" (henceforth IS).

11. *Morgenstunden* and *An die Freunde Lessings* (JA III.2 1–175 and 177–218—henceforth *Morgenstunden* and *Freunde*, respectively), with JA III.2 xi–xcv, translated as "Introduction to *Morning Hours* and *To the Friends of Lessing*."

12. *Sache Gottes, oder die gerettete Vorsehung* (JA III.2 219–60—henceforth *Sache Gottes*), with JA III.2 xcvi–cx, translated as "Introduction to *God's Cause, or Providence Vindicated*" (henceforth IGC).

one philanthropists and academic luminaries. Financial support came from the House of Mendelssohn & Co. Three senior German-Jewish scholars[13] shared overall editorial responsibility and chose five younger collaborators. The five included Strauss, who was assigned coeditorship of two volumes containing Mendelssohn's writings on philosophy and aesthetics (JA II and III.1) and sole editorship of a volume containing his writings related to the controversy over Lessing's putative Spinozism (JA III.2).[14] By 1933, six volumes were in print, including the two that Strauss had coedited. Four more were in progress, including Strauss's remaining volume.

With the collapse of the Weimar Republic and its replacement by the Nazi regime, funding for the volumes in progress soon dried up. Nevertheless, work on them continued, at the urging of the sponsors and the editors-in-chief. By 1937, each of the four volumes was complete in manuscript. One of them came into print the next year, a volume of Mendelssohn's Hebrew writings edited by Haim Borodianski/Bar-Dayan. But the Gestapo seized and evidently destroyed most of the copies. Publication of JA now reached a standstill. Of the three unpublished manuscripts that remained, only two—including Strauss's JA III.2—would survive World War II and find their way into the resumed series. As for the third unpublished manuscript, I have recounted its particular fate in a translator's footnote to Strauss's introduction to Mendelssohn's *Morning Hours* and *To the Friends of Lessing*.[15]

Not until the mid-1960s did a new publisher, Günther Holzboog, acquire the rights to JA under the imprint of Friedrich Frommann Verlag of Stuttgart–Bad Cannstatt. In 1971, Holzboog began reissuing the seven previously produced volumes in facsimile reprint (including the one that had barely escaped total destruction in 1938) and publishing the remaining ones. The new editor-in-chief was Alexander Altmann, like Strauss an escapee from Nazi Germany and, by 1971, author of a magisterial intellec-

---

13. Ismar Elbogen (1874–1943), Julius Guttmann (1880–1950), and Eugen Mittwoch (1876–1942). For brief biographies of Elbogen and Guttmann, see *Studies in Jewish Thought: An Anthology of German Jewish Scholarship*, ed. Alfred Jospe (Detroit: Wayne State University Press, 1981), 419–20. For a brief biography of Mittwoch, see *Africa: Journal of the International African Institute* 14 (1943): 3.

14. Besides Leo Strauss, the others were Fritz Bamberger (designated editor for JA I, the first of JA's three-volumes-in-four of Mendelssohn's writings on philosophy and aesthetics, and coeditor with Strauss for JA II and III.1), Haim Borodianski/Bar-Dayan (designated editor for JA XIV and XVI, containing Mendelssohn's writings in Hebrew and his correspondence in Hebrew and Yiddish), Simon Rawidowicz (designated editor for JA VIII, originally containing Mendelssohn's writings on Judaism in German), and Bruno Strauss (designated editor for JA XI–XIII, containing Mendelssohn's correspondence in German).

15. See IMH XXXVIII.150.

tual biography of Mendelssohn.[16] Altmann had made use of Strauss's manuscript of JA III.2 for his biography and other writings on Mendelssohn[17] and now set about to supervise its publication. Meanwhile Strauss had become terminally ill. During the months before his death in October of 1973, he was able to proofread the pages of JA III.2's introductions, but not its Mendelssohnian texts and editorial apparatus (the variant readings he had compiled and the detailed editorial annotations he had supplied for those texts). Altmann completed the proofreading himself, and JA III.2 finally appeared in 1974.

III

Third, there is the story of Strauss's turning from his highly respected study of Spinoza's *Theologico-Political Treatise*[18]—written, as he later said autobiographically, by "a young Jew born and raised in Germany who found himself in the grips of the theologico-political predicament"—to the study of Mendelssohn as the philosophical founder of modern Jewish thought.[19] By the mid-1930s, Strauss had already written in considerable breadth and depth on both Jewish thought and modern philosophy. These topics, taken together, form the immediate backdrop to Strauss's Mendelssohn reflections.

Besides his Spinoza book, Strauss's writings on Jewish thought included not only youthful essays and position papers on Zionism and related matters,[20] but especially sober analytical appraisals of well-known contemporary and near-contemporary Jewish thinkers, notably the historian Simon Dubnow,[21] the philosophical theologian Franz Rosenzweig,[22] Sigmund

---

16. Alexander Altmann, *Moses Mendelssohn: A Biographical Study* (University, Ala.: University of Alabama Press, 1971); henceforth MMBS.

17. Altmann, *Moses Mendelssohns Frühschriften zur Metaphysik* (Tübingen: J. C. B. Mohr Paul Siebeck, 1969), henceforth MMFM; Altmann, *Die trostvolle Aufklärung: Studien zur Metaphysik und politischen Theorie Moses Mendelssohns* (Stuttgart–Bad Cannstatt: Friedrich Frommann Verlag Günther Holzboog, 1982), henceforth MMTA.

18. *Die Religionskritik Spinozas als Grundlage seiner Bibelwissenschaft: Untersuchungen zu Spinozas Theologisch-politischem Traktat* (Berlin und Wien: Akademie-Verlag, 1930); LSGS I 1–354; translated in 1965 as SCR.

19. Cf. SCR 1, 13–14, or LAM 224, 237.

20. See LSGS I 299–306, 311–21, 337–61; these and others are translated in LSEW 64–75, 79–89, 106–37.

21. "Soziologische Geschichtsschreibung?" *Der Jude: Eine Monatsschrift* (Berlin) 8 (1924): 190–92; LSGS II 333–37; "Sociological Historiography?" LSEW 101–6.

22. "Franz Rosenzweig und die Akademie für die Wissenschaft des Judentums," *Jüdische Wochenzeitung für Kassel, Hessen und Waldeck* 6.49 (December 13, 1929): n.p.; LSGS II 363–64; "Franz Rosenzweig and the Academy for the Science of Judaism," LSEW 212–13. Strauss dedicated his Spinoza book (note 18, above) to Rosenzweig's memory.

Freud,[23] and the Neo-Kantian philosopher Hermann Cohen[24]—as well as of non-Jewish thinkers, notably the comparative religion scholar Rudolph Otto[25] and the biblical historian Paul de Lagarde[26]—on biblical and post-biblical Judaism. Three essays in connection with Spinoza's Jewish origins considered, in turn, Cohen's interpretation of Spinoza's Bible science,[27] Spinoza's Bible science as compared with that of his predecessors',[28] and Spinoza's theologico-political bequest to Jews.[29] In addition to the four essays he incorporated into *Philosophy and Law: Contributions to the Understanding of Maimonides and His Predecessors*, a book on medieval Jewish thought,[30] Strauss published related essays on a no longer extant writing by Maimonides' Muslim predecessor Farabi,[31] on Maimonides' and Farabi's political science,[32] on Maimonides' view of providence,[33] and on Maimonides'

23. "Die Zukunft einer Illusion," *Der jüdische Student* 25.4 (August 1928): 16–22; "Sigmund Freud, *The Future of an Illusion*," LSEW 202–11.
24. See note 36, below. Writing autobiographically in 1962, Strauss described Cohen as "the center of attraction for philosophically minded Jews who were devoted to Judaism . . . the master whom they revered" (SPPP 233; cf. SCR 15, or LAM 240).
25. "Das Heilige," *Der Jude* 7 (1923): 240–42; LSGS II 307–10; "The Holy," LSEW 75–79.
26. "Paul de Lagarde," *Der Jude* 8.1 (1924): 8–15; LSGS II 323–31; "Paul de Lagarde," LSEW 90–101.
27. "Cohens Analyse der Bibel-Wissenschaft Spinozas," *Der Jude* 8 (1924): 295–314; LSGS I 363–86; "Cohen's Analysis of Spinoza's Bible Science," LSEW 140–72.
28. "Zur Bibelwissenschaft Spinozas und seiner Vorläufer," *Korrespondenzblatt des Vereins zur Gründung und Erhaltung einer Akademie für die Wissenschaft des Judentums* 7 (1926): 1–22; LSGS I 389–414; "On the Bible Science of Spinoza and His Precursors," LSEW 173–200.
29. "Das Testament Spinozas," *Bayerische Israelitische Gemeindezeitung* 8.21 (November 21, 1932): 322–36; LSGS I 415–22; "The Testament of Spinoza," LSEW 216–23.
30. *Philosophie und Gesetz: Beiträge zum Verständnis Maimunis und seiner Vorläufer* (Berlin: Schocken Verlag, 1935); "Einleitung [Introduction]; "Der Streit der Alten und der Neueren in der Philosophie des Judentums (Bemerkungen zum Julius Guttmann, *Die Philosophie des Judentums*)" [The Quarrel of the Ancients and the Moderns in the Philosophy of Judaism: Notes on Julies Guttmann, *The Philosophy of Judaism*]; "Die gesetzliche Begründung der Philosophie (Das Gebot des Philosophierens und die Freiheit des Philosophierens)" [The Legal Justification of Philosophy: The Commandment to Philosophize and the Freedom of Philosophizing]; "Die philosophische Begründung des Gesetzes (Maimunis Lehre von der Prophetie und ihre Quellen)" [The Philosophical Justification of the Law: Maimonides' Doctrine of Prophecy and Its Sources]; LSGS II 3–123; *Philosophy and Law: Essays Toward the Understanding of Maimonides and His Predecessors*, trans. Fred Baumann (Philadelphia: Jewish Publication Society, 1987); or *Philosophy and Law: Contributions to the Understanding of Maimonides and his Predecessors*, trans. Eve Adler (Albany: SUNY Press, 1995). *Philosophie und Gesetz*'s last chapter was published separately as "Maimunis Lehre von der Prophetie und ihre Quellen," *Le monde orientale* (Uppsala) 28 (1934): 99–139.
31. "Eine vermißte Schrift Fârâbîs" [A Missing Writing of Farabi], *Monatsschrift für Geschichte und Wissenschaft des Judentums* 80 (1936): 96–106; LSGS II 167–76.
32. "Quelques remarques sur la science politique de Maimonide et de Fârâbî," *Revue des études juives* 100 (1936): 1–37; LSGS II 125–58; "Some Remarks on the Political Science of Maimonides and Farabi," trans. Robert Bartlett, *Interpretation* 18 (1990–91): 3–30.
33. "Der Ort der Vorsehungslehre nach der Ansicht Maimunis," *Monatsschrift für Geschichte und Wissenschaft des Judentums* 81 (1937): 93–105; LSGS II 179–90; "The Place of the Doctrine of

epigone Isaac Abravanel.[34] Finally, Strauss also composed two unpublished lectures on the religious and intellectual situations of the present[35] and a third on Cohen and Maimonides.[36]

Strauss's publications on modern philosophy included his doctoral dissertation on Jacobi.[37] The close familiarity he acquired, then and since, with the writings of the philosophers and theologians of the German Enlightenment from Leibniz to Kant shows up in his extensive editorial annotations to JA II, III.1, and III.2, which contain pertinent citations to and quotations from many less-celebrated but instructive figures of the period.[38] Because Strauss often makes references to these in the numerous citations embedded his ten introductions, the present translation reproduces all the editorial annotations he refers to explicitly, along with many he refers to implicitly, and includes them in appendix 2 of this volume.[39] That is not all. Strauss also reviewed books of contemporary philosophical interest

---

Providence According to Maimonides," trans. Gabriel Bartlett and Svetozar Minkov, *Review of Metaphysics* 57 (2003–4): 537–49.

34. "On Abravanel's Philosophical Tendency and Political Teaching." In *Isaac Abravanel*, ed. J. B. Trend and H. Loewe (Cambridge, U.K.: Cambridge University Press, 1937), 93–129; LSGS II 195–227.

35. "Religiöse Lage der Gegenwart" [Religious Situation of the Present] (1930), LSGS II 377–91; "Die geistige Lage der Gegenwart" [The Intellectual Situation of the Present] (1932), LSGS II 441–59.

36. "Cohen und Maimuni" (1931), LSGS II 393–436; "Cohen and Maimonides," trans. Martin D. Yaffe and Ian Moore, in MW.

37. *Das Erkenntnisproblem in der philosophischen Lehre Fr. H. Jacobis* [The Problem of Knowledge in the Philosophical Doctrine of F. H. Jacobi] (1921), LSGS III 237–92. See also *Auszug aus der Inaugural-Dissertation* [Extract from the Inaugural Dissertation] (1921), LSGS III 293–98; Strauss's "Extract" is translated in LSEW 53–61.

38. These include: Thomas Abbt (1738–66), Johann Bernhard Basedow (1723–90), Alexander Gottlieb Baumgarten (1714–62), Pierre Bayle (1647–1706), Georg Bernhard Bilfinger (1693–1750), Charles Bonnet (1720–93), Roger Joseph Boscovich (1711–87), Jean Pierre de Crousaz (1663–1750), Johann August Eberhard (1739–1809), Jean Henri Samuel Formey (1711–97), Christian Garve (1742–98), Johann Melchior Goeze (1717–86), Johann Christoph Gottsched (1700–1766), Johann Georg Hamann (1730–88), Johann Gottfried Herder (1744–1803), Isaak Iselin (1728–82), Johann Heinrich Lambert (1728–77), Johann Caspar Lavater (1741–1801), Johann Bernhard Merian (1723–1807), Pierre Louis de Maupertuis (1698–1759), Christoph Friedrich Nicolai (1733–1811), Ernst Platner (1744–1818), André Pierre le Guay de Prémontval (1716–64), Hermann Samuel Reimarus (1694–1768), Friedrich Gabriel Resewitz (1729–1806), Friedrich Justus Riedel (1742–85), Johann Joachim Spalding (1714–1804), Johann Nikolaus Tetens (1736–1807), Voltaire (1694–1778), William Warburton (1698–1779), Christian Wolff (1679–1754).

39. The German originals of JA II, III.1, and III.2 format Strauss's citations as running (parenthetical) notes. The present translation reformats these as footnotes, and occasionally expands, updates, corrects, and repositions them as appropriate. Where Strauss's footnotes (as these may now be called) refer to JA's editorial apparatus, appropriate cross-reference is made to the "supplement" to that particular footnote as may be found in appendix 2 of this volume. For a fuller explanation of how this volume formats and cites Strauss's footnotes, see section III of the translator's preface.

by scholarly luminaries in Weimar Germany. In addition to Otto and Lagarde (mentioned earlier), these include the sociologist Karl Mannheim,[40] the philosopher Julius Ebbinghaus,[41] and especially the legal theorist Carl Schmitt.[42]

To these should be added a published article[43] and a pair of manuscripts[44] on Thomas Hobbes. One of the manuscripts, on Hobbes's political science, was immediately translated from German into English for publication. The other, on Hobbes's critique of religion, remained unfinished and was not published or translated during Strauss's lifetime.

Last but not least, there is Strauss's ongoing engagement with the philosophical, theological, and literary writings of Lessing, about whom he was planning to write in depth.[45] As he would recall autobiographically during spontaneous public remarks in 1970 concerning his studies that led to his 1930 Spinoza book and beyond: "Lessing was always at my elbow...."[46]

IV

Finally, there is also the story of Strauss's scholarly friendship with Alexander Altmann (1906–87). This story includes their differing assessments

---

40. "Der Konspektivismus" (1929; not published during Strauss's lifetime); LSGS II 365–75.

41. "Besprechung von Julius Ebbinghaus, *Über die Fortschritt der Metaphysik*," *Deutsche Literaturzeitung* 52 (December 27, 1932): 2451–53; LSGS II 437–39; "Review of Julius Ebbinghaus, *On the Progress of Metaphysics*," LSEW 214–16.

42. "Anmerkungen zu Carl Schmitt, *Der Begriff des Politischen*," *Archiv für Sozialwissenschaft und Sozialpolitik* (Tübingen) 67.6 (August-September 1932): 732–49; LSGS III 217–38; "Comments on Carl Schmitt's *Der Begriff des Politischen*," in SCR 331–51; also in Heinrich Meier, *Carl Schmitt and Leo Strauss: The Hidden Dialogue*, trans. J. Harvey Lomax (Chicago: University of Chicago Press, 1995), 91–119.

43. The article, "Einige Anmerkungen über die politische Wissenschaft des Hobbes: Anlässlich des Buches von Z. Lubienski, Die Grundlagen des ethisch-politischen Systems von Hobbes," was published in French translation as "Quelques remarques sur la science politique de Hobbes," *Recherches philosophiques* 2 (1933): 609–22; for the original German, see LSGS III 243–78; translated as "Some Notes on the Political Science of Hobbes" in HCR 121–36.

44. *Hobbes' politische Wissenschaft in ihrer Genesis* (1935); translated as *The Political Philosophy of Hobbes: Its Basis and Genesis* (henceforth PPH); the German original was eventually published, with a new preface by Strauss, as *Hobbes' politische Wissenschaft* (Neuwied am Rhein und Berlin: Hermann Luchterhand Verlag, 1965) and is reprinted in LSGS III 3–192; for an English translation of the new preface, see Strauss, "Preface to *Hobbes' politische Wissenschaft*," trans. Donald Maletz, *Interpretation* 8 (1979): 1–3. *Die Religionskritik des Hobbes: Ein Beitrag zum Verständnis der Aufklärung* (1933–), LSGS III 263–370; translated as *Hobbes's Critique of Religion: A Contribution to Understanding the Enlightenment*, in HCR 23–114.

45. See LS's letter to Alexander Altmann of May 28, 1971, reproduced in Altmann's "Vorbemerkung" [Preliminary Remark] to JA III.2, translated in the present volume; also LS's "Vorbemerkung" to his unwritten *Eine Erinnerung an Lessing* [A Reminder of Lessing], LSGS II 607–8; translated in appendix 1 of the present volume. See also ET 52–59 (reprinted in RCPR 64–71).

46. "A Giving of Accounts," originally published in *The College* (Annapolis, Md.) 22:1 (April 1970): 1–5; reprinted in JPCM 457–66. For the remark quoted, see JPCM 462.

of Mendelssohn's thought and behavior in connection with the Pantheism Controversy—including Mendelssohn's private letters and published writings in response to Jacobi's shocking charge about Lessing's covert Spinozism, and Jacobi's letters and publications in rejoinder—which culminated and in fact ended Mendelssohn's life's work. Altmann calls respectful attention to his scholarly disagreement with Strauss concerning the controversy. In his preliminary remark to JA III.2, Altmann reproduces three personal letters Strauss wrote to him about their disagreement. Because the disagreement is instructive for understanding Strauss's argument as a whole, I have translated Altmann's preliminary remark and placed it before my translations of the ten introductions as an appropriate lead-in.

In what follows, then, I begin by commenting extensively on the scholarly issue Altmann raises but leaves unresolved in his preliminary remark. I go from there to analyze Strauss's ten introductions one by one. Wherever appropriate, I point out how a given introduction also prepares the way for what Strauss finds in Mendelssohn's writings apropos the Pantheism Controversy. I conclude by indicating how Strauss's understated references to three philosophical figures that hover in the background of his account of the controversy—Hobbes, Rousseau, and Nietzsche—anticipate the pivotal roles his later writings ascribe to them as regards the overall course of modern political philosophy, and how the philosophical figure at the heart of the controversy—Spinoza—shows up in Strauss's autobiographical preface to the English translation of his 1930 Spinoza book as regards the state of Jewish thought in our time.

ALTMANN'S DIFFERENCES WITH STRAUSS

I

The three letters reproduced in Altmann's preliminary remark are Strauss's appreciative replies concerning two separate publications that Altmann had sent him during the early 1970s. Strauss's letter of May 28, 1971, comments on an article by Altmann arguing that Jacobi misinterpreted Lessing's covert Spinozism—which Jacobi reported discovering during private conversations with Lessing in the summer of 1780 and disclosed to Mendelssohn three years later in a devious manner designed to embarrass Mendelssohn.[47] Strauss's letters of September 9 and 15, 1973, comment on

---

47. "Lessing und Jacobi: Das Gespräch über den Spinozismus" [Lessing and Jacobi: The Conversation about Spinozism]," *Lessing Yearbook* 3 (1971): 25–70; reprinted in MMTA 50–83.

Altmann's recently published Mendelssohn biography, particularly his detailed account of the emergence of *Morning Hours* and its sequel *To the Friends of Lessing*, Mendelssohn's philosophical responses to Jacobi's disclosure.[48] These two subjects—the historical emergence of *Morning Hours* and *To the Friends of Lessing* and their philosophical content—occupy the two halves of Strauss's penetrating account of the run-up to the Pantheism Controversy in his introduction to those two writings (henceforth IMH). IMH is by far the longest (eighty-four pages in JA III.2) and most comprehensive of his ten Mendelssohn introductions. It is also the most complex and subtle one, drawing together as it does many loose strands of what he says in the other nine. Strauss's letters to Altmann about this introduction are thus a window to them all.

In the 1973 letters, Strauss says that were his health and age to permit, he might *"conceivably"* revise what he had written in 1936–37 about the emergence of *Morning Hours* and *To the Friends of Lessing* in the light of what Altmann now shows. When pressed by Altmann for clarification, Strauss explains that he himself may have put too much trust in an anecdotal report by J. F. Reichardt, the music director of the Berlin Opera and a friend of Jacobi's, that speaks of Mendelssohn's nervous behavior during Reichardt's visit to his home on December 13, 1785, and of Mendelssohn's self-deprecating remark in the course of their conversation to the effect that his own early (Jewish) education, unlike Jacobi's, did not include the notions of "gentleman" and "point of honor." Reichardt's visit occurred during the initial shock wave felt by readers following the publication of Jacobi's *On Spinoza's Doctrine, in Letters to Mr. Moses Mendelssohn*—his public exposé of Lessing's putative Spinozism—and Mendelssohn's nearly simultaneous *Morning Hours*, first conceived in anticipation of Jacobi's exposé but completed too late to preempt it. It was also three weeks before Mendelssohn's untimely death, following his overexposure to cold weather while hand-delivering the manuscript of *To the Friends of Lessing* to his publisher that New Year's Eve. Altmann's disagreement with Strauss here has to do with whether Mendelssohn's nervous behavior and self-deprecating remark are to be understood as signs of his severe personal stress due to the scandal, as Strauss suggests in 1936–37. According to Altmann, the nervous behavior was merely a chronic symptom of the debilitating disease that Mendelssohn had been suffering for the past fifteen years, and the self-deprecating re-

---

48. See MMBS 553–759.

mark no more than a modest joke that the cordial Mendelssohn was making at his own expense.[49]

In the 1971 letter, Strauss says that Altmann and he agree that there is more to Lessing's covert ("esoteric") views than Jacobi managed to notice, although they disagree on what that more is. Strauss mentions that he had originally planned to treat "the center of Lessing's thoughts *de Deo et mundo*"[50] either in a concluding part to IMH or in a separate article. As things happened, however, Strauss was unable to follow through and could only "refer [his] better students strongly to Lessing and say at a fitting opportunity what [he] owed to Lessing." Even so, Strauss adds: "The decisive points are still as clear to me now as they were then."

The three letters, taken together, suggest the following. Under Altmann's friendly prodding, Strauss at the end of his life was open to rethinking what he had written in the 1930s about the historical emergence and philosophical content of Mendelssohn's *Morning Hours* and *To the Friends of Lessing*. Strauss's motivation here is somewhat complex. Whereas he would, if he could, reopen his inquiry into the emergence of those two writings with a view to what he might have miswritten about Reichardt, he would reopen his inquiry into their content with a view to what he had not yet written about Lessing. As we shall see when we look at IMH more directly, Strauss's two inquiries, historical and philosophical, are two sides of a single, more far-reaching inquiry. They are united by Strauss's wish to clarify Mendelssohn's inherently controversial defense of Lessing's Spinozism as such. This would include clarifying what was at stake for Mendelssohn not only personally—as Lessing's close friend who, if Jacobi was correct, nevertheless remained in the dark about Lessing's deepest philosophical thoughts—but also theologically and politically, as the philosophical founder of modern Jewish thought and, at the same time, as his own test case for the prospect of a non-ghettoized life for Jews as Jews in modern times that might include close friendships with non-Jews like Lessing. To say all this somewhat differently: Strauss writes as Mendelssohn's theologico-political heir. He seeks to illuminate the combined private and public perplexities that Mendelssohn bequeathed to subsequent Jewish thought and life—which, even or especially under the pressure of his controversy with Jacobi, Mendelssohn never quite succeeded in illuminating for himself.

---

49. MMBS 268–71, 732–39, 745–46.
50. Lat.: about God and the world.

Accordingly, the differences between Strauss and Altmann do not show up merely in Strauss's possible misreading of Reichardt and his involuntary silence about Lessing. To spell out those differences more fully, I start instead, as Strauss and Altmann do, from the controversy over Lessing's Spinozism as it comes to sight in *Morning Hours* and *To the Friends of Lessing*.

II

Mendelssohn himself calls attention to Spinoza in eye-catching ways not just once but twice in his philosophical writings. In his earliest publication, *Philosophical Dialogues* (1755), his fictional interlocutors vindicate Spinoza, whom they take to be an atheist, by considering whether Leibniz, their own philosophical authority, drew his key doctrine of preestablished harmony from Spinoza's "system."[51] In *Morning Hours* and its sequel, on the other hand, Mendelssohn engages in a radical critique of Spinoza's system, though he subsequently adds that it is capable of being reformulated as a morally harmless Pantheism. Central to the disagreement between Altmann and Strauss is the question of whether Mendelssohn's two separate treatments of Spinoza are entirely consistent. There are also the related questions of whether they are consistent with Spinoza—and, of course, with Lessing. As we shall see, these same questions are complicit in the complicated coming into being and overall aim of *Morning Hours*. Focusing on them brings into view, as well, the fault line in the foundations of Mendelssohn's synthesis of Judaism with modern philosophical thought as Strauss (though not Altmann) sees it.

At first glance, Mendelssohn's Spinoza critique in *Morning Hours* seems incidental to its overall aim. Most of its seventeen chapters are aptly described by its subtitle, *Lectures on the Existence of God*. According to Mendelssohn's preface, the "Lectures" originated as early-morning home instruction in (Leibnizian) natural theology for his teenage son and two other young Jews. But the Thirteenth through Fifteenth Lectures turn abruptly to a somewhat disconnected topic. The Thirteenth Lecture offers a broad and, by its own lights, not necessarily original refutation of Spinoza's system. The Fourteenth Lecture then considers a "refined" or "purified" version of that system, now construed as Pantheism, which Mendelssohn divulges as having been covertly subscribed to by his late friend Lessing: readers of Lessing's highly provocative, widely admired philosophical dramas, literary criticism, and theological polemics had previously assumed

---

51. See IMH xxiin66.

that he was a Leibnizian. Finally, the Fifteenth Lecture supplies a moral defense of Lessing's "purified" Spinozism for its putative compatibility with the practical teachings of religion. The sudden and self-contained character of the Thirteenth through Fifteenth Lectures, along with Mendelssohn's announced private motivation for having formulated his Lectures in the first place, suggests to Strauss that this writing might never have been published, written, or even conceived except for a pressing need to insulate Lessing's philosophical legacy from the shocking charge of covert Spinozism, understood as atheism.

Jacobi first confronted Mendelssohn with Lessing's Spinozism in a cleverly underhanded way—by letters to a mutual friend, a third party who saw fit (as Jacobi expected she would) to act as go-between. The third party was Elise Reimarus, daughter of the late Hermann Samuel Reimarus, the notorious anonymous author of the so-called "Wolfenbüttel Fragments." These were posthumous excerpts from her father's unpublished *Apology or Defense for the Rational Worshipers of God*,[52] a radical-Rationalist critique of revelation-believing Christianity. Lessing had serialized the excerpts as "Fragments of an Unnamed" and introduced them with provocative "Counterpropositions" of his own as librarian at the Ducal Library at Wolfenbüttel, where the "Fragments" had (he said) turned up.[53] In the Fifteenth Lecture of *Morning Hours*, which like the Fourteenth Lecture is written as a narrated dialogue, Mendelssohn introduces as fictional interlocutor a longstanding friend and admirer of Lessing[54] who, while denying that Lessing had ever been a Spinozist, traces Lessing's defection from Leibnizian natural theology to his editorial involvement with the Fragmentist.[55] By inserting this last assertion inside a larger panegyric to the effect that Lessing's defection was nevertheless perfectly compatible with his exemplary devotion to Christian morality, Mendelssohn's interlocutor aims to gloss over and repair any blemish to Lessing's reputation caused by Jacobi's exposé. For all that, Mendelssohn ends the Fifteenth Lecture by amicably correcting his interlocutor—and, indirectly, Jacobi—on a pertinent biographical detail. Mendelssohn, or rather his persona, quotes extensively from Lessing's

---

52. *Apologie oder Schutzschrift für die vernünftigen Verehrer Gottes*. See Strauss's editorial annotation to *Morgenstunden* 125.27–126.2 (translated in IMH xivn26).

53. LM XII 303–304, 428–50 (Nis 61–82).

54. The interlocutor resembles Elise Reimarus's brother J. A. H. Reimarus, author of *Über die Gründe der menschlichen Erkenntniß und der natürlichen Religion* [On the Bases of Human Cognition and of Natural Religion] (Hamburg, 1787). See Strauss's editorial "Annotations and Additions" to *Morgenstunden*, 159.2–5 (translated in appendix 2, supplement to IMH xlivn193).

55. See IMH lxxxviin390.

youthful fragment "The Christianity of Reason"[56] as evidence that Lessing had been advocating "purified" Spinozism since long before his involvement with the Fragmentist.

Altmann takes Mendelssohn at his final word in the Fifteenth Lecture to the effect that he had known about and respected Lessing's adherence to "purified" Spinozism all along. Strauss, however, has his doubts. Unlike Altmann, Strauss finds in the literary incoherence of *Morning Hours* a philosophical incoherence as well—the result, he suggests, of Mendelssohn's ongoing failure to reflect on his underlying presuppositions. Even so, Strauss goes on to show how the sudden and intense pressure of Jacobi's disclosure brought Mendelssohn closer than ever before to reflecting on those presuppositions. In my subsequent comments here on the Thirteenth through Fifteenth Lectures of *Morning Hours*, I shall spell out these differences between Altmann and Strauss more fully.

III

As Strauss points out, the Thirteenth Lecture's refutation of Spinozism says nothing about whether Spinozism is to be understood as atheism or as Pantheism—even though its chapter heading mentions Pantheism rather than atheism. The refutation itself boils down to three arguments. One argument points out an incongruity in Spinoza's basic notion of substance; the other two arguments point out incongruities that result even or especially if one accepts Spinoza's basic notion of substance. All three arguments seem meant to apply, by default, to both Spinozism as Pantheism and Spinozism as atheism.

First, Spinozists are said to claim that "we ourselves" and the external world of which we are aware through our senses are not self-subsisting things but mere modifications of a single self-subsisting thing, or substance, which is infinite in both bodily extent (*extensio*) and power of thought (*cogitatio*). The one substance is also the same as God. Everything is, in short, one thing; and that one thing is, in turn, everything. Mendelssohn objects, however, that this conception of substance is a dubious departure from commonsense, an arbitrary overstatement. Spinoza confuses the self-subsistent feature of substance, its individuality vis-à-vis everything else, with its self-sufficiency, or nondependence on anything else. He trades on a semantic ambiguity. "Substance" in its plain meaning, as the self-subsistent, allows for the possibility of an indefinite plurality of substances. Only "substance"

---

56. "Das Christenthum der Vernunft" (1753). See IMH XLVIII.201.

in its hyperbolic, Spinozist meaning—as "that which is in itself and . . . whose concept does not need the concept of another thing from which it has to be formed"[57]—leads to the ultimately untenable view that there can be just one, all-inclusive substance.

Second, then, Spinoza is said to follow Descartes in conceiving of the bodily attribute of the one substance simply as extension. Mendelssohn objects that extension, even when one adds to it the concept of impenetrability, can account for nothing more than the material common to all body. It cannot account for the form of this or that organized body—the pattern of its purposive movement or its rule-governed behavior as an individual organism. Extension as such neither moves nor engenders movement.

Third, Mendelssohn also objects that the mere power of thought, however infinite, cannot account for "goodness and perfection, pleasure and displeasure, pain and gratification, in general everything that belongs to our faculty of approval and of desire."[58] Thought as such neither approves nor desires, nor does it engender either approval or desire.

Now, both Altmann and Strauss note Kant's dismissive comment on what he calls the "maxim" or "artifice" informing Mendelssohn's Spinoza critique here, namely, Mendelssohn's stated inclination "to explain all the quarrels of the philosophical schools as mere quarrels about words, or at least to derive them originally from quarrels about words."[59] Kant counters crisply that no philosophic quarrel is ever simply verbal: "in matters that have been quarreled over for quite some time, especially in philosophy, at bottom it has never been a quarrel about words, but always a genuine quarrel about things."[60] Altmann defends Mendelssohn against Kant by quoting a passage from Spinoza's *Ethics* that Mendelssohn himself quotes in the Fourteenth Lecture,[61] to the effect that, in Spinoza's opinion at least, many disputes are indeed no more than verbal.[62] Strauss, however, quotes a further statement of Kant's concerning an attempt by Mendelssohn elsewhere

---

57. Spinoza, *Ethica*, pt. I, def. 3 (Geb II 45; cf. WhSt 3).
58. *Morgenstunden* 108.25–27; cf. DaDy 78.
59. *Morgenstunden* 104.30–33; cf. DaDy 75.
60. "Einige Bemerkungen zu Ludwig Heinrich Jakobs Prüfung der Mendelssohn'schen *Morgenstunden*" [A Few Remarks on Ludwig Heinrich Jakob's Examination of the Mendelssohnian *Morning Hours*], IKW IV 482. See IMH LXX.
61. *Morgenstunden* 121.8–12; cf. DaDy 88.
62. ". . . very many controversies originate . . . because human beings do not correctly explain their own mind or because they interpret another's mind poorly. For, in truth, while they are contradicting each other most, they are thinking either the same thing or different things, so that they impute to the other errors and absurdities which aren't there." *Ethica*, pt. II, prop. 47 schol. (Geb II 128–29; cf. WhSt 86–87).

to reduce a philosophical controversy to a verbal one: according to Kant, it "is as if [Mendelssohn] wanted to stop a tidal wave with a wisp of straw."[63] The underlying issue between Altmann and Strauss here is whether Mendelssohn is able to take the full measure of Jacobi's challenge concerning Lessing's putative Spinozism within his own purview as a professed Leibnizian. Altmann does not see that Mendelssohn has much difficulty in doing so. Strauss, in contrast, does. Mendelssohn's appeal to verbal differences, or more broadly to commonsense, is, Strauss suggests, a sign of his implicit recognition that systematic argument as such fails to meet the challenges he faced when confronted by philosophical and theological disagreements in general, and Spinozism in particular, which are, after all, practical as well as theoretical challenges.

IV

The Fourteenth Lecture consists of an imaginary dialogue between Mendelssohn and Lessing, on the fictional supposition that Lessing might have been present during the Thirteenth Lecture's refutation of Spinoza and now speaks in his own defense as a Spinozist. What follows, then, are the fictional Lessing's rehabilitating or "purifying" of Spinozism, and Mendelssohn's subsequent reply.

The fictional Lessing (henceforth "Lessing") concedes the second and third of the aforementioned points of criticism, but not the first. That is to say, "Lessing" grants, with Mendelssohn, an indefinite plurality of actual things, each of which is a source of its own purposive movement. He also grants each actual thing's inherent ability to exercise approval, or choice of the best, alongside the bare "thought" or awareness embedded to some degree or other in it. Still, conceding these two points does not require "Lessing" to abandon the remainder of the Spinozist claim—Spinoza's denial of the "objective" existence of things, that is, of their substantiality apart from their "representation" or concept in God.[64] "Lessing's" argument here seems cribbed from the real-life Lessing's youthful fragment "On the Actuality of Things Outside God" (1763),[65] which raises the question of whether or how God may be said to have a concept of things actually existing outside His

---

63. Kant, *loc. cit.*, on Mendelssohn's "Über Freiheit und Nothwendigkeit" [On freedom and necessity], (JA III.1 343–50).
64. *Morgenstunden* 116.7; cf. DaDy 84.
65. "Über die Wirklichkeit der Dinge ausser Gott," LM XIV 292–93; quoted in its entirety in Strauss's editorial annotations to *Morgenstunden* 116.6–15 and 117.8–118.18 (at JA III.2 302–3); Nis 30–31. See IMH xcvn459.

understanding, given that those actual things would have to correspond completely to the true and adequate concepts He has of them anyway. In Lessing's (and "Lessing's") language, God's concepts are the "archetypes" of actual things. That is, prior to their actualization, things exist in God's understanding as not-yet-realized possibilities whose realization in conformity with the laws of nature is, even so, altogether perspicuous to God. The question that "Lessing" raises, then, is: What is the basis for claiming that the actualized things, so understood, are "outside" God? Must not all the features or "predicates"[66] of those things insofar as we can in principle conceive or represent them—complete "with the infinite series of their successive modifications and variations"[67]—be present in God beforehand? And would not all this include, as a matter of course, whatever it is that makes for the difference between things insofar as they are merely possible and those same things insofar as they are actual—what the real-life Lessing calls "the complement of [their] possibility"?[68] If so, would it not be both inconsistent and redundant to say that actual things, so understood, are *also* "outside" God?

Mendelssohn's reply is that there are "undeceptive signs that distinguish me as an object from me as a representation in God; me as an archetype [sic] from me as an image in the divine understanding."[69] The "most telling" sign of "my substantiality outside God, my archetypal [sic] existence," is my own, individual "awareness of myself, combined with complete ignorance of everything that does not accordingly fall within the circle of my thought." Given that God is the most perfect being, however, it follows that "the thought in God . . . which has a limited being for its object cannot, in [God], arrive at any individual, as it were torn-off awareness."[70] As in the Thirteenth Lecture, so too here, Mendelssohn offers a commonsense rebuttal to the systematic argument attributed to "Lessing's" Spinoza: each individual's existential awareness of his own ignorance is both undeniable and irreducible to anything else—that is to say, in Mendelssohn's word, "archetypal."

Altmann defends Mendelssohn's rebuttal by merging its appeal to commonsense with Leibnizian systematics as follows.[71] Things become actu-

---

66. *Morgenstunden* 117.20 and 24; cf. DaDy 85.
67. *Morgenstunden* 117.13–15; cf. DaDy 85.
68. The expression is Christian Wolff's. See his *Ontologia* §174. Cf. All 69–71.
69. *Morgenstunden* 117.36–118.16; cf. DaDy 85–86.
70. *Morgenstunden* 120.21–34; cf. DaDy 87. The foregoing Mendelssohnian passages are cited by Strauss in IMH LXXI–LXXII.
71. See MMBS 693–94.

alized as a result not just of God's knowing or thinking them, but also of His approving or choosing them. The full panoply of actual things is thus chosen by God as the best of all possible worlds. Yet this best of all possible worlds also includes things that are chosen for their being merely relatively best, that is to say, better than other possible things, the latter having been knowingly rejected by God: the absolutely best set of things, viewed wholesale, includes some second-rate things when these are viewed individually, or retail. Things chosen for their being relatively best, then, while known and approved by God, can never be part of God, in whom only the absolutely best can exist. Hence, Altmann concludes, the relatively best must exist "outside" God.

Strauss, however, notes in Mendelssohn's rebuttal a radical inconsistency, of which Mendelssohn seems oblivious. In the passages just quoted, Mendelssohn unreflectively[72] switches the location of archetypes from God to individual selves. Suddenly each self is no longer an image of which God's concept is the archetype, but vice versa: God's concept of each self now becomes the image of which that self is the archetype. That this switch is able to occur without warning and remain unaccounted for in any systematic way indicates an unexamined presumption, a "hidden presupposition" on Mendelssohn's part. At a minimum, the presupposition is that God and the individual self are equal in respect of being the site of archetypes. Theologically speaking, this equality is supported by, or at least consistent with, Mendelssohn's view that God is not only a consummately understanding being but also an undemandingly benevolent being, who creates and provides for human beings solely for their happiness as individuals in this life and the next, rather than for, say, His own eternal glory and righteousness.[73] It should be added here that, as regards the doctrine of God's undemanding benevolence, Mendelssohn remains somewhat at variance with his highest philosophical authority Leibniz, as well as with Lessing, who both defend the traditional theological doctrine of eternal punishments in hell, that is,

---

72. Altmann defends Mendelssohn's switch as follows (MMBS 867n35): "While Lessing applied the term *Urbild* ['archetype'] to the concept of a thing in the divine mind, Mendelssohn, who wished to differentiate between the intradeical and extradeical existence of things, called the extradeical, real thing *Urbild* and its ideal existence in God's intellect by the term *Bild* ('image'). He thus reversed the traditional terminology without, however, intending to deny that the intradeical concept of a thing was in fact the archetype of the real thing. His unorthodox terminology is clearly designed to rebut Lessing's argument, and should not be construed to have any further purpose."

73. See note 212, below.

of inescapable and unceasing punitive justice post mortem for evildoers.[74] Be that as it may, Strauss goes on to say that Mendelssohn's hidden presupposition about the equality between God and human individuals also finds expression in unexamined statements in other writings of his to the effect that God's "rights can never come into quarrel and confusion with ours"[75] and that each individual is, in Mendelssohn's words, a "citizen in God's State" with, as it were, constitutional rights over against God.[76] In these statements, Mendelssohn is, to be sure, indebted to Leibniz, who likewise speaks of individuals as citizens in the City of God[77]—but, given Mendelssohn's theological disagreement with Leibniz on the question of eternal punishments,[78] the debt is less a strictly theological one than it is a political-philosophical one. Strauss concludes from all this that Mendelssohn's metaphysical effort to secure the substantiality of things in general outside God turns out to rest on the unexamined presupposition of the irreducible autonomy of each individual in particular outside God.

The difference between Altmann and Strauss here has to do with whether Mendelssohn's confrontation with Lessing's putative Spinozism can be spelled out more or less adequately in terms of metaphysical argumentation (Altmann) or whether instead it collapses into theologico-political individualism (Strauss). This difference extends as well to how we are to understand Mendelssohn's practical defense of Lessing's Spinozism in the Fifteenth Lecture of *Morning Hours*.

V

Mendelssohn defends Lessing's Spinozism qua Pantheism in the Fifteenth Lecture by saying that it differs from Leibnizian theism only by a metaphysical "subtlety" that has no effect on moral practice. It remains for now to consider this defense in the light of the difference between Altmann and Strauss concerning the integrity of metaphysics as Mendelssohn understands it. Altmann's view, as found in his biographical study of Mendelssohn and other writings, can be reduced to four points. By leaving things for the moment at what amounts to a list of comparisons between Altmann and

---

74. Mendelssohn confronts Leibniz (and indirectly Lessing) on this issue in *Sache Gottes* (1784). See my remarks on IGC, below.
75. *Jerusalem* 127; Ark 59.
76. E.g., *Phädon* 112–13; *Sache Gottes* §60.
77. E.g., *Système nouveau de la nature* §8 (Ger IV 479–80; Wie 110–11 or ArGa 145 or FrWo 147–48).
78. See IGC xcvi–cx.

Strauss, I can do no more (though perhaps no less) than point to the deeper issues connected with Mendelssohn's founding of modern Jewish thought, in the light of their unresolved latter-day scholarly controversy.

In the first place, then, according to Altmann, "Only the pressure of Jacobi's report had forced Mendelssohn to attach importance to the Spinozistic leanings that Lessing had seemingly betrayed."[79] Altmann, in other words, doubts whether Mendelssohn took Lessing's Spinozist leanings all that seriously except for the practical stakes involved. Strauss, on the other hand, is not so quick to separate the practical stakes here from the inherently philosophical issues. For that reason, Strauss does not exactly agree with Altmann on the scope and limits of the practical stakes. The likely practical consequences of Jacobi's impending public exposé concerning Lessing's Spinozism would include not only the gloating of Lessing's theological enemies, but also Mendelssohn's personal humiliation as a result of Jacobi's documented insinuation that, notwithstanding their years of close friendship, Lessing had been deliberately reticent toward him in sensitive philosophical matters. But these consequences and how we are to understand them, Strauss suggests, have to do with the further question of who, Mendelssohn or Jacobi, had the better understanding of Lessing—and, of course, of Spinoza. Differently stated, Strauss holds that the practical stakes are bound up, as well, with an assessment of Mendelssohn's strictly philosophical merits as the founder of modern Jewish thought. This last is a persistent sub-theme of Strauss's overall investigation of the Pantheism Controversy, in a way that it is not for Altmann. Altmann is more inclined to view the controversy in an antiquarian way. For Strauss, it is an ongoing theologico-political issue whose ripple effects extend, for example, to his own, pressing situation as a Jewish escapee from the Germany of the 1930s,[80] where Jewish life in its assimilation to German life had been radically shaped by Mendelssohn's oeuvre. It is part of what the later Strauss had in mind when, as I mentioned earlier, he described himself autobiographically as a young German-born, German-educated Jew who found himself in the grips of a theologico-political predicament that was bequeathed to a considerable extent by Mendelssohn.[81]

Second, Altmann says that Mendelssohn's fictional interlocutor in the Fifteenth Lecture "is presented as the spokesman of a view of Lessing with

---

79. MMBS 694.
80. Consider Strauss's contemporaneous (1937) preface to his unwritten book on Lessing (translated in appendix 1).
81. See notes 19, above, and 397, below.

which Mendelssohn would have loved to identify himself, and with which he had identified himself before Jacobi intruded on the scene."[82] That is, in the wake of Jacobi's report of Lessing's Spinozist atheism, Mendelssohn himself could hardly agree with the interlocutor's presentation of Lessing as a morally admirable adherent of religious Rationalism like the Fragmentist, however much he might wish to project this image to save Lessing's public reputation. Here Strauss agrees with Altmann, though on grounds that are not coextensive with Altmann's. Altmann takes at face value Mendelssohn's claim that Lessing's "Christianity of Reason" is a Spinozist document—even though, as Strauss points out, there is not much that is particularly Spinozist about it. It looks to be a string of more or less Leibnizian aphorisms. The aphorism that most closely resembles a Spinozist thought[83] reads:

> To envisage, to will, and to create are identical in God's case. One can therefore say that everything God envisages, he also creates.[84]

Whether Lessing's thought here—the identity of thinking and willing and creating in God—is Leibnizian or Spinozist would depend on whether God is to be understood, on the one hand, as an intelligent being or, on the other hand, merely as the all-encompassing, all-producing substance, of which to speak as "envisaging" and "creating" would be to speak equivocally, at least from the viewpoint of commonsense. "Purified" Spinozism—the view that Mendelssohn finds in Lessing's aphorism (according to Altmann) or retrofits to it (according to Strauss)—merges those two alternatives: the intelligent "creator" of everything never actually lets go of anything. Altmann argues that Mendelssohn is correct in attributing this view to "Christianity of Reason" and calling it Spinozist. Strauss, in contrast, finds the attribution doubtful: Mendelssohn, making do with the limited resources at his command as a lifelong Leibnizian, instead projects a modified version of his own Leibnizianism onto Lessing.

Third, Altmann, like Strauss, sees a need to account for the rhetorical prominence Mendelssohn gives to the Fifteenth Lecture's fictional interlocutor, who promulgates the pre-Jacobian, morally salutary if not exactly true image of Lessing as a religious Rationalist. For Altmann, that image, being at variance with the view that Mendelssohn himself promulgates at the end of the Fifteenth Lecture—of Lessing as an advocate of "purified"

---

82. MMBS 695.
83. See IMH xc1n441.
84. *Morgenstunden* 133.32–33; cf. DaDy 97.

Spinozism—nevertheless serves as an appropriate backdrop for contextualizing Lessing's advocacy. "Christianity of Reason" is said to belong to a series of Lessingian writings that outspokenly vindicate views that had been unjustly vilified. The list includes not only the poetic drama *Nathan the Wise*, Lessing's vindication of providence in the face of the anti-Leibnizianism popularized by Voltaire's *Candide*, but also Lessing's aphoristic "The Education of the Human Race," his vindication of revealed religion in the wake of the Fragmentist's historical criticism of biblical revelation, as well as Lessing's "Counterpropositions" on the "Wolfenbüttel Fragments." In short, Altmann understands Mendelssohn's account of Lessing's advocacy of "purified" Spinozism as being Mendelssohn's enumeration of one more instance of Lessing's lifelong "gallantry,"[85] or moral high-mindedness. So far, Strauss does not disagree. For a fuller understanding of what Mendelssohn does and does not attribute to Lessing's high-mindedness, however, Strauss sees a need to probe Lessing's strictly philosophical dimension in its own terms as well, which Mendelssohn himself fails to do. In the light of the foregoing, Strauss's Lessing turns out to be what one may provisionally call, for want of a better term, a histrionic[86] philosopher rather than a systematic one, as Mendelssohn supposes. I shall say something more about this in connection with the fourth, and final, item on my list.

Finally, then, Altmann comments that Mendelssohn "stubbornly refused to recognize the significance of 'The Education of the Human Race' in opening up new horizons beyond the concept of natural religion in which history had no place."[87] That is, Mendelssohn withheld his approval from whatever in Lessing did not fit with his own philosophical system. On this point Altmann and Strauss agree, except that Altmann speaks of Mendelssohn's shortcoming here as at bottom moral—namely, Mendelssohn's stubbornness in refusing to recognize something new and possibly improved—whereas Strauss sees it as instead philosophical, namely, his distinctively modern presupposition that philosophy is necessarily a matter of systematic demonstration. Strauss emphasizes that Mendelssohn owes this presupposition to Leibniz, who notes the absence of demonstration in Plato and Aristotle and the other ancient philosophers[88] and calls attention

---

85. MMBS 696–97; cf. 577–78.
86. Cf. IMH xixn56, with note 274, below. Also, Friedrich Nietzsche, *Jenseits von Gut und Böse* §28 (KSA V 46–47; *Beyond Good and Evil*, GaKa 230–31): Nietzsche speaks of Lessing's *Schauspieler-Natur* ("histrionic nature").
87. MMBS 698.
88. Leibniz, *Nouveaux Essais* IV, ch. 2, §9 [Ger V 352; cf. ReBe 371]; IMH LXII.

to the methodological superiority of his own philosophizing in his *Theodicy* by speaking of it as "my system."[89] In particular, Mendelssohn owes to Leibniz the fact that he speaks and thinks of Spinoza entirely in terms of the latter's "system"—a term Spinoza himself never uses, though I must immediately add that the term is nevertheless implicit to a considerable extent in Spinoza's way of arguing in the *Ethics*,[90] and Strauss suggests that it is likewise implicit in Descartes's *Meditations* as a founding document of Rationalist (or Cartesian-Spinozist-Leibnizian) philosophy.[91] Yet in Mendelssohn's case identifying philosophy with demonstration or system turns out to be in tension with his efforts at reconciling philosophy with Judaism. On the one hand, he follows Leibniz et al. in holding that the ontological proof of God—a pillar of Descartes's, Spinoza's, and Leibniz's "systems"— eliminates the need, or even the possibility, of revealed truths. According to Mendelssohn, this is to be desired since revealed truths are not clearly and distinctly knowable and so do not appear to supply a firm theological basis for the Torah and Jewish practice, whereas at the same time they encourage superstition. On the other hand, the teaching of the Torah is not demonstrative; strictly speaking, that is to say, it is not a system but, by its own lights, revealed law. The resulting tension between philosophy qua system and Judaism qua revealed law is what I earlier referred to as the fault line in the foundations of Mendelssohn's Jewish thought. As we shall see while following the details of Strauss's Mendelssohn introductions, Mendelssohn's various attempts to resolve that tension culminate in *Morning Hours* and *To the Friends of Lessing*, where he judges the merit of philosophy itself by the non-philosophical or extra-philosophical standard of sound commonsense.[92] Still, his ultimate failure to resolve the tension shows up in his inability to come to grips with Lessing's thought and, concomitantly, with Spinoza's. Strauss's entire Mendelssohn oeuvre seems devoted in one way or another to pointing this out. Altmann, by contrast, seems content to understand Mendelssohn's Jewish thought more or less within the horizon that Mendelssohn himself bequeaths.

Let us now look at each of Strauss's ten Mendelssohn introductions in turn.

---

89. See Leibniz, *Théodicée*, Préface, toward the end (Ger VI 40–45 *passim*; Hug 64–69 *passim*); IMH LXVI.
90. On Spinoza's rhetoric in the *Ethics*, see Richard Kennington, *On Modern Origins: Essays in Early Modern Philosophy*, ed. Pamela Kraus and Frank Hunt (Lanham, MD: Lexington Books, 2004), 205–28, with SCR 28–29 or LAM 253–55.
91. IMH LXIII.
92. See IMH LXVII, LXVIII, LXXXI, and LXXXVI.

MENDELSSOHN AND LESSING ON PHILOSOPHY AND POETRY: POPE A METAPHYSICIAN! (1755)

The question of what Lessing thought and when he thought it comes up in the very first of Strauss's Mendelssohn introductions—his introduction to *Pope a Metaphysician!* (henceforth IPM).

Pope a Metaphysician! is a collaboration between the young Mendelssohn and the young Lessing. IPM's jam-packed three paragraphs deal, successively, with three interrelated topics: what prompted it, what its coauthors intended, and who wrote what in it.

What prompted *Pope a Metaphysician!* was, as IPM shows, the Berlin Academy's essay contest for 1755, announced in 1753. Contestants were to compare Alexander Pope's doctrine that "Everything that is, is right," in his didactic poem *Essay on Man* (1733–34), with Leibniz's philosophical "Optimism,"[93] the metaphysical doctrine that this world is "the best of all possible worlds."[94] Shortly before the contest deadline, Lessing and Mendelssohn decided not to submit their collaboration as an entry after all, but to publish it anonymously as a philosophical pamphlet. The pamphlet contains some scathing remarks against the Academy,[95] and Strauss suggests that it was Lessing rather than Mendelssohn who added these during the final editing.[96] Readers at first identified Lessing as the sole author (even though the pamphlet's foreword states plainly that it was coauthored).[97] Evidently any differences between the coauthors did not particularly show up in the eyes of their original readership.

How Lessing and Mendelssohn's intention went beyond the Academy's, IPM indicates as follows. Shortly after the contest announcement, the Leibnizian Johann Christoph Gottsched wrote a pamphlet accusing the Academy of seeking a pretext for publishing anti-Leibnizian views. Gottsched's pamphlet called attention to an earlier controversy concerning Pope and Leibniz—though Strauss finds nothing to indicate that recollection of the

---

93. On this term, see IPM xviiin15.
94. Cf. Leibniz, *Théodicée* I, §8–9 (Ger VI 107; Hug 128) and *passim*, with, e.g., "Réponse aux reflexions contenues dans la seconde Édition du Dictionnaire Critique de M. Bayle, article Rorarius, sur le système de l'Harmonie préétablie" (Ger IV 556; FrWo 244); "Principes de la nature et de la grâce" §§9–10 (Ger VI 602–3 [Wie 528–29 or ArGa 210 or FrWo 262–63]); *Monadologie* §§53–60; (Ger VI 615–16; Wie 543–545 or Sch 156–57 or FrWo 275–76).
95. See *Pope!* 76.25–77.9; Gal 58.
96. Cf. notes 105ff., below.
97. *Pope!* 45.13–15; Gal 46. Cf. Altmann, MMBS 46.

controversy influenced the Academy's choice of essay topic. In 1737, the anti-Leibnizian Jean Pierre de Crousaz had accused Pope of promulgating a morally suspect metaphysical determinism derived from Leibniz. Pope's defender William Warburton had replied by, among other things, denying the poet's dependence on Leibniz altogether.[98] Lessing and Mendelssohn—perhaps, Strauss surmises, after being alerted to the Crousaz-Warburton controversy by Gottsched's pamphlet—approach the 1755 contest with a view to vindicating Leibniz at Pope's expense. Unlike the other contestants (and in de facto agreement with Warburton's disclaimer), they doubt the Academy's presupposition that Pope's and Leibniz's doctrines are essentially the same or can be matched up neatly for purposes of comparison. They therefore find the Academy's essay topic inherently skewed. They point out an unbridgeable difference between philosophy and poetry. Whereas philosophy is "a system of metaphysical truths,"[99] that is to say, logically demonstrated assertions about God and the world and human beings that are not necessarily reducible to sense-experience, poetry consists of aesthetic language, that is to say, language immediately connected with and pleasing to the senses. Here Strauss is quick to rebut the hasty inference (by the historian Adolph von Harnack)[100] that Lessing and Mendelssohn mean to draw a hard and fast line between philosophy and poetry. On the contrary, not only do Lessing and Mendelssohn speak of Pope as a "philosophical poet";[101] they go on to explain how didactic poetry like Pope's is possible. The poet, they argue, uses aesthetic language to convey moral doctrines that are convincing to philosophers and nonphilosophers alike, independently of logical demonstration. Poetry communicates those doctrines in a "living" or immediately effective manner. Admittedly, Lessing and Mendelssohn's underlying distinction between theoretical knowledge (as demonstrated logically) and "living knowledge" (as communicated aesthetically) is neither self-explanatory nor adequately spelled out in *Pope a Metaphysician!* On the one hand, then, Strauss refers his reader to Mendelssohn's *Treatise on Evidence* and his own introduction to it (henceforth ITE), where he will analyze the distinction further and subsequently (in IMH) show it to be symptomatic of a crisis in Cartesian-Leibnizian philosophy.[102] On

---

98. See IPM xviiin11.
99. See IPM xviiin21.
100. IPM xviiin22.
101. *Pope!* 50.27ff.; Gal 48.
102. See ITE xlviiiff., with IMH lxff.

the other hand, he also quotes Lessing's *Treatise on Fables* in support of the distinction.[103] In all this, Strauss refrains from saying whether the two co-authors are in complete agreement as regards their fuller understanding of that distinction. Even so, a detailed annotation in Strauss's editorial apparatus to *Pope a Metaphysician!* quotes passages from Lessing's approximately contemporaneous "Vindications of Horace," which adumbrate the distinction between poetry and philosophy in Horace's terms quite apart from Leibniz's.[104]

Separating Lessing's contribution to the writing of *Pope a Metaphysician!*[105] from Mendelssohn's[106] becomes possible in hindsight, by comparing their other writings during that period of their respective authorships. IPM notes that both authors blamed national arrogance for Englishmen's tendency to overestimate Pope and Frenchmen's tendency to underestimate Leibniz.[107] Both are also said to share a predisposition to combat the Academy's anti-Leibnizian sentiment—Mendelssohn more for the sake of protecting Leibniz's good name,[108] Lessing more for the sake of protesting any unfairness on the part of the Academy.[109] What separates Lessing from Mendelssohn, Strauss argues, comes out in *Pope a Metaphysician!*'s denial that Pope's doctrine of the hierarchical ordering of being is a Leibnizian doctrine at all.[110] That this denial was probably written by Mendelssohn rather than Lessing, Strauss infers from the fact that Lessing had espoused the same doctrine in 1753, in §17 of "Christianity of Reason," to which Mendelssohn had objected

103. IPM xvIIInn30–31, xIxn33. Cf. *Jerusalem* 178–79; Ark 112–13.
104. See Strauss's annotation to *Pope!* 51.27–36, translated in appendix 2, supplement to IPM xvIIIn24.
105. See IPM xIxnn40–41.
106. See IPM xIxn39.
107. Warburton was English (see IPM xvIIn2). Influential French members of the Academy included Maupertuis (IPM xvIIn17, IPM xvIIn18, ITE xLvIIn25), Prémontval (IPM xvIIn13), and Voltaire (cf. ITE xLvIIIn29). In 1751, Lessing (who resided in Berlin from 1748 till 1755) met Voltaire (who resided there from 1747 till 1753) and translated his *Shorter Philosophical Writings* (1752) into German.
108. The "Fourth Dialogue" of Mendelssohn's contemporaneous *Philosophical Dialogues* is devoted to defending Leibnizian philosophy (JA I. 29–39 or 367–77; cf. Dah 121–29). Cf. note 110, below, with IPM xIxn34, and ITE xLvIn12.
109. See IPM xIxn36.
110. Altmann, MMBS 46–48, argues that Mendelssohn's denial here is against his better knowledge and is a deliberate in-joke at the Academy's expense, i.e., is deliberately tongue-in-cheek. In his editorial annotation to *Pope!* 62.19–63.21 (reproduced in appendix 2, supplement to IPM xxn42), Strauss lists various Leibnizian passages where this doctrine, along with that of the interaction of all cosmic elements, may be found, and adds: "Only this much is correct, that the discussion of the hierarchical ordering is comparatively more frequent in Pope than in Leibniz." Strauss also points out that Mendelssohn himself espouses the doctrine of the hierarchical order of being in *Phädon* 105.4ff. and *Seele* 233.

at the time.[111] Strauss concludes IPM by adding that Mendelssohn's objection did not result in Lessing's abandoning that doctrine, even if it did coincide with his leaving "Christianity of Reason" unfinished, since the doctrine in question shows up again in 1780, in §73 of Lessing's "The Education of the Human Race."[112] Because Mendelssohn will make much of "Christianity of Reason" in his eventual defense of Lessing during the Pantheism Controversy, Strauss postpones further discussion of it till IMH.[113]

In sum, *Pope a Metaphysician!* gives the outward impression that the two coauthors were simply "brother[s] in Leibniz" (to use an expression of Mendelssohn's that Strauss adduces in IMH).[114] But IPM brings out small differences between them that did not surface publicly then and there. Strauss thereby indicates that, from the very beginnings of their friendship, Lessing's philosophizing was perhaps independent of Leibniz's system in a way that Mendelssohn's was not. Lessing, for one, seems to have been quite aware of this difference—at least according to two statements made during his conversations with Jacobi in the summer of 1780, as later reported by Jacobi (and recounted by Strauss in IMH). One statement occurred after Jacobi had expressed his "amazement" that in the *Treatise on Evidence* the otherwise clear-headed and meticulous Mendelssohn could have been so zealous in endorsing the ontological proof of God, about which Jacobi was expressing his doubts to Lessing at the moment.[115] According to Jacobi, Lessing's reply consisted of excuses on behalf of Mendelssohn and led to Jacobi's asking Lessing "whether he had ever declared his own system" to Mendelssohn—to which Lessing replied that he almost did in connection with a disagreement between them over the subject matter of §73 of "The Education of the Human Race"[116] but, as Lessing reportedly went on to say, "we never came to closure, and I let it go at that."[117] In a second statement as reported by Jacobi, Lessing described Mendelssohn as "a bright, accurate,

---

111. See IPM xxnn44–46. As Strauss points out, Mendelssohn's letter to Lessing of February 1, 1774, indicates that the particular doctrine to which Mendelssohn was objecting was that of the Trinity. In his reply to Mendelssohn of May 1, 1774, which recollects their intra-Leibnizian controversy of some twenty years earlier, Lessing attributes to Leibniz the view that "it is incontestably better to defend an unphilosophical cause very philosophically than to want to reject and reform it unphilosophically" (JA XII.2, 40–41, 47). Cf. notes 1, above, and 382, below, with IMH LIIn228.
112. See IPM xx. Cf. IMH xxivn87, LXXXIvn399, LXXXVIIIn428. I have translated the Lessingian passage in appendix 4.
113. IMH xlviff., lxxx, xciff.
114. IMH lxxxiii, citing Mendelssohn's letter to Lessing of May 1763 (JA XII.1 9).
115. Strauss quotes the fuller passage at IMH xxiv.
116. See note 112, above.
117. See IMH xxivnn87–88.

superior mind" but not a "metaphysical" one: "Mendelssohn needed philosophy, found what he needed in the predominant doctrine of his time, and clung to it," yet for absorbing "systems" other than his own (*sc.*, Leibnizianism) "he had neither calling nor instinct"; he "lacked the philosophical resourcefulness that was precisely Lessing's outstanding character trait°."[118] While acknowledging that the foregoing words sizing up Mendelssohn's philosophical capabilities are Jacobi's and not necessarily Lessing's own, Strauss nowhere in his Mendelssohn introductions finds them to be entirely mistaken.

MENDELSSOHN'S CRITIQUE OF ROUSSEAU: "EPISTLE TO MR. LESSING IN LEIPZIG" (1756)

The "Epistle to Mr. Lessing in Leipzig" is an appendix to Mendelssohn's translation from the French of Rousseau's *Discourse on the Origin and Foundations of Inequality among Men* (1753). Before analyzing the content of Mendelssohn's appendix, Strauss's introduction to it (henceforth IEL) summarizes how it came about.

Lessing's move from Berlin to Leipzig in the fall of 1755 left unresolved some philosophical disagreements the two friends were having in oral conversations about the *Discourse*. Meanwhile, Mendelssohn had promised to translate the *Discourse* into German and append his own critical reflections concerning it. He would then send both the translation and the appendix to Lessing, who would see to their publication. Mendelssohn's appendix takes the form of an open letter to Lessing. It spells out his own views about the *Discourse*, though not those of Lessing's to which he is responding. In the circumstances, Strauss limits himself in IEL to examining Mendelssohn's views apart from Lessing's.[119]

IEL shows how Rousseau's argument both attracts and escapes Men-

---

118. Strauss quotes the fuller passage at IMH xxvi–xvii.

119. Something of Lessing's view of Rousseau's *Second Discourse* at the time comes out in his letter to Mendelssohn of January 21, 1756 (JA XI 34): ". . . I really don't yet know what sort of concept *Rousseau* attaches to this word [*sc.*, "*perfectibilité*"], because up till now I've been leafing through his treatise [*sc.*, the *Discourse*] rather than reading it. I only know that I attach a completely different concept to it than one that's turned out to follow from what you've concluded from it. You take it as an *effort* to make oneself more perfect, and I understand merely the condition of a thing by virtue of which it can become more perfect, a condition that all things in the world have and that was unavoidably necessary for their continuation. I believe the creator must have made everything he made capable of becoming more perfect if it was to remain in the perfection in which he created it. The savage, for example, wouldn't remain a savage for long without perfectibility, but would very soon become nothing better than some sort of irrational beast; he therefore received perfectibility not in order to become something better than a sav-

delssohn. What attracts Mendelssohn is Rousseau's social critique, his denunciation of the evils that come with life in political society. For all that, Mendelssohn is both puzzled and annoyed by the inference Rousseau is seen to draw from his critique—namely, that sociality is not natural to human beings, who were better off in a "state of nature" prior to the emergence of society. Strauss goes on to point out what Mendelssohn overlooks that would have clarified Rousseau's (admittedly problematic) inference. Here too, as in IPM, Strauss anticipates what IMH will elaborate more fully concerning Mendelssohn's blind spots.

What escapes Mendelssohn, IEL shows, is the basis on which Rousseau formulates his social critique. Mendelssohn does not get much further than noting contradictions in Rousseau's argument. He is nonplussed by Rousseau's apparent failure to think things through more consistently or systematically, in the manner of the Leibnizian natural theology to which he himself subscribes.[120] He remarks, for example, that to say, as Rousseau does, that what distinguishes human beings from the brutes is "perfectibility" is tantamount to saying, contra Rousseau, that the perfecting of man's capacities in society is grounded in nature after all.[121] He also finds it odd how Rousseau can complain unremittingly about the evils of society, when at the same time all the extreme[122] political reforms Rousseau would like to see—radically republican ones[123]—are said to be found in Geneva (his native city, to which he dedicates the *Discourse*).[124] Here and throughout, Mendelssohn overlooks Rousseau's underlying premise. Strauss indicates how that premise comes to the surface in Rousseau's novel assertion that what distinguishes human beings is not understanding, as in the philosophical tradition he is rebelling against, but freedom.[125] On this premise, the all-too-human passions that emerge with human society come from sociality as such rather than from, say, sensuality. That is why Rousseau can describe man in the state of nature, unlike social man, as completely free of passions, all of which are said to result from comparing or measuring oneself with others, hence from the vanity that emerges with social rank and

---

age, but in order to become nothing less." (The emphases are Lessing's.) For Strauss's remarks on the mature Lessing's view of Rousseau, see ET 58–59 (reprinted in RCPR 70–71).

120. Cf. *Sendschreiben* 92 with NRH 274–76, the mature Strauss's commentary on and critique of the Mendelssohnian passage. I have translated the passage in appendix 3.

121. See IEL xxiiin14. Cf., however, the mature Strauss's comment at NRH 265–66.

122. Mendelssohn calls them "*schwärmerischen*." On this term, see IEL xxiiin15 and IMH LXIVn297.

123. On Mendelssohn's antirepublicanism, cf. IMH xix.

124. See IEL xxiiin16. Cf., however, NRH 253–54.

125. See IEL xxiiin18.

privilege. Rousseau thus faults and justifies the passions simultaneously: they are at once vain self-indulgences and socially necessary (though otherwise unwarranted) constraints on individual freedom.[126] Mendelssohn is oblivious of Rousseau's radical innovation here. Strauss finds the obliviousness especially noticeable in Mendelssohn's passing criticism to the effect that Rousseau's description of freedom as "the noblest gift of heaven" can apply "much more naturally . . . to the use of reason." While this criticism is correct as far as it goes, Strauss observes, Mendelssohn misses the opportunity to extend it to Rousseau's argument as a whole.[127]

Strauss concludes IEL by quoting with approval Mendelssohn's suspicion that Rousseau must have inherited his standpoint from "a multitude of gloomy enthusiasts" who deliberately exaggerated present-day evils in order to "raise the splendor of a glorious future all the more in our eyes."[128] Were Mendelssohn to have confronted Rousseau radically by starting with this suspicion, Strauss intimates, he might have been able to come to terms with the subtleties of Rousseau's argument more adequately. Earlier in IEL, however, Strauss calls attention to an ongoing tendency in Mendelssohn that keeps him from taking that step. He cites Mendelssohn's complaint that Rousseau embeds a simple truth—the defectiveness of our current political institutions—in an extraneous, overstated, "strange system," when the simple truth, expressed "cautiously enough," would do.[129] Strauss comments:

> Truth [for Mendelssohn] is *not* paradoxical, and every philosophers' quarrel ultimately goes back to a quarrel over words, to a difference in

---

126. See IEL xxiin17. Rousseau's umbrella term for the passions is *amour-propre* ("self-esteem"); Strauss in IMH uses the German equivalent *Eigenliebe*. See, on this term, IMH xxviiin101.

127. See IEL xxiiinn19–21. On Rousseau's radical innovation as spelled out in Strauss's subsequent writings, see the epilogue to the present essay.

128. See IEL xxiin23. Cf. IGC cvii.

129. See IEL xxiin12. The Mendelssohnian passage from which Strauss is quoting (*Sendschreiben* 101) reads, in part: "Hobbes has remarked that men in the state of nature would be bound by no laws to do anything at all and that in such a case very many errors must have arisen, since men had not yet introduced any property, distributed any goods, and come up with any arrangement among themselves. He only needed *to present* this opinion *not cautiously enough* a single time in order to make the point, or perhaps to persuade himself, that he could do away with the inner lawfulness of actions all at once." (The emphases are mine, M.D.Y.— cf. Mendelssohn's word "presentation" in quotation marks in the sentence of Strauss in the block quotation that follows next in this essay.) As regards the first of Mendelssohn's two assertions here, Strauss's editorial annotation *ad loc.* cites *De Cive* I.10 (MoL II 164–65; MoE II 9–11) and Epistle Dedicatory (MoL II 138–39; MoE II vi–vii). As regards Mendelssohn's second assertion, Strauss's editorial annotation *ad loc.* comments: "Formulations that could be understood in this sense are found, e.g., in *De Cive* XII.1 [MoL II 284–86; MoE II 149–51]."

"presentation"—this is established from the beginning for the later philosopher of sound commonsense.[130]

Strauss's comment recalls IPM's account of Mendelssohn's distinction between philosophical (demonstrated) truth and its nonphilosophical (aesthetic) presentation, a distinction to be revisited in more detail in ITE and IMH. Here in IEL, a variation of that distinction shows up in Mendelssohn's view that truth, being simple, is or ought to be uncontroversial—so that the disagreements among philosophers must be said to originate instead in the imprecision of the ordinary, commonsense language in which the truth is stated.[131] In his introductions to come, Strauss will show how Mendelssohn's general tendency to meet (or perhaps avoid) the difficulties resulting from the putatively demonstrative character of philosophy, by resorting to non-philosophical solutions like the foregoing, shadows his entire philosophical oeuvre. In ITE, for example, Strauss will describe how Mendelssohn tries to solve the difficulty of reconciling the metaphysical truths demonstrated in the Cartesian-Leibnizian manner with the "historical experience" of an irreducible diversity of competing metaphysical systems.[132] As we shall see when we look at ITE more directly, the *Treatise on Evidence*'s solution is as follows: just because human beings recognize immediately the importance of what metaphysics is about for underwriting their "way of life, happiness, and opinions,"[133] each tends to embrace metaphysical doctrines on his own, albeit in accord with his individual preferences and weaknesses rather than in accord with demonstrated truths; yet metaphysical doctrines arrived at in that way are susceptible to doubts and, once doubted, can no longer fulfill their practical role as motivational support for carrying out one's ethical obligations—unless or until such doubts are overcome by means of metaphysical demonstrations. This solution has a high price, however. Insofar as Mendelssohn now comes to judge the merit of such demonstrations by practical criteria, he compromises their strictly theoretical integrity. Or rather, as IMH will document more fully and more generally, the integrity of metaphysical demonstrations is thereby shown to be dubious and unstable, as may be seen by following the course of Mendelssohn's philosophical writings overall.[134] IMH will track his career-long

---

130. IEL xxii. (The emphasis is Strauss's.)
131. Cf. notes 59 and 60, above.
132. ITE xlviii–liii.
133. *Evidenz* 295 (Dah 277), quoted at ITE xlix.
134. IMH xiv, xlix–l, lxiv–lxix.

series of less-than-satisfactory attempts to reconcile metaphysical demonstrations with the practical or commonsense concerns prompting them. Strauss's survey of those attempts will bring out how, in his final writings, Mendelssohn's pressing need to defend, first, his Judaism and then Lessing's putative Spinozism draws him to the verge of coopting metaphysical demonstrations altogether into the service of commonsense—that is to say, of effacing the line between philosophy and mere apologetics or ideology.[135]

Rousseau reappears in IMH as well. During IMH's analysis of Jacobi's radically libertarian political views, lurking as they do in the background of the Pantheism Controversy, Strauss will observe that Jacobi, who professedly admired the arguments of "the classic of despotism, Thomas Hobbes," nevertheless "speaks against despotism with a decisiveness reminiscent of [Hobbes's trenchant critic] Rousseau."[136] Subsequently, IMH will note how Jacobi's histrionic manner of arguing—his dramatic back-and-forth appeals to and attacks on Hobbes, Rousseau et al.—"was really unintelligible to [Mendelssohn]," even though, Strauss will add understatedly, "he was familiar with it firsthand from Lessing."[137] Above all, Strauss will wonder to what extent Rousseau's argument enters into Jacobi's implicit justification of his underhanded, brutal, dishonest, and cowardly treatment of the unsuspecting Mendelssohn. In Strauss's words, Jacobi's "moral cowardice"

> becomes more identifiable when it is defined more closely as a mixture of self-pity with a brutal disregard for others. Its root is an unrestrained self-esteem that takes on the appearance of love of freedom. For the indulging of self-esteem one may blame Rousseau, who throughout his whole oeuvre had supplied a justification for this emotion that charmed the century, although or because he was combating it as the detestable source of detestable institutions....[138]

That is to say, since Rousseau's rhetorically engaging castigation of self-esteem (*amour-propre*, in Rousseau's language) as the contemptible be-all and end-all of bourgeois society was at the same time a vindication of that passion that caught the eye and turned the heads of his Enlightened readers; therefore a sensitive, impressionable, self-centered, and vain Jacobi

---

135. See IMH LXIVff.
136. IMH XVIII.
137. IMH XXX.
138. IMH LVII. Strauss goes on to exonerate Rousseau for Jacobi's brutality; he ascribes it instead to Jacobi's utter lack of "*générosité*." See section (5) of my remarks on IMH-1, below.

could indulge in it with a free conscience, even or especially during his shameless ambushing of Mendelssohn. Finally, IMH will mention Rousseau in connection with the very first of Mendelssohn's attempts to look beyond philosophy to offset the strictly philosophical shortcomings of Cartesian-Leibnizian metaphysical demonstrations—in his letters *On the Sentiments* (1755), where he appeals for that purpose to the additional authority of aesthetic appreciation or, more exactly, to "taste": ". . . in this original choice of his," Strauss will remark, "the essence of the 'civilized,'[139] pre-Rousseauian eighteenth century comes to sight."[140] The implication here is that even though—or just because—the morally refined, gentlemanly[141] Mendelssohn is not up to keeping pace intellectually with Rousseau, he remains untainted by what he himself calls, in a private letter to Lessing from which Strauss quotes in IEL, Rousseau's morally unconscionable "refus[al of] morality to civilized man."[142] In short, Strauss finds in Mendelssohn's failure to comprehend Rousseau a sign of Mendelssohn's thoroughgoing moral superiority to the intellectually precocious Jacobi.

MENDELSSOHN'S JUSTIFICATION FOR PHILOSOPHY BEFORE THE FORUM OF JUDAISM: *COMMENTARY ON MOSES MAIMONIDES' "LOGICAL TERMS"* (1760)

Strauss's one-paragraph introduction to Mendelssohn's *Commentary on Moses Maimonides' "Logical Terms"* (henceforth ILT) is little more than a promissory note. Strauss informs the reader that he has translated a selection from Mendelssohn's commentary—a chapter-by-chapter exposition of Maimonides' introduction to logic, together with the Maimonidean text[143]—from

---

139. For this term, see note 142, below.
140. IMH LXIV–LXV. Cf. Strauss's suggestion that Mendelssohn would have found Jacobi's two novels *Allwill* and *Woldemar* at least as unsatisfactory as he did Rousseau's *Julie* (IMH xxx, with xxxn115).
141. Cf. IMH LVI, with LXVn303.
142. Mendelssohn to Lessing, December 26, 1755 (JA XI 27), quoted at IEL xxi.
143. The full Arabic text of the Maimonidean original (written in 1151) was not available in Mendelssohn's time. "Two complete Arabic manuscripts were edited, with a Turkish translation, by Mubahat Türker in *Ankara Üniversitesi Dil ve Tarih-Coğrafya Fakültesi Dergisi* 18 (1960): 40–64 . . . An earlier critical edition, containing the Arabic text of the first half of the *Logic* (all that had hitherto been available), medieval translations of the whole work by Moses ibn Tibbon, Ahitub, and Vivas, and an English translation, was edited by Israel Efros under the title *Maimonides' Treatise on Logic: The Original Arabic and Three Hebrew Translations*, ed. and trans. Israel Efros (New York: American Academy for Jewish Research, 1938)." (Joshua Parens and Joseph C. Macfarland, eds., *Medieval Political Philosophy: A Sourcebook, Second Edition* [Ithaca, NY: Cornell University Press, 2011], 181.) Mendelssohn uses Moses ibn Tibbon's translation of the Maimonidean text (Haim Borodianski/Bar-Dayan, "*Vorbemerkung*," JA XIV VI).

Mendelssohn's Hebrew into German.[144] He indicates that the translated selection will have to do for now (1931), until the full Hebrew text of Mendelssohn's commentary and an in-depth introduction to it are available in JA in the future. As has already been mentioned, Haim Borodianski/Bar-Dayan's edition of the Hebrew text appeared in 1938, in the last of the seven JA volumes to be published in pre–World War II Germany; the volume survived the Gestapo's seizure of most of the copies and eventually reappeared in facsimile reprint in 1972.[145] The promised in-depth introduction did not appear till 2004; it is by Heinrich Simon, moreover, and is mostly historical and philological rather than philosophical.[146] We are therefore left mostly on our own as regards whether or how the translated selection is meant to fit with the overall drift of Mendelssohn's thought as spelled out in Strauss's other introductions.

ILT does offer a brief rationale for each of the items selected—the preface, chapter 7 (on the syllogism), and excerpts from chapters 4 and 11. According to ILT, the excerpts from chapters 4 and 11 were selected because Mendelssohn refers to these same passages in his Hebrew treatise *The Soul*, which Strauss has also translated.[147] Chapter 7 was selected because of Mendelssohn's praise of Maimonides' treatment of the syllogism there for its remarkable brevity and clarity.[148] And the preface was selected because it undertakes to justify philosophy, particularly logic, before the forum of Judaism—just as, in a comparable way, Mendelssohn's *Jerusalem* (1781) undertakes to justify Judaism before the forum of philosophy. I must limit my consideration of Mendelssohn's philosophical justification for Judaism here to noting where *Jerusalem* comes up for further mention in Strauss's introductions to the *Phädon* (henceforth IP) and to *God's Cause* (henceforth IGC), as well as in IMH.[149] Meanwhile I shall look at the preface's Jewish justification for the study of logic, for the further light it may shed on what

---

144. See JA II 197–230. For an English rendering of Strauss's translation, with added footnotes showing his German equivalents for Hebrew words of particular philosophical interest in the Mendelssohnian text, see www.press.uchicago.edu/sites/strauss/.

145. See JA XIV 23–119, with note 15, above.

146. See JA XX.1 xxxvii–xlviii. A recent German translation of Mendelssohn's entire *Commentary* by Reuven Michael may be found at JA XX.1 33–175; it does not seem particularly cognizant of Strauss's translation (cf. the translator's remarks at JA XX.1 xlix–l with the entirely perfunctory acknowledgment of Strauss at li). A recent English translation of a selection from Mendelssohn's preface (JA XIV 27–30) may be found in Got 231–36.

147. See *Seele* 204 and 210. For an English rendering of Strauss's translation, see www.press.uchicago.edu/sites/strauss/.

148. See *Logik* 219.

149. IP xixn46, xxn52; IMH lxii, lxvi–lxvii, lxxiii, lxxxvi; IGC ciii, cviin79, cx.

we have already seen Strauss point to as the problematic interface between philosophic demonstration and commonsense in Mendelssohn's oeuvre. The preface's own summary of its justification for the study of logic reads as follows:

> ... without doubt, He who has graced man with discernment has planted the rules of rational thinking in his heart and prescribed infallible laws for him by virtue of which he grasps one thing from another and understands the hidden from the known, and so knows truth. For since He has created man in His image, He has without doubt wished man to grasp those rules and avail himself of them in order to contemplate the works of God, reflect on His Torah, and understand its interpretations and deep secrets. Therefore, whoever investigates those rules does the will of his Master; and it would be a great injustice to hold that such a person concerns himself with nullities or dabbles in profane books.[150]

That is to say, God has placed unerring rules of rational thinking in man, for him to learn and use in contemplating God's works, in reflecting on the Torah, and in understanding its deep, hidden meanings. Broadly speaking, Mendelssohn's argument to this effect is in three stages—exegetical, philological, and dialogical. These have to do, respectively, with (1) the meaning of the Hebrew word *higgayon*, (2) the identification of *higgayon* with the Latin word *logica*, and (3) Maimonides' exemplary piety and his competence as an exponent of Aristotle's logic.[151] At no stage does Mendelssohn take openness to the study of logic on the part of Judaism for granted. On the contrary, he acknowledges numerous objections to that study, which his overall argument is designed to counter.

(1) The preface begins with an exegetical argument about the meaning of the word *higgayon* and its cognates as found in various biblical and rabbinic passages quoted by Mendelssohn. The passages show that the word in question has two meanings. Sometimes it means meditation, or inward thought.[152] At other times it means utterance, or outward speech.[153] This

---

150. *Logik* 207.
151. *Logik* 199–203, 203–5, and 205–7, respectively.
152. Josh. 1:8, Ps. 77:13, 143:5 and 49:4 (*Logik* 199).
153. Job 27:4, Ps. 37:30, Is. 59:3, Ps. 115:7, Job 37:2, B.T. *Sanhedrin* 90a (*Logik* 199); Ps. 9:17, 92:7 (*Logik* 201–2); B.T. *Berachot* 28b (*Logik* 202).

ambiguity is not accidental, Mendelssohn argues. Speech and thought are inseparable, like body and soul. A body whose soul has been separated from it is lifeless, and a soul no longer clothed in the body is imperceptible to mortals; correspondingly, speech without thought is mere noise, and thought by itself is fleeting and cannot reveal itself or "cause an impression in the outside world"[154] except by means of bodily movement. Nevertheless, the bond between thought and speech is mysterious, as both rabbinic and modern scientific authorities agree: both acknowledge that the interaction between mental representations and bodily movements occurs by way of the brain, yet neither is able to clarify how representations emerge from such movements or vice versa. Finally, the deep dependence of inward thought on outward speech is evident in the difference between sensory representations and intellectual representations: whereas sensory representations have to do with particulars, intellectual representations have to do with universals; but arriving at the latter requires an act of abstraction, and this can occur, says Mendelssohn, only when one represents to oneself the letters or sounds of the spoken words that signify the particular sense objects from which one is abstracting.

Remarkably, in none of the passages Mendelssohn quotes do both meanings of *higgayon* show up in the same instance. In Ps. 37:30,[155] for example, the verb *yihgeh* refers to wise utterances that come from the mouth of the just—that is to say, to speech rather than thought. In Ps. 9:17, on the other hand, the expression *higgayon sela*[156] refers, in connection with what has preceded in that verse,[157] to the appropriateness of reflecting on the wondrous ways of providence whereby God exercises justice in punishing evildoers according to their evildoings—that is to say, to thought rather than speech. Admittedly, in the talmudic passage at *Berachot* 28b that Mendelssohn quotes for its containing an admonition to restrain one's children from *higgayon*, this word might appear to have both meanings at once. According to Rashi, whose authoritative explanation of the passage Mendelssohn also quotes, *higgayon* in this instance could mean either independent reflection on the literal meaning of Scripture (as opposed to authoritative rabbinic explanations) or childish chatter—that is to say, either thought or speech. Nevertheless, Mendelssohn does not attribute to Rashi the view that both

---

154. *Logik* 199–200.
155. "The mouth of the just one utters wisdom."
156. "... O, the great thought."
157. "Thus is the Eternal known; the justice that he has created. — / The blasphemer must become entangled in the work of his own hands...."

meanings are intended, only that either meaning is possible. In short, Mendelssohn's assertion that the word *higgayon* is not simply equivocal is based more on his account of the relation between thought and speech than on the quoted passages themselves. His exegetical argument, it seems, is driven by an independent philosophical argument.

(2) This impression is corroborated by the second, or philological, stage of Mendelssohn's argument—his identifying *higgayon* with *logica*. He says little more here than that the identity is well-known to the philosophically informed. He does go on to offer a philological clarification. Namely, since Latin originally had no single word combining the meanings of speech and thought, Latin speakers coined a word to serve as the equivalent of the Greek *dialectica* ("dialectics"), which Greek speakers had coined from the verb *legein*, meaning both "to tell" and "to consider" (that is, to speak and to think). More exactly, the Latin *logica* is derived from the Greek *logos*, a noun that, like the Hebrew *higgayon*, sometimes signifies speaking, sometimes thinking—and sometimes, Mendelssohn adds, the science of thinking truly and correctly.[158] At any rate, translators who began translating philosophical books from other languages into Hebrew around the time of Maimonides et al. saw fit to use *higgayon* as synonymous with *logica* and *dialectica*. Evidently the prior importation of the strictly philosophical connotations of the Greek word into a Latin word served as precedent for the further importation of those connotations into the Hebrew word. By explaining the equivalence of *higgayon* with *logica* and *dialectica* in this way—that is to say, philologically—Mendelssohn narrows the question concerning the justification of the philosophical study of logic into a question concerning the merit of having philosophical books about logic available in Hebrew for pious Jewish readers.

Accordingly, the chief merit of books about logic is said to be that one can thereby acquire the means for grasping the infinite wonders of creation in order to know God's greatness and sublimity and to thank Him for His ongoing benevolence toward all creatures great and small. As for how logic functions in this regard, Mendelssohn's description is rather terse, not to say cryptic. By means of logic, he says,

> the soul ... ascends from the first concepts that are well-known to each human being ... and from representation to representation until it finally arrives at the most sublime inquiries and ... tastes of ... the won-

158. *Logik* 203.

drous wisdom . . . for which each intelligent, God-fearing person has a longing. . . .[159]

In other words, starting with simple, commonsense concepts, logic enables the human soul to infer incrementally and securely to other, more abstract concepts that are consistent among themselves and with the original concepts, until it reaches the sought-for concept of a God on which everything else may be seen to depend. Since Mendelssohn spells out this process in more detail in his *Treatise on Evidence*,[160] which is addressed to non-Jewish readers who by and large take the study of logic for granted, we might ask why he does not do so in even more detail here. This question answers itself. In addressing pious Jewish readers who ex hypothesi do not take the study of logic for granted and who therefore require a justification for its acceptance, Mendelssohn for rhetorical purposes stays as close as possible to the terms with which those readers are familiar. He pleads his case in the language of the Torah. Doing so, he is able or rather required to season his argument with biblical allusions—as I have indicated indirectly in the description of the chief merit of logic that I have just quoted, by leaving ellipses where Mendelssohn himself has inserted biblical or quasi-biblical expressions. In Mendelssohn's fuller description, the soul that "arrives at the more sublime inquiries" does not merely "taste of . . . the wondrous wisdom . . . for which each intelligent, God-fearing person has a longing." Rather, "with the end of the staff that it has in its hand" it "tastes of the honey" of that wisdom, a wisdom that moreover is "reserved for honest persons who walk straightforwardly" and for which the longing of each intelligent, God-fearing person is "strong as death," etc.[161] Generalizing from Mendelssohn's use of biblical and quasi-biblical expressions here, we may say that a consequence of his philological account of the identification of *higgayon* with *logica* and *dialectica* is the recasting of the expressions just quoted, and others, as synonyms or adornments of terms previously found only in philosophical books written in Latin or Greek. To state this another way: from the point of view of Mendelssohn's argument, the biblical passages alluded to in his description of logic's chief merit—as well as the passages he quotes at the start of the preface, where *higgayon* or some cognate refers to inward

159. *Logik* 204.
160. Cf. note 115, above.
161. As Strauss points out in the editorial annotations to his translation, these expressions allude to I Sam. 14:43, Prov. 2:7, and Song of Songs 6:7, respectively (see www.press.uchicago.edu/sites/strauss/, *ad loc.*).

thought,[162] and other such passages—are to be viewed as the Torah's way of presenting theological doctrines that might equally be arrived at by logical inferences alone.

But if so, we may ask, does the philosophical study of logic then make the Torah itself theologically expendable? That is, to the extent that philosophical terms and biblical expressions may now be said to be interchangeable for theological purposes, are philosophy and the Torah mutually necessary after all? Mendelssohn acknowledges this objection. He gives two ad hominem rebuttals. First, those whose study of logic has led them to conclude that the Torah's insights were no longer needed have ended up in intellectual error and moral confusion. Second, the study of logic remains indispensable even or especially for observant and believing Jews, who still need to think clearly when interpreting the Torah's theological teachings and its detailed legal prescriptions. Mendelssohn's rebuttals amount to an admonition to his Jewish reader that rejecting either philosophy or the Torah would not be in his self-interest. He underscores the ad hominem character of this admonition by going on to imagine someone objecting that he could be wise without making use of the rules of logic—to which Mendelssohn replies that it would be like saying he was going to see the stars in the sky without making use of his eyes, or to converse and write without making use of the rules of grammar; he would have to be joking! This brief narrated dialogue culminates the second stage of the preface's argument and anticipates the third stage, which is written explicitly as a (narrated) dialogue between Mendelssohn and his reader.[163] Here Mendelssohn will reply to a more far-reaching objection, having to do with the study of logic as such and not merely its practical consequences.

(3) The third stage of the preface's argument consists of two narrated speeches, a long one by Mendelssohn himself and a short one that Mendelssohn supposes to be on the mind of his reader and inserts at the beginning of his own speech. The reader's speech contains a series of questions expressing his worry as a pious student of the Torah. The worry is that logic was created by the pagan Aristotle, whose books have been forbidden by the rabbis for containing an overabundance of misleading and faulty views.

---

162. "And you shall meditate on it [*sc.*, the Torah] day and night" (Josh. 1:8); "And the meditation of my heart is understandings" (Ps. 49:4); "And I have meditated on all your actions" (Ps. 77:13, 143:5).

163. Actually, the preface as a whole turns out to be addressed to its intended reader explicitly: cf. Mendelssohn's eventual uses of the second person at *Logik* 203 (= *HaNefesh* 27, 28) and 205 (= *HaNefesh* 29).

Mendelssohn addresses this worry at length. He offers the reader three reassurances about logic, given that its exponent in this case is not Aristotle but Maimonides, who is praised as both exemplary in his piety and competent in his understanding of Aristotle. First, since Maimonides has "purified"[164] or separated Aristotle's teaching about logic from his misleading and faulty views, the reader need not bother with Aristotle directly. Second, whereas other branches of philosophy, including physics, metaphysics, and ethics, generate endless controversies—"which as is well-known are grounded in differences of times, circumstances, temperaments, and habits"[165]—, logic instead resembles mathematics and astronomy in resting on reliable proofs. Finally, the rules of logic per se do not lead to error or apostasy, since they are quite remote from the principles of religion and the foundations of the Torah, and moreover have nothing to do with commandment and prohibition. In the remainder of his preface, Mendelssohn goes on to suggest how the study of logic—by means of Maimonides' book with Mendelssohn's commentary—might be integrated into his reader's pious study habits. He adds that it was because Maimonides' book is impenetrable to beginners on account of its brevity, and because previous commentators have explicated it incompetently on account of their inexperience in logic, that he decided to write his own commentary on it.

With Mendelssohn's dialogical reassurances, I have come full circle as regards my reason for looking into the preface. I wanted further light on the problematic interface between philosophic demonstration and practical concerns in Mendelssohn's oeuvre as Strauss understands it. Here in the preface, Mendelssohn's reassurances were needed because of his intended reader's ongoing worry about how philosophical demonstrations would fit (or fail to fit) with Jewish piety, despite the exegetical and philological arguments that had preceded. The dialogical format of Mendelssohn's reassurances leaves it open whether or not his reader has been fully persuaded, however. Before moving on from the preface, then, let me summarize the unresolved issues. They are both theological and moral. On the one hand, the study of logic according to Mendelssohn, though not identical with inquiry into the principles of religion and the foundations of the Torah, would nevertheless enable his reader to arrive at theological conclusions by means of demonstrations alone; yet it is not clear how far such conclusions would serve to clarify the Torah's doctrines as traditionally understood—

---

164. *Ibid*. Cf. note 11, above.
165. *Logik* 206–7.

or how far they would end up merely replacing them. On the other hand, while the rules of logic, as Mendelssohn says, have nothing to do with commandment and prohibition, the reader who arrives at theological doctrines by way of demonstrations rather than by way of the Torah as traditionally understood may well need to think again, or have doubts, about God's support for the Torah's own commandments and prohibitions—with possibly deleterious effects on his moral practice.

As I have already indicated,[166] these same issues will reappear in a non-Jewish setting in (and beyond) Mendelssohn's *Treatise on Evidence* and Strauss's ITE, to which I now turn.

MENDELSSOHN'S SELF-DISTANCING FROM METAPHYSICS:
TREATISE ON EVIDENCE IN METAPHYSICAL SCIENCES (1764)

Mendelssohn's *Treatise on Evidence in Metaphysical Sciences* won first prize in a 1763 Berlin Academy essay competition. (Famously, it edged out Kant's submission.)[167] ITE shows how the *Treatise on Evidence* emerged, what it argues, and why it is significant.[168] These topics overlap, for reasons we shall see.

It emerged in response to the competition question asked by the Academy: Can the truths established by metaphysical demonstrations have the "evidence,"[169] or force of conviction, of mathematical truths?[170] At stake was whether metaphysics is capable of demonstrating, in a logically airtight and epistemically credible manner, the first principles of natural theology and morals. "Evidence" here has two interrelated senses: whether metaphysical demonstrations can be as "certain," or irrefutable, as mathematical ones; and whether they can be as "perspicuous," or lucid. A yes answer to the Academy's question would mean that metaphysical demonstrations, like mathematical ones, could prove on inspection to be inherently convincing (that is, perspicuous as well as certain). A no answer, on the other hand, would still leave open the possibility that metaphysical demonstrations could have enough certainty to be convincing for theological and/or moral purposes.[171] Differently stated, the question was whether in principle meta-

---

166. Cf. note 133, above, and my remarks occasioning the note.
167. See ITE xlvi.
168. ITE xlv–xlvii, xlvii–xlviii, and xlviii–liii.
169. I.e., "evidentness." See the translator's remark at ITE xlvn3.
170. For the academy's full wording, see ITE xlv, with appendix 2, supplement to ITE xlvn4.
171. Cf. ITE ln48.

physical demonstrations not only warrant assent but somehow compel it. Mendelssohn's answer is yes and no. As he puts it, metaphysical truths have the certainty of mathematical truths but not their perspicuity.[172] Strauss finds this answer somewhat incoherent. ITE probes the *Treatise on Evidence*'s argument to try to account for the incoherence.

Before examining its explicit argument as such, Strauss notes that Mendelssohn entered the essay competition to combat the current antimetaphysical sentiment in Germany, which the Academy had been promoting until recently.[173] Strauss adds that all his life Mendelssohn identified metaphysics with the doctrines of the first-generation Leibnizian Christian Wolff[174] and that he considered these definitive and impossible to improve on. Even so, Strauss indicates how in his defense of metaphysics Mendelssohn is forced to distance himself from Wolff and Leibniz, and indeed the philosophical tradition as a whole, by ascribing to metaphysical demonstrations a further, extraneous meaning. Here, and not merely in the *Treatise on Evidence*'s explicit argument, is where ITE locates the source of its incoherence—and, at the same time, its larger significance.

As for the explicit argument, ITE shows how it is meant to rebut the critique of metaphysics spelled out most prominently by Pierre Louis de Maupertuis, a recent president of the Academy.[175] Maupertuis had claimed that only in mathematical sciences are certainty and agreement of opinions possible. His justification for this claim was that only the objects of mathematics—that is to say, numbers and extension—are capable of more or less; these alone, therefore, are amenable to addition and subtraction (and so can be both certain and perspicuous); in contrast, the objects of metaphysics—that is to say, qualities—can be added and subtracted only insofar as their effects are connected with numbers and extension.[176] Mendelssohn rebuts Maupertuis's claim by means of Wolffian arguments: (1) the basis of mathematical certainty is, in turn, the principle of contradiction; (2) quantity and quality—and, accordingly, mathematical and metaphysical demonstrations—are mutually entailed, by a "precise kinship and reciprocal bond";[177]

---

172. *Evidenz* 272 (Dah 255).
173. Cf. IPM XVI–XVII, ITE LII–LIII, IMH LX–LXXI.
174. Cf. IPM XIXn34.
175. See ITE XLVIIIn24. Dahlstrom dismisses Strauss's argument here on the too-narrow grounds that Maupertuis had not been president since 1756 and had died in 1759 (Dah XXVI). As for why Mendelssohn might avoid mentioning Maupertuis's name in any case, consider IPM XV, with XVIIIn17 and XIXn34.
176. This view is also found in David Hume; see ITE XLVIIn26.
177. See ITE XLVIIIn28.

hence (3) a "science of qualities"[178] is indeed possible, given the differential calculus and its application to qualities (as intensive magnitudes).

But there is more to the *Treatise on Evidence*'s argument, as ITE goes on to show. Whatever the merits of Maupertuis's critique of metaphysics, it had a surface plausibility. This had to do with the "historical experience"[179] of Mendelssohn's mid-eighteenth-century contemporaries concerning metaphysics' fate, namely, that all previous attempts to arrive at certain and perspicuous demonstrations of metaphysical truths had failed. Such attempts were now seen—and not just by Maupertuis, but also by Condillac, Voltaire, and d'Alembert before him[180]—as a series of idiosyncratic, mutually contradictory systems, each the passing product of its proponent and its time. Nor was this view limited to those who rejected metaphysics. "Even those who consider metaphysical concepts to be convincing and irrefutable," Strauss quotes Mendelssohn as saying, "must nevertheless concede that so far these have not been given the evidence of mathematical proofs. . . ." Mendelssohn must therefore try to account for metaphysics' lack of evidence all along. Initially, as Strauss notes, he does so by appealing to the non-perspicuity of metaphysical truths, which he says resemble those of the differential calculus in this regard. But as Strauss points out, this explanation denies rather than addresses the difficulty—especially since Mendelssohn also says that among the "many" who reject metaphysics are "discerning minds who have given sufficient proof of their competence."[181] To account for the rejection of metaphysics by those who are otherwise competent, then, Mendelssohn supplements his initial explanation by appealing to "subjective" factors.[182] As we have already seen when looking briefly at ITE during our discussion of IEL,[183] he says that human beings embrace metaphysical doctrines apart from any or all demonstrations—that is to say, idiosyncratically and in conformity with their moral and intellectual weaknesses—just because they recognize the importance of such doctrines for guiding their way of life, happiness, and opinions. Accordingly, what prevents human beings from being receptive to metaphysical demonstrations, aside from any lack of perspicuity on the part of metaphysics itself, is their own moral

---

178. This expression comes from Alexander Baumgarten (a disciple of Wolff); see ITE XLVIIIn29.

179. See ITE XLVIII–XLIX.

180. See ITE XLVIIInn30, 32, 34.

181. See ITE XLIXn37. Altmann, in contrast, defends Mendelssohn's explanation (MMBS 118ff.).

182. See ITE XLIXn39.

183. See note 133, above.

and other convictions as bound up with the non-demonstrated doctrines that are seen to undergird those convictions. If we include the Bible among these non-demonstrated doctrines, we may say that here the *Treatise on Evidence* confronts, in its own way, the tension between biblical theology and philosophical demonstrations that Mendelssohn's preface to his *Commentary on Moses Maimonides' "Logical Terms"* confronts in a strictly Jewish setting.

Strauss emphasizes that none of the foregoing implies that Mendelssohn sees a need to undertake a reform of metaphysics, however.[184] The implication is rather that Mendelssohn must adjust his otherwise Wolffian defense of metaphysics to accommodate the further fact that human beings avail themselves of metaphysical doctrines they happen to find convincing for moral and related purposes independently of demonstrations. As ITE goes on to show, this adjustment results in an unannounced and unaccounted-for reinterpretation of the very metaphysics he is defending.

Mendelssohn reinterprets in particular Wolff's concept of "living knowledge." We have already seen this concept in IPM, where it referred to the immediate effectiveness of didactic poetry in communicating moral doctrines to its addressees.[185] Wolff defines it as knowledge that motivates one to act morally—that serves as a "motor of the will," in Wolff's expression.[186] Yet any knowledge that would have this effect must be certain; and according to Wolff it can be certain only if the knower grasps the principles motivating his actions as demonstrated truths. Wolff adds that one must also grasp how the principles apply in particular situations, so that besides the a priori (or demonstrated) knowledge of moral principles, one must have an a posteriori (or empirical) knowledge consisting of examples where those principles are realized. Strauss's point here is that Wolff identifies practical conviction with complete theoretical conviction, a priori and a posteriori. Mendelssohn, in contrast, separates practical conviction from theoretical conviction. Without explicitly acknowledging his divergence from Wolff, he equates "living knowledge" merely with those non-demonstrated doctrines that are sufficiently convincing to motivate moral actions.[187] Correspondingly, he also reinterprets Wolff's concept of conscience. Wolff

---

184. Strauss does point out that Mendelssohn speaks of a still unmet need for "essential signs" in metaphysics (i.e., symbols or language that would give metaphysical terms the precision found in mathematical terms). See ITE Ln44.
185. See IPM XVIII–XIX.
186. See ITE L–LI.
187. See ITE LIn51.

defines conscience as "the judgment about whether our actions are good or evil."[188] From this definition, Wolff infers that we are not always able to judge what we ought to do or refrain from doing in accordance with the requirements of conscience (that is to say, by applying the relevant moral principles),[189] given that all too often the relevant details of the moral situations in which we find ourselves are not fully known to us then and there; hence we must be content with only probable judgments. Mendelssohn, however, speaks of conscience's independence from reason. Conscience, he says, as "a skill at differentiating good from evil by means of indistinct inferences," must replace reason in situations where, not having a distinct grasp of all the relevant details at the moment, we are in danger of becoming morally obtuse by postponing action indefinitely while we wait for further information.[190] According to Mendelssohn, the "inner feeling" that we need to respond to pressing moral demands in a timely way despite our having only indistinct knowledge motivates us "far more intensely and vividly" than "the most distinct inferences of reason."[191]

In short, Strauss finds the *Treatise on Evidence*'s significance less in the specifics of its argument than in its general drift. While sharing his contemporaries' doubt about the force of conviction of metaphysical demonstrations, Mendelssohn discounts such doubt by upgrading the importance of the indistinct, non-demonstrated, yet "living" knowledge that serves as a trusted guide for human life. This upgrade lets him grant the nonperspicuity of metaphysical demonstrations without having to give up his lifelong attachment to Leibniz-Wolffian metaphysics or think about a reform of metaphysics. Even so, it forces Mendelssohn to reinterpret the meaning of metaphysics as such. He now assigns to metaphysical demonstrations a practical role—namely, defending the newly upgraded "living" knowledge whenever our being convinced of it is threatened. Mendelssohn will say more about this role in his *Phädon*.

ITE's final remarks concern the *Treatise on Evidence*'s unresolved incoherence. Where, Strauss asks, does the threat originate that metaphysical demonstrations are now to defend against? Since the *Treatise on Evidence* is silent here, Strauss can only look around for Mendelssohn's implicit answer. He recalls the resistance that Mendelssohn says metaphysical demonstrations run into in the face of human beings' prior moral and other convictions.

---

188. See ITE LI–LII.
189. On Wolff's concept of "correct conscience," see ITE LIIn56.
190. See ITE LII.
191. Cf. IP XXIV–XXV.

Meanwhile he notes a future statement of Mendelssohn's, in *To the Friends of Lessing*, to the effect that the (non-demonstrated but "living") truths metaphysics seeks to defend are just as perspicuous and certain to sound commonsense as any proposition in geometry.[192] Strauss infers that if such is also Mendelssohn's view in the *Treatise on Evidence*, or to the extent that it is, the aforementioned resistance to metaphysically demonstrated truths must therefore extend to sound commonsense's versions of those truths as well. But if so, then it is that resistance, rather than metaphysics' putative lack of perspicuity, that explains metaphysics' historical fate. Why, Strauss wonders, does Mendelssohn himself not draw this inference? Strauss's answer is that, as much as Mendelssohn is open to doubting the perspicuity of metaphysical demonstrations of the Leibniz-Wolffian sort, he remains convinced of their certainty. In Strauss's words, the underlying cause of the *Treatise on Evidence*'s manifest incoherence is Mendelssohn's "unbroken conviction . . . about natural religion's noblest truths having been demonstrated by Leibniz and Wolff."[193] In his introductions to come, Strauss will show how this conviction is put to the test during the controversies Mendelssohn soon faces, both theological and philosophical, as a result of his *Phädon* and subsequent writings.

MENDELSSOHN'S UPDATING OF PLATO: *PHÄDON* (1767)

In his *Phädon*, Mendelssohn recasts Plato's *Phaedo* to suit the literary taste of his German-speaking contemporaries and updates its proofs for the immortality of the soul. IP examines the connection between the Mendelssohnian proofs and the "living knowledge" already discussed in the *Treatise on Evidence*—except that the *Phädon* drops this term in favor of the broader term "sound commonsense."

The key points IP makes are these: (1) Mendelssohn's initial interest in Plato's *Phaedo* was not its proofs for immortality so much as its rhetorical artistry and its dramatic presentation of Socrates as a role model for adherents of "rational religion."[194] (2) Mendelssohn redesigns the dramatic setting found in Plato's dialogue, to fit with rational religion's doctrine of God's undemanding benevolence.[195] (3) In doing so, he softens the sternness with

---

192. See ITE LIIIn63. Mendelssohn's statement is also quoted in IP XVIII.
193. ITE LIII. Strauss's wording recalls the title of H. S. Reimarus's *The Noblest Truths of Natural Religion* (see IMH XIVn26, with notes 50–52, above).
194. See IP XIII–XVIII.
195. See IP XVIII–XIX.

which the Platonic Socrates faces death, even as he tightens up the proofs themselves.[196] (4) His subsequent epistolary controversy with Johann Gottfried Herder exposes the historically transitory character of the doctrine of immortality being promoted and defended in the *Phädon*.[197]

(1) According to the documentary evidence IP brings up, Mendelssohn composed his *Phädon* in two stages, roughly corresponding to the major premise and the conclusion of his overall argument for immortality. Overall, the *Phädon*—following Leibniz, Wolff et al.—aims to prove immortality on the basis of immutability. Immutability (or imperishability) refers to the soul's mere persistence as an individual substance. Immortality, on the other hand, includes the soul's ongoing awareness of its individual past and present. Logically speaking, the link between the soul-substance's imperishability and its immortality is its simplicity (or indivisibility and hence immateriality)—the subject of the minor premise of Mendelssohn's overall argument. Thus the theses to be proved in the three "Dialogues" that compose the *Phädon* are the soul's imperishability, simplicity, and immortality, respectively. In any event, a three-year break occurred somewhere between the writing of the First and Third Dialogues. IP cites several pieces of evidence for the break. These include the replacement of Mendelssohn's proof for the soul's simplicity as found in his initial draft for the book, which he eventually discarded;[198] two letters by Mendelssohn to his friend Isaak Iselin in Basel indicating that he had sent the first half of his *Phädon* to Iselin as an entry in a Swiss essay competition but had not received Iselin's reply to his question about whether what he had written so far was worth completing;[199] and a letter from Mendelssohn to his friend Thomas Abbt attributing the resumption of his writing to Abbt's doubts about immortality.[200] Strauss's main point in all this is that Abbt's doubts are instructive for how the *Phädon* ultimately turned out.

In the book review quarterly he coedited with Mendelssohn and Friedrich Nicolai,[201] Abbt had written a critique of the argument for immortality found in the Leibniz-Wolffian theologian Johann Joachim Spalding's popular pamphlet *The Destiny of Man*.[202] A friendly controversy ensued in the form of letters between Mendelssohn and Abbt, followed by

---

196. See IP XIX–XXX.
197. See IP XXX–XXXIII.
198. See IP XIV–XV, XVII.
199. See IP XV–XVI.
200. See IP XVI–XVIII.
201. See IP XIIIn6, also XVI–XVII.
202. See appendix 2, supplement to IP XVIn32.

Mendelssohn's published reply to Abbt in defense of Spalding.[203] Abbt and Mendelssohn each describe themselves as renewing the controversy between their respective theological authorities, Pierre Bayle and Leibniz, which had occurred two generations earlier.[204] Strauss points out, however, that they renew it on narrower grounds than those of their predecessors. Both Abbt and Mendelssohn argue as second-generation epigones. Neither confronts the basic issue between Bayle and Leibniz in its own terms—as Strauss himself will eventually do in IMH and IGC.[205] Meanwhile, from the fact that the theological doctrine and conviction Mendelssohn expresses in the *Phädon* agree with those expressed in Spalding's pamphlet, Strauss finds their intent to be the same as well. It is to defend immortality against skepticism. Skepticism—whether grounded in the view that immortality is a matter of religious faith and is not amenable to rational proof, as in Abbt's case, or in the "sophistry"[206] of the anti-metaphysical (or materialist) views being disseminated in Germany by the French *philosophes*[207] associated with the Berlin Academy, as we saw in IPM and ITE[208]—is the live issue for Mendelssohn, as for Spalding. Strauss implies that defending against "sophistry" is the more pressing side of the issue for Mendelssohn, given that the steady popularity of Spalding's pamphlet since its appearance half a generation earlier indicates an ongoing need to bolster its midcentury German readership's "living knowledge" of theology, which was being undermined indirectly if not directly by the francophone voices in the Academy.[209] As Strauss puts it in IP, the doctrine and conviction expressed by Spalding, and concurrently under attack, were "the common coin of the German Enlightenment, standing as it did on the soil of Leibniz-Wolffian philosophy."[210]

(2) What Mendelssohn shares with Spalding and his like-minded readers is summed up by the term "rational religion." Negatively expressed, the term refers to religion not guided by revelation. Yet rational religion has positive doctrines as well, including the immortality of the soul. According to Mendelssohn, rational religion's doctrines are all provable by reason alone. More fundamentally, however, they are also said to be familiar to

---

203. See IP xvi–xviinn33–34, with the previous note.
204. Abbt appeals to Bayle as "an enemy to systems," and Mendelssohn in turn invokes the "spirit of the great Leibniz." See IP xviinn35–36.
205. See IMH lxxiv, IGC cv–cx.
206. Cf. IP xviin37, with IP xviiin44.
207. See the translator's remark at IPM xviiin23.
208. See IIS xxxvi, IPM xviff., ITE xlvii–xlviii.
209. Cf. ITE lii–liiinn62–63.
210. IP xvii; cf. IGC ci.

sound commonsense prior to and apart from rational proof, having been passed down from time immemorial. Sound commonsense, it is held, has always and everywhere found the doctrines of rational religion to be true, inasmuch as they are indispensable for human happiness. In this context, IP quotes statements of Mendelssohn's in *Jerusalem* and *Morning Hours* as well as in the *Phädon* to the effect that even though human beings would be "most pitiful" if the hope of immortality were denied to them, they have nevertheless been created by an "all-benevolent and all-wise Being," by whom they are "loved most tenderly" and who "softly dispenses" the means for their happiness.[211] The underlying theological notion here—as IP points out and as IMH and IGC will spell out more fully—is that God is not a demanding, summoning God who acts above all with a view to His own power, glory, and punitive anger, Calvin to the contrary notwithstanding.[212] The God of rational religion is consummately benevolent.[213] Hence death could not possibly be the baleful termination of life, much less a transition to eternal punishments in hell.[214] It must instead be the threshold to a post mortem continuation of this-worldly life, where divine providence has wisely and benevolently arranged for each individual soul to extend its pursuit of happiness—that is to say, its moral and intellectual self-improvement—indefinitely.[215]

IP's focus is not primarily theological, however, but "anthropological."[216] The strictly human implications of rational religion's doctrine of God's benevolence show up, to begin with, in the difference between Mendelssohn's version of the dialogue's dramatic setting and Plato's version.[217] In characterizing that difference, IP avails itself of a term Mendelssohn uses in a statement already quoted concerning divine providence: Mendelssohn "softens" Plato's drama.[218]

(3) The "softening" is seen in the various alterations Mendelssohn makes to what Plato's own dialogue says about death and dying. Whereas the Pla-

---

211. IP XVIII–XIXnn45–48.
212. IP XIX. Strauss emphasizes that the disagreement with Calvin here is not merely intraecclesiastical but characterizes the Enlightenment as such. Cf. SCR 193–214.
213. Cf. LSGS III 318–19 (HCR 67–69).
214. Cf. IP XIXn50.
215. Cf. IP XXX–XXXI, with *Seele* 209–13.
216. IP XIX–XX. IP's theological themes are taken up in IGC.
217. IP XXI–XXIV.
218. See IP XIXn46. The statement is from Mendelssohn's *Jerusalem* (cf. note 149, above). Mendelssohn begins it by characterizing his description of divine providence as being "According to the concepts of true Judaism..."; Strauss interpolates that for Mendelssohn these coincide with those of rational religion. See also the statement criticizing Plato from Mendelssohn's introduction to the *Phädon*, which Strauss quotes in full at IP XX.

tonic Socrates says that the body is an obstacle to philosophy such that truth is attainable only insofar as one frees oneself from the body, that is to say, dies (*Phaedo* 61b–69e), Mendelssohn remarks that he cannot go along with Plato's Pythagorean depreciation of the body here but has kept this passage "merely out of a liking for Plato's conquering eloquence."[219] Whereas the Platonic Socrates says that if the soul were to die with the body, death would be a victory for the wicked since they would then lose their wickedness (107c), the corresponding Mendelssohnian statement is rather that if the soul were mortal, there would ultimately be no reason for being good.[220] And whereas the Platonic Socrates worries that his interest in his own immortality puts at risk whether he can discuss it philosophically and not merely wish it to be true since it is personally consoling (91a–c), the Mendelssohnian Socrates "wagers" that it is true precisely because it is, among other things, consoling.[221] In general, as IP goes on to show in detail, Mendelssohn drops the Platonic Socrates' "sternness" in the face of death and, "contrary to Plato's explicit meaning," makes Socrates' dying into a "poignant spectacle."[222] Strauss lists a dozen instances from the dialogue's opening pages where Mendelssohn imports and renders Plato's Greek sentences so as to infuse emotive overtones not present in the original. Thus Plato's "to remember Socrates" (58d) becomes "to remember *my* Socrates" (the emphases here and subsequently are IP's); Plato's "no pity overcame me, as one who is present at the death of a man befriended" (58e) becomes "*I felt* no pity, no *such uneasiness* as we are used to feeling when a friend *fades in our arms*"; Plato's "he died ... so fearlessly" (*ibid.*) becomes "so quiet was his behavior *in the hour of death*"; etc. Correspondingly, Mendelssohn's Socrates does not face death with the same philosophical equanimity as Plato's Socrates does. Instead, where Plato's Socrates believes that to philosophize correctly means caring for nothing besides dying and being dead (64d), Mendelssohn's believes only that it means applying one's life to "becoming more familiar with death ..."; and where Plato's Socrates devotes his life to contemplating something (66d), Mendelssohn's merely prepares himself "to *embrace* the truth."

Given that Mendelssohn's drama is less stern than Plato's, IP asks, why does Mendelssohn need proofs that are more rigorous than Plato's? IP answers by looking at why the Mendelssohnian Socrates' interlocutors want

---

219. See IP xxn53.
220. See IP xxin56.
221. See IP xxin57.
222. IP xxi; cf. IGC cviii. The emphases in the following quotations from Mendelssohn are Strauss's.

proofs in the first place. It is not that they are unfamiliar with the doctrine of immortality, or even doubt its truth. But there are moments when they cannot (in their words)[223] "represent it to [themselves]" with enough "liveliness" for it to have the force of conviction for them. At such moments, their "peace of soul" is endangered. What they want from Socrates, then, is to reassure themselves of that truth by means of a "simple series of unshakeable reasons" that they can "remember at all times." That is to say, they need a "chain of distinct inferences" that is as uncomplicated, certain, free of tendentiousness, and close to commonsense as possible, so as to make the consoling truth as accessible and unforgettable as possible. The rigor of the proofs is meant to secure what the *Treatise on Evidence* would call the "living knowledge" of their addressees.

For that reason, as IP goes on to show,[224] Mendelssohn does not limit himself to recycling Plato's proofs, such as they are. He draws as well from the philosophical tradition. Broadly understood, the *Phädon*'s proofs are Platonic (in the logical connection between imperishability and simplicity that governs the First and Second Dialogues) and Leibnizian (in the difference between imperishability and immortality that governs the transition from the First and Second Dialogues to the Third Dialogue). Yet in detail they are neither. Mendelssohn says as much in his appendixes to later editions of the *Phädon*. IP's further remarks concern what Mendelssohn reports in the appendixes and elsewhere about how he has adapted the traditional proofs and why.

As regards the First Dialogue's proof for the soul's imperishability, Strauss takes issue with Kant, who claims to have refuted it.[225] According to Kant, Mendelssohn started with "the usual argument" to the effect that the soul is not susceptible to dissolution, or gradual ceasing-to-be; he then discovered that this argument left the soul's "necessary continuance" in doubt; accordingly, he had to bring in a further argument to the effect that the soul is not susceptible to vanishing, or sudden ceasing-to-be, either. But IP shows how Kant gets Mendelssohn's proof backwards. Mendelssohn, says Strauss, starts instead by proving that nothing in nature is susceptible to vanishing; he then proves that any dissolution would require a vanishing at some point; only then does he conclude that the soul in particular is not susceptible to dissolution.[226] Nor, IP adds, is this proof meant to counter

---

223. See IP xxvnn74–75. Cf. ITE L–LII.
224. IP xxv–xxvi.
225. See IP xxvi–xxvii.
226. See IP xxvIn81.

any prior doubts about the key metaphysical concept, namely, that nothing vanishes; rather, as Mendelssohn says in a private letter from which IP quotes, his proof is addressed to non-metaphysicians who "possess sound commonsense and wish to reflect" and to whom he must therefore introduce metaphysical concepts gradually—as he does when introducing the principle that no leap occurs in nature.[227] Strauss infers from all this that, *pace* Kant, Mendelssohn in the First Dialogue deviates from "the usual argument" only for the sake of making his proof as universally understandable as possible with as few presuppositions as possible.

As regards the Second Dialogue's proof for the soul's simplicity,[228] IP shows how Mendelssohn had two precedents to choose from besides the Platonic one: a proof traceable to Descartes, and another traceable to Plotinus. He rejected the Cartesian (or quasi-Cartesian)[229] proof even though he found it personally "convincing," since it was too technical for his purpose. He liked the Plotinian proof, which inferred the soul's immateriality on the basis of the simplicity, and hence indivisibility, of both thinking and thought—in contrast to the Cartesian proof, which conceived the soul's immateriality only in terms of its non-extendedness. He combined the Plotinian proof with the Platonic one after finding an inadequacy in the Platonic Socrates' reply to an objection by his interlocutor Simmias. At *Phaedo* 92e–93b, Plato's Simmias objects to immortality on the ground that although the soul appears to be different from the body, this appearance does not rule out the possibility that the soul is nothing more than a harmonious mixture of bodily elements whose existence is bound up with the body's. Mendelssohn focuses on Simmias' initial question there: can a composite do or suffer anything other than what it is composed of? Mendelssohn's answer to this question, like Plato's, is no. But it is more complicated than Plato's, since Mendelssohn cannot quite go along with Simmias' question in its own terms. He objects to Simmias' objection with a further question:

> But why is it that a rule-governed whole can be composed out of non-rule-governed parts, a harmonious concert out of non-harmonious tones, or a powerful state out of powerless members?[230]

---

227. See IP xxvi–xxviin82.
228. IP xxvi–xxix.
229. Cf. Strauss's editorial annotations to *Phädon 3* 152.9–18, *Unkörperlichkeit* 167.22 and *Unkörperlichkeit* 167.25–27—each of which I have reproduced in IP xxviin84—with the remarks on these in my account of IdL, below.
230. *Phädon 3* 153.21–24 (cf. Nob 155).

By Mendelssohn's admission, he poses this further question as a Leibnizian—being committed, as he says, to the view that "movement is to arise from such forces as are not movement, and extension from properties of substances that are something quite other than extension." Mendelssohn's further question thus amounts to asking: on what non-composite basis is a composite able to act otherwise than what it is composed of? His answer, to begin with, is also Leibnizian: on the basis, he says, of the thinking that collects the elements of the body into a whole such that they appear otherwise than mere bodily elements. Here Strauss immediately restates Mendelssohn's answer in terms that no longer advertise its Leibnizian provenance: the fact that the soul appears to be different from anything material could not possibly be a consequence of the body's material components, since the soul's activity is a condition of the composite's appearing otherwise than those components in the first place. Strauss then goes out of his way, or so it seems, to editorialize that he considers this proof to be the most precise of any he has ever seen. He even quotes at length an informed authority among Mendelssohn's contemporaries who shares that opinion.[231] Finally, he emphasizes that Mendelssohn's originality here consists merely in how he presents the proof rather than in its content, which has numerous precedents among Mendelssohn's contemporaries. As it turns out, Strauss's overall point is that Mendelssohn's proof as he presents it is not exactly Leibnizian after all, since here too, as in the *Phädon*'s First Dialogue, Mendelssohn is guided by his overall aim of supplying proofs that are as universally intelligible and free of special presuppositions as possible. Ultimately, then, Strauss characterizes the Second Dialogue's proof as an "inner critique of materialism"—a critique that is, and is meant to be, accessible and understandable quite apart from Mendelssohn's professed Leibnizianism. In IP's words, Mendelssohn's proof merely "reminds" would-be materialists, who like everyone else "must differentiate between being and appearance, between primary and secondary qualities, of the difficulty that clings to this difference under the materialist presupposition."[232]

As for the Third Dialogue's proof of the soul's immortality, it too limits itself to showing the difficulty inherent in the materialist alternative, as Strauss indicates.[233] If the soul were mortal, Mendelssohn argues, then this life would be the highest good; but a state has a right to demand (under cer-

---

231. See IP xxixn90, with the accompanying text. Cf. also IP xxx.
232. See also Strauss's handwritten addendum reproduced in IP xxixn92.
233. IP xxix–xxx.

tain circumstances) that a citizen sacrifice his life; yet if life were the highest good, the citizen would be equally right to resist—in which case there would result the absurdity of a clash of equal rights! In particular, a criminal rightfully condemned to death would have the right to do whatever he could to save his life, even through violence against the state—a right he would have gained through his crime! As in the Second Dialogue, so too here, Mendelssohn's proof proceeds by way of indicating the difficulty of sustaining materialist premises to the contrary.

(4) Herder, who claimed to be the *Phädon*'s closest reader, objected not to Mendelssohn's proofs per se, nor to their refutation of materialism, but to the rational religion they were meant to underwrite.[234] Whereas Mendelssohn assumes that life after death is a further stage that enables the individual soul to progress toward moral and intellectual perfection, Herder doubts that such progress is all that simple. Perfecting any one power of the soul, Herder insists, always comes with a corresponding deterioration of some other power; overall, the soul stays at the same stage of perfection; its present life is self-contained and does not point beyond itself; even death is a moment of this life only. Herder's disagreement with Mendelssohn, Strauss suggests, is less a matter of argument than of the presuppositions their respective arguments seek to vindicate. "Herder's opinion" says Strauss,

> was based on the belief, coming into dominance for more than a century by now, in the eternity of life as "*this*" life, *in* which death acts as a moment of life itself, whereas Mendelssohn is still totally dominated by the original despair in light of the possibility that a man passes away as a person. . . .[235]

That is to say (in the language of the *Treatise on Evidence*), Mendelssohn unlike Herder is defending what we might call yesterday's "living knowledge" about death and dying, and not necessarily today's or tomorrow's. Strauss reinforces this point by quoting a well-known literary historian: Herder, says Rudolf Unger, puts the

> old, dualistic concept of death and immortality out of power . . . through the *Stirb und Werde* born out of the *Lebensgefühl* of an immanent view of God and the world.[236]

---

234. IP xxx–xxxii.
235. IP xxxii. The emphases are Strauss's own.
236. See, for this and the following, IP xxxiinn99–101.

In translating Unger's German sentence here, I have retained two expressions that I managed to put into English in IP, though I needed the help of my translator's footnotes to do so. The expression *Stirb und Werde*, which I rendered literally there as "Die and Come-to-be," alludes to the last stanza of Goethe's lyric poem *"Selige Sehnsucht"* (Blissful longing), which describes how a moth is consumed by the candle flame it is inherently attracted to: the culmination of its life and the undergoing of its death are one and the same. As regards the expression *Lebensgefühl*, I could not render it quite so literally except rather awkwardly as, say, "feeling of life" or, worse, "sense of living"; and although I considered the English expressions "intuitive feeling" and "intuitive sense," I ended up with "live sense." By keeping the word "live" in front of my own reader, I wanted to suggest the likelihood that while quoting Unger's words, Strauss is recalling the Mendelssohnian expression *lebendige Erkenntnis* (living knowledge) and inviting his reader to wonder with him whether what Mendelssohn understands by it is ultimately able to bear the weight he wishes to place on it.

Strauss ends IP by pointing out that Herder's objections to the *Phädon* were identical to Abbt's objections to Spalding's *The Destiny of Man* and that, in his subsequent "Annotations to Abbt's Friendly Correspondence" (1781), Mendelssohn published the material he had wanted to work into a revised version of the *Phädon*'s Third Dialogue in answer to Abbt (who had died in 1766). Strauss quotes from the foreword to the 1781 writing, where Mendelssohn expresses regret at having had to publish his "Annotations" prematurely: he no longer has the time or strength, he says, to follow them out properly or bring them into the form in which the most important part of them—concerning the destiny of man—should have been used in the latter (or last?) part of the dialogue.

AFTER THE *PHÄDON*: *TREATISE ON THE INCORPOREALITY OF THE HUMAN SOUL* (1774, 1775)

Strauss's introduction to Mendelssohn's *Treatise on the Incorporeality of the Human Soul* (henceforth IIS) deals with its emergence rather than its content. As IIS indicates, it is a follow-up to the *Phädon*. It addresses the question of the soul's imperishability (including its incorporeality), in response to controversies generated by the *Phädon*'s reception. Mendelssohn never completed a *Treatise on Incorporeality* as such, however. Instead, the book known by this title consists of four separate essays plus a fragmentary introduction, or "Entrance"—not Mendelssohn's word for it but that of Joseph

Grossinger, a Viennese admirer who put the essays together with the "Entrance" and published them in Latin translation in 1774 and in the original German (omitting the "Entrance") in 1775. Strictly speaking, then, it is not exactly a "*Treatise*," though this name for it has stuck.

IIS tries to dispel some confusions about the *Treatise on Incorporeality*'s original language and date of publication. These were promulgated by scholars then and since who, among other things, ignored information plainly supplied by Grossinger's editorial preface concerning what language Mendelssohn first wrote it in (German, not Latin) and misdated it as "around 1760." As for the dating, a 1760 or so appearance is manifestly impossible, as Strauss shows in some detail: the longest of the *Treatise*'s four essays is Mendelssohn's reply to an essay by d'Alembert that was published only in 1767 (or 1768, in a second edition); and an extant manuscript of the *Treatise* bears the date 1774. Two pieces of evidence do point to a pre-1774 dating, however: Grossinger's preface mentions that the *Treatise* originated thanks to an unnamed "Prussian Royal Highness" who perhaps, Strauss speculates, was Friedrich the Great's sister, since she had conversed at length with Mendelssohn during her visit to Berlin around New Year's of 1772; and Mendelssohn's physician Marcus Bloch reports that Mendelssohn produced three different scholarly writings that same year.

Strauss's only direct reference to the *Treatise on Incorporeality* in his other introductions is for the purpose of corroborating that Mendelssohn looked to Plotinus as a resource for his proof of the soul's immateriality in the *Phädon*.[237] Here in IIS, Strauss characterizes the *Treatise* as "the *Phädon*'s confrontation with materialism," since—in the light of what we have already seen in IP—"the moderate Enlightenment's doctrine of immortality was threatened most strongly and most obviously by materialism."[238]

AFTER THE *PHÄDON*, CONTINUED: "ON A HANDWRITTEN ESSAY OF MR. DE LUC'S" (1779)

Strauss's one-paragraph introduction to Mendelssohn's "On a Handwritten Essay of Mr. de Luc's" (henceforth IdL), like IIS, deals only with its emergence. It was Mendelssohn's response to the Swiss physicist Jean André de

---

237. See IP xxvIIn85.
238. See *Phädon 3* 149.24–36 (cf. Nob 152), together with the remarks on Spalding, etc., at IP xvIff.

Luc's request for feedback on a sketch for a treatise he was planning on materialism. De Luc's treatise never appeared as such; instead, he absorbed it into a larger work on geological and human history. After receiving Mendelssohn's permission to quote his remarks in the larger work, de Luc included the latter half of them in a French translation, which he introduced by acknowledging Mendelssohn's kindness in having written them. Strauss concludes IdL by emphasizing that Mendelssohn's remarks were about de Luc's original sketch, not about what de Luc ended up writing in the larger work.

There is no direct reference to Mendelssohn's remarks on de Luc in any of Strauss's other introductions. Strauss does refer to them in passing in an extensive editorial annotation on Mendelssohn's interpretation of the "Cartesian" proof of the soul's immateriality, which I have interpolated among the annotations to IP.[239] In that annotation, Strauss shows how Mendelssohn's version of Descartes's proof differs significantly from Descartes's own version in the latter's *Meditations on First Philosophy*. I shall summarize Strauss's argument in his annotation (and in other annotations to which it makes cross-references), since the difference between Mendelssohn and Descartes here turns out to be emblematic of Strauss's overall understanding of Mendelssohn.

Strauss argues as follows: Like the secondary authorities on whom he evidently relies,[240] Mendelssohn misconstrues Descartes's proof. According to Mendelssohn, the proof amounts to showing how the soul's existence cannot be accounted for on materialist premises.[241] Mendelssohn assumes here that Descartes's proof rests on the presupposition that the existence of matter is secure. But he overlooks that Descartes doubts this presupposition in advance of the proof, inasmuch as Descartes has already doubted the existence of the corporeal world on the ground that it is more uncertain than the existence of the mind.[242] Instead, says Strauss, Descartes's proof rests on the following two presuppositions: (1) the clear and distinct ideas of soul and body are wholly disparate; (2) anything we conceive clearly and distinctly exists in reality exactly as we conceive it. From these two presuppositions, taken together, Descartes concludes that soul and body, being

---

239. See appendix 2, supplement to IP xxviin84.
240. See Strauss's editorial annotation to *Unkörperlichkeit* 165.27–167.2, translated in appendix 2, supplement to IP xxixn91.
241. Cf. note 237, above.
242. Cf. *Meditations* I and II (Hef 86–117). Cf. LSGS III 348–64 *passim*; HCR 94–109 *passim*.

clearly and distinctly conceived as wholly disparate substances, are therefore wholly disparate in reality. Now, Mendelssohn considers the former presupposition uncontroversial, though not the latter.[243] He calls the latter presupposition, together with the conclusion that soul and body are wholly disparate substances, Descartes's "well-known first principle." By excluding from Descartes's "well-known first principle" the presupposition that the clear and distinct ideas of soul and body are wholly disparate, however, Mendelssohn inadvertently revises Descartes's understanding of clear and distinct knowledge.[244] He assimilates Descartes's epistemology to Locke's. Yet Locke, in contradistinction to Descartes, denies that we can infer that soul and body are two wholly disparate substances, on the ground that we have no clear and distinct knowledge of substance in the first place.[245] From this denial, Locke unlike Descartes infers that the immortality of the soul is indemonstrable. Even so, Mendelssohn suspects that the indemonstrability of immortality may not be Locke's final view.[246] Strauss endorses Mendelssohn's suspicion, as far as it goes, by noting that despite Locke's explicit doubt about the demonstrability of the doctrine of immortality, he nevertheless continues to profess this doctrine "quite energetically."[247] In any event, Strauss takes the occasion here to point out the difference between "Locke himself and the French Enlightenment, insofar as the latter propagated Locke's ideas in the service of radical unbelief."[248]

The connection between this last statement and Strauss's overall understanding of Mendelssohn so far is as follows. Mendelssohn's coopting of philosophical arguments in the service of "living knowledge" has a certain precedent in the coopting of Locke's arguments in the service of radical unbelief by the *philosophes* of the French Enlightenment. The German Enlightenment differs from the French Enlightenment—to which it is nevertheless indebted, as the francophone official-language of the Berlin Academy indicates—in being "moderate" on questions of religion. Here one might recall, as a sign of the difference between the German and French Enlightenments,

---

243. Cf. *Seele* 219–22.
244. Here Strauss cites *de Luc* 197.14–23 as well.
245. *Essay Concerning Human Understanding*, I, ch. IV, §18 (Nid 95).
246. That is to say, having overlooked the difference between Locke's understanding of clear and distinct knowledge (which excludes the possibility of clear and distinct knowledge of substances) and Descartes's (which does not), Mendelssohn suspects that Locke's view of immortality may be more or less identical with Descartes's—and his own—after all.
247. Annotation to *Unkörperlichkeit* 167.25–27. Even so, unlike Strauss in a later writing, Mendelssohn does not go on to consider whether Locke may have continued to profess it out of deliberate "caution" rather than sincere conviction; see NRH 203ff., especially 206–9.
248. Loc. cit.

the "rational religion" defended in Spalding's *The Destiny of Man*. As Strauss has already said during his discussion of Spalding in IP, the German Enlightenment (in contrast to the French Enlightenment) stands on the soil of Leibniz and his disciple Wolff.[249] Leibniz in his *Theodicy* had sought to reconcile the truths of religion with the scientific truths of modern Enlightenment by means of his philosophical system—the same system to which Mendelssohn adheres, in its Wolffian version, two generations later. But by Mendelssohn's time Leibniz's system has shown itself to be not as "evident" as may have been hoped. The ongoing attacks on Leibniz-Wolff's system by francophone members of the Academy, which we first met up with in IPM in connection with *Pope a Metaphysician!*, and the various adjustments Mendelssohn himself keeps having to make in defense of that system, indicate that neither Leibniz's own arguments nor those of his first- and second-generation disciples were able to defeat the competing (anti-metaphysical and anti-theological) views of their French ("Cartesian") counterparts. These were at best kept at bay. Meanwhile, as we noted in ITE (and anticipated in IEL), Mendelssohn soon found himself forced to downgrade philosophy itself to the role of defending "living knowledge" (or, eventually and more generally, "sound commonsense"). In IMH and IGC, Strauss will show how the instabilities that show up in both Mendelssohnian philosophy in particular and Cartesian-Leibnizian philosophy in general are two aspects of the same instability. It is the instability inherent in the thought of the German Enlightenment itself insofar as Leibniz may be said to be its philosophical founder.

PRESENTING THE *PHÄDON*'S THOUGHTS TO JEWISH READERS: *THE SOUL* (PUBLISHED POSTHUMOUSLY)

The Soul consists of two posthumously combined treatises Mendelssohn wrote in Hebrew—one on the problem of immortality, the other on the psycho-physical problem.[250] Both treatises were translated into German shortly after their publication in 1787. Strauss found those translations to be too defective for inclusion in JA, however.[251] His brief introduction to the combined treatises (henceforth IS) indicates why they are important enough for him to have retranslated them himself. He says he was guided in his word choices wherever possible by Mendelssohn's own German terminology. Translator's footnotes in my own English version of his

249. See note 238, above.
250. See note 10, above.
251. IS XLI.

translation,[252] therefore, correlate Mendelssohn's key Hebrew terms with Strauss's German equivalents as appropriate.

Brief as it is, IS makes four points about *The Soul*'s content, citing the text as translated by Strauss to document each point. My own brief summary of IS here is guided by his four citations.[253]

(1) As its internal evidence shows, *The Soul*'s "First Treatise,"[254] like the *Treatise on Incorporeality* and *"*On a Handwritten Essay of Mr. de Luc's," is a follow-up to the *Phädon*. When considering various views concerning the soul's moral and intellectual progress after death, and endorsing the view that such progress is not continuous or without relapses, Mendelssohn in the "First Treatise" refers his reader to the fuller discussion of this view in his *Phädon*.[255]

(2) Before conceiving the *Phädon*, Mendelssohn had wanted to write a treatise in Hebrew on the problem of the immortality of the soul for pious Jewish readers who could not or would not read German books. In that treatise, as he says in a 1768 letter quoted by Strauss, he would have taken every opportunity to renounce the Platonic *Phaedo* as an irrelevant distraction to the adherents of the "true religion."[256] Subsequently, however, Mendelssohn decided to make the *Phädon*'s thoughts available also to Jewish readers, even though it was written from the standpoint of "rational religion" rather than of the revelation-believing Jewish tradition. Strauss suggests that Mendelssohn could nevertheless say to himself that letting Jewish readers benefit from the *Phädon*'s thoughts would satisfy a religious obligation on his part, given his underlying conviction that Judaism's doctrines and those of rational religion ultimately coincide. As IS indicates in a footnote, this conviction shows up in the "First Treatise's" opening statement that it will treat the doctrine of the immortality of the soul "insofar as it is a foundation of the Torah."[257]

(3) Whereas in the *Phädon* Mendelssohn writes for a popular readership, in *The Soul* he writes for a more traditional and scholarly readership—as is evidenced, for example, in the "First Treatise's" systematic way of sorting out the options for conceiving moral and intellectual progress after death.[258]

---

252. See www.press.uchicago.edu/sites/strauss/.
253. In addition, Strauss cites *The Soul* at ILT XLI and IGC cn27 and civn62, and in his editorial annotation to *Pope!* 62.19–63.21, translated in appendix 2, supplement to IPM xxn42.
254. *Seele* 203–13.
255. *Seele* 212–13, with *Seele* 212n88.
256. IS XL.
257. *Seele* 203.6–7.
258. See IS XLn9's reference to *Seele* 211.30–213.3.

(4) Finally, as IS mentions, the "Second Treatise"[259] contains Mendelssohn's only detailed statement on the problem of the synthesis of soul and body. Here Mendelssohn is mostly just restating standard Leibniz-Wolffian doctrine, except that he deviates from Leibniz-Wolff in his argument concerning reward and punishment.[260] Since this deviation shows up more fully in *God's Cause*, Strauss postpones considering it further till IGC.

CONFRONTING LESSING'S PUTATIVE SPINOZISM: *MORNING HOURS* (1785) *AND TO THE FRIENDS OF LESSING* (1786)

Strauss divides IMH into two parts. Part I (henceforth IMH-1) deals with the emergence of *Morning Hours* and *To the Friends of Lessing*—by showing, among other things, how they are in effect a single writing. Part II (henceforth IMH-2) analyzes their content. In what follows, I comment on each part separately. Since I have already anticipated much of IMH while recounting Altmann's scholarly disagreement with Strauss about the Pantheism Controversy, I limit myself now to sketching its main contours. As regards each part, I begin by enumerating the main points. I then add a synopsis of Strauss's argument for each point. Meanwhile, I supply footnotes containing further amplifications and cross-references with a view to encouraging readers to examine the details of Strauss's argument (and Mendelssohn's) more directly.

I

IMH-1 makes five main points.[261] (1) *Morning Hours*' own account of its emergence does not disclose the real reason for its emergence, namely, Jacobi's duplicitous report of Lessing's Spinozism, which was intended to disrupt Mendelssohn's original plan to write *Something about Lessing's Character*, a philosophical eulogy of his late friend. (2) Jacobi had two inextricable motives for disrupting Mendelssohn's plan—a philosophical motive having to do with his dissatisfaction with the moderate Enlightenment, which Mendelssohn epitomized for him, and a personal motive having to do with who should carry on Lessing's legacy, Mendelssohn or himself. (3) Mendelssohn soon modified his first, dismissive reaction to Jacobi's disruption, partly out of consideration for Elise Reimarus, the go-between in the

---

259. *Seele* 214–33.
260. *Seele* 213.33ff.
261. For the following, see IMH XI–XVII, XVII–XXX, XXX–XLV (with XLVIII–LI), XLV–LI and LI–LVIII, respectively.

private epistolary controversy that eventually resulted in Mendelssohn's *Morning Hours* and Jacobi's *Spinoza Letters*, each of which was meant by its author to take his opponent by surprise. (4) Defending Lessing's putative Spinozism by construing it as Pantheism ("purified" Spinozism) occurred to Mendelssohn only late in the controversy, despite his claim in *Morning Hours* to have known about it all along. (5) Jacobi's *Spinoza Letters* disabled Mendelssohn's entire defense and crushed his self-esteem by making public Lessing's habitual reticence toward Mendelssohn.

(1) Strauss shows how "from the beginning" the controversy over Lessing's putative Spinozism "was animated and distorted by the prejudices of the two men involved."[262] On the one hand, Jacobi's initial letter to Elise Reimarus about Lessing's Spinozism was a series of deliberate misrepresentations. IMH-1 quotes the letter and lists how each of its assertions runs contrary to Jacobi's behavior then and afterward.[263] Jacobi's letter was thus meant not to inform Mendelssohn but to trap him into a public controversy that Jacobi knew he could win. On the other hand, Strauss does not find Mendelssohn free of deviousness either. In his preface to *Morning Hours*, Mendelssohn asserts that his aim is simply to present lectures on the existence of God (as announced in the book's subtitle). IMH-1 cites the biographical and other evidence, inconclusive as it is, in support of Mendelssohn's assertion.[264] Yet Mendelssohn avoids mentioning his book's true aim, which is to defend Lessing's posthumous reputation preemptively before Jacobi's report became public.

The difficulty Strauss faces in tracing the emergence of *Morning Hours* and *To the Friends of Lessing* is thus bound up with the fact that Jacobi in his attack on Mendelssohn, and Mendelssohn in his defense, each go out of their way to cover their tracks.

(2) To sort out the tangle of philosophical and personal motives animating Jacobi's attack, IMH-1 draws from an earlier controversy with Mendelssohn over Jacobi's *Something that Lessing Said* (1782). Here Jacobi appealed to an oral statement of Lessing's to the effect that "the arguments against Papal despotism either are no arguments at all, or else they are two or three times as valid against the despotism of princes."[265] He expands Les-

---

262. IMH xv.
263. See IMH xv–xvii.
264. See IMH xii–xiv.
265. See IMH xviiin38. I have quoted Strauss's paraphrase of the statement Jacobi reports, as found in ET 58 (reprinted in RCPR 70).

sing's statement into a polemic against any and all despotism.²⁶⁶ Jacobi is a political liberal *avant la lettre*.²⁶⁷ Although his polemic against despotism is reminiscent of Rousseau's, the nerve of his argument is Hobbesian. Jacobi's admiration for Hobbes, which stops short of endorsing Hobbes's despotic conclusions, has to do with the seriousness, rigor, and honesty of Hobbes's argument.²⁶⁸ In this, Strauss remarks, Jacobi "knows himself to be of one mind with Lessing"²⁶⁹ not only politically, in opposing despotism, but also philosophically, in holding that "the inner consistency of the thought" is "more important than the accidental correctness of the result."²⁷⁰

The immediately ensuing controversy over *Something that Lessing Said* ended in a victory for Jacobi, and Strauss wonders why Jacobi did not leave Mendelssohn alone after that. Mendelssohn had drafted some objections and sent these to Jacobi, who with Mendelssohn's consent had part of them published together with another reader's objections; Jacobi then published a reply.²⁷¹ Mendelssohn objected to what he saw as a double bias in Jacobi's argument—a papist bias in arguing against the rights of princes, and a democratic bias in shifting the issue of prince versus pope to that of prince versus people.²⁷² Jacobi countered that to call his argument either papist or

---

266. Jacobi's basic presupposition here is, in Strauss's words, "the elementary rights of man," that is to say, "unconditional claims that would be the source and legitimate basis of the state and to which obligations would remain subservient" (IMH XVIII; cf. also, on Jacobi's presuppositions, IMH LXXVII; on Mendelssohn's, IMH XXVII, XL, XLVI, LXX, LXXI–LXXV).

267. As Strauss notes, Jacobi is guided by the ideal of a political constitution that would limit the power of princes and popes alike so as to leave individuals entirely free to exercise their passions as they wish except for laws protecting property. For Jacobi, he adds, true religion and true virtue are voluntary, not compulsory; compulsion is needed only for governing individuals' passions insofar as these are not guided by "reason"—where Jacobi's citations to Hobbes indicate that this term is understood entirely in the sense of the Enlightenment. On the connection between "reason" and Enlightenment as spelled out in Strauss's subsequent writings, see the epilogue to the present essay. As for the political conclusions themselves that Jacobi draws from the voluntariness of religion and virtue (and which we might be inclined to characterize as libertarian), Strauss calls them "astonishing" (IMH XVIII; cf. IMH LI–LIV, LVI–LVII).

268. See IMH XIX.

269. Cf. also IMH XXIV.

270. IMH XIX.

271. See IMH XIXnn49–50. The objections were edited by Jacobi and, at Jacobi's request, published anonymously by Christian Dohm in the periodical *Deutsches Museum*, which Dohm coedited (Altmann, MMBS 599). For Dohm as an advocate for the civil emancipation of the Jews in Germany, see *Jerusalem* 145, 146n, 200 (Ark 77, 79n, 135), with MMBS, especially 449–71.

272. Mendelssohn, says Strauss, "is manifestly dominated by the original Enlightenment's mistrust of the *vulgus hominum*, given over as they are to the delusion of the priests, and . . . for that reason is not willing to let the alliance between (enlightened) despotism and philosophy totter" (IMH XIX; cf. XXIV, XXVI–XXVII, XXIX–XXXII, XXXVII–XLII, LIII–LIV, LVI–LVII, LVII–LVIII, LXIV–LXIX, LXXI, and *Jerusalem* 103–4, 146–48 [Ark 34–35, 78–80].)

democratic was to misconstrue it.[273] Mendelssohn also objected to Jacobi's taking a deliberately paradoxical statement of Lessing's, however appropriate such a statement might be for purposes of conversation, as if it were a clear and distinct statement appropriate for philosophical instruction.[274] Jacobi's reply emphasized most strongly by far the superior pedagogical merit of conversation whose aim is to improve one's interlocutor in the highest manner by awakening in him the search for truth.[275] Given Jacobi's apt rejoinders, Strauss finds it "almost inexplicable" that this "preliminary skirmish" could have "left a sting in him."[276] On reflection, however, Strauss notes that the controversy was "incomparably more important" for Jacobi than for Mendelssohn. Publishing Mendelssohn's objections to *Something that Lessing Said* was Jacobi's doing rather than Mendelssohn's and allowed the younger, less well-known Jacobi to have "created . . . the occasion" for a public reply. The remainder of IMH-1's discussion of Jacobi's motivation considers the likelihood that it was Mendelssohn's comparative indifference to that controversy that "irritated [Jacobi's] noblest and at the same time his most contemptible impulses in the highest degree." Following out this consideration leads Strauss to look at what Jacobi himself acknowledges owing to Mendelssohn and Lessing, respectively.[277]

On the one hand, Jacobi recalls how as a twenty-year-old he had looked forward to reading Mendelssohn's prizewinning *Treatise on Evidence* but was disappointed with what struck him as its excessive reliance on the on-

---

273. Altmann (MMBS 601) suggests that Jacobi found it incomprehensible that he could have been accused of either a democratic bias, given that he had already repudiated all despotism (and a democratic regime could be a despotism wielded by the democratic majority), or a papist bias, given that Mendelssohn had not bothered to raise the question of whether the papacy was a democracy. "In point of fact," Altmann adds with a view to underscoring Jacobi's incomprehension while at the same time vindicating Mendelssohn's objections, "this particular question *had* been put to Jacobi in Mendelssohn's written remarks, but it had been omitted from the printed text." (See note 271, above.)

274. Here, Strauss observes, Mendelssohn could not help letting his critique of Jacobi pass over into a critique of Lessing's own histrionic philosophizing—of the latter's so-called "theater logic" (see IMH xixn56), an expression originally applied to Lessing in a non-complimentary way by his theological adversary Johann Melchior Goeze (see IMH xxiiin76; cf. All 107ff.). For Mendelssohn's philosophical pedagogy, in contradistinction to Lessing's, see *Jerusalem* 158ff. (Ark 91ff.), including Mendelssohn's criticism of "Education of the Human Race" (*Jerusalem* 162–64; Ark 95–97).

275. Strauss suggests that there is a rather complex irony to Jacobi's reply: addressed as it was to the "German Plato" for whom the dialogues of Plato were "of only limited present-day relevance," it was being advanced instead—peacefully yet incisively—on the basis of "the dialogues of Lessing's" (see IMH xxn57). Cf. the previous note.

276. IMH xx, with xxviii.

277. In his subsequent *David Hume on Belief* and his *Spinoza Letters*, respectively. See, for the following, IMH xxi–xxx.

tological proof of God. His disappointment prompted him to study the ontological proof further on his own, both to expose what was wrong with it and to explain why others were nevertheless persuaded by it. Tracing its historical precedents led him to Spinoza. The ontological proof, he eventually concluded, is the most extreme expression of the tendency to prove everything—to demonstrate everything by way of clear and distinct concepts and to take nothing for granted, a tendency that, if followed out forthrightly, ends up in Spinozism, that is to say, in atheism and fatalism. Since Leibniz-Wolffian philosophy, like Spinozism, rests on demonstration, it too ends up in atheism and fatalism.[278] The only way to avoid these "absurd consequences" according to Jacobi is to hold firmly to "knowledge of ignorance," the original truth underlying demonstration and presupposed by it. Because this truth is not the result of logical demonstration but is a matter of sound commonsense, it cannot be arrived at except by "believing" it beforehand by means of a *salto mortale* or leap of faith. In contrast, the tendency to prove everything stems from arrogance or self-centeredness— from the will to be dependent on nothing outside oneself, hence to control the truth rather than obey it. Here Strauss notes the affinity between Jacobi's opposition to "metaphysical despotism" as epitomized in Spinoza and his opposition to political despotism as epitomized in Hobbes. In both cases, Jacobi preferred the arguments of the "despots"—Hobbes in politics, Spinoza in metaphysics—over those of the less radical, more moderate Leibniz-Wolffians like Mendelssohn, who were seeking a middle-ground between demonstration and sound commonsense.

On the other hand, Jacobi's personal conversations with Lessing during the summer of 1780 confirmed what he had already gathered from reading Lessing's philosophical and theological writings of the past decade.[279] Namely, Lessing no longer adhered either to traditional theology or to the

---

278. Jacobi's critique of Cartesian-Spinozist-Leibnizian philosophy had been preceded by what he had read in Leibniz and Mendelssohn themselves. Leibniz had described Spinozism as "exaggerated Cartesianism" (see IMH xxiin65). Mendelssohn had located Leibniz's doctrine of "preestablished harmony" in Spinoza—together, Jacobi inferred, with "even more of Leibniz's basic doctrines" (see IMH xxii–xxxiiin74). Cf. also LSGS I 260 (SCR 204): ". . . Spinoza is convinced that the denial of sin, and the theological principles which bear out this denial, are capable of being demonstrated by strictly scientific means. Calvin's radical doubt of theory undermines this position. Even if all the reasoning adduced by Spinoza were compelling, nothing would have been proven. Only this much would have been proven: that on the basis of unbelieving science one could not but arrive at Spinoza's results. But would this basis itself thus be justified? It was Friedrich Heinrich Jacobi who posed this question, and by so doing lifted the interpretation of Spinoza—or what amounts to the same thing, the critique of Spinoza—on to its proper plane."

279. See IMH xxiii–xxiv. Cf. All 80–120.

natural theology (or "rational religion") of the Leibniz-Wolffian Enlightenment. Among other things, he confided to Jacobi that his admiration for Leibniz had to do with Leibniz's "grand style of thinking" rather than with this or that opinion or apparent opinion of Leibniz's. While acknowledging both Jacobi's thorough grasp of Spinoza and his general philosophical resourcefulness, he dismissed playfully Jacobi's argument about fatalism and the need for a *salto mortale*. He also expressed himself in such a way that Jacobi could take him to be a Spinozist.[280] Finally, he recommended that Jacobi get to know Mendelssohn as the friend he valued most. It was during the follow-up to this recommendation that Lessing "provided Jacobi with full clarity" not only about fundamental philosophical differences between himself and Mendelssohn concerning natural theology, but also about his deliberate reticence toward Mendelssohn as regards those differences.[281]

On the basis of the foregoing, IMH-1 reconstructs Jacobi's philosophical-personal motives as follows.[282] The fact that Jacobi brought up his youthful disappointment with Mendelssohn's reliance on the ontological argument in a conversation with Lessing seventeen years later indicates how Mendelssohn represented for him the shortcomings of Leibniz-Wolffian demonstrative philosophy. Nor, in Jacobi's view, were these shortcomings offset by Mendelssohn's efforts in the *Treatise on Evidence* to do justice as well to the popular (teleological) proofs of God.[283] Instead he saw Mendelssohn as inconsistent in wanting to hold fast to two incompatible alternatives—demonstration and sound commonsense. Jacobi found such inconsistency both unintelligible and intolerable. Accordingly, he shifted the point of his attack from the "self-centeredness" underlying political and metaphysical despotism to the "ambivalent enablers" of such despotism, Mendelssohn in particular.[284] Being "a sensitive-emotional nature, of no common intellectual passion,"[285] Jacobi took Mendelssohn's critique of *Something that Lessing Said* personally. He saw it as an indifference on Mendelssohn's part to the truth that he, Jacobi, was pursuing. He was particularly annoyed at Mendelssohn's complacency in interpreting a statement of Lessing's, of which he had learned only though Jacobi, so as to "make it innocuous for

---

280. See subsection (3) of IMH-1 and subsection (5) of IMH-2, below.
281. See notes 115–18, above.
282. See IMH xxiv–xxvi.
283. Nor, Strauss adds, by those in his aesthetic investigations to prove the (conditional) priority of "sensuously perfect representations" over clear and distinct concepts (IMH xxv).
284. Cf. IMH xxvi with xcv.
285. IMH xxvii.

his own standpoint."[286] He was also miffed at Mendelssohn's underestimating his own (Jacobi's) philosophical abilities. Last but not least, having learned of Lessing's ongoing reticence toward Mendelssohn, he found himself in possession of secret information that, when divulged, would assure him of victory.

(3) Oddly, Mendelssohn's more than two-year correspondence with Jacobi mentions neither Lessing's "Christianity of Reason" nor the "purified" Spinozism he attributes to Lessing in *Morning Hours* on the basis of it. Strauss combs through the correspondence for clues about when and how these distinctive features of *Morning Hours* must have occurred to Mendelssohn in the run-up to the book. The correspondence consists of twenty or so letters (depending on how one counts their enclosures) written between July 21, 1783, and October 4, 1785, mostly either to, through, or by Elise Reimarus (and/or her brother), including six by Jacobi and nine by Mendelssohn. Strauss probes these as they unfold chronologically.

Mendelssohn's initial response to Jacobi's first communication to Elise Reimarus alleging Lessing's Spinozism was to dismiss it as merely anecdotal. He assured her that Lessing did not understand himself "so simply" in terms of "the system of any man" unless he was either "no longer himself at the time, or in his special humor for asserting something paradoxical."[287] He did find Jacobi's allegation "highly disagreeable," both personally and for the gloating it was likely to provoke among Lessing's theological enemies. But he did not see it as an obstacle to writing *Lessing's Character*, provided that Jacobi would supply more details. Ultimately, Strauss considers this initial response sufficient to ward off Jacobi's allegation of Lessing's Spinozism as such.[288] To be sure, Mendelssohn had not yet read Jacobi's detailed report of his conversations with Lessing, where Jacobi quotes him as stating, "There is no philosophy other than the philosophy of Spinoza." But Jacobi failed to point out in his first communication (or ever) that by this statement Lessing, as Strauss says, "had in no way expressed himself unreservedly in favor of Spinozism." A moment earlier in the conversation, Lessing had said that he knew of no one else besides Spinoza to name himself after *if* he had to name himself after someone. And when a few moments later Jacobi denied that his own credo was in Spinoza, Lessing replied that he hoped that it was not in any book.

286. IMH XXIX.
287. See IMH XXX–XXXI.
288. See IMH XXIII, XXXI, XC–XCI.

All the same, Strauss adds that Mendelssohn could not dismiss the possibility that Lessing, while not exactly a Spinozist, might in his speculative endeavors have distanced himself from Leibniz in the direction of Spinoza. As Strauss goes on to show, Mendelssohn was prompted to confront this possibility partly from his firsthand reading of Jacobi's report and partly from the influence of the Reimarus siblings. By sending Mendelssohn his detailed report via Elise Reimarus unsealed, Jacobi had made it available to her and her brother J. A. H. Reimarus as well. The latter, in a separate note to Mendelssohn that Elise Reimarus then sent him alongside Jacobi's report, did not question the report's reliability. Instead he cautioned Mendelssohn against saying too much about Lessing's Spinozism in his planned writing and hoped that Mendelssohn would "put those delusions that confused the great Spinoza and others after him into a brighter light some day."[289] Remarkably, in his reply to the Reimarus siblings after reading the report (and J. A. H. Reimarus's note), Mendelssohn did not question its reliability either. Nor did he mention any "purified" Spinozism of Lessing's.[290] Rather, he now saw a need to separate himself from Lessing. He considered treating Lessing's Spinozism as a cautionary example of the dangers of philosophical speculation unguided by sound commonsense[291] and postponed the working out of *Lessing's Character* until he could clarify his thoughts about Spinoza with the help of Jacobi and J. A. H. Reimarus.[292] Some weeks later, he informed Elise Reimarus of his decision to work out a Spinoza critique[293]

---

289. See IMH xxxvi. Strauss quotes with approval his JA coeditor Bruno Strauss's remark that the latter statement of J. A. H. Reimarus's was "a first encouragement for *Morning Hours*," inasmuch as Mendelssohn's book was originally conceived as a refutation of Spinoza.

290. IMH xxxiv–xxxv. Mendelssohn also judged favorably Goethe's poem "Prometheus," which Jacobi reports having given Lessing to read prior to their conversations. In *To the Friends of Lessing*, in contrast, he would judge it unfavorably; see IMH xxxivnn139–142. Strauss notes that Mendelssohn had no difficulty understanding Jacobi's implicit purpose in sharing the poem with Lessing: in the light of the theistic tradition, Jacobi et al. saw Spinoza's atheism as Promethean in being a rebellion against God.

291. So *Morning Hours* and *To the Friends of Lessing* would eventually argue; see IMH xxxvii, with note 88, above.

292. Given the ongoing effects of his debilitating disease, Strauss suggests, Mendelssohn felt too weak to undertake the Spinoza critique alone. Cf. Altmann, MMBS 264–71.

293. Strauss sees a threefold significance here: (1) Mendelssohn has given in to Elise Reimarus's pressure to respond to her "fear in the face of a public announcement of Lessing's final sentiments" (IMH xxxvi). (2) Because his critique involves "going back to the first concepts . . . , mainly what substance, truth, and cause are, which what objective existence is seems to come down to mostly . . . ," he announces for the first time the theme and scope of the "Prior Cognition" (First through Seventh Lectures) of *Morning Hours* (IMH xxxviii). (3) That the focus of his critique is to be "objective existence" means that Mendelssohn has now departed from the commonplace view of Spinozism as atheism (according to which God is merely the sum of all finite things) in the direction of the view of Spinozism as divine solipsism or Egoism (according to which finite things do not exist outside the divine understanding)—the view he had originally

and returned Jacobi's report to her brother with a request for feedback. About three and a half months after that, he informed her that, health and leisure permitting, he would abandon *Lessing's Character* altogether in favor of the Spinoza critique.[294] He also expressed a preference for taking on "a definite adversary, with whom we start out from a certain point, presuppose certain principles as given, and then investigate something further."[295]

A few more months passed before Mendelssohn informed Jacobi (via Elise Reimarus) of his plan to write a Spinoza critique. He sent Jacobi a set of Spinoza criticisms he had formulated on the basis of the Spinoza interpretation contained in Jacobi's report. He added the title "Objections of Mr. Jacobi."[296] In return, Jacobi sent Mendelssohn a copy of his "Letter to Hemsterhuis" as a precursory reply to the "Objections."[297] Several months later, Mendelssohn informed Elise Reimarus that a book manuscript containing his Spinoza critique was now in progress, though he had not yet dealt with Spinoza but only with "a sort of revision of the proofs of the existence of God in general."[298] He asked her to request Jacobi's permission "to make public use of his philosophical letters some day."[299] He also asked her to inquire into when he might expect Jacobi's full reply to the "Objections."

---

formulated in his *Philosophical Dialogues* and will use to refute Spinozism in *Morning Hours* (IMH xxxviii, xli). Nevertheless, Strauss adds, he is still far removed from *Morning Hours*'s distinction between authentic or commonplace Spinozism and Lessing's "purified" or acosmic Spinozism.

294. IMH xxxvii–xxxix.
295. See IMH xln167.
296. Mendelssohn's criticisms, says Strauss, are "characterized by a complete misreading of the questions raised by Jacobi." Instead of taking into account Jacobi's own conception of Spinoza as spelled out in the report (Spinozism as fatalism and, ultimately, materialism), Strauss observes, Mendelssohn's "Objections" depart from the commonplace conception (Spinozism as atheism according to which God is merely the sum of all finite things) in the direction of the conception he had originally set forth in his *Philosophical Dialogues* (Spinozism as the denial of the "objective existence" of a world outside God, hence as divine solipsism or "Egoism"). Meanwhile Mendelssohn cannot disregard his own, Leibnizian attribution to God of understanding (*intellectio*)—in contrast to Spinoza himself, who, as Jacobi had emphasized, attributes to God only thought (*cogitatio*) and extension (*extensio*). As a result, he confuses Jacobi's conception of Spinoza with the commonplace conception and suspects Jacobi of being an obscurantist. See IMH xl–xlii.
297. Strauss ascribes the following significance to Mendelssohn's reading of Jacobi's "Letter to Hemsterhuis" as regards the emergence of *Morning Hours*: (1) Like the Fourteenth Lecture of *Morning Hours*, the "Letter" is written in the form of a dialogue. (2) Beginning as it does by distinguishing between Spinoza's "system" and his "geometrical method," it may be presumed to have "again brought Mendelssohn close to the thought of distinguishing explicitly between authentic Spinozism and a more complete form of Spinozism freed from the fetters of the geometrical method (a 'purified' Spinozism)." (3) As in his earlier exposition of Spinozism in the report of his conversations with Lessing, so too in the "Letter," Jacobi emphasizes Spinoza's denial of divine intelligence. See IMH xliii.
298. See IMH xliii.
299. IMH xliv.

He wanted "to hear soon if possible," he explained, "since I must arrange my presentation accordingly."

Owing to a sudden six-week illness of Jacobi's, three more months passed before Mendelssohn received the full reply he had requested—albeit just after he had sent off a letter to Elise Reimarus revising his earlier request for it. He now asked her instead to request that Jacobi "not . . . rush with the response to my 'Objections.'"[300] Another three months later, he asked her to inform Jacobi that a publication concerning their correspondence would appear following the upcoming Leipzig bookfair. In it he hoped "to establish . . . the *status controversiae* and in that way to introduce the quarrel [between them] properly."[301] Two and a half months after that, on October 4, 1785, he sent Jacobi a copy of his newly published *Morning Hours* with a cover letter that concluded by asking for Jacobi's "heartfelt affection and friendship."[302] No sooner was it en route than Mendelssohn—who until then had been confident of having preempted Jacobi by publishing his own account of Lessing's Spinozism first—received a copy of Jacobi's already published *Spinoza Letters*.[303]

What draws Strauss's particular attention in the foregoing is Mendelssohn's sudden reversal in asking Jacobi not to rush with his response to the "Objections."[304] Strauss finds the reversal "surprising in the greatest degree." What had happened, Strauss wonders, during the time since Mendelssohn had asked for Jacobi's response "soon if possible"? What had happened, as IMH-1 goes on to show, was the reemergence of Lessing's "Christianity of Reason" into Mendelssohn's purview. Its reemergence, though independent of the actual correspondence, coincided with the final stage in the writing of *Morning Hours* as documented by the correspondence.

(4) Strauss dates the reemergence of "Christianity of Reason" by the fact that *Morning Hours* cites it in the version found in a collection of Lessing's unpublished theological manuscripts edited posthumously by Lessing's brother for a volume that was to appear in time for the 1785 Easter bookfair in Leipzig.[305] Although Lessing's brother had sent Mendelssohn the original manuscripts two years earlier, in April or May of 1783, to ask whether

---

300. See IMH XLIV–XLV.
301. See IMH L–LI.
302. See IMH LI.
303. For the immediate run-up to Jacobi's decision to publish without informing Mendelssohn, see subsection (5), below.
304. IMH XLIV–XLV.
305. See IMH XLV–XLIX.

they were worth publishing, Strauss finds no evidence that Mendelssohn at that time singled out "Christianity of Reason" or recognized it as a Spinozist document. Not until reading Jacobi's detailed account of his conversations with Lessing, in August of 1783, was he prompted to take seriously the possibility of Lessing's Spinozist leanings. And not until April of 1785 did he read the Lessing manuscripts in their published version.

Reading "Christianity of Reason" in its published version, moreover, occurred just as Mendelssohn was about to receive, as part of Jacobi's response to the "Objections," a specific reply to his criticism of Spinoza for "want[ing] to let the limited emerge out of the aggregate of the unlimited."[306] Jacobi's reply was that, *pace* Mendelssohn, the sum of all finite things for Spinoza is no mere aggregate but "a whole whose parts can only be in it and in accord with it, and be thought in it and in accord with it." This reply was indispensable for how Mendelssohn came to formulate *Morning Hours*' Pantheistic ("purified") alternative to his prior notion of Spinozism as divine solipsism—a notion Mendelssohn had conceived in his *Philosophical Dialogues* of 1755 and had appealed to in his "Objections." Of the "purified" Spinozism attributed to Lessing in *Morning Hours*, Mendelssohn now says—departing from his prior notion and in quasi-agreement with Jacobi's reply—that "the one necessary being" (that is to say, "God or nature") is "infinite in its unity and in accord with its power."

(5) Jacobi learned of Mendelssohn's intent to publish what would turn out to be *Morning Hours* from Elise Reimarus in late May of 1785.[307] He rejected the advice of his friends Hamann and Herder that he publish his conversations with Lessing by themselves, apart from his correspondence with Mendelssohn. Instead Jacobi preferred to let the events he had set in motion "take their historical course quietly."[308] After waiting two more months in vain for Mendelssohn's acknowledgment of his reply to the "Objections" (which he had sent to Mendelssohn in late April) and remaining unsure of what Mendelssohn would say in *Morning Hours* either about Lessing's Spinozism or about Jacobi himself, he decided in July of 1785 to preempt Mendelssohn by publishing his own record of the correspondence, with a conclusion devoted to a critique of the Enlightenment. To undercut Mendelssohn's credibility as regards Lessing, he included in the record Lessing's statement concerning his habitual reticence toward Mendelssohn.

306. See IMH XLVIII–XLIX.
307. See, for the following, IMH LI–LVIII.
308. See IMH LI–LII, with LVIInn258, 261.

Strauss describes how devastating Jacobi's disclosure of Lessing's reticence was to Mendelssohn personally.[309] The deep anguish discernible in Mendelssohn's letter to Kant of October 16, 1785, and in a related passage in *To the Friends of Lessing*, Strauss suggests, can be accounted for only as the shock effect of Mendelssohn's sudden exposure to a barrier that had separated him from Lessing all along; it cannot be accounted for as mere annoyance over Jacobi's having outwitted and outmaneuvered him. Mendelssohn's "unreserved friendship with Lessing" was, as Strauss puts it, "the oldest and most trustworthy bridge that connected him with [the non-Jewish] world at all, the testimony most precious to him of the possibility of complete understanding between men of opposite background." Nor, Strauss adds, can Mendelssohn's residual distrust of that world be traced to mere "pathological sensitivities" on his part, since on the contrary he was "as free of [these] as any human being can be" and "bore no greater distrust than what is justified sufficiently by the experiences of the Jews at all times."[310] Here Strauss seems to have in mind as well his own Germany of the 1930s,[311] as he goes on to say that even though the "natural hatred against the Jews" did not yet have at its disposal the principle of nationalism (as, of course, Nazism did have), nevertheless "the anti-Jewish theory and practice of the Christian Churches [which show up in Mendelssohn's theological adversaries Bonnet and Lavater et al.][312] supplied it with weapons scarcely less effective."

IMH-1 concludes by reflecting on the moral cowardice that tainted Jacobi's intellectual daring.[313] That Jacobi as a tactician was far superior to Mendelssohn, Strauss sees mirrored in the ineptness of Mendelssohn's countermeasures. Jacobi's cowardice, on the other hand, shows up in his self-pity[314] mixed with his brutal disregard for others[315]—a mixture Strauss traces to Jacobi's uninhibited self-esteem that presented itself as love of freedom (as in his *Something that Lessing Said*). While Strauss suggests that the self-esteem is attributable to the combined influence of Rousseau and "the general

---

309. IMH LIII–LVI.
310. Consider Strauss, SCR 1–7 or LAM 224–31.
311. Consider Strauss's preliminary remark to his unwritten book on Lessing, dated 1937 and conceived as his personal farewell to his native Germany (see appendix 1). Cf. SCR 2 or LAM 225–26.
312. See IMH LIVn240. Jacobi "had let himself get carried away" with an appeal to Lavater at the conclusion of his *Spinoza Letters* (IMH LV).
313. See, for the following, IMH LVI–LVII.
314. See, e.g., IMH XXVIIInn104–5, XXXIIIn133.
315. See, e.g., IMH LVIIn261.

revolutionary movement of that time,"[316] Jacobi's brutality needs a further explanation. Strauss locates it in "the complete absence [in Jacobi] of the *'générosité'* that, however questionable, formed the revolutionary spirit's patent of nobility."[317] Probing Strauss's statement here, we may recall that Descartes, for one, had identified "generosity" with "esteem[ing] nothing more highly than doing good to other men"[318] and had appealed to it as the virtue proper to scientists carrying out and disseminating their research in the service of universal popular Enlightenment.[319] Strauss suggests in this way that, had this virtue such as it is been present in Jacobi, it might have curbed the brutality and dishonesty inseparable from his elaborate sneak attack on Mendelssohn.[320] In contrast, Mendelssohn's tactical ineptitude testifies to his basic guilelessness and, Strauss editorializes, "calls forth our compassion rather than our protest."

II

IMH-2 analyzes the content that distinguishes *Morning Hours* and *To the Friends of Lessing* from Mendelssohn's earlier writings,[321] including his reflections on truth, appearance, and error in *Morning Hours'* introduction,[322] his critique of Spinozism and his related attempt at a new proof of God, his critique of Jacobi's philosophy of belief, and especially his interpretation of Lessing's philosophical endeavors. Mendelssohn's reflections on truth, appearance, and error draw IMH-2's attention first, since these lay the groundwork for discussions of the (problematic) relationship between philosophical speculation and sound commonsense that "run through the two writings like a scarlet thread" and, in so doing, serve to unify them as a whole.[323] Accordingly, the two writings document "the final crisis of modern metaphysics of the Cartesian-Leibnizian stamp." They contain "the solutions to this crisis that were being taken up within Mendelssohn's pur-

---

316. IMH LVII.
317. See IMH LVII. Cf. also Strauss, PPH 36–37.
318. Descartes, *Les passions de l'âme* §156 (AT XI 447–48; *Passions of the Soul*, trans. Vos 105). Similarly, "generosity" for Spinoza is "the longing by which, solely on the basis of the dictate of reason, each endeavors to help others and join them to himself in friendship" (*Ethica*, pt. III, prop. 59 schol. [Geb II 188; cf. WhSt 145]).
319. Cf. Kennington, *On Modern Origins*, 197–201.
320. See *inter alia* Jacobi's own statement to that effect, quoted at IMH LVII, to which, Strauss says, "[Jacobi's] conscience did not raise an objection."
321. See IMH LIX–LX.
322. I.e., First through Seventh Lectures, subtitled "Prior Cognition."
323. IMH LIX–LX.

view." IMH-2's analysis of *Morning Hours* and *To the Friends of Lessing* is thus, at the same time, an analysis of those "solutions":[324] (1) the philosophy of sound commonsense, (2) Spinozism, (3) Jacobi's philosophy of belief, and (4) the philosophizing of Lessing.

(1) Leibniz's metaphysics recommended itself to Mendelssohn, in preference to the Neo-Platonism with which he identified premodern metaphysics, for its putatively superior concept of the value of the human body as a "divine creation" and for its demonstrations that each human soul is guided by special providence in this world and is destined for eternal happiness in the next.[325] Unlike the earlier metaphysics, modern metaphysics in general (and Leibniz's in particular) rested on "the conviction that God has created man for man's happiness without placing all too high demands on him"—a conviction accompanied by demonstrations of the existence of God as "a supremely benevolent being." In this connection, Mendelssohn himself speaks of his "rather Epicurean" theism. He means that (in IMH-2's words) it removes "the terrors of superstition and the despair of unbelief" by vindicating "an, as it were, just claim to a further progress to higher perfections [*sc.*, after death]" without requiring human beings to scale back their claims to happiness in this life.

Central to Strauss's analysis here is that Mendelssohn never questioned the presuppositions of his modern (Leibnizian) metaphysics, only the adequacy of the particular demonstrations integral to it.[326] IMH-2 thus shows how Mendelssohn's ongoing confrontations with the difficulties arising from the demonstrative character of modern metaphysics took place within a narrower purview than they might have if it had occurred to him to question those presuppositions—as it had occurred to Lessing to question them.

Strauss traces the difficulties to Descartes's project to replace our "prejudices" about the world with a "clear and distinct" understanding of the world.[327] Descartes's project was designed to secure human beings' peace of mind by disseminating truths about the world such as are ascertainable through scientific demonstration. A lingering difficulty here, however, was that the demonstrated truths could be properly expressed only in the language of mathematical physics—yet this language could not be fully absorbed into "popular" language as required for the purpose of "Enlighten-

---

324. IMH LX.
325. See, for the following, IMH LVIII–LXIII.
326. Cf., however, IGC c1ff.
327. See, for the following, IMH LXIII–LXIV.

ment." Since commonsense could therefore only go so far in assimilating the truths being transmitted to it by Cartesian-Leibnizian metaphysics, it soon dismissed that metaphysics as obscurantist and looked around for new alternatives. These alternatives entered Mendelssohn's purview as the philosophy of sound commonsense (to which he himself gradually inclined) and the other three "solutions" listed above.

Mendelssohn arrived at the philosophy of sound commonsense after going through three prior stages.[328] I have already mentioned (in my remarks on IEL) how in his early *On the Sentiments* Mendelssohn looked to "taste" as the needed complement to metaphysical demonstration. In Strauss's formulation: "whereas reason is the authoritative faculty in the realm of the theoretical and the moral, reason is subject to another authority [namely, taste] in the realm of the beautiful"—a division of authority that Mendelssohn favored initially, Strauss suggests, as a "civilized" thinker in the pre-Rousseauian sense of the term. In his *Treatise on Evidence*, however, Mendelssohn had to confront the difficulty that metaphysical demonstrations of ethical principles were "less illuminating, less perspicuous, than even those in the first principles of metaphysics or natural theology." As we have already seen (in ITE), he argued there that although such demonstrations, while certain, were not perspicuous, this difficulty could be offset by assigning to metaphysical demonstration the practical role of defending ethical principles that already commanded assent as "living knowledge," whenever those principles came under attack from "hairsplitting doubts." Yet subsequently, being forced by Bonnet and Lavater to defend his Judaism and his Rationalism at the same time, Mendelssohn in his writings against them, and above all in his *Jerusalem*, did so by construing Judaism as a "rational religion." Given that the biblical teaching itself is not demonstrative, however, his defense of Judaism was possible (in IMH-2's words) "only in such a manner as to limit considerably the significance and legitimacy of demonstration." Hence Mendelssohn's final view of the relation between demonstrative philosophy and sound commonsense, in *Morning Hours* and *To the Friends of Lessing*, is that (as IMH-2 says) "reason . . . has to be subjugated to sound commonsense, without whose guidance it necessarily errs; the sound commonsense of the simple-minded is the authority for reason."

(2) Although Spinoza wrote a generation before Leibniz, it was Leibniz who inadvertently prepared Germany for Spinozism, as IMH-2 shows.[329]

---

328. See, for the following, IMH LXIV–LXIX.
329. See, for the following, IMH LXX–LXXV.

The metaphysical presuppositions by which Leibniz's *Theodicy* justified creation and providence also justified Determinism and Optimism—doctrines akin to Spinoza's, which denied divine creation and special providence in favor of something like emanationism or kabbalism. On the one hand, then, the German reception of Spinozism in the late-1700s was a sign of "a considerable progress in unbelief."[330] On the other hand, it was also a sign of "the reawakening of speculative seriousness," following decades when scientific materialism and other non- or anti-metaphysical doctrines held sway. As Mendelssohn saw, however, there remained the difficulty of how Spinozism would be absorbed into the concepts of sound commonsense. With its denial of divine creation and special providence, Spinozism was much more threatening to Mendelssohn's position than doctrines like scientific materialism, which he had confronted in his earlier writings. Not surprisingly, then, Mendelssohn's confrontation with Spinoza "forced him into a more radical meditation on his own presuppositions than any other confrontation carried out by him." Even so, Mendelssohn never undertook to confront Spinoza directly; *Morning Hours* mostly recycles the standard Spinoza critique of his fellow Leibniz-Wolffians. The Spinoza critique peculiar to him is instead a critique of Lessing's "purified" Spinozism—a circumstance that corroborates the argument of IMH-1 that Mendelssohn's real motive for *Morning Hours* was his interest in Lessing.

I have already summarized what IMH-2 says about Mendelssohn's critique of Spinozism, and the "hidden presupposition" underlying that critique, while comparing Strauss with Altmann earlier.[331] Here I merely recall the inference Strauss draws from the fact that, in the course of criticizing Spinozism for its failure to account for the self, Mendelssohn casually switches between conceiving the self as an image whose archetype is a thought of God's and, vice versa, conceiving that same thought of God's as an image whose archetype is the self. At this point, says Strauss, Mendelssohn comes as close as he ever does to recognizing his presupposition that God and the human self are in some sense equals. More exactly, to

---

330. Here Strauss contrasts the Mendelssohn-Jacobi controversy of the late 1700s with the Leibniz-Bayle controversy of the early 1700s. The earlier controversy turned on whether a natural theology that contradicted belief in revelation in every important detail was in harmony with a revelation-believing religion that was still unshaken in the popular mind (Leibniz saying yes, Bayle saying no). The later controversy turns on whether doctrines arrived at via demonstrations that also lead to atheism are equivalent to doctrines based on "belief" construed as naturally theistic (Mendelssohn saying yes, Jacobi saying no). In the later controversy, the possibility of demonstrating God's existence by starting from creation or nature is no longer taken for granted, and revelation as such is no longer part of the discussion. Cf. LSGS II 10–15; PL 23–26.

331. See, for the following, notes 68–73, above.

counter Spinozism's denial of divine creation and special providence, Mendelssohn can only oppose to it, or rather presuppose following Leibniz, the view that all selves (or, to use Leibniz's term, "monads") are to be thought of as citizens in the City of God, understood on the analogy of a constitutional monarchy whose individual subjects have, in principle, autonomous rights over against their Chief of State.[332] Mendelssohn elaborates this view further in his confrontation with Leibniz in *God's Cause*—although as IGC will show, he does not come to grips with its full implications there either.

(3) Mendelssohn's philosophical position is closer to Jacobi's than to Spinoza's.[333] Both Mendelssohn and Jacobi agree that metaphysics' attempts to demonstrate belief's concept of God have collapsed, and both identify metaphysics with modern metaphysics. They differ in how their respective appeals to "belief" (Jacobi) and "sound commonsense" (Mendelssohn) are meant to offset that collapse. For Mendelssohn in *Morning Hours*, the convictions to be demonstrated by reason are the same as those of sound commonsense. For Jacobi (in his controversy with Mendelssohn, anyway), the two sets of convictions differ fundamentally, since reason is proud (in wanting to control the truth rather than obeying it) whereas belief is humble (in obeying the truth rather than wanting to control it). Mendelssohn objects to Jacobi's position[334] as he understands it that to make belief the basis for reason is to blur the difference between them, hence to promote prejudice and superstition. But Strauss indicates how Mendelssohn misunderstands Jacobi here. If the conclusions of reason in its defense of the existence of God and the immortality of the soul are interchangeable with the convictions of sound commonsense (as they are for Mendelssohn), then these convictions could appear as self-evident truths and therefore as not in need of further justification by independent rational speculation. If, however, the convictions in question are instead matters of deliberate, self-conscious belief (as they are for Jacobi), then they might well imply knowledge of ignorance and thereby motivate independent rational speculation. Contra Mendelssohn, Strauss infers, belief as Jacobi understands it "is much less of a danger to speculation than sound commonsense is."

Strauss traces Mendelssohn's misunderstanding of Jacobi in part to Ja-

---

332. The Sixteenth Lecture's related proof for God's existence, which "passes instinctively" from the incompleteness of our self-knowledge to the incompleteness of our knowledge of anything else, likewise starts by privileging the self "as the most indubitable case of an actual thing." See IMH LXXV.
333. See, for the following, IMH LXXV–LXXVII.
334. Since Mendelssohn in *Morning Hours* says nothing about his correspondence with Jacobi, he makes Bernhard Basedow the target of this objection instead; see IMH LXVIIn323.

cobi's misleading manner of expression, which in turn is grounded in Jacobi's obliviousness of the full implications of his Spinoza critique. Jacobi criticizes Spinoza for failing to account for human thought's ability to direct human action: "in all things," says Jacobi of Spinoza, "action precedes reflection, *which is only the action in its° continuation.*"[335] This same view, Strauss adds, is the presupposition of Jacobi's overall criticism of the Enlightenment. But Jacobi's criticism of the Enlightenment is unsustainable. For if, as Jacobi puts it, "every age has its own truth, . . . its own living philosophy, which presents the age's predominant way of acting *in its continuation,*"[336] then what basis is there for judging the distinctive shortcomings of the Enlightenment (or of any historical period, for that matter)? Here Strauss finds Jacobi's thought to be at bottom self-contradictory. Jacobi, we may say, is in this regard a historicist *avant la lettre*.[337]

(4) IMH-2's concluding paragraphs assess Mendelssohn's defense of Lessing. To begin with, Strauss probes why Mendelssohn avails himself of the dialogue form in the Fourteenth and Fifteenth Lectures of *Morning Hours*. He does so, Strauss argues, to prepare the public for the shock of Jacobi's impending exposé of Lessing's Spinozism by letting readers absorb in advance a weakened version of that shock. As we have already seen,[338] the Fourteenth Lecture is in the form of an imaginary dialogue between Mendelssohn[339] and Lessing on the fictional supposition that Lessing had been present to hear Mendelssohn's refutation of Spinozism in the Thirteenth Lecture. Objecting to the inadequacy of Mendelssohn's refutation, "Lessing" discloses his "purified" Spinozism and offers the reassurance that it is distinguished from the theism of the Leibniz-Wolffian Enlightenment only by a metaphysical subtlety that has no effect on morals. The Fifteenth Lecture too is in the form of an imaginary dialogue, in this case between Mendelssohn and a fictional "Friend D.," a longstanding close acquaintance of Lessing's who is well-versed in Lessing's writings and who doubts Mendelssohn's claim in the Fourteenth Lecture that Lessing was a "purified" Spinozist. D. suggests instead that Lessing abandoned Leibniz-Wolffian theism for the radical-Rationalist Christianity of the Fragmentist. Correct-

335. See IMH LXXVII (the emphasis is Jacobi's). Cf. PPH 105.
336. *Ibid.* (the emphasis is Jacobi's).
337. For the later Strauss's critique of historicism, see especially NRH 9–34, WPP 56–77.
338. See notes 64–70, above.
339. Strauss calls the intra-dialogical Mendelssohn "M.," to indicate the distinction between the opinions voiced by him within the dialogue and those of Mendelssohn himself apart from the dialogue.

ing D. within the parameters of the dialogue, Mendelssohn replies that Lessing had been a "purified" Spinozist all along and cites as documentary evidence Lessing's "Christianity of Reason." The Fourteenth and Fifteenth Lectures thus aim to reduce the shock of the public disclosure of Lessing's Spinozism in two ways—by making the disclosure part of a fictional dialogue and by reassuring the reader that Lessing's "purified" Spinozism was morally harmless.

Still, Mendelssohn's dialogical presentation does not offer a straightforward answer to the more basic questions: what is his actual view of Lessing's philosophizing, and is it accurate? These questions occupy the remainder of IMH-2.

Mendelssohn's actual view, says Strauss, can be arrived at only from "occasional, if always sparse statements of his [in his other writings and his correspondence] . . . applied as a standard for the critique of the portrayal in *Morning Hours*."[340] Chief among these is Mendelssohn's characterization of Lessing, in a letter to him in May of 1763, as a "brother in Leibniz." Strauss finds no evidence that Mendelssohn had any reason to doubt this characterization before reading Jacobi's report of his Lessing conversations in the autumn of 1783. Rather, given Mendelssohn's initial response on receiving Jacobi's first communication from Elise Reimarus in August of 1783—namely that, *pace* Jacobi, Lessing did not understand himself "so simply, without any closer determination, in terms of the system of any man"—Strauss infers that until then Mendelssohn must have viewed Lessing as no more than an independent-minded Leibnizian. Nor could Mendelssohn help knowing, from reading "Leibniz on Eternal Punishments" and "The Education of The Human Race," that what prompted Lessing's abandonment of Leibniz-Wolffian theism was his preference for what Strauss calls Leibniz's "genuine" doctrine and not, as Friend D. is made to say, for the radical-Rationalist theism of the Fragmentist.[341] Hence, Strauss infers, Mendelssohn in *Morning Hours* must have ascribed "purified" Spinozism to Lessing "just because

---

340. IMH LXXXIII.
341. Strauss characterizes D.'s assertion as "the popular, exoteric version of the opinion that Mendelssohn had of Lessing's belief originally, i.e., until Jacobi's communication . . . the Lessing for the school and home use of the Enlightenment" (IMH LXXXVIII–LXXXIX). In this context, Strauss indicates that Jacobi has a point in doubting (or, in Jacobi's case, mocking) D.'s attempt to infer on the basis of *Nathan the Wise* that Lessing personally subscribed to a theistic doctrine of providence as opposed to a Spinozist *amor fati* (Strauss uses this Nietzschean expression for "love of fate"). On "love of fate" in Nietzsche and Spinoza as spelled out in Strauss's subsequent writings, see the epilogue to the present essay.

he could not possibly represent before the public that his late friend had distanced himself even further from the predominant view [than D. asserts he had]." This is proved, says Strauss, by Mendelssohn's allowing "purified" Spinozism to be presented only by the fictional Lessing, by his ascribing "purified" Spinozism to the actual Lessing only after he has "completely destroyed" D.'s assertion, and by his ascribing it "only in a certain roundabout way," namely, by identifying "purified" Spinozism with Pantheism.[342]

In sum, then, the substance of Mendelssohn's reply to Jacobi's thesis that Lessing was a Spinozist is twofold. First, Lessing's philosophizing cannot be reduced to any "system." Second, Lessing's having "purified" Spinozism means that his philosophizing is at bottom independent of Spinozism.[343] Strauss finds both these claims accurate, as far as they go. In addition, however, Mendelssohn claims longstanding personal familiarity with Lessing's "purified" Spinozism. Strauss contests this claim by examining, in turn, three writings from Lessing's and Mendelssohn's early periods as authors: Lessing's "Christianity of Reason," which Lessing had "read aloud" to Mendelssohn "right at the beginning of [their] acquaintance"; Mendelssohn's *Philosophical Dialogues*, whose Second Dialogue aims to show how "Spinoza's system could be consistent with reason and religion"; and Lessing's "On the Actuality of Things Outside God," which was addressed to Mendelssohn personally.

In "Christianity of Reason," the young Lessing "distanced himself from Leibniz's doctrine by the adoption of Spinozistic thoughts"—namely, by asserting that "to envisage, to will, and to create" are "one thing in God" (§3) and perhaps also that "there *could possibly* be infinitely many worlds, if God were not always thinking the most perfect one" (§15). Still, says Strauss, there is nothing to show that Mendelssohn ever thought of Lessing as a Spinozist at that time.[344]

Mendelssohn's *Philosophical Dialogues*, a writing influenced stylistically by Lessing, construes Spinozism as the doctrine that "all visible things down to this hour were to be found merely in the divine understanding."[345] Admittedly, this doctrine is the same as the "purified" Spinozism of *Morning Hours*, and Mendelssohn puts it in the mouth of a fictional interlocutor who resembles Lessing, who asserts that Leibniz adopted his doctrine of preestablished harmony from Spinoza, and who "behaves toward Leibniz

---

342. IMH LXXXIX–XC.
343. *Ibid.*
344. IMH XCI–XCIII.
345. IMH XCIIIn449, with XXXVIIIn157.

as a doubting admirer and an admiring doubter."[346] Nevertheless, Strauss notes that the real Lessing during this period presents himself as a Leibnizian rather than a Spinozist. Despite Lessing's glowing praise of the *Philosophical Dialogues* at the time of its publication, his letter to Mendelssohn of April 17, 1763, expresses doubts about Mendelssohn's tracing the doctrine of preestablished harmony to Spinoza and wonders "that no Leibnizian has taken up against you yet." Also, there is Mendelssohn's aforementioned letter to Lessing the following month that characterizes him as "a brother in Leibniz."[347]

And even if Mendelssohn wrote the Fourteenth Lecture of *Morning Hours* with Lessing's "On the Actuality of Things Outside God" in mind, Strauss argues, he could not have thought of Lessing as a "purified" Spinozist when Lessing wrote it in 1763, given that he also characterized Lessing that year as a "brother in Leibniz." Furthermore, had Mendelssohn come to that thought prior to Jacobi's first communication to Elise Reimarus, some vestige of it would have shown up in his answer to Jacobi.[348] Nor would Lessing himself have undertaken to "purify" or "refine" Spinozism except to supply what he elsewhere calls, with reference to Horace, "a lovely quintessence" whereby one might avoid "every suspicion of freethinking"—that is to say, except to provide "exoteric" cover for the inner freedom of thought that characterizes philosophizing in Horace's (and Lessing's) sense.[349] Perhaps, Strauss editorializes, Lessing himself "would not have been ashamed" of Jacobi for having noted as much in his *Against Mendelssohn's Accusations in His "To the Friends of Lessing."*[350]

CONFRONTING LEIBNIZ: *GOD'S CAUSE* (1774; NOT PUBLISHED DURING MENDELSSOHN'S LIFETIME)

As the *Phädon* was Mendelssohn's recasting of Plato's *Phaedo*, so *God's Cause* is his recasting of Leibniz's *Causa Dei*.[351] *Causa Dei* is the appendix to Leibniz's *Theodicy* (1710), his systematic defense of God's justice. In *Causa Dei*,

---

346. The interlocutor, Neophil, is seen to admire Leibniz's philosophical prudence in ways that anticipate Lessing's "Leibniz on Eternal Punishments" and "Vindication of Wissowatius" (IMH XCIII–XCIV).
347. IMH XCIII–XCIV.
348. IMH XCIV–XCV.
349. See IMH XCVn464, with Strauss's editorial annotation to *Pope!* 51.27–36, translated in appendix 2, supplement to IPM XVIIIn24. Also, note 382, below.
350. IMH XCV, with LXXXVII–LXXXIX.
351. For the full title of Leibniz's Latin appendix, see IGC XCVI.

Leibniz compresses his *Theodicy*'s overall argument into 144 Latin aphorisms. These include compressed versions of the *Theodicy*'s defenses of the Christian doctrines of sin and grace and of eternal punishments post mortem for the wicked. Mendelssohn begins the eighty-four aphorisms of *God's Cause* by imitating his Leibnizian model rather closely. As Strauss points out, §§1–69 of *God's Cause* are mostly a literal translation of Leibniz's Latin into Mendelssohn's German, except where Mendelssohn departs from his model now and then to correct doctrines he finds unacceptable in *Causa Dei* and to substitute Jewish references for Leibniz's Christian references. This is not surprising, since, as Strauss notes, Leibniz is Mendelssohn's highest philosophical authority. Yet Mendelssohn departs from his Leibnizian model altogether and formulates his own aphorisms, even where in substance he agrees with Leibniz, once *Causa Dei* turns thematically to the Christian doctrine of sin and grace, from §70 on. By then, Mendelssohn has also polemicized against Leibniz on eternal punishments, in §§55–60. Mendelssohn's polemic draws Strauss's particular attention. Since *God's Cause* is the only writing where Mendelssohn attacks his highest philosophical authority, in it "the views peculiar to him are brought out in the sharpest possible way."[352] These views, IGC goes on to say, are not Mendelssohn's alone. They are "the common coin of the later German Enlightenment,"[353] for which the success of Leibniz's system is "a self-evident possession." Ultimately, IGC finds the differences between *God's Cause* and *Causa Dei* to be "a thoughtful expression" of how the Enlightenment in Germany has progressed since Leibniz.

As IP examined the substantive differences between Mendelssohn and Plato by starting from where the *Phädon* departs from its Platonic model, so IGC examines the substantive differences between Mendelssohn and Leibniz by starting from where *God's Cause* departs from its Leibnizian model. IP characterized the *Phädon* as a "softening" of Plato's "sternness" as regards the immortality of the soul.[354] Similarly, we may say that IGC characterizes *God's Cause* as a softening of Leibniz's sternness as regards God's justice— except that its focus is theological rather than "anthropological," as was IP's. Theologically speaking, Strauss finds that the differences between Leibniz and Mendelssohn cannot be arrived at quite so straightforwardly. IGC

---

352. IGC CI, with CVIII–CIX.
353. Cf. IP XVII.
354. See IP XIX–XXIV.

considers various ways of characterizing those differences:³⁵⁵ (1) whereas Leibniz is a Christian, Mendelssohn is a Jew; (2) whereas Leibniz defends religious orthodoxy, Mendelssohn advances religious Enlightenment; (3) whereas Leibniz emphasizes God's wisdom, Mendelssohn emphasizes God's benevolence; (4) whereas Leibniz writes for philosophical readers, Mendelssohn popularizes Leibniz for theological readers. Each of these characterizations is seen to be true as far as it goes, though none tells the whole story.

(1) That *God's Cause* is not simply Mendelssohn's confrontation qua Jew with Leibniz qua Christian is shown as follows. Besides attacking Leibniz, *God's Cause* also disparages Christian doctrines as such. Strauss infers from this that *God's Cause* was not meant for publication.³⁵⁶ At the same time, he rebuts the presumption that *God's Cause* is either a fragment or else a draft or preliminary study for some other Mendelssohnian writing.³⁵⁷ Instead Strauss considers what might have prompted Mendelssohn to write *God's Cause* as a self-standing book at all.³⁵⁸ First, he notes, *God's Cause* has the same subject—the problem of theodicy—as the Third Dialogue of the *Phädon*, which, as IP has shown, Mendelssohn originally wrote in response to Abbt's objections concerning the Leibniz-Wolffian doctrine of providence and afterward planned to revise in response to Herder's objections concerning that Dialogue but never got around to.³⁵⁹ Second, given Mendelssohn's use of Hebrew citations in it, *God's Cause* must have been written for Jewish readers, or rather, in the absence of any intent to publish, for Jewish readers he knew personally. Finally, Mendelssohn wrote *God's Cause* in 1784, at or around the time he was also instructing his teenage son Joseph and two other young men in natural theology.³⁶⁰ From these considerations, Strauss infers that what prompted *God's Cause* might well have been Mendelssohn's need to rethink the problem of theodicy for the same purpose he reports in his preface to *Morning Hours*, namely, that of guiding his son (and two other Jewish Leibnizians-to-be) "at an early age to the knowledge of God."

(2) That Mendelssohn has written *God's Cause* from the point of view

---

355. See IGC xcvii–ci, ci–ciii, ciii–cv, cv–cx, respectively.
356. IGC xcvii–xcviii.
357. IGC xcix–ci.
358. Since *God's Cause* remained not only unpublished but also without any direct report of the circumstances of its emergence except that Mendelssohn wrote it in 1784, Strauss is left to infer how it emerged from its content alone (IGC xcvi).
359. See IP xvi–xvii, xxxff.
360. See IMH xii–xiii.

of advancing religious Enlightenment rather than defending religious orthodoxy, Strauss gathers from the following.[361] While dropping Leibniz's Christian references, Mendelssohn does not always replace them with Jewish references. He makes far fewer such references and takes them less seriously than Leibniz. Unlike Leibniz, he also avoids specifically religious terminology. Particularly illuminating in all this is that where Leibniz defers explicitly to "the truly Orthodox,"[362] Mendelssohn substitutes "the true religion of reason" (§2). Here Mendelssohn distances himself qua man of reason from Leibniz qua religiously orthodox.[363] His self-distancing from religious orthodoxy helps explain an otherwise incongruous fact. Namely, Mendelssohn opens his polemic against Leibniz by charging him with accepting a doctrine of mercenary morality—what Mendelssohn calls the "universal popular ethical doctrine" to the effect that "every virtue would result in a reward"—rather than the "higher ethical doctrine of the wise" that the reward for virtue is simply virtue (§55).[364] Taken at face value, the charge is unsustainable, as Strauss points out. Not only do Leibniz and Christian doctrine agree with Judaism in ranking nonmercenary morality above mercenary morality, but from what Mendelssohn says elsewhere he would have to concede that Judaism too must occasionally adapt its ethical doctrines to the vulgar imagination.[365] Mendelssohn's charge makes sense, then, only as the expression of an underlying "struggle."[366] As Strauss goes on to show, the struggle is less about virtue and reward than about vice and punishment—more exactly, about the harshness of punishments. Since the terms of the struggle are not fully spelled out in *God's Cause* itself, Strauss soon turns to its deep background in Leibniz's *Theodicy*.

(3) The struggle shows up in *God's Cause* as a disagreement over whether the harshest possible punishment—eternal damnation—is theologically justifiable. As Strauss documents, Mendelssohn assumes Leibniz's concep-

---

361. IGC CI–CII.
362. Strauss indicates parenthetically, as well as in the remainder of IGC, that Leibniz's explicit deference to religious orthodoxy is not his final word. Cf. the remarks of Mendelssohn's Neophil (a character in his *Philosophical Dialogues* who is meant to resemble Lessing) on Leibniz, which Strauss quotes at IMH XCIV.
363. Strauss ascribes Mendelssohn's tendency to distance himself from religious orthodoxy to his being "a philosopher [*Weltweise*] in the style of the eighteenth century" (IGC CII; cf. IPM XVIIIn23).
364. IGC CII–CIII.
365. See IGC CIIInn53–54.
366. Cf. IP XVII, where Strauss attributes to Mendelssohn and his fellow adherents of "rational religion" a "struggle not only against the scholastic tradition, but against tradition simply, against 'prejudices' simply, especially against the traditions of the revealed religions."

tion of justice as benevolence governed by wisdom.[367] Here Leibniz puts the emphasis on God's wisdom. This means that the main purpose of creation is the beauty and order of the universe. Correspondingly, human happiness consists in the contemplation of the universal order. By his own lights, then, Leibniz can in principle justify even the most extreme human suffering by showing it to be compatible with that order. Mendelssohn, in contrast, emphasizes God's benevolence. This implies that the suffering of any human individual would be unjustified unless it benefited, or contributed to the happiness of, that same individual. Hence Mendelssohn denies that God punishes anyone eternally. In the language of Leibniz's *Theodicy*,[368] Mendelssohn can justify no more than a "corrective" punishment that lasts until the evildoer turns away from the evil for which he is being punished.[369] Leibniz, on the other hand, can justify as well a "retributive" punishment that satisfies both the evildoer's victims and the wise who contemplate it—as beautiful music or good architecture, says Leibniz, satisfies cultivated minds.[370]

To see what led to Mendelssohn's disagreement with Leibniz over whether God's wisdom takes precedence over God's benevolence or vice versa, Strauss probes the theological controversy between Leibniz and Bayle that prompted Leibniz's *Theodicy* in the first place.[371] Bayle aimed to counter the "despotic" privileging of God's sovereignty and glory characteristic of supralapsarian Calvinism. He did so by arguing, independently of positive (Christian) theology, that God in His perfection could have created the world out of benevolence alone. If so, Bayle inferred, creation would

---

367. See IGC CIIIn56. See also *Jerusalem* 115 (cf. Ark 46): "Wisdom combined with benevolence [*Güte*] is called *justice*."

368. For the Leibnizian passage, see IGC CIV.

369. Thus, "corrective" justice would serve to promote ongoing moral and intellectual self-improvement post mortem. It is the Mendelssohnian alternative to the commonplace "mercenary" morality he has accused Leibniz of accepting, according to which the afterlife is conceived simply in terms of payoff and/or payback for one's moral behavior and/or misbehavior in this life. Cf., however, Lessing, "Leibniz von den ewigen Strafen," LM XI 480–81 (Nis 55–56), with the following note.

370. Since the evildoer's victims may not be wise, i.e., unlike the wise may not see or be able to see their being victimized in the light of the universal order, therefore satisfying them would require, as Strauss says, "a twofold manner of communicating truths, an esoteric and an exoteric one" (IGC CV). According to Lessing, Leibniz identifies the biblical imagery of hellfires, etc., as "exoteric" truths in the form of parables designed to admonish concerning the "natural" consequences that would follow from sin even without the threat of hell. "But," adds Lessing, "if a higher wisdom has nevertheless held such an extraordinary threat to be necessary, then it has recognized that it is just as advisable to express oneself about it entirely in accordance with our present sensibilities"—that is, to use Lessing's word, "exoterically" ("Leibniz von den ewigen Strafen," LM XI 480; cf. Nis 54). See also note 382, below.

371. IGC CV–CVIII.

serve the happiness, or absence of suffering, of human beings. Accordingly, God would have no need to punish human beings, just as perfectly benevolent fathers would have no need to punish their children: rather than chastise them with rods, says Bayle,[372] such fathers would motivate them with sweets. As Strauss points out, Bayle meant his argument ironically and skeptically.[373] The undeniable experience of suffering in the world, Bayle saw, disfavors any theology of pure benevolence and favors instead a dualistic theology like Marcionism or Manicheanism, which views the world as a "vale of sorrows."[374] By indicating in this way that a theology of pure benevolence, though logically consistent, is empirically doubtful, Bayle was casting doubt on both positive theology and natural theology. Leibniz aimed to restore natural theology in the face of Bayle's doubt. He did so by retaining Bayle's principle of benevolence yet restricting its scope. In Leibniz's system, the principle of benevolence is governed not by the principle of sovereignty and glory, nor by the principle of justice, but by the principle of wisdom—that is to say, contemplation of the beauty and order of the universe. To this change in the basic theological concepts, Leibniz added three others. First, he relaxed the requirement that God's benevolence be demonstrated by experience, in favor of the lesser requirement that it merely be confirmed by experience—namely, by the progress of modern science. On this basis, he neutralized and displaced the "otherworldly" tendencies of Bayle's theology of pure benevolence by arguing instead that this world is the best of all possible worlds. Second, however, in governing the principle of benevolence by the principle of wisdom rather than by the principle of justice, Leibniz sanctioned Bayle's de facto suppression of the classical meaning of justice (as found, say, in Ulpian).[375] Instead of being the steadfast will to give each his due, justice "dissolved into the two moments of wisdom and benevolence," as Strauss puts it, and "evaporated."[376] Leibniz did try to keep the strictly punitive ("retributive") feature of jus-

---

372. Strauss cites "Origène," remark E (DHC III 544n57). Bayle, in turn, cites Lucretius (*De rerum natura* I 935ff., IV 11ff.), who speaks of physicians honey-coating the rim of a cup containing bitter medicine so that the lips of the children for whom it is prescribed will be tricked into swallowing it before they can spit it out.

373. On Bayle's prudent manner of deliberately scattering impious, obscene, or subversive arguments among wide-ranging historical and critical discussions, see Ralph Lerner, *Playing the Fool: Subversive Laughter in Troubled Times* (Chicago: University of Chicago Press, 2009), 14–15, 63–88.; as regards the present example, see 84n11.

374. Bayle, *loc. cit.* Here Strauss recalls the Mendelssohnian passage with which he concludes IEL.

375. See IGC cviiin80.

376. IGC cvii.

tice; but punishment now became, aside from the mere disciplining of the evildoer, no more than a beautiful spectacle. Finally, by incorporating Bayle's principle of benevolence into his system, Leibniz made it viable. Hence Mendelssohn's disagreement with Leibniz over the relative priority of benevolence and wisdom remains an intra-Leibnizian disagreement.[377] It was Leibniz's system—more than Judaism in particular and rather than religious orthodoxy in general—that allowed Mendelssohn to take seriously the principle of benevolence, which Bayle meant ironically and skeptically, and to free it somewhat from the principle of wisdom by which Leibniz governed it.

(4) Mendelssohn, then, differs from Leibniz as a second-generation popularizer from his philosophical teacher. Strauss adduces comparable passages in Leibniz's *Theodicy* that show how Mendelssohn's very formulations of his reservations against Leibniz, whatever they may owe to Bayle (and Abbt), are of Leibnizian provenance.[378] Thus, Leibniz too argues that individual selves (qua "monads") are utterly free and self-sufficient beings ("the sole and true atoms of nature"); that each self has an inherent right even over against God to pursue its higher perfections; that each is a citizen in the City of God and can reasonably demand that God govern the universe with a view to its individual self-interest;[379] and that justice is to be understood in terms of the rights or claims of individuals as such, rather than in terms of obligations imposed on individuals as such.[380] If Mendelssohn differs in emphasis from Leibniz, he does so just because he takes for granted doctrines that are hard-won yet open to further question. We have already seen how the questionableness of Leibniz's theological achievement shows up during Mendelssohn's own time—in Abbt's invoking the spirit of Bayle, in the ongoing reverberations of the francophone voices in the Berlin Academy, and especially in Lessing's abandonment of the theism of the moderate Enlightenment.[381] Like his fellow adherents of "rational religion," however, Mendelssohn remains convinced that Leibniz's system is preferable for its having overcome both superstition and unbelief once and for all. IGC thus concludes, somewhat understatedly, by ascribing to Mendelssohn an "incomparably" stronger interest in the practical implications of the changes that Leibniz brought about in the basic theological concepts

377. See IGC CIII.
378. IGC CIX–CX.
379. Cf. IGC CIXn95.
380. Cf. NRH 183–86.
381. Cf. IP XVI–XVIII, IMH XXIIIff. *passim*.

than Leibniz himself. Leibniz designed the changes, Strauss suggests, with a view to reclaiming the rights of man from religious orthodoxy—though he did so ultimately as a philosopher, a "lover of wisdom" in the ancient sense of the term,[382] whose interest was in contemplating the beauty and order of the universe, rather than as "a philosopher in the style of the eighteenth century."[383] Mendelssohn, who writes as a philosopher in the latter sense, emphasizes how (thanks to Leibniz) those rights are to be reclaimed in practice.[384]

EPILOGUE: MORE ON HOBBES, ROUSSEAU, NIETZSCHE—AND SPINOZA

I conclude, as promised, by indicating how Strauss's references to Hobbes, Rousseau, and Nietzsche (and Spinoza) anticipate the pivotal roles his later writings ascribe to them as regards the overall course of modern political philosophy (and modern Jewish thought).

In tracing Jacobi's view of religion and virtue as essentially voluntary to his view of human beings as essentially rational, IMH added parenthetically that his appeals to Hobbes show that he understands "reason" entirely in terms of the Enlightenment.[385] Elsewhere Strauss connects Hobbes's understanding of reason with his understanding of Enlightenment as follows. Hobbes devises and bequeaths a notion of reason as an instrument to serve the passions. His premise is Machiavellian. It is that reason in the common-sense meaning of the term—as found in the preaching of the theological tradition and the moralizing of the philosophical tradition—is impotent when it comes to ensuring obedience to the moral and political prescriptions it dispenses, even or especially the most reasonable ones. But a solu-

---

382. Cf. Lessing, "Leibniz von den ewigen Strafen," LM XI 470 (cf. Nis 46): "Leibniz . . . in the firm conviction that no opinion can be accepted which is not true from a certain aspect, on a certain understanding . . . very often had the complaisance to turn and twist an opinion as long as it took him to make this aspect visible, this certain understanding conceivable. . . . With that, he did no more and no less than what all the ancient philosophers used to do in their *exoteric* speech. He observed a sort of prudence for which, it is true, our most recent philosophers have become much too wise. He willingly set his system aside and sought to lead each individual along the way to truth on which he found him." (The emphasis in the foregoing is Lessing's. The translation of Lessing's second and third sentence here is Strauss's; see ET 53 or RCPR 65, with ET 57–59 or RCPR 69–71.)

383. Strauss's word for "philosopher" here is *Weltweise*; see IPM xviiin23.

384. IGC's concluding sentence calls particular attention in this regard to Mendelssohn's *Jerusalem*. Strauss's various citations to it in his introductions are listed in note 149, above.

385. IMH xvii–xviii, with note 267, above. See, for the following, NRH 166–202, with SCR 86–97, PPH 80–81, 91–93, 106–7, 112, 130, 136–37, 149–50, 158–61, LSGS III 344–48 (HCR 90–94), WPP 47–52, 170–96, TWM 83–91 *passim*.

tion may be found if moral and political standards are lowered. Hobbes downsizes the moral and political problem into a technical one. According to Hobbes's new dispensation, a solid political order can be constructed by starting with individuals apart from and prior to society—in a "state of nature." Hobbes reasons that it is in their pressing interest as individuals to leave the state of nature and form a political society designed to protect the exercise of their passions, especially the most powerful passion, the passion for self-preservation, since self-preservation is fundamentally in danger otherwise. The main obstacle to constructing such a society is not technical, however, but educational. It is the "prejudices" traceable to the aforementioned theological and philosophical traditions, to which individuals remain naturally susceptible. So there is a persistent need to remove those prejudices by "enlightenment"—that is to say, by the ongoing accumulation and popular diffusion of the "technical" knowledge of nature arrived at by the methods of Baconian-Galilean science, which would progressively displace such prejudices from moral and political life. In Strauss's words, what characterizes Machiavelli and Hobbes and their early-modern successors is "the reduction of the moral and political problem to a technical problem"—to be solved by the calculations of reason in its delimited use as a problem-solving instrument—together with "the concept of nature as in need of being overlaid by civilization as a mere artifact," where civilization is construed as receptive in principle to modern-scientific enlightenment.

Hobbes looms large in Strauss's subsequent consideration of Rousseau as well. IEL called attention to the radical innovation of Rousseau's whose significance escaped Mendelssohn—namely, his replacing "reason" by "freedom" as human beings' specific difference.[386] Elsewhere Strauss examines how this innovation fits with Rousseau's attempt to correct a basic difficulty inherited from Hobbes. The difficulty is twofold. On the one hand, since individuals in the Hobbesian state of nature are presumed to be capable of calculating their self-interest, they must be "rational" and hence, unaccountably, already social. On the other hand, the society formed by the Hobbesian social contract degrades moral and political life. It fosters universal affluence and peace but neglects nonmercenary virtue, by favoring (enlightened) despotism. Hobbes views individuals as *bourgeois* rather than as citizens. In doing so, however, he fails to overcome the gulf between human beings as they are and as they ought to be. Rousseau re-

386. IEL XXII–XXIII. See, for the following, TWM 89ff. with PPH 160–61, NRH 252–94, WPP 50–54, 191.

models Hobbes's project from the ground up so as to enable the *is* and the *ought* to coincide. In contrast to Hobbes, he removes all vestiges of civilization from the state of nature by making individuals there prerational or subhuman and, accordingly, not competitive but compassionate with one another. What distinguishes them from other animals at that point is their mere "perfectibility," that is to say, their malleability. The steps toward civil society are not planned or premeditated, therefore, but result from a series of natural accidents. Reason emerges in the process—as the by-product of what Rousseau's successors came to call History. The coincidence of the *is* and the *ought* occurs historically wherever, through the exercise of reason, human beings govern themselves by laws in accordance with the general will. In Rousseau's remodeled version of the social contract, no individual can impose his private will on society without proposing what he has in mind in the form of a law suitable for the free assent of his fellow citizens; the promulgated law's formal rationality, that is to say, its generality or universality, guarantees that it is what it ought to be. Even so, for Rousseau as for Hobbes, laws constrain individual freedom in the interest of mere self-preservation; hence Rousseau infers—as we saw in IEL—that society is not good for human beings as such. For Rousseau, self-preservation is good only because what is being preserved is the goodness, or sweetness, of existence itself as experienced in its pure form in the state of nature. As Strauss shows, this means that happiness as the blissful experience of that sweetness is possible for civilized human beings only in a diluted form and only at the fringes of society—notably for "artists" or, alternatively and primarily, for individuals who commune with nature in solitude.

Because Rousseau's radical remodeling of Hobbes's Enlightenment project has the effect of extending its influence further, Strauss speaks of Rousseau as initiating a second "wave" of modernity, following the first wave initiated by Machiavelli and continued by Hobbes.[387] And just as the wave initiated by Rousseau was the outcome of his confronting a crisis—a difficulty pervading moral and political life and thought—that emanates from Hobbes, so a third wave is initiated by Nietzsche as the outcome of his confronting a crisis that emanates from Rousseau. According to Strauss, Nietzsche's wave brings in tow its own crisis, which is our current crisis as well. It has to do with the rise following Rousseau of what Nietzsche calls the "historical sense"—the tendency to reduce the principles of human

387. TWM 94ff., with NRH 252–53, WPP 50, 54.

thought and action to the historical setting, or culture, in which they happen to emerge. I shall say more about this in a moment.

Nietzsche made a cameo appearance in Strauss's Mendelssohn introductions.[388] IMH used his expression *amor fati* ("love of fate") to describe Spinoza's determinism, while examining why Jacobi mocks Friend D.'s attempt to infer Lessing's natural theology from *Nathan the Wise*. In this context, IMH was restating more fully what IPM had intimated in passing. Namely, Lessing's philosophical poems (which include the poetic drama *Nathan*) resemble Horace's in three ways: in seeking "a lively impression" rather than "a deep conviction"; in appealing to various philosophical "systems" to express various truths as appropriate; and in leaving "everywhere . . . untouched those hairsplittings that have no influence on morals." For these reasons, IMH was arguing, any inference from *Nathan* to Lessing's supposed personal conviction as between a theistic doctrine of providence and a Spinozist "love of fate" would hardly be conclusive, as Jacobi saw rightly enough with all his morally dubious mocking. Admittedly, readers may wonder why IMH did not pause to spell out Nietzsche's expression further, especially since Strauss's subsequent writings have much to say about him both in his own terms and in relation to Spinoza. My suggestion is that, here and throughout, Strauss is emulating Lessing (and Horace) in the ways just mentioned. He confines himself to articulating philosophical issues forcefully, eloquently, and especially economically so as never to lose touch with the moral questions that animate them. (The question prompting him in the present case was, as I've said, Why does Jacobi mock Mendelssohn?) In making this suggestion, I am assuming two things. First, what applies to Lessing's poetic dramas also applies to the "theater logic" characteristic of his other writings. Second, while Strauss's introductions are philological and historical investigations of a high order, they are at the same time philosophical inquiries of a high order that are, by his own account, indebted to Lessing as a role model.[389] At any rate, these two assumptions have guided my interpretive essay all along. My remaining remarks will indicate how Strauss's emulation of Lessing also characterizes pertinent statements of his elsewhere about Nietzsche and Spinoza as regards "love of fate." Since I do not claim to be able to convey secondhand the full forcefulness and elo-

388. See, for the following, IMH LXXXV–LXXXIX, including LXXXVIIIn424, with IPM XVII–XIX, especially XVIIIn24, and IMH XIX–XX, XXIII, XXIV, XXVI, XXVII, XXXI, XXXV, XLV–XLVI, LIII, LV, LXXXIV, LXXXV–LXXXIX, XC–XCV.

389. See notes 45–46, above.

quence of Strauss's statements—the first two of the three aforementioned features his writing shares with Lessing's—I limit myself by and large to indicating how those statements exhibit the third feature, his never losing touch with the moral questions that animate them.

Strauss elsewhere considers Nietzsche's doctrine of "love of fate" under the rubric of the latter's closely related doctrine of "eternal return."[390] He shows how it emerges from Nietzsche's confrontation with the crisis concerning the "historical sense" bequeathed by Rousseau and his German Idealist successors, Hegel above all, but not adequately understood by them. Strauss argues as follows. Hegel tried to settle the antagonism left by Rousseau—between nature as the ground for the blissful experience of the sweetness of existence, on the one hand, and morality, politics, rationality, and history, on the other—by conceiving history as a rational and reasonable process culminating in the rational state based on the recognition of the rights of man. For Hegel, this same process also culminates in the complete secularization of Christianity—its full reconciliation with, shaping of, and embodiment in secular history. Post-Hegelian thought rebelled against the notion of a culmination of history, however, in favor of the belief that history is unfinished and unfinishable. Nevertheless, it kept the now groundless belief that history is rational or progressive. Nietzsche confronts the self-contradictory conception of history besetting post-Hegelian thought by returning to the antagonism between society and nature as conceived by Rousseau. Yet unlike Rousseau he denies any escape from society to nature, and of course unlike Hegel he denies any final reconciliation between the individual and society. For Nietzsche, human beings are naturally cruel, not compassionate as for Rousseau. History as Nietzsche conceives it is then a more or less random series of cultures, each of which is framed by ideals, or overarching values imposed on human beings. These in turn originate in free human creative acts, or projects, such that the series cannot be arranged into a system, nor the individual cultures into a genuine synthesis. The new conception of history makes possible a radically new project. Nietzsche calls it the transvaluation of all values. He means the creation and imposition of new ideals unlike any previous ones. Historically speaking, all previous ideals were mistakenly thought to have had objective support in reason, nature, or the divine. The new ideals, in contrast, are to originate consciously and wholly in human creativity or, to use Nietzsche's

---

390. See, for the following, TWM 94–98 and WPP 54–55, with NRH 26, 65, 195, 320–21, SCR 12–13 or LAM 236–37, SPPP 180–90.

term, in the "will to power"—a creativity that characterizes not just what human beings do but what they are and what they share as such with all other beings.

Here Strauss points out the difficulty that pervades Nietzsche's project. Exercising the will to power so as to impose the new ideals is inseparable from the cruelty involved in overpowering others in the process. Even so, Nietzsche looks to vindicate the new ideals by dint of their originating in a human being of the future with the highest will to power. This human being Nietzsche calls the Over-man. Unlike the human beings of the future as envisioned by Marx, the Over-man is not necessitated by or deducible from history, but only made possible by history as a creative project for which Nietzsche seeks to prepare his readers. He means to counteract the specter of what he calls the Last-man—human beings of the future as envisioned by modern egalitarian movements, including both communism and liberal democracy. The Last-man has a high standard of living, materially speaking, but lacks any higher ideals or aspirations and is therefore utterly degraded and contemptible as a human being. Still, as Strauss notes, the society ruled by Nietzsche's Over-man is like the society of Marx's human beings of the future in marking the end of the rule of chance, such that for the first time human beings will be masters of their own fate. The pervasive difficulty, then, concerns what justifies the Over-man in preference to the human beings of the future as envisioned by Marx or, for that matter, by liberal democracy. While the society to be founded by the Over-man is to resemble the great societies of the past in being hierarchic or aristocratic, Nietzsche cannot be satisfied with appealing to these as historical precedents, given that it is to originate in the as it were infinitely creative will of the Over-man. Nor can he appeal, like Plato, to nature as the standard for judging the order of rank among human beings that would underwrite aristocratic rule. All that remains for Nietzsche, then, is merely to affirm the eternally unfinished and unfinishable course of history in all its details—that is to say, of fate—for making the Over-man possible as a freely willed project. Nietzsche's "love of fate"—his "eternal Yes-saying to everything that was and is"[391]—is no more (though no less) than the indispensable postulate for the coming of the Over-man. In other words, Nietzsche deliberately presupposes, or wills, the "eternal return" or ceaseless repetition of everything that has been fated to occur historically, just because it has prompted the philosophical reflections leading to the possibility of the Over-man in preference to the Last-

391. SPPP 180.

man. Strauss, however, laments that Nietzsche abuses his "unsurpassable and inexhaustible power of passionate and fascinating speech" to preach morally irresponsible doctrines, including "the sacred right of 'merciless extinction' of large masses" of human beings, for the sake of that possibility. Whereas the distinctive political legacy of the first wave of modernity, Strauss observes, was the theory of liberal democracy and that of the second wave was communism, that of the third wave is fascism (including, of course, Nazism): "[having] left [his readers] no choice except that between irresponsible indifference to politics and irresponsible political options," says Strauss of Nietzsche, "he thus prepared a regime which, as long as it lasted, made discredited democracy look again like the golden age."

Finally, in his autobiographical retrospective on his Weimar years, Strauss touches on "love of fate" in Spinoza.[392] The immediate context is Strauss's wondering why Weimar Jews were inclined to celebrate Spinoza in light of the notorious fact that he had been excommunicated by the (orthodox) synagogue in Amsterdam and subsequently lived as a non-Jew, though without ever converting to Christianity. Strauss finds two answers worth reflecting on. On the one hand, Weimar Jews celebrated Spinoza for underwriting Jewish assimilation. On the other hand, they celebrated him for underwriting Jewish self-identification as a separate nation. "Love of fate" comes up in Strauss's reflection on the second of these answers, albeit not by that designation, as we shall see. While the two answers are somewhat at odds, they are not entirely disconnected. I must therefore summarize Strauss's reflection on each in turn.

On the one hand, Strauss observes, Spinoza can be said to have underwritten Jewish assimilation by the influence of his philosophical "system" on subsequent German thought. Spinoza's system is characterized, to begin with, by a novel conception of God. In the wake of the modern (Machiavellian) project of Bacon, Descartes, and Hobbes to make human beings the masters and owners of nature—that is to say, to make philosophy or science essentially practical—Spinoza aims to restore the dignity of speculation or contemplation. As Strauss remarks, one cannot think of conquering nature if nature is the same as God. Yet Spinoza's restoration is based on the modern-scientific conception of nature, including its denial of natural ends, or final causes. Like the ancient and medieval Neo-Platonists, Spinoza views everything as proceeding from God, as the many from the One. Un-

---

392. See, for the following, SCR 15–18, 29–31, or LAM 239–43, 255–57, with WPP 171, JPCM 90–93. Also note 277, above.

like them, however, he conceives the process not as a descent or decay but as an ascent or unfolding. The highest knowledge for Spinoza, as Strauss notes, is not knowledge of God as the one substance but knowledge of individual things or events understood *sub specie aeternitatis* (that is to say, with a view to their timeless features). Strauss thus ascribes to Spinoza the invention of the kind of philosophical system that conceives the production of individual things or events as a progress. In this most important respect, he adds, Spinoza prepares German Idealism—a synthesis of Spinoza's philosophy with Kant's. Concomitantly, Strauss goes on to say, Spinoza arrives at a novel conception of human dignity. As Spinoza updates Neo-Platonic theology, so too he updates ancient republicanism—by becoming the philosophical founder of liberal democracy, a specifically modern regime based on a natural right of every human being as the source of all possible duties. This regime, as Strauss points out, allows much more freedom to the passions and relies much less on the power of reason than does ancient law generally or, say, Aristotle's polity in particular. Spinoza unlike Aristotle denies that human beings have any natural end; instead he construes human beings' end as "rational"—as the result of human beings' figuring it out for themselves. In this way, he prepares the modern notion of the "ideal" that we have just seen in Nietzsche. The historical consequence of Spinoza's two radical innovations, theological and political, was a novel sort of religion, or religiosity, that could unite Jews and Christians since it was not based on any positive revelation that might divide them. In Strauss's words, Spinoza became "the sole father" of "a new kind of Church . . . which was to be universal in fact and not merely in claim"; its rulers were "not priests or pastors but philosophers and artists" who would transform Jews and Christians into "cultured human beings who because they possessed Science and Art did not need religion in addition." In thus displacing religion by "culture," Strauss concludes, Spinoza significantly shaped the non-Jewish world so as to open it up to Jews who were willing to assimilate themselves to it. Such, at any rate, was the broader outcome traceable to Spinoza's formal reception in Germany with the publication of Jacobi's *Spinoza Letters*, to which Strauss also refers in the present context.

On the other hand, Spinoza can equally be said to have underwritten Jewish national self-identification—that is to say, Zionism—as the result of his revolt against official Judaism. Here Strauss finds something akin to "love of fate" in the deep Jewish background to Spinoza's revolt. Official Judaism, Strauss remarks, was both legalistic and rationalistic. Its rationalism—its assertion that God created and governs the world *sub ratione boni* (with a view to the good)—had strong outside support from classical political philosophy,[393] particularly from the Platonic conception of God as an artificer who makes the universe by looking up to the unchanging, lifeless ideas. Spinoza revolted against all this in the name of what Strauss calls "profound subterranean Judaism"—that of the biblical prophets as opposed to the priests and, more generally, of the inspired as opposed to the uninspired, hence "of the absolutely free or sovereign God of the Bible—of the God who will be what He will be, who will be gracious to whom He will be gracious and will show mercy to whom He will show mercy[,] ... who forms light and creates darkness, makes peace and creates evil."[394] Strauss goes on to sketch how the "profoundly understood divinity of the Bible" underlies various doctrines peculiar to Spinoza. These include his enthusiastic embrace of Paul's doctrine of predestination, though without its Christian-spiritual implications. Strauss lists other such doctrines as well. He characterizes these collectively as Spinoza's "lift[ing] Machiavellianism to theological heights": since God's might is His right, therefore the power of every being is as such its right too; evil passions display God's right and might no less than do other things we find admirable and delight in contemplating; good and evil differ only from a human point of view; not only is there is no justice or injustice, duty or guilt, in the state of nature, but the state of nature persists with the establishment of civil society, so that pangs of conscience are simply feelings of displeasure when plans go wrong; no vestiges of divine justice are to be found except where just men reign; finally, human acts themselves are modes of the one, mysterious God whose mysterious love is revealed in eternally and necessarily bringing forth not only love, nobility, and saintliness, but also hatred, baseness, and depravity, and, Strauss adds, "who is infinitely lovable not in spite of but because of His infinite power which is beyond good and evil." Strikingly, Strauss uses this last expression, "beyond good and evil," without quotation marks and without explicitly calling attention to its Nietzschean provenance,[395] to introduce the foregoing list of doctrines as well as to conclude it. I suspect that by framing the list with a recognizably Nietzschean expression, Strauss means to suggest that the kinship between the biblical doctrine in question and Spinoza's doctrines extends to Nietzsche too. I shall speculate

---

393. For this term, see especially WPP 27–40, 78–94, with NRH 81–164.
394. SCR 17 or LAM 242. Cf. Is. 45:7, with the blessing immediately following the *Bar'chu* in the traditional Jewish morning liturgy (as found in, e.g., *The Authorised Daily Prayer Book*, ed. Joseph H. Hertz [rev. ed.; New York: Bloch, 1948], 108–9).
395. Cf. SPPP 174–91, with SCR 271n5, 272n25, 272n28, or LAM 257n5, 258n25, 258n28.

more on this in a moment. Meanwhile, since Spinoza's "God or nature" is here said to be no less lovable for the fact that His actions are eternal and necessary (rather than personal and providential), the doctrines listed also invite the overall description "love of fate." I should add that nothing that has been said just now in connection with what Strauss has called the Bible's "profoundly understood divinity"—or, if I may, its "love of fate"—is meant to imply that Spinoza views the Bible as anything other than a human document or set of documents. For Spinoza, contra official Judaism, the Jewish people is the source of the Torah, not the other way around.[396] It was on this premise, bequeathed as such by Spinoza, that Strauss's Zionist contemporaries celebrated him for underwriting the "inspired" quality of the Jewish people—understood (in Strauss's words) "as an organism with a soul of its own"—as the basis for Jewish national identity.

Strauss's autobiographical retrospective culminates by pointing to a thread that links the Bible, Spinoza, and Nietzsche as regards the "theologico-political predicament" in which he found himself as a young German-born, German-educated Jew.[397] The link is as follows. Earlier in his retrospective, Strauss calls attention to Nietzsche's critique of modern atheism. According to Nietzsche, the denial of the biblical God demands as a matter of intellectual probity—that is to say, of rational consistency—the denial of biblical morality, which has no other support than the biblical God. Nietzsche infers that in the circumstances the biblical virtues of mercy, compassion, egalitarianism, brotherly love, and altruism must give way to the qualities of the Over-man—cruelty and the like. The main exception, as Strauss points out, is intellectual probity itself, a virtue of biblical origin. Nietzsche sees intellectual probity at work historically in destroying biblical theology and as an ongoing component of the morality of the Over-man. Nevertheless intellectual probity itself has no other support than belief in the biblical God! Nietzsche's penetrating critique of the self-contradictoriness of modern atheism, along with the unsatisfactoriness of his own response to it, prompts Strauss to reflect further on the difference between modern and premodern atheism. The classic, premodern exponent of atheism, he argues, was Epicurus, whose moral teaching was hedonistic and whose theoretical doctrines aimed at no more than liberating the mind from the terrors associated with religious fear, the fear of death, and the fear of natural necessity. Epicureanism, whose critique of religion precedes and

396. Cf. SCR 5–6 or LAM 229, with PAW 194n106.
397. See, for the following, SCR 12–13, 29–30, or LAM 236–37, 255–56, with JPCM 95–99. Also, SCR 37–52, LAM 76–139.

is presupposed by modern atheism, was thus "cautious or retiring." Modern atheism, in contrast, starts with the enterprise (begun by Hobbes et al.) of making ourselves the masters and owners of nature, that is to say, of liberating ourselves from all nonhuman bonds. This enterprise requires revolutionary political struggle and has the effect of transforming the Epicurean into an "idealist"—an activist prepared, as Strauss says, "to fight and die for honor and truth" while working for that liberation. Yet with all the systematic progress of modern civilization in pushing back nature and subjugating it to humanly imposed laws, it soon becomes apparent (starting, we might say, with Rousseau) that the ultimate goal of liberating ourselves entirely from those bonds remains hopelessly elusive. At that stage, says Strauss, the religious "delusion" is rejected not because it is terrifying but because it is comforting—or, more exactly, because it is a false comfort inasmuch as it disguises the true hopelessness of that goal and the corresponding forsakenness of human beings. If I have followed the thread of Strauss's argument here correctly, he is saying that the atheism of Nietzsche's time and beyond, by its own lights, not only vindicates Spinoza's atheism but outdoes it by dispensing with the need to revolt against biblical orthodoxy and claiming instead to have overcome orthodoxy radically by exposing the true roots of the human belief in God—that is to say, of human beings' futile attempt to cover over their putative hopelessness and forsakenness—as what we might call an affront to intellectual probity. Strauss's response to this claim, however, is that, being based on intellectual probity, it amounts to an appeal to biblical morality, whose validity in turn depends on belief in the biblical God, whereas arguments parading as rational but based on belief are, in Strauss's words, "fatal to any philosophy."

As regards this last point: the difference between intellectual probity and philosophy, or more broadly between the modern conception of reason and reason simply speaking, shows up in Strauss's Mendelssohn introductions, in its way, in the difference between what Mendelssohn and Lessing each took from Leibniz. Mendelssohn, as we saw, took Leibniz's "system" (in its Wolffian version) as unimpeachable in its rational consistency. He differed only in emphasizing its practical implications for further implementing what Strauss elsewhere spells out as Hobbes's Enlightenment project. Lessing, on the other hand, returned to what Strauss calls Leibniz's "genuine" doctrine, which turns out to be independent of this or that "system."[398] Still elsewhere, Strauss calls attention to the key Lessingian statement about

---

398. IMH LXXXIV. See, for the following, PAW 182, with note 382, above.

Leibniz. Leibniz, says Lessing, was firmly convinced that any or every received opinion has some truth to it when looked at from a certain aspect or on the basis of some understanding, and very often was accommodating enough to twist and turn an opinion until he could bring out that aspect or that understanding. Lessing adds that, in this, Leibniz did exactly what the ancient philosophers did in their "exoteric" (popular or public) statements—a prudent practice that modern philosophers have come to think beneath them. Namely, he was willing "to set his system aside" and instead "sought to lead each individual along the way to truth on which he found him." My concluding suggestion is therefore that, as Lessing thus seems to have taken Leibniz as a role model in his philosophical independence as regards current opinions and doctrines, so Strauss seems to have taken Lessing. His Mendelssohn introductions cross-examine the give and take of opinions and doctrines that he brings forward as a philological-historical editor, so as to present these for the rational or philosophical consideration of the thoughtful reader whose theologico-political starting point Strauss analyzes in his autobiographical retrospective.

INDEX OF PROPER NAMES

Abbt, Thomas, 19–21, 22n79, 32–33, 34n39, 49, 150, 159, 171, 174–75, 188, 200, 202, 225n38, 265–66, 273, 301, 305
Abelard, Peter, 198
Abravanel, Isaac, 225
Adelung, Johann Christoph, 10n23, 16n15, 77n101, 113n297
Allison, Henry E., xv n4
Altman, William F. H., xv n4
Altmann, Alexander, xiv, xvi, 3–5, 18n3, 26n56, 44n88, 57n3, 58n11, 79n114, 87n150, 88n153, 104n236, 118n323, 180, 222–23, 226–41, 244n110, 261n181, 279, 282n273, 294
Aquinas, Thomas, 199
Aristotle, 112, 115n304, 240, 253, 257–58, 313
Arkush, Alan, xv n5
Arnauld, Antoine, 177
Arnheim, Fritz, 54n17
Arrian, 180
Auerbach, Jakob, 149n19, 150–51
Augustine, 164, 182–83, 199, 203

Bamberger, Fritz, 11n34, 115n308, 168, 194, 222n14
Barbier, Antoine Alexandre, 187
Bartholmèss, Christian, 163
Basedow, Johann Bernhard, 118, 127, 194–95, 225n38, 295n334
Baumgarten, Alexander Gottlieb, 22, 26n56, 171, 225n38, 261n178
Baumgarten, Siegmund Jakob, 174
Bayle, Pierre, 33, 73, 120, 138, 143, 156–59, 180, 188, 225n38, 242n94, 266, 294n330, 303–5
Beck, Lewis White, xiv n2
Becker, Sophie, 111n285
Beiser, Frederick C., xiii–xv
Bell, David, xv n4
Bilfinger, Georg Bernhard, 211, 225n38
Bloch, Marcus Eliezer, 54, 274

Bonnet, Charles, 104, 116, 148, 225n38, 290, 293
Bonnot, Étienne. *See* Condillac, Abbé of
Borodianski/Bar-Dayan, Haim, 87n150, 222, 252
Boscovich, Father Roger Joseph, 160n94, 212, 225n38
Bourel, Dominique, xv n4
Brandis, Christian August, 149n19
Brandt, Frithiof, 45n90
Brasch, Moritz, 149n19
Brocke, B. H., 8n11
Brunswick, Duke of (Karl Wilhelm Ferdinand), 60, 148n17

Calvin, Jean, 36, 156, 267, 283n278, 303
Cartesian. *See* Descartes, René
Caterus, Johannes, 177
Chrysippus, 164
Clarke, Samuel, 180
Cohen, Hermann, 122n348, 224, 225
Condillac, Abbé of (Étienne Bonnot), 22, 180, 261
Cooper, John Gilbert, 201n
Crousaz, Jean Pierre de, 8–9, 164, 168, 225n38, 243
Cudworth, Ralph, 43n83, 110, 178, 180, 183

Dahlstrom, Daniel, 27n62, 88n153, 138n427, 260n175
d'Alembert, Jean Lerond, 22, 51, 53, 172–73, 261, 274
de Jariges, Philipp Joseph, 184
de Luc, Jean André, 55–56, 220, 275
Descartes, René, 42–43, 71, 74 107n254, 110, 113, 176–77, 233, 241, 243, 249, 251, 270, 275–76, 277, 291–93, 312
Diderot, Denis, 29
di Giovanni, George, xv n4
Diodorus, 198
Dohm, Christian, 281n271
Dubnow, Simon, 223

320　INDEX

Ebbinghaus, Julius, 226
Eberhard, Johann August, 75, 159n82, 225n38
Edelmann, Johann Christian, 196
Elbogen, Ismar, 222n13
Emden, Rabbi Jacob, 115n304
Epicurus, 111, 113n293, 292, 315

Farabi, Abu Nasr al-, 224
Febronius, Justinius, 66n39
Febvre, Lucien, 95n196
Ferdinand, Karl Wilhelm. *See* Brunswick, Duke of
Fischer, Moses, 18n6
Fittbogen, Gottfried, 123n351, 132n394
Formey, Jean Henri Samuel, 7n4, 20, 23n39, 174, 225n38
Fragmentist. *See* Reimarus, Hermann Samuel
Freud, Sigmund, 223–24
Friedländer, David, 52–53, 57, 179
Friedrich the Great (Friedrich II of Prussia), 53n13, 54, 55n4, 174, 187

Garve, Christian, 44, 48, 104n238, 105n242, 179, 180, 225n38
Gerstenberg, Heinrich Wilhelm von, 180–81
Goedeke, Karl, 52n8
Goethe, Johann Wolfgang von, 47n97, 84, 273, 286n290
Goetschel, Willi, xv n5
Goeze, Johann Melchior, xii, 72, 75, 225n38, 282n274
Gottlieb, Michah, xiv n2
Gottsched, Johann Christoph, 8–9, 164, 180, 225n38, 242ff.
Green, Kenneth Hart, xviii–ix
Grossinger, Joseph, 50–51, 53, 54, 274
Guttmann, Julius, 136n414, 222n13

Hamann, Johann Georg, 7n8, 29, 102, 103, 225n38, 289
Hegel, G. W. F., 127n375, 310
Heinemann, J., 61n14
Hemsterhuis, François, 182, 190, 287
Hennings, August, 62n20, 66n36, 117n321, 187
Herder, Johann Gottfried, 41n75, 46–49, 63n25, 77, 102, 108n261, 150, 225n38, 265, 272–73, 289, 301
Herz, Elkan, 148n15, 148n17
Herz, Marcus, 49

Hettner, Alfred, 149n19
Hobbes, Thomas, xiv–xv, 66–67, 71, 79, 127n375, 190, 198, 226, 227, 248n129, 250, 281, 283, 306–8, 312, 316
Holzboog, Günther, 222
Homberg, Herz, 186
Horace, xv, 81n1121, 137, 167, 244, 299, 309
Huet, Pierre Daniel (Huëtius), 139n429, 177
Humboldt, Wilhelm von, 186
Hume, David, 21n26, 93, 171, 188, 260n176

Iselin, Isaak, 30n12, 31–32, 60, 180, 182, 225n38, 265

Jacobi, Friedrich Heinrich, xi, xiii, xiv–xv, xvi, 4n7, 5, 59n1, 63–108, 109, 110, 117, 120 126–32, 136–42, 145, 187, 188, 190–91, 221, 225, 227–29, 231–32, 234, 238–39, 245–46, 250–51, 279–92, 294–99, 306, 309, 313
Janssens, David, xiv n4
Jaquelot, Isaac, 184–85
Jenisch, Daniel, 186
Jerome, 202
Jospe, Alfred, 136n414

Kafih, Yosef, 116n317
Kant, Immanuel, 9, 19–20, 22n29, 42, 49, 87, 104, 106, 120, 158n77, 160n94, 171, 191, 192, 233–34, 259, 269–70, 290, 313
Kayserling, Meyer, 116n317, 149n19
Kennington, Richard, 241n90
Klotz, Christian Adolph, 48, 175, 176, 181–82
Köhler, J. Bernhard, 175–76
Krüger, Gerhardt, 3n3

Lagarde, Paul de, 224, 226
Lambert, Johann Heinrich, 21, 109, 183, 225n38
Lavater, Johann Caspar, 104, 106, 116, 148, 225n38, 290, 293
Lazier, Benjamin, xv n5
Leibniz, Gottfried Wilhelm, xii–xiii, 7–13, 22, 28, 31, 32, 33, 41, 43–44, 55n4, 58, 60n6, 71–73, 74, 75, 76, 78n106, 87, 102n228, 109–10, 111–12, 113, 116, 117, 120, 124, 133–34, 141–42, 143–45, 146–61, 163, 164, 165–66, 168–69, 170, 182–83, 184, 193, 197–201, 202–4, 205–8, 209–10, 211, 219, 221, 230, 231, 234–37, 239–41, 242–47, 249, 251, 260, 263, 264, 265–66,

269, 271, 277, 279, 283–84, 286, 287n296, 291, 292–95, 296, 297, 298–306, 316–17
Leitzmann, Albert, 186
Lerner, Ralph, 304n373
Lessing, Gotthold Ephraim, xi–xiii, xiv, xv–xvi, xviii, 4–5, 7–13, 14, 15n10, 19n5, 20n12, 20n17, 21n23, 29n6, 30, 59, 62–66, 68–69, 72–87, 89–91, 93–98, 100–106, 109, 110, 115n302, 117, 121, 128–45, 155n65, 162, 163, 166, 167–70, 175, 181, 186–87, 189, 190–91, 195, 196–97, 213n1, 214–15, 219–21, 222, 226–32, 234–47, 250, 251, 264, 279–94, 296–99, 302n362, 303nn369–70, 305, 306n382, 309–10, 316–17
Lessing, Karl Gotthelf, 20n17, 75n95, 98, 186ff., 189, 288ff.
Levi, Raphael, 41n75, 42n80
Lévy-Bruhl, Lucien, 79n113
Lindner, Hermann, 7n8
Locke, John, 26n56, 134, 177, 178, 193, 276
Lord, Beth, xiv n2
Lucretius, 111, 179, 304n372
Luise Ulrike (queen-widow of Sweden), 54
Luzzatto, Simone, 34n40

Machiavelli, Niccolò, 190, 306, 307, 308, 312, 314
Maimonides, Moses, xviii, 18, 110, 115n304, 116, 196, 200, 220, 221, 224, 225n38, 251–53, 255, 258
Malebranche, Nicolas, 165–66
Manicheans/Manicheanism, 138, 157, 159, 304
Mannheim, Karl, 226
Marcion/Marcionism, 157, 304
Marie, Countess. *See* Schaumburg-Lippe, Countess of
Martin, Henri-Jean, 95n196
Masters, Roger D., 77n101
Maupertuis, Pierre Louis de, 9, 21–22, 165, 166, 169, 171, 225n38, 244n107, 260–61
Meier, Heinrich, xvii n8, 3n3, 162n1, 226n42
Mendelssohn, Brendel, 61n16
Mendelssohn, Joseph, 60–61, 151, 186, 301
Merian, Johann Bernard, 20, 170–71, 225n38
Meyer, Ludovicus, 82, 188
Michael, Reuven, 18n3, 252n146
Michaelis, J. D., 163
Misch, Georg, 53n13
Mittwoch, Eugen, 222n13
Moore, Henry, 180
Mosheim, Johann Lorenz von, 178, 180
Müchler, J. G., 53

Newton, Isaac, 182
Nicolai, Christoph Friedrich, 20n7, 29, 32n25, 46, 48, 61, 62n20, 74n92, 90, 102n225, 105, 174–75, 178, 180–81, 186, 225n38, 265
Nietzsche, Friedrich, 138, 227, 240n86, 297n341, 306, 308–12, 313, 314–16

Oldenburg, Henry, 188
Origen, 202
Otto, Rudolph, 224, 226

Palme, Anton, 192
Pascal, Blaise, 73, 79, 188
Platner, Ernst, 196, 225n38
Plato, xv, 7n5, 29–31, 33–34, 36–39, 41, 43–44, 46, 57, 69, 110, 111, 146, 164, 176, 181, 194, 202, 210, 220, 221, 240, 264–65, 267–70, 278, 282n275, 299, 300, 311
Plotinus, 43, 178, 270, 274
Pope, Alexander, 7–13, 164–65, 166–67, 169–70, 219, 242–44
Prémontval, André-Pierre le Guay de, 8, 142n444, 163, 164n1, 169, 225n38, 244n107
Prudentius, Aurelius Clemens, 202
Pythagoras, 36

Rashi, 254
Rawidowicz, Simon, 87n150, 104n239, 222n14
Rehberg, August Wilhelm, 184, 196
Reichardt, J. F., 5, 104n240, 105n241, 106n247, 108n256, 228–29
Reicke, Rudolph, 9n14
Reimarus, Elise, xii, xiii, 63–65, 80, 80n116, 81n117, 81n122, 82ff., 84, 85, 86, 87, 90, 93, 94, 95–96, 98, 99n215, 100, 101n223, 102, 103, 105, 107, 121n339, 130–32, 133, 135, 138, 139, 140, 141, 231, 279, 280, 285, 286–88, 289, 297, 299
Reimarus, Hermann Samuel, xii, 63n26, 86, 131–33, 134–39, 225n38, 231
Reimarus, J. A. H., 80n116, 83, 84, 86, 87, 89, 94, 96, 98n204, 100, 107, 121n339, 130–32, 138, 139, 189, 231n54, 285, 286
Resewitz, Friedrich Gabriel, 48, 115n308, 225n38
Riedel, Friedrich Justus, 48, 175, 176, 181–82, 225n38

322 INDEX

Rosenstock, Bruce, xiv n6
Rosenzweig, Franz, 223
Rousseau, Jean-Jacques, 14–17, 67, 77n101, 79, 80n115, 107, 115, 213, 219–10, 221, 227, 246–51, 281, 290, 293, 306–8, 310, 316

Schaumburg-Lippe, Countess of (Marie), 50–51, 53
Schaumburg-Lippe, Count of (Wilhelm), 53
Schlegel, Dorothea, 61n16
Schmitt, Carl, 226
Scholz, Heinrich, 64n29, 83, and *passim*
Seneca, 168, 201
Shaftesbury, Earl of (Anthony Ashley Cooper), 112, 164, 181, 204
Simon, Heinrich, 18n3, 252
Socrates, 29, 33–34, 36–40, 46, 193–94, 201n, 264–65, 268–70
Spalding, Johann Joachim, 33, 49, 175, 180, 225n38, 265–66, 273, 274n238, 277
Spinoza, Benedict, xi–xvi, 4n7, 60n6, 63–64, 66, 71–73, 75, 78n106, 79–82, 84–103, 105–7, 108n258, 109–10, 119–33, 136n414, 137–45, 164, 182, 184–85, 188, 190–91, 195–96, 201, 221, 222, 223–24, 226, 227–35, 237–41, 250, 279–80, 282–99, 306, 309, 312–16
Strauss, Bruno, 8n12, 9n17, 19n6, 20n12, 32n29, 86, 87n150, 118n323, 163, 164n1, 165, 170, 174, 222n14, 225, 286n289
Sulzer, Johann Georg, 55

Tetens, Johann Nikolaus, 109n272, 118, 192, 225n38
Thales, 164
Timm, Hermann, xv n4

Tschirnhaus, Ehrenfried Walther von, 188
Twersky, Isadore, 116n317

Ulpian, 211, 304
Unger, Rudolf, 47n99, 272–73

Vallée, Gérard, xv nn4–5
Veit, Simon (Witzenhausen), 61n16
Voltaire, 22, 39n68, 138, 159, 172, 204, 225n38, 240, 244n107, 261
von Harnack, Adolf, 10n21, 243
von Platen, August, 41n75, 182
von Schütz, Friedrich Wilhelm, 186
Vorst, Conrad, 198

Warburton, William, 8–9, 164, 225n38, 243, 244n107
Wegelin, Jakob, 29
Wessely, Aron, 61n18
Wessely, Bernhard, 61
Wessely, Hartwig, 57
Wilhelm, Count. *See* Schaumburg-Lippe, Count of
Winkopp, Peter Adolph, 119n329
Wolff, Christian, xiii, 21–22, 24–28, 32, 92, 116, 121, 134, 159n81, 168–69, 172, 185, 187–88, 192, 195–96, 201, 209, 211, 225n38, 235n68, 260, 261n178, 262–65, 277, 316
Wolzogen, Ludovicus, 177
Wycliff, John, 198

Zeller, Eduard, 153n54, 154n57
Zimmermann, Johann Georg, 55, 93n183, 94n191, 180, 186